MW01614744

Outrigger Canoeing
'A Paddler's Guide'

'So far as the development of the sport is concerned, it is expanding at such a rate that technical information needs to be presented in a whole new format in order that improved learning strategies and cohesion may be created for paddlers, coaches and anyone interested in furthering their knowledge of the sport; whether isolated on a Pacific Island or in the madness of a busy Westernised Metropolis.'

Outrigger Canoeing
'A Paddler's Guide'

A Kanu Culture production, published by Batini Books, written and researched by Steve West.

Publishing Information

© Steve West, Batini Books 2010
First Edition Published 2006
Second Edition Published 2010
Photography *Steve West* unless otherwise indicated.
Layout and Design *Steve and Mandy West*
Illustrations Bobby Woods (So Cal) Paul Ritchings (Aust)
www.kanuculture.com

Content for this book derived from past conversations, interviews, recordings and submissions with and from; *Chris Maynard, Todd Bradley, Jim Foti, Jackie Taylor, Terry Wallace, Kawika Sands, Al Ching, Tay Perry, Billy Danford, Walter Guild. Additional inspiration from Danny Sheard, Nicole Wilcox, Sue Sheard Mindy Clarke and many others.*

Bibliography

Holmes, Tommy, *The Hawaiian Canoe*. Honolulu. Editions Limited. 1981.
Thorne, Alan and Raymond, Robert, *Man on the Rim: The Peopling of the Pacific*. Australia. Angus & Robertson 1989.
Chun, Naomi, *Hawaiian Canoe-Building Traditions*. Honolulu. Kamehameha Schools Press, 1995.
Toro, Andras. *Canoeing: An Olympic Sport*. San Francisco. Olympian Graphics. 1986.
West, Steve, *Level 1 Coaching Manual. AOCRA.* Australia. Batini Books. 2000.
Evan, Jeff, *Waka Taua: The Maori War Canoe*. New Zealand. Reed Publishing, 2000.
Haddon and Hornell, *Canoes of Oceania*. Honolulu. Bishop Museum Press. 1975.
West, Steve, *Kanu Culture.* Volumes 1-10 Australia. Batini Books. 1995.
West, Steve, *The Art and Skill of Steering*. Australia. Kanu Culture Publishing. 2006.
Court, John, *A Sporting Chance.* United Kingdom. Staffordshire University. 2001.
Summerlin, Annette, *Canoe Racing and Paddling in Hawai'i.* Honolulu. University of Manoa. 1994.

ISBN 978 0 09586554 2 2

Outrigger Canoeing
'A Paddler's Guide'

Contents

Steve West

My Thanks To
Tahiti Tourism
Air Pacific
Air Tahiti Nui
Fiji Tourism
Palau Tourism
Marianas Tourism
Hamilton Island Resort
Infront Communications
Susan Boyd
Harvie Allison
Sue Sheard
Chris Maynard
Jim Foti
Todd Bradley
Colin Philp
Jackie Taylor
Kialoa Paddles
and to my
beautiful wife
Mandy.

I could write this from the third person and let you believe someone else wrote about my virtues and vices and why I am eminently qualified to present this offering to you. But I won't, I'll leave that job to me.

What I can tell you is that my life has always depended upon a relationship of being on, near, or in the water and the joy to be found in the physicality ocean sports provide in their raw, pure, unpredictable form. Here's some former and present qualifications and roles:

British Windsurfing Display Team
UK Board Sailing Open Sea Examiner
Royal Yachting Association Senior Instructor
International Windsurfing Schools Instructor
First windsurfer to sail on the River Nile.
Co-Founder of the UKs Around Hayling Island Race
Level 1 Coaching Principles (Aust)
Level 2 Coaching Principles (Aust)
Level 1 Outrigger Canoeing Coach (Aust)
Elements of Shipboard Safety (Coxswains)
Co National Coaching Director (Aust) with C. Maynard (5yrs)
Co National Coaching Director (Fiji) with C. Philp (5yrs)
Founder of AOCRA Coaching / Author of Manuals
Founded Kanu Culture 1994
Author of 12 Books on the subject of Outrigger Canoeing
Founding member and Vice President Mooloolaba OCC 1990
Former Vice President Australian Outrigger Canoe Racing Association
Former Secretary Australian Outrigger Canoe Racing Association.
Team New Zealand Crew 1998 New Caledonia
Former International Polynesian Canoe Federation Delegate.
2009 AALS (UK) Authored the Good Practice Guide for SUP
2009/10 UK SUP Coaching Development
2010 UK Outrigger Canoeing Development
2010 Team Starboard Racing Team UK (SUP)

I've won a few major races along the way, and many 'chocolate medals' - silvers and bronze, some of which were more enjoyable than 'wins'. Of over 15 years of competing in the Hamilton Cup Australia, I finished out of the top 5 crews on but a few occasions, testimony to the men with whom I was fortunate to paddle with.

Winner Masters Division of Moloka`i Hoe 1998/99
Winner Masters Division of Hamilton Cup 1998/99/07
Winner Masters Division 16km Round Hamilton Island 1998/99/07
Winner Cairns To Port Douglas (OC1) 2008 with C. Maynard
Runner up Hauraki Hoe New Zealand 1998/2003
Runner up Catalina Classic 1998 (Mixed Division)

Have raced in these events either once, twice or on multiple occasions. The Hawaiki Nui Va`a I have raced twice, followed it five times and the toughest by far, especially the 2nd day, 60km iron.

Catalina, Moloka`i Hoe, Hawaiki Nui Va`a, Hamilton Cup, Micronesian Cup, Gold Coast Cup, Bay of Islands NZ, Hauraki Hoe NZ, Ouvea to Poindimie New Caledonia, Fiji International and no doubt, some I've forgotten.

Most of my paddling years have been spent either in seat 1, 2, 5 or 6. My favourite if I had to be honest, is seat 5 in big water with a top crew. In 2007 our Mooloolaba Masters crew consisting of Chris Maynard, Danny Sheard, Grant Kenny, 'Lemmo', Darren Mercer and myself won the around Hamilton Race. Sitting in seat 5 behind these guys in the hands of Danny Sheard was an epic experience I will never forget. We were fast, but did not beat the record we set in 1998, with Danny Sheard and Grant Kenny also in that crew.

Introduction

This body of work, I consider but a humble offering to what I believe to be a truly noble sport, wherever and whenever practiced by those who understand its mystery on all of its levels. I can think of no other sport so all encompassing, offering to the adventurer, the journeyman, the maverick, the dreamer, a journey through life through active participation, rich on so many levels, from the cultural to the spiritual, from the physical to the metaphysical.

This offering is in essence a culmination of many journeys, many meetings, many experiences and I hope worthy of this noble sport. I remain outspoken on some key issues, to which end I make no apology as my aim is not to win friends and influence, but to present the issues as I have come to know them, whether of a cultural, traditional or political nature. I am not an 'expert' per se, merely intrigued to discover and share what I learn.

Fifteen years of travel throughout the Pacific has given me rare insights and enlightenment regarding key issues and rights of ownership over many claims and it continues to concern me that many paddlers form deep seated cultural notions and pre-conceptions without having left the immediate sphere in which they live.

For those who belong to a va`a-culture within the Pacific, their voice is rarely heard and as so often happens throughout history, there seems a pervading euro-centric slant wherever there has been intervention of European culture onto that of another, rarely if ever, vice-versa. European intervention may have eroded the practice of va`a paddling and building in many regions of the Pacific and though reinstated it was not always done so in such a way which would have pleased the elders and traditional owners of the sport.

On the face of it, va`a paddling, is the late bloomer as far as paddle sports go. Though it has been around as a design concept for thousands of years, certainly pre-dating the kayak, there have been certain forces at play preventing it from rapid global expansion in the same way kayaking, dragon boating and open canoe paddling have developed.

As a paddle sport, va`a paddling, has created a catalyst by which *Va`a Cultures* of Oceania can focus a re-awakening of a cultural identity and pride. For many peoples of Oceania, va`a paddling is an activity of great significance, a fundamental part of the cultures of Oceania, commanding respect, ritual and remembrance, serving to keep the legend of the va`a and it's people alive.

For those who find themselves involved with the sport, whose cultural origins are not of a *Va`a Culture,* realise that the design of this paddle craft is considered to be one of the most accomplished of all maritime designs. Take time to understand why this is and your participation will take on new meaning. To participate without empathy with the va`a and without an understanding of its origins, will make your experience only half fulfilled.

Universally, va`a racing has undergone a rapid change in recent years, from its laid-back 'Island Style' roots, towards a more stressed out, fast paced, technologically advanced sport; but not without some continuing resistance. On the upside, improved user friendly equipment has been developed in spite of pervading questionable design restrictions in some regions of the world, providing the potential for wider global appeal and greater enjoyment. Whatever the attraction for you the paddler, some effort to nurture an appreciation of the craft's origins together with a respect for the cultures who developed their many different forms, will greatly enhance your experience and connection with the sport as a whole.

I do not embrace this sport as Hawaiian per se (though there are distinct differences between va`a and wa`a types) but essentially Polynesian. And as if to confuse even more, Melanesian and Micronesian as you begin to understand that proud cultures from these regions, indeed older than Polynesia, also associate with and have a powerful affinity to the va`a. The va`a is perhaps more profoundly associated and encompassed by the scope of Oceania and not just one region within it.

Furthermore, since Hawai`i was populated by voyages from the Marquesas and Tahiti, it stands to reason that the Tahitian va`a pre-dates the Hawaiian wa`a and that any modification over time of these first Tahitian va`a to arrive in Hawai`i are mere modifications. Unfortunately, this fact seems overlooked to the extent that today, Hawaiian and Tahitian artisans are no longer free to disseminate knowledge regarding design, as rulings of dubious intent have effectively halted the evolution of the Hawaiian wa`a in any meaningful way. Juxtaposed to this, the Tahitians continue to evolve their va`a designs free from constraint as is just and appropriate.

Much of the contents relating to the technical consideration of va`a paddling in this book are fundamentally arrived at by intuitive notions and many, many hours of discussion, observation and participation. The science is presented not through physics or complex formula and theory, but more in lay-mans terms, which I hope anyone and everyone can comprehend.

The photos are predominantly as they happen, few are staged. Sincere thanks to *Harvie Allison* for supplying some truly amazing photography. His support of *Kanu Culture* over the years has been overwhelming. My thanks also to *Joss* of Hawaii, who has been, *Our man in Hawai`i,* for many years and through his imagery has helped elevate the profile of the sport and also to California's *Daphne Hougard.*

My list of thanks would fill another book and for fear of omitting someone over the course of these years, I decline to attempt it. But to all those who have helped and supported me and *Kanu Culture* over the years, my deepest thanks, there is a part of you in this book.

Steve West

Kanu Culture, Founder and Editor
AOCRA National Coaching Director [Australia] 2002-2006
FOCRA Coaching Consultant [Fiji National Squad] 2000 - 2006

Wa`a (Hawai`i) and Va`a (Tahiti)

Throughout this publication, in accordance with respect for traditional names, as the *kayak* is to the *Inuit,* so too the *wa`a* (va-a) or *va`a* (va-a) is to the Hawaiians and Tahitians respectively. Therefore, where appropriate, *outrigger canoe* is replaced with either *wa`a* (Hawai`i) or *va`a* (Tahiti) respectively; va`a is used as the predominant term for the sport as a whole. The descriptive Hawaiian name for an outrigger canoe is *wa`a kaukahi.* Through most of French Polynesia, va`a is used to describe most existing canoe types with the exception of the Marquesas, where *vaka* is more popular, as it is in the Cook Islands – though va`a is still understood. In Samoa, va`a is still used as a general term, while in New Zealand, *waka ama* is in common use, though *amatiatia* was the traditional name used to describe a canoe with outrigger assembly in Aotearoa.

Typically, euro-centric researchers and subsequently those of European decent who assisted in the development of contemporary wa`a racing (Hawai`i) choose to use *outrigger canoe,* ironically perpetuating a common disregard for the Hawaiian language and ultimately for the wa`a itself, a practice continued to this day. By choice, I choose not to contribute or perpetuate the practice in the context of this publication. Validating a genuine concern of reviving an ancient Hawaiian pastime would not preclude the correct use of the Hawaiian language when describing the craft, at least one would assume so, but is was however for the most part overlooked.

It is an arguable fact, that the rudder steered solo and duo hybrid va`a hoe of Tahiti, modified by Anglo-Hawaiians could be considered the only craft worthy of being called by another name, in so much as they have no traditional basis or equivalent; contemporary in all but the use of an outrigger assembly and use of single blade.

There are many island groups of Polynesia, Micronesia and Melanesia participating in the sport of *outrigger canoe racing,* however the *International Va`a Federation* reiterates the need to use a culturally appropriate word to identify the canoe type we are concerned with. As participants in the sport, consider the long-term implications of failing to use the correct term of wa`a or va`a as it relates to the future development and uniqueness of the craft itself. By using these terms, a clear distinction is made in terms of the canoe type, origin and sport itself.

Origins of The Word 'Canoe'

The word *canoe* originated from an *American Indian* word *kenu* - meaning dugout. *Kanu* is the neo-Melanesian word for *canoe* and also the German, to which end Papua New Guineans adopted this via German missionaries. When *Christopher Columbus* happened upon the natives of the *Cariban West Indians* of *Haiti* paddling hollowed out tree logs and propelled with paddles, the name was ultimately recorded with a Spanish lilt as *canoa* and subsequently *canoe,* brought into popular use in 1555. Far more than an issue of semantics, there is an urgent need to address issues of the application of culturally accurate names for differing canoe and kayak types.

The Oceania Va`a

'Of humankind's inventiveness in the challenge to travel near or far, the va`a was to the ancient cultures of Oceania, what the wheel was to western culture. As a method of transportation, its impact and significance was on the grandest of scales.'

Canoes of all manner of shape, size, construction and material, designed to function in a variety of aquatic environments, are present in most parts of the world. Va`a, which include an outrigger framework, are uniquely different from other types of 'canoe'. Whether possessing a single or double-outrigger, double hulled, paddled or sailed, they were at their most prolific and developed to their highest form throughout the islands and cultures of Oceania (Melanesia, Micronesia, Polynesia) – though also present in Madagascar, the Comoro Islands, East Africa, Southern India, Sri Lanka, the Maldives and Indonesia.

Origins – From Raft to Va`a

Much speculation exists about the origin of the outrigger concept. Being made of organic material, archaeological finds of any accurate age are few and far between, and do not provide any definitive chronological evolutionary evidence nor resolution of cultural ownership. The Hawaiian wa`a variance is but one of hundreds of designs and certainly not the place of origin in terms of the concept.

Originating in Southeast Asia, a seafaring migration into the Pacific Basin set in motion the first significant steps towards the birth and evolution of an advanced maritime technology. The abundance of bamboo throughout Southeast Asia provided early sea-farers with an ideal material for water-craft construction, especially since it is lightweight, strong, buoyant, impermeable and easy to manipulate. Poles lashed together formed the basis for these early voyaging craft powered by oars, paddle or sail. In time, such rafts underwent design modifications and much larger bamboo craft, up to 15 metres, were designed and constructed for the purpose of extended journeys to new lands.

Fijian Dug-out, Fiji Museum, Suva.

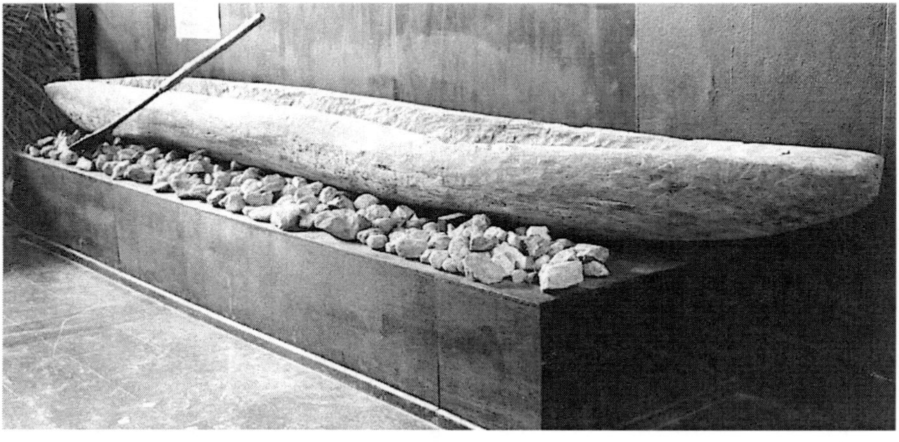

Raised stanchion assembly Bora Bora and below a modern day trimaran based on a double outrigger canoe design of Micronesia.

It is assumed that tree logs were used to create the first floating platforms, propelled over the water by use of a long pole, pushed into the riverbed for leverage - what we know as 'punting'. Considerable time passed before the creation of suitable tools, which used with fire in some instances, enabled the logs to be hollowed-out, creating the 'dugout canoe' and therefore the basis of the va`a.

It has been suggested that a rafting community has existed in Indonesia for 60,000 years, during which time sailing rigs and hollowed timber va`a hulls were developed. Around 20,000 years ago, raft rigs were progressively attached to these hulls with the use of lashings, internal lugs and fittings. From this, the evolution of the va`a, both single (outrigger frame on one side only) and double (outrigger frame on both sides) and the double-hulled voyaging canoe where progressively developed.

Expert opinions differ regarding the exact sequence of modifications which led to the development of the outrigger framework. But it is assumed that since a hollowed-log was inherently unstable, the natural ingenuity of these maritime cultures would have led them to experiment with the three basic options; the single and double outrigger concept and the double-hulled va`a.

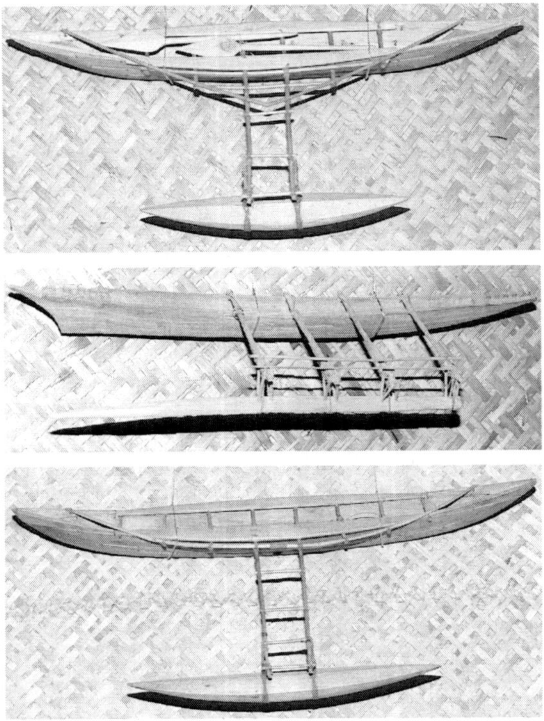

Three differing single-outrigger va`a designs from the Pacific. *Captain Cook Museum* Auckland, New Zealand. The single-outrigger va`a, presumed to be a modification of the double-outrigger va`a, designed so the hull would not become suspended between swells. The Micronesians were considered early pioneers of this design and its use is evident throughout the Philippines and Indonesia, the origins of the Micronesian people. This design was then also applied to paddle-craft.

During the populating of the Pacific Rim, cultures adapted the va`a to suit a range of environments, i.e. rivers and coastlines, while a Northwards migration into the frigid and inhospitable waters of the Arctic Circle led to the advent of the closed deck kayak. Venturing out into the vastness of the Pacific Ocean was left until last. The open ocean provided the greatest challenge of all and required the va`a to be more robust and stable to cope with the forces it would face.

Substantial modifications were required in order to develop a more stable craft and it was at this point that maritime technology entered a new cycle, one which was developed over thousands of years, culminating in the last and greatest migratory exploration and settlement of the planet; the islands of Polynesia.

Outrigger Assembly - Experimentations and Limitations

Though it was assumed that the double-outrigger sailing va`a would be the most stable and seaworthy craft, there were problems associated with handling the mountainous deep-water seas. With increased swell and wave size as well as the space between deep-water swells, the hull was often left suspended, airborne between two swells, with the two flimsy outriggers supporting the hull's weight.

The *E Ala* a small Hawaiian voyaging wa`a. The double-hulled va`a were used by the Polynesians during their epic seafaring voyages because of their seaworthiness and strength.

The va`a with double-outrigger was therefore not considered adequate for deep-water sailing where it would encounter large ocean swells. The solution was to remove one of the outriggers and to increase its size and weight, thus increasing its counterbalance affect. How this solution was reached is unclear, but it resolved a major design problem and allowed seafarers of this region to venture into deeper waters.

The conclusion has been made that the va`a with single-outrigger is considered a more recent design, because it is a more advanced concept and not the most obvious, logical solution in stabilising the primary hollowed timber hull. This seemingly simple, yet significant leap in technology meant that va`a could now withstand reasonably rough and hazardous open ocean conditions. The addition of a sail meant that sea travel between islands was now possible. The pace of life quickened and the opportunity for new oceanic migrations on a grand scale was created.

The Advancement of the Dugout Canoe

The development of the va`a hull ensured that they were no longer make-shift, and their construction now required specialised tools, the careful selection of a suitable tree, hours of hard, precise tooling and refinements in the art and skill of wood carving. The adze became the standard tool of the trade, designed to hollow out tree logs. It is a short-handled tool with a wooden shaft and axe-like head that was normally made of stone or more commonly in Melanesia of giant clam shell, and later in New Zealand of greenstone *jade*.

With the advancement of the va`a and outrigger framework, many of the limitations associated with the hull were overcome, notably that va`a could now be made extremely rigid and strong enough to cope with rough sea conditions. The size of the va`a then became limited only by the size and availability of suitable trees.

This increase in outrigger weight meant that the load-bearing properties of the va`a and the points of attachment needed to be strengthened. In doing so, they raised the sides of the va`a by attaching planks. They were now able to build larger, deeper, stronger and more seaworthy sailing and paddling va`a than the size of the tree dictated with planking added to the bow, stern and sides.

A Migration Outwards into the Pacific

'The ancient Polynesian played a major role in a drama that tops any wonder of the classical ancient world: the settlement of Polynesia, humankind's final push Eastward into the most remote reaches of the Pacific Island world. This drama was played across thousands of mile of sea and lasted for thousands of years.

It began in Indonesia and Melanesia around 2000BC, when a group of highly skilled mariners and traders, known to archaeologists as the 'Lapita People' began to explore islands West of the Admiralty archipelago, moving quickly through Fiji and New Caledonia to Samoa and Tonga by about 1200BC and then deeper into Polynesia.

Around 500BC, the ancestors of the "The Men" (as today's Marquesans refer to themselves) sailed Eastward from Tonga or Fiji, to discover a remote string of jagged volcanic islands poking into the Pacific sky 780 miles Northeast of Tahiti: the islands which we know as the Marquesas.

By about 100AD or so, Marquesans mariners had pushed on to Hawai`i and by 500AD had established settlements on Easter Island (Rapa Nui), Mangareva, and possible some of the Tuamotu atolls.' Rose Corser, Director Museum of Polynesian Seafarers, Taiohae, Nuku Hiva, Isles Marquesas.

Marquesan voyaging va`a, Nuku Hiva, Marquesas.

All of this was only possible when va`a technology and navigation had advanced far enough to enable these Eastern-Austronesians to venture further Eastward into the Pacific. It must also be noted there was a move Northwards, resulting in the settlement of Micronesia and ultimately the development of the Chamorro culture, whose origins are Indonesian.

These early mariners and settlers took with them the skills to manufacture a variety of va`a types, which they went on to do, using the available raw materials. A variety of va'a types were ultimately required for a range of purposes, i.e. fishing, trading, venturing, as well as warfare and as a basic form of transportation.

Hawaiian voyaging wa`a, *Makali`i.*

Tahitian voyaging va`a, *Raia`tea*, Tahiti.

Hawaiian voyaging wa`a, *Molo`kiha.*

The African Dugout Canoe

No historical account of the dugout canoe's origin would be complete without the inclusion of its wide distribution throughout Africa. As there was an original transmigration of peoples across from Africa into

India then Southeast Asia, the dugout canoe, though not developed to the same degree as the Oceanic va`a, could have originated in Africa. Indeed many scholarly writings make mention of East Africa and Madagascar in particular.

The dugout canoe formed an intrinsic part of many African cultures in tropical regions where rainfalls were high, and river and coastal based-cultures thrived, especially on the West Coast of Africa. In May 1987, a Fulani herdsman discovered a *Dufuna Canoe* near the River Yobe in Nigeria. It was carbon-dated as being over 8000 years old and made from African mahogany, a black wood. It is the third oldest dugout canoe ever discovered, the other two originating in the Netherlands and France.

'It is highly probable that the Dufuna boat does not represent the beginning of a tradition, but had already undergone a long development, and that the origins of water transport in Africa lie even further back in time'. Peter Breunig of the University of Frankfurt, Germany.

Sacredness, Significance and Ceremony

Throughout the Pacific, the adze became a sacred and valued tool amongst va`a carvers, it is known in Hawai`i as kalai wa`a. Blessed, kept in a sacred place and used with reverence by those who shaped the va`a from logs, the adze is recognised as one of the most significant tools created and remains in widespread use around the world. The cultures of Oceania acknowledged the significance and sacredness of trees within the context of their maritime culture.

Trees were selected by priests (and often continue to be today) on the basis of their individual mana or spirit. They were blessed before being felled and carved, with the first cut being made by a

sacred ceremonial adze. Upon completion, the va`a was blessed once more and named at its naming ceremony. This succession of acts, bestowed upon no other item to the same degree, made the end product a sacred item.

Deep in a Huahine rainforest in French Polynesia, a priest blesses a sacred Bread Fruit tree before it is ceremoniously cut down to be carved into a va`a. Having provided for the village for many years, its ultimate fate is sealed.

The axeman feel the tree's 'mana' or life force, make a prayer and pass on their message to the tree before felling.

The process of felling then begins with thundering blows.

Once the tree has fallen, the axeman stares skyward where there once was a canopy of green, then reflects back on his actions and the significance.

A study of the va`a of Oceania, is as much a study of ethnology and the migration of a seafaring people, as it is of the development of an amazingly advanced maritime culture. The story culminates with the development of the voyaging va`a, a craft more advanced in all respects than the galleons of Europe that did not appear in the Pacific for another 1500 years, after most of Polynesia had already been colonised by Polynesian va`a of a double-hulled configuration.

Note: The double-hulled voyaging va`a of Samoa, considered the departing point for the Polynesians epic journeys into the Pacific, were known as va`a tele.

All Polynesian people are descendants of at least one great va`a journey and it is this fact that makes their commitment to the sport of va`a racing of great significance, as can also be said for the peoples of Melanesia and Micronesia, where highly advanced sailing va`a and navigational skills existed.

Colonialism

The va`a has been the focal point and essence of most ancient Oceanic cultures. Without its creation, the survival and transmigration of people across the Pacific would not have occurred in the manner in which it did. With arrival of the Europeans, came the subsequent introduction of western values, religions, diseases and the overwhelming material attractions of a western lifestyle, each contributing to the degradation and loss of many of the formidable skills associated with va`a construction and seamanship. Consequently, there followed a loss of cultural identity, for it was these very skills which provided the people with pride, strength, belief and purpose.

It was inevitable, as the need for va`a construction ceased and values changed, many traditional wood carving skills died. The adze was laid aside and with it a skill that had been handed down through generations. With a lack of demand for the creation of va`a, craftsman felt no need to teach their children a useless craft.

Today, the cultures of Oceania are rediscovering their ancestor's ancient skills of va`a building. With this is a revival of the skills of wood carving and of the traditional ceremony involved throughout the process of building; the blessing of the tree selected for felling, the blessing of the va`a before its maiden voyage, and the everyday ritual which revolved around the importance of the va`a within the community and culture.

Nuku Hiva Marquesas Islands - Team *Outrigger Australia*.

Peoples of the Va`a

'Polynesian culture was the last of the great Oceanic cultures to flourish and develop. The inherent skills of va`a architecture, seamanship and navigation acquired through the pioneering maritime skills of the Melanesians and Micronesians, undoubtedly paved the way for the Polynesian voyages across the vast expanse of the Pacific Ocean.'

First European Pacific Crossings

The Pacific Ocean was originally named *The Great South Sea,* by Spaniard *Vasco Nunez de Balboa* in 1513. However, it was to be renamed seven years later by *Fernando Magellan* who, after rounding Cape Horn in treacherous conditions, was relieved by the sudden tranquillity of the vast ocean into which he sailed, renaming it *Pacific Ocean* – calm and peaceful. He was to sail across its vast expanse to the Philippine Islands, without sighting a single one of the many thousands of tiny isolated islands and atolls. He wrongly concluded that it was a vast and empty expanse of water.

Little did he know that 1500 years prior, the Polynesian seafarers had already begun their voyages of exploration of the Pacific which they went on to inhabit. The area between Hawai`i to the North, Easter Island to the East and New Zealand to the South is known as the 'Polynesian Triangle'.

The lack of recognition that Polynesian seafarers have received within the context of European record keeping is astonishing. Many so called definitive historical works documenting great maritime achievements of exploration, fail to give the Polynesians a mention. Books that profess to document the history of sea-craft, skim lightly over the subject of the va`a. Maritime history and exploration records would have to put the Melanesian, Micronesian and Polynesian development of va`a technology and open ocean navigation as the most astounding of all.

In truth, many of the European explorers who bumbled their way across the Pacific, nearly 1500 years after the Polynesian's first voyages, were mere amateurs by comparison. They were just out to gain a little notoriety should they happen across an island or two and thereby lay claim to it for King and country.

It is unfortunate that this Euro-centric perspective of human achievement should be recorded this way. It portrays a blinkered and limited view of maritime technological history and exploration while failing to provide the Polynesians and other cultures of Oceania with the respect that they deserved.

Captain James Cook, one of the most noted and legitimate recorders of first European contact with the Polynesians was clearly impressed with their seafaring skills and with what he saw; noting in 1769, that the canoes were much faster than The *Endeavour*.

Voyaging va`a were 55-60 feet (16.76-18.28m) long with V-sectioned hulls. The hulls were constructed of timber frames or dugout logs with sennit (braided coconut-fibre) used to lash on the wide planks to make up the sides, and then caulked or sealed with breadfruit sap.

European galleons were slow and inefficient for the purpose of voyaging and discovery when compared to the double-hulled voyaging va`a of the Pacific or indeed any other form of sailing va`a.

Such is the enormity and sparseness of the Pacific Ocean that one cannot help but think that the Polynesians must have been infinitely more knowledgeable and attuned to their ocean environment than the luckless European explorers who followed them. Luck could not have been in such good supply to favour and account for all the Polynesian achievements and discoveries.

Mooloolaba Australia. *Captain Cook's Endeavour* Replica in background. Ancient ways relived.

Ancient petroglyph, Hawai`i.

The Shaping of Polynesian Culture and Early Voyages

It is assumed that time spent together in geographic isolation was necessary to develop a common Polynesian language and culture. The first settlers arrived from Eastern Melanesia settling in Tonga, then Samoa roughly 3500 years ago, or 1500BC. Tonga and Samoa are considered to be the cauldron of Polynesian culture. One theory asserts that Polynesian culture was of Indian origin, with a migration into Indonesia before moving on to Tonga then Samoa after a period of around 500 years. Archaeological excavation of a particular style of pottery, known as *Lapita*, provided a link in tracing the migration of people across the Pacific, supporting this Melanesian and Indonesian origin.

There are many theories surrounding the initial voyages of the early Polynesians. One theory states that it began with voyages heading eastward from the shores of Samoa, in va`a of hollowed logs and planks, with sails made of woven leaves, making the first landfall on the Marquesan Island of Nuku Hiva some 2000 years ago (122BC).

From the Marquesas, the Polynesian Marquesans embarked on further ventures across the Pacific. Often this need to move was a result of over population or internal warfare, with the defeated forced to find new lands: Easter Island (Rapu Nui) 2,400 miles (3,862 km), Hawai`i 2,200 miles (3,540 km) via the Society Islands (principally Tahiti and Raiatea), and then on to New Zealand another 3,200 miles (5,149 km).

Theory states that the settlement of Hawai`i was made with the arrival of six va`a, which had set out from Tahiti-Nui, thought to be Borneo. Hawaiian legend supports the Hawaiian people's homelands as Tahiti and the Marquesas Islands. Other theories support a Micronesian origin, based on the type of va`a that were present in Hawai`i - the double hulled va`a and single outrigger with a direct method of attaching the boom to the float and having only two booms. Coincidentally, the ancient name of Havai`i is echoed in the names of several islands throughout Polynesia, the most notable is Savai`i of Samoa.

Similarities in physique, language, legends, va`a design, gods, jewellery and artefacts confirm the links between Polynesian people of different island regions. Their va`a voyages took them to virtually every habitable speck of land in the 'Polynesian

Triangle', making them one of the most significant of all seafaring cultures. With the help of the wind filling their mat sails and paddling during the lulls, they could cover 100-150 miles (160-241 km) a day on the open ocean. Once islands were colonised, paddle powered va`a went on to be fashioned in a variety of designs on all Polynesian Islands, both single and double outrigger and double-hulled.

Polynesians had learned about food preservation and nutrition, and were able to store provisions for journeys that would enable them to cover distances of 5000 miles (8046 km). The Micronesians and Polynesians had learned that warm trade winds created cloud over land masses and that, where they broke up as they drifted downwind, indicated the presence of an atoll. Tinges of the colour green in the clouds can be reflections of the clear shallows of a lagoon, even though the island is well out of sight. Small clues and knowledge such as this made it possible for these voyagers to locate islands which Europeans were later to sail right past.

While these clues may answer some questions, they give rise to many others. The most intriguing question of all was what navigational techniques they used to guide them safely and repeatedly across thousands of miles of ocean within pinpoint accuracy.

The Polynesian Triangle

by Kipeni Su`apa`ia, Ph.D., 1962

'In the central and eastern Pacific, there is a large triangular area known as the 'Islands of Wonders' where the happy and charming Polynesians live. They inhabit the "Polynesian Triangle, which includes such popular groups as Hawai`i, New Zealand, Samoa, Tonga, Tahiti (or Society), Cook and Marquesas Islands. In it are also smaller and scattered groups, such as Ellice, Tuvalu, Phoneix, Tokelau, Austral, Tuamotu and the Equatorial Islands. There are also rarely visited islands, such as Futuna, Wallis, Niue, Pitcairn, Rapa, Mangareva, Henderson and Easter Island. The word "Polynesia" means many islands – it comes from the Greek words 'poly' which means 'many' and 'nesos' which means 'island'.

Loading Taro onto voyaging canoe in Huahine, French Polynesia.

The triangle is formed by drawing a line from Hawai`i to New Zealand, bending westward to include the Ellice Islands (Tuvalu) and passing between Fiji and Tonga. This North to South line forms the base of the triangle with Easter Island is the apex, located 4,000 miles to the East. The Marquesas lie almost in the centre of the eastern line; from Easter in the South to Hawai`i in the North. Samoa, Tonga, Tahiti and the Cook Islands are surrounded by the triangle. New Zealand, the most southern group of Polynesian Islands is where the Maoris live. The striking unity of the languages spoken in these different islands, as well as sufficient similarities in their arts, culture, custom and tradition, allow the world scientists and anthropologists to agree that the Polynesians are a racial unit.'

Voyaging Crews Determined by Physical Prowess

Because of the rigours of travelling thousands of miles over open ocean, male and female crew members were carefully selected. Those chosen needed to have sufficient muscle and stamina as well as ample fat to protect them from the chilling effects of salt spray and wind, and the constant drenching that could occur.

This selection process ensured a positive survival rate and goes a long way to explaining the physical size of some Polynesians, which separates them from other Pacific Island and Pacific Rim peoples. The settlement and procreation of new generations of Polynesians on discovered islands with such formidable stock, gave rise to generations of massive human beings. Taken a step further, it could be said that the voyaging canoe helped to 'shape' the Polynesian people.

Rediscovering Voyaging Skills

Today, many maritime skills are being rekindled, recorded and recreated as part of an ongoing project to learn more about the early Polynesians and to enable today's Polynesians to discover their origins and traditions. *The Bishop Museum* of Honolulu began a quest to ensure the Polynesian culture was effectively documented and recorded for future generations. Today it is recognised as the leading authority on Polynesian culture.

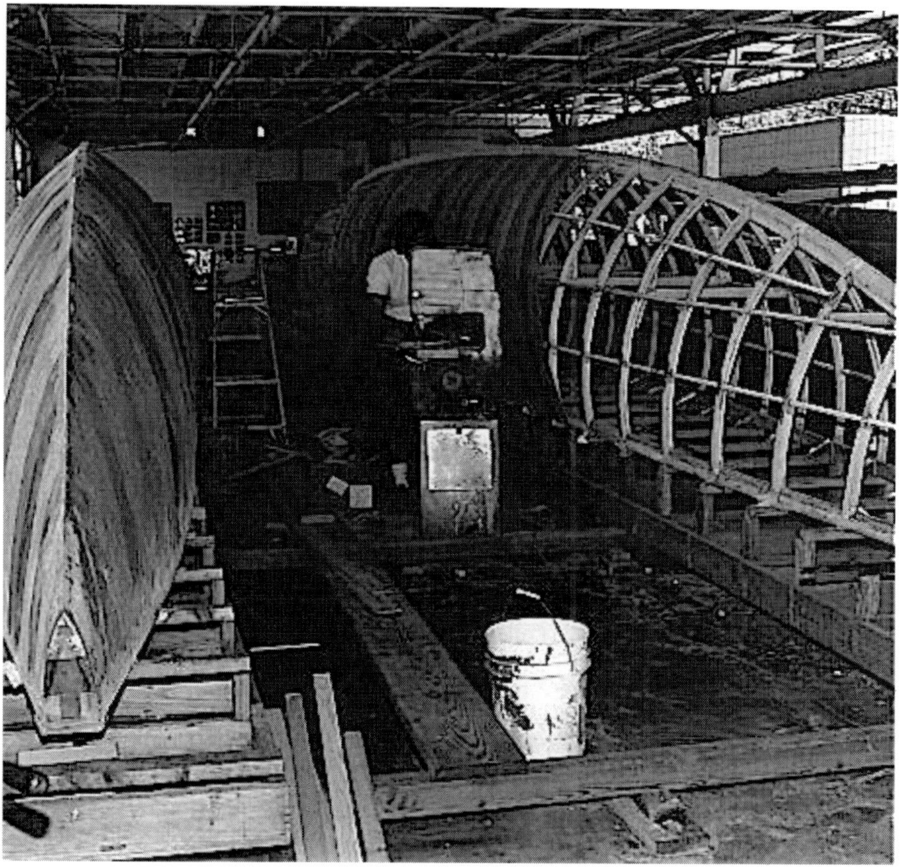

The *Molo`kiha*, voyaging canoe twin hulls under construction. The building of voyaging wa`a and the retracing of ancient trade and migration routes using traditional navigation techniques, has renewed cultural pride and status to Polynesian peoples.

The question of whether Polynesia was settled by windblown castaways or by navigational skill has been put to the test over the last twenty years. *Hokule`a,* a Hawaiian double-hulled wa`a, made its maiden voyage in 1976, with a round-trip between Hawai`i and Tahiti, and has since gone on to amass over 35,000 nautical miles (56,325 km). More recently, in 1995 the *Hawai`i Loa,* made entirely from organic materials, hollowed logs, plaited sails and held together by sennit (woven coconut fibres), set out to retrace the voyages of the Marquesans to Hawai`i - the voyage of the first Hawaiians.

The Hawaiian Outrigger Canoe Voyaging Society (HOCVS) has also embarked on an incredible and unprecedented multi-year journey, with the eventual goal of paddling a six-person Hawaiian wa`a from the most Southern of the Hawaiian

Traditional Hawaiian fishing wa`a from which racing wa`a developed.

Islands to the Northernmost atoll - Kure. Their purpose is to perpetuate through education and experience the Hawaiian culture of traditional long distance wa`a voyaging.

These voyages have proved beyond doubt that navigation was based on star path navigation, wind direction and an ability to distinguish swell direction and motion in relation to the course they were steering. Even in overcast conditions where sun, moon or stars could not be seen, experienced navigators could set a course based on the feel of the ocean swell as it rolled and pitched the canoe beneath them.

Polynesians regularly negotiated one of the longest traditional sea routes in the Pacific using these same navigational techniques for round-trips between Hawai`i and Tahiti, a distance of roughly 6,000 miles (9,655 km).

The voyaging va`a was, as artist, researcher and one of the founders of the Polynesian Voyaging Society, *Herb Kewaunee Kane* puts it, *'The spaceship of the Hawaiian ancestors'*. That initial voyage made by the Samoans – the first Polynesians – began the greatest of maritime ventures, resulting in the exploration and settlement of Polynesia.

Similarity of Va`a Design Across the Pacific

Around 450 AD, the original settlers of Hawai`i, the *kanaka maoli,* brought with them the design concepts of the double-hulled va`a and a va`a with a single outrigger, which had the float lashed directly to two booms.

From this transmigration of maritime technology, today we have a variety of racing va`a, which have their roots in Hawai`i as well as the Tahitian and Marquesan Islands. Developed and streamlined from traditional single outrigger fishing canoes and those used as basic modes of transportation, the va`a has progressively risen again from an almost forgotten time as Hawaiian, Tahitian and Marquesan and other cultures of Oceania renew their associations and connections.

Single, double, three-person, four-person, six-person, eight-person and the double va`a of twelve and sixteen are all being raced today, the biggest variation existing in Tahiti where many different forms of va`a are paddled and raced.

Significance of Contemporary Va`a Racing

Today's six-person racing va`a is a close relative of the traditional coastal fishing wa`a of Hawai`i, with a single-outrigger design. However, its origins stretch further back in time to the settlements of Tahiti, the Marquesas and perhaps even before this. Though it is designed for paddling, many also included a sailing rig and today there is a resurgence of wa`a sailing in Hawai`i, often using conventional racing wa`a modified to accommodate the mast. Va`a racing has evolved into a powerful way for the cultures of Oceania to rekindle and keep alive the legacy and legends of all va`a and the cultures who embraced and developed them into their many and varied forms.

Contemporary va`a racing is intrinsically linked to this past and the cultures from which it came. As it grows in popularity throughout the pacific region, there will inevitably be an ever increasing cross-over between cultures, between those who are European in origin and those who are indigenous to Oceania.

This is brought about by travel to contests within the Pacific region and by the diversity of ethnicity of va`a club memberships, making it unique to the sport. At this time in humankind's progress, surrounded by hype and technology, it's good to be a part of something that has a greater purpose than sport alone.

as one
The ancient oceanic craft and skill of outrigger canoe paddling is an art that symbolizes strength, discipline, determination and teamwork involving mind, body, soul and canoe working together harmoniously as one.

'In essence, va`a racing is not a glamour sport but a cultural one. You cannot help but feel a twinge of the primitive welling up in your emotions as you and five other paddlers, paddle your hearts out across a deep blue ocean; each in time to the paddle rhythm; salt spray mixed with sweat thick on your skin; and the heady sweet smell of the ocean pervading the air.

Paddling in a va`a gets you far out to sea into a truly oceanic environment; amongst the swells, the cobalt blue of the ocean depths, the seabirds, the dolphins, the whales, the sharks and turtles.

The motion of the va`a, the slap of the ama as it slides over an ocean swell and the great sense of harmony that you can achieve, lost in the rhythmic pulse of your paddling, is a feeling that truly transcends time. You slide back a few hundred years to a time when life was very much different than it is today; a world of va`a and legends, of tribal warfare and sacred rights, a time when the Hawaiians and Tahitians were masters of this craft both as craftsmen and paddler.'

Bora Bora Pounding

Ceremony

The va`a was considered by many cultures of Oceania as a living entity, providing a direct link to their entire existence. It was a means of harvesting food from the ocean, a way to travel near or far, and on occasion, a vehicle for warfare and recreation.

Felled and hollowed out, the living tree in some sense underwent a process of death and rebirth, as it was transformed from tree to va`a through the hands of 'its creator', and it held with it a great deal of spiritual significance. This was not the case for all va`a forms, as there existed a correlation between the size of the va`a, the effort required in its creation, the sourcing of the raw material, and the purpose for which it was intended.

Va`a of particular significance were named and consecrated at an official ceremony, the final act before the canoe was launched. Today, these practices are still performed but have been somewhat modified, a relief as human sacrifice was not uncommon, particularly if the va`a was for a high chief. The essential belief was that the ceremony ensured good fortune for both va`a and those who ventured to sea in it.

Out of respect for keeping the notion that the va`a, whether fibreglass or timber, is considered 'alive' and not inanimate, the following protocol are encouraged;

- **Do not jump or step over the va`a when on land – walk around.**
- **Do not sit on the va`a.**
- **Do not swear when in the va`a.**
- **Avoid standing up in the va`a - To avoid damaging hull floor.**
- **On land, the va`a must be positioned facing out towards the ocean, a practice more about being prepared for possible invasion and ease of launching than respect.**

Many clubs wanting to incorporate ceremonies as part of club protocol are often confused about where to begin and concerned about not offending. These ceremonies extend to blessing ceremonies - blessing a va`a pre-race, blessing an event, a canoe naming ceremony, a burial ceremony (deceased paddlers) or simply as an act of remembrance and thanks. Confusion regarding such ceremonies is understandable as without someone familiar with such rituals, the task often becomes somewhat hit and miss. Whether some act of reverence out of ignorance is better than none, is questionable as it's easy to offend without knowing.

Paddler's saying prayer before the race. Huahine, French Polynesia.

There is a curious juxtaposition of western religious practices versus that of the beliefs of early Oceanic cultures. Pre and post missionary intervention meant that the way ceremonies were conducted would have varied considerably, especially in terms of the essential 'content'. Once missionaries arrived in Hawai`i in 1820 for example, traditional, local rituals were outlawed along with other Hawaiian practices. Once the missionaries' stranglehold on the land and people lost its potency, around the 1880s, ceremonies were reintroduced. But after fifty years of cultural intervention, a residual Christian under-tone remained, and ceremonies were no longer strictly of a traditional nature.

Blessing ceremony before the start of the *Queen Lili`uokalani* race. Kona, Hawai`i. Young Moari paddlers in New Zealand (Aotearoa) issue a challenge to competitors.

Hawai`i was of course not alone in this intervention, as most islands of the Pacific endured the same experience. Today's ceremonies often include the local pastor or equivalent. Unfortunately, I have witnessed some truly dismal performances where the individual concerned, not surprisingly, had little or no historic perspective of the significance of the va`a and subsequently no empathy or emotional attachment, through no fault of their own, other than a lack of cultural affinity. The net result was that while words gushed forth, intent, clarity and sincerity were missing, leaving you feeling empty and hollow, and with a sense that some disrespect had resulted.

Actively educating your theologian so he or she is fully acquainted with the significance of what they are being asked to perform, would surely go a long way in bringing more depth to the ceremony. It would not be unreasonable to create your own wording to pass on to the individual charged with the responsibility of performing the ceremony. After all, wedding vows are often written out by the intended couple, so why not extend this to canoe ceremonies? Ultimately, there seems to be no offence in 'localising' your ceremony to accommodate your own cultural needs and understanding of the process. The important thing is that there is depth and sincerity, as well as an effort made to connect the paddlers with the va`a.

Naming Ceremonies and Name Selection

by Kawika Sands

Performing traditional, Hawaiian-style ceremonies, incorporating 'local' perspectives and content or performing a completely local ceremony, are all fine, no matter where you live. My reasoning for this relates to one familiar debate in Hawaiian cultural discussions, exactly when did Hawaiian culture become 'Hawaiian'?

Going back in time, the *kanaka maoli* the first inhabitants of the Hawaiian archipelago, brought with them Tahitian and before that Marquesan culture. Then there is the journey back through Samoa and on back to Southeast Asia. All along this path, the existing culture changed and developed and probably changed again.

Therefore, it can be argued that Hawaiian culture, as we know it, is the latest 'photograph' of the development of this branch of Polynesian culture. That being the case, the ceremony has also changed along the way. It follows that if the ceremony has changed from the past to present-day, it's not surprising that it will continue to change wherever the wa`a takes it.

However, I will argue that one who pretends to be in any way conversant with Hawaiian customs and language, and presumes to use a Hawaiian term, ought to know the proper pronunciation.

Selecting Wa`a Names

(Hawai`i)

You are of course free to name your canoe as you wish. However, traditionally speaking, since the wa`a is regarded to have mana (spirit) of it's own and is to be considered one of the ohana (family) you should give the same consideration as if you are naming a child of your own.

In Hawaiian traditions it is not unusual to name it for the surrounding waters or lands, the people or persons who are responsible for it's acquisition, the ones for which it is intended, for inspirational or historical reasons and so on. However, trying to translate a name or phrase into Hawaiian for naming purposes can be a little tricky.

When there is no direct translation, it is necessary to look at the meaning of the phrase as a whole to be translated instead of the individual words. In suggesting the name *Sea Dragon,* as one club wanted to name its wa`a, I pointed out there was no direct equivalent in Hawaiian for *Dragon*. The closest is *Mo`olele* (Mo`o = lizard, Lele = leap, jump or fly). In suggesting the name *Ming* (a Chinese word meaning 'Moonlight') for a person, I gave *Malamalamaokamahina* (Malamalama = radiant, O = of, Ka = the, Mahina = moon) or *Malama* for short. *Malama* can also mean 'care, keep, heed or beware.'

This brings up the important issue of secondary or alternate meanings. The Hawaiian language is notorious for this, as the meanings of words often depend of exactly how they're used. For example, *Aloha* has about 50 different meanings.

Leilani **– Heavenly Flower. Waikiki, Hawai`i**

Beware of Double Meanings When Naming a Wa`a

by Jane Bockus (Hawai`i)

When *Keauhou Canoe Club* held the *ho`ola`a wa`a* dedication of our new koa wa`a, built by *John Kekua* and *Bobby Puakea,* several names were suggested. Club members were given the opportunity to choose which name they liked best. Prior to presenting the names, the list was submitted to several *kupuna* (elders) for comment.

The name *Kahuna* was proposed, meaning 'breath of life'. *Herb Kane*, noted historian, artist and a member of the founding board of *Keauhou* (formerly *Kauikeaouli*) Canoe Club, pointed out the double meaning here - as well as 'breath of life' *Kahuna* can also mean the last breath of life or 'last gasp'. Needless to say, *Kahuna* was not included in the proposed name list, and *Makaki Kai'* (Sea Wind) was dedicated.

Wa`a Naming

by Tay Perry (Hawai`i)

I don't think that every Hawaiian name given to a canoe or other object needs to be referenced to a place name. I know, however, that this is often the case for names and I see absolutely nothing wrong with tying a wa`a to a location. Some examples of wa`a built prior to the 1960s related to localities, *Mokulua, Papaloa, Hönaunau, Kamala, Waipuna o Kona, Niumalu* and others.

Kehuka' simply means *Sea Spray* and as far as I know does not have place name ties. I was involved in the building of that wa`a and the name was suggested by *Mary Pukui* through *Dorothy Barerre* of the *Bishop Museum*. I do not know any of the *kaona* meaning in that name, although there might have been some. Unfortunately, I don't think that the wa`a exists any longer, as I have not heard of it's whereabouts for the past twenty years.

Wa`a of similar vintage had

Early morning race prayer, Marquesas Islands. Sacred Tei fronds tied to rear manu, for good fortune and Honu (turtle) tattoos.

names such as, *Leilani, Kakina, Hanakeoki, Malia, Lanakila, Hoolale, Manuiwa, Hokulele, Paoa, Uila* and *Kaualani.* These had no obvious connection to a particular place. The *Kakina, Hanakeoke, Hökulele* and *Paoa* and possibly *Leilani* were named after specific people. These were, *Lorrin Thurston,* someone named *George, Star Weaver, Duke Kahanamoku* and someone named *Leilani* respectively.

Also some old koa wa`a had names such as, *White Horse, Princess, Royal Hawaiian* and *Captain,* which obviously were not in the Hawaiian language, but certainly were totally Hawaiian wa`a.

An Ancient Hawaiian Wa`a Naming Prayer

The following is from *Na Pule Kahiko.* Ancient Hawaiian Prayers, *June Gutmanis*, Honolulu, Editions Limited, 1983.

Translations: 'O Mokuhali`i, Kupa`aike`e, Lea', Mokuhäli`i - A God of Canoe Makers, Küpä`aike`e - Swivel Head Adze God, Lea - Goddess of Canoe Makers.

English

'Here is the pig,
A payment, a gift, an offering,
A sacrifice to all of you.
The wa`a (name) is completed,
A (type of wa`a) floating in the sea.
It is his fish to seek, to obtain wealth.
Look very closely all of you.
Beware of the coral heads,
The stone hills of the reef,
The waves, the billows of the ocean.
All of you direct the wa`a to places of deep sea,
That the wa`a goes over the waves of the sea.
That the wa`a may go till weather worn,
Till worn out and covered with limu and
The cane sounds.
`Amama. It is free of taboo.'

The reference to the 'cane sounds' relates to when someone is old and must use a cane stick and makes the sound of, 'tap, tap, tap'.

Hawaiian

E Mokuhäli`i,
Küpä`aike`e, Lea Eia ka pua`a, He uku,
He makana, he `älana, He möhai ia `oukou.
Ua pa`a ka wa`a (inoa)
(`ano) a e ho`olana `ia aku ana i ke kai
O kana i`a e huli ai i ka loa`a a me ka waiwai.
E nänä pono loa `oukou
E maka`ala i na püko`a,
na pu`upohaku o kähi laupapa
Na nalu, na `ale o ka moana.
Ho`oholo no `oukou i ka wa`a ma kähi
hohonu o ke kai, I hele ai ka wa`a a nalukai
A `äpalu, a ulu ka limu pakaiea,
a kaniko`oko`o.
`Ämama, ua noa. Pau.

Pakaiea = A type of limu (seaweed) Kaniko`oko`o.

Sunrise, Halo O Lano, starting point of the Moloka`i Hoe. A rock temple, iconic in form and intent, constructed by paddlers.

'Imparting Brains' to the Wa`a

Source: Hawaiian Canoe-Building Traditions,
Kamehameha Schools Bernice Pauahi Bishop Press, Honolulu 1995.

It was normal to float the wa`a prior to a naming or consecrating ceremony. This formal ceremony was called, *lolo `ana ka wa`a i ka halau' Lolo `ana ka wa `a*, translates to 'imparting brains to the wa`a.' Performed correctly, the service was made to ensure the safety of the wa'a and owner.

With the wa`a placed in the *halau* (shelter) a *pua`a hiwa* (black pig) *niu hiwa* (coconuts) *kumu* (red fish) *`uala* (sweet potatoes) *kalo* (taro) and sometimes a *`ilio* (dog) were placed before the *kahuna kalai wa`a* (wa`a builder) and wa`a. The offerings were for the gods.

The *kahuna kalai wa`a* would then pray in silence. During this period of silence, if there was a disturbance, it was considered that the wa`a was imperfect. If there was no disturbance, the *kahuna kalai wa`a* would declare the wa`a ready.

The wa`a would then be put in the water for a short fishing trip. If red fish were caught, it was considered a good omen. After returning to shore, the fish would be offered and more prayers followed. On occasion, a live pig was placed in the hull of the wa`a. If the pig went to the front of the wa`a it was considered good, if it then went on to jump out from the front, it was declared a wa`a of exceptional qualities.

Burial Ceremonies

It's not uncommon that departed long-time watermen and women would be cremated and have their ashes spread upon the ocean in which they played. Nor is it uncommon for a remembrance ceremony to be held, without the formality the spreading of ashes. Like most Polynesian ceremonies, sunrise appears to be the most poignant time to hold such ceremony. Paddling onto the water before the sun rises, wa`a can come together in silence. Once the sun has risen, words can be spoken by whomever needs to express their self – often regarding the life of that person, but it can also be to express an apology to or regrets. The idea is to create positive *mana* energy and to let that person go in peace. Symbolically, prayer is followed by the practice of throwing flower *leis* into the ocean.

Watermen's Burial Poem

Bury me deep in the clear blue sea
Where the crashing waves will spray over me
Where my soul will rise with the risen sun
And be surfing (paddling) still when the day is done.

Hawaiian Historical Perspective

The va`a has been the principal mode of transportation in Oceania for thousands of years. While its direct role in everyday life throughout the Pacific region has diminished, giving way to the outboard motor and boats of contemporary design, va`a racing has created a renewal of the passion and an assurance that the legend of the va`a will live forever.

Hawaiian Wa`a Racing - Origins and Wa`a Types

Wa`a racing evolved as a natural extension of the ancient Hawaiian's everyday relationship with the single-outrigger wa`a, which was used primarily for coastal fishing. While the ocean supplied most of their food, it also provided for their sport and recreation.

Prestige was gained by the village whose canoe team was victorious. Popular amongst neighbouring villages and island communities, betting was one of the primary driving forces behind wa`a racing. And it was not always for trivial things, sometimes there were major possessions at stake such as land and wives. In some respect, wa`a racing took the place of warfare, as the competitive nature of the sport i.e. the gruelling physical and mental demands, made it a reasonable substitute for battle.

Chiefs chose the strongest and most respected paddlers to represent them in races with the promise of special status within the community should they be victorious. Races often began far out from shore with the first wa`a to arrive on the beach declared the winner.

Wa`a used in races were of varying length, weight, width, and even differed in the number of crew. Because of this, teams were clearly either doomed before the start or at a distinct advantage, an issue not resolved until the 1960s with the design and manufacture of the *Malia* class fibreglass wa`a.

When *Captain Cook* first landed at *Kealakekua Bay* in 1779, 3000 wa`a carrying some 15,000 Islanders paddled out to greet the strange bulging vessel. Over those initial years of contact and co-habitation with the Hawaiian peoples, European visitors were continually astounded by the Hawaiian's athletic abilities and skills on the water but particularly by their paddling skills.

Missionary, *Hiram Bingham* was obviously fascinated by the mechanics of wa`a paddling and noted, *'...nine or ten athletic men in each of the coupled canoes, making regular and effective strokes, each raising his head erect and lifting one hand high to throw the paddle blade forward beside the canoe, the rowers, dipping their paddles and bowing simultaneously and earnestly, swept their paddles back with naked muscular arms, making the brine boil, and giving great speed to their novel and serviceable sea-craft.'*

Intervention

Despite this admiration, Christian missionaries, in their enthusiasm to save the souls of this heathen race, were quick to discourage wa`a racing and other traditional water sports, such as surfing, among their new converts. It was believed that too much frivolity and gambling, an intrinsic part of the wa'a race, were not the way to salvation. By the turn of the twentieth century these aquatic activities were all but wiped out, as paddlers replaced their paddles with bibles and hymnbooks.

Modesty and an adherence to puritanical ethics became the standard of behaviour for the Polynesians; freedom lost in the playgrounds of their gardens and oceans. Wa`a paddling and surfing were not the only casualties of this bleak period of Hawaiian history as many other ancient arts, crafts and beliefs were eroded.

Reinstatement of Contemporary Racing

During the mid 1800s, after some fifty years of adherence to the missionary's wishes, a defiant resurgence of interest in aquatic sports began. A 'boat race' was held May 20, 1859 in honour of the first birthday of *Prince Kalakaua* of Hawai`i, son of *King Kamehameha IV* and *Queen Emma*. Following this and before Kalakaua's ascension to the throne in 1875, aquatic events were held at regular intervals. A great lover of water sports, *King Kalakaua* (1874-1891) encouraged the revival of both sailing and paddle races with the commencement of an annual November regatta.

A Hawaiian revivalist, he encouraged the return of Hawaiian traditions such as the *hula* dance which the missionaries called the 'heathen dance'. He also composed the national Hawaiian anthem the *Hawai`i Ponoi* (now the state song) sung before the Moloka`i to O`ahu marathon race. It must be noted that many of the early regattas featured barges (row boats) of western-design with few wa`a entries. Without question the Hawaiian people felt a need to reconnect with their past as the influence of the missionaries began to decline.

The Hawaiians needed little encouragement to be enticed back to their ancestral and traditional water sports. By the early 1900s, regattas began to evolve with a similar format to those performed a hundred years prior to the arrival of the missionaries. In 1908, the most significant step towards the formal rebirth of outrigger wa`a racing and surfing occurred with the founding of the *Outrigger Canoe Club* by a small group of *haole* (European) businessmen. It was a shame they choose not to call it the, *'The Wa`a Club'*. The aim was to establish a foundation from which wa`a racing and surfing could be rekindled throughout the Islands after such a long stagnation.

Also founded in 1908 was *Hui Nalu Surfing Club*. It was formally chartered by a group of Hawaiian surfers to promote surfing and swimming and by 1910 began pitting its own wa`a crews against the *Outrigger Canoe Club*. This club rivalry was to become the catalyst for the establishment of other clubs.

With its resurrection, wa`a racing became not only a healthy pastime, but the salvation of a Hawaiian cultural activity that had been an intrinsic part of their way of life and a link with their heritage. The first regatta devoted entirely to the wa`a was held in 1922 and divisions existed in W2, W4 and W6. It was not until the 1940s that it was agreed that racing needed to have formalised rules and regulations to avoid some of the disagreements which were arising as wa`a racing became much more than just a social event.

Rides for the Tourists - The Legend of the Waikiki Beach Boys

by Greg Heller

Led by pioneers such as *George Freeth* and *Duke Kahanamoku*, turn-of-the-century (Waikiki) *Beach Boys* helped revitalize an ancient surfing culture that had languished under oppressive European constraints. Surfing and wa'a paddling hadn't completely vanished, but were frowned upon as frivolous and immoral when European civilization took root in Hawai`i during the 1800s. Fortunately, a small band of watermen persevered and went on to see the ailing pastime into the 20th century.

Around 1901, when the first tourist resorts were being completed at Waikiki, these men found their calling. They earned their livelihood from surfing instruction and wa`a rides for tourists. As more resorts were completed and *Honolulu* tourism started to boom, surfing with the *Beach Boys* became a major attraction.

Under these conditions, surfing and subsequently wa`a rides would be introduced to the world through the writings of *Jack London*. In Waikiki with his wife in 1907, *London* met journalist / organizer *Alexander Hume Ford*. *Ford* took *London* surfing and introduced him to 23-year-old *Freeth*, the most accomplished surfer of the time. *London* was so entranced by surfing, and *Freeth* in particular, that he wrote a piece for *Woman's Home Companion* depicting the *'Royal Sport for the Natural Kings of Earth'*.

This vintage postcard, which I found in a Honolulu antique shop, reads: 'Surfboarding and exciting outrigger canoe rides are popular Hawaiian water sports at sunny Waikiki Beach. Diamond Head crater, in the background, is seen from the air while approaching Honolulu on United Mainliner Stratocruisers'.

The *Beach Boys* of Waikiki - entertaining visiting tourist to the island of O`ahu since the early 1990s providing canoe rides. 'Canoe-Surfing' is the quintessential Hawaiian thing to do for the visitor. Top 1950s, below 1990s and still going strong.

Wa`a (canoe) surfing has been a part of the Waikiki beach scene for many years. Prior to the 1960's, the *Outrigger Canoe Club* located on the beachfront, was very active in providing rides for travellers from all walks of life (becoming the thing to do when in Waikiki) using converted fishing wa`a and some purpose-built surfing wa`a. This was to change in the early 1960s when the *Outrigger Canoe Club* was relocated.

Wa`a rides became formalised with hotel beach services cashing-in on and perpetuating them. Along the beachfront, fibreglass surf wa`a await the tourist and vendors shout out to attract a crew to venture out into the Waikiki surf. If nothing else, it is at least a truly Hawaiian experience for the tourist and serves to keep one of the Hawaiian's traditional pastimes alive and well, even though some of the *Aloha Spirit* has long since waned.

The *Ala Wai Canal* O`ahu

***Ala Wai Canal* Waikiki.**

Built in 1922, the *Ala Wai Canal* was constructed to divert the streams that flowed into Waikiki to the detriment of the Hawaiian farmers who had their water drained away from them. Located immediately behind the hotels and shops of Waikiki, the *Ala Wai Canal* has become a popular venue for outrigger canoe clubs and as a training ground for all manner of paddle-craft.

Long and straight, flanked on one side by parks and a golf course, the canal is home to various canoe clubs, providing a perfect location from which to operate with easy access to the ocean via the *Ala Wai Yacht Harbour* and on to open water. Most famous of these, the *Waikiki Surf Club* relocated here from the Waikiki beachfront when the lease expired on their long-standing site, which was subsequently sold and developed.

The *Outrigger Canoe Club*, founded in 1908, was also located for many years on Waikiki beach. In 1963, the lease on their site was due to expire and was acquired by *Roy Kelley* who went on to build the first of the *Outrigger Hotels, Outrigger Waikiki,* in 1967. *'Duke's Barefoot Bar & Restaurant'* named after, Hawai`i's most famous waterman Olympian and indigenous Hawaiian, *Duke Kahanamoku* and the colourful surfing and canoeing legacy of Waikiki, commemorates those early days, located on the beachfront beneath the hotel.

Waikiki Surf Club's* unmistakable red and yellow wa`a on the *Ala Wai.

The *Outrigger Hotels Group* is now the largest in Hawai`i. The *Outrigger Canoe Club* relocated to *Outrigger Beach* at the foot of *Diamond Head* on a two-acre site and was officially opened on 4 January 1964. The club has extensive facilities that include dining and bar services, fitness centre, volleyball courts and much more. Its dedication plaque at the clubhouse entrance reads:

'Let this be a place where man may commune with sun and sand and sea, where good fellowship and aloha prevail, and where the sports of old Hawai`i shall always have a home.'

Aloha

An involvement with the sport of va`a will ultimately take you beyond the physical to a spiritual view of the world as embraced by the Polynesians. The notion of 'Aloha' is one of these worlds. Visit Hawai`i and you're likely to hear it a couple of hundred times a day. It is said that it is more than a word; it's a way of life.

Fundamentally, it is an extraordinarily complex notion of what love, life, compassion and understanding alludes to being. Many wa`a clubs incorporate this notion as a part of their constitution. I once heard it described as not being about politeness, repression of instinct, or sensibility, but about bone deep emotion. It grows out of a feeling, not limited by written language, but out of the senses and of primal instinct. The ancient Hawaiians discovered Hawai`i out of such instinct, which Europeans loosely termed as good-fortune and chance.

Aloha is an emotional prism, spawned from an affinity with the ocean, to an extent that European culture has never quite grasped. While Europeans built stiff-ships to withstand the pounding of the ocean, Polynesians built wa`a from organic materials designed to morph and flex with the ocean. They shaped wa`a hulls and sails to go with the wind, not against. They designed for speed, not necessarily comfort. Essential ingredients included physical prowess, a sense of play and adventure with nature, elevated instincts and a zest for a life lived on the edge; based on a fundamental philosophical and spiritual notion that it is better to work with nature than against it.

Aloha per se is a sense of spirit which alludes to faith in self, life, the universe and fundamentally an acceptance that nature is bigger than the sum of the whole of humanities collective thoughts and concerns. Just how it relates to wa`a racing is ultimately what you make of it.

In the context of present day Hawai`i, aloha is endemic, yet fundamentally elusive; a worn out clichéd anachronism for the most part, with little real meaning being that the tourist industry and many locals, have embraced, branded, commercialised and buggerised it to the point of non-sense. Competitive sport and the notion of aloha, is a concept diametrically opposed and while some paddlers certainly live and race with the *aloha spirit*, I have witnessed many who do not.

Hawaiian Acacia Koa Wa`a

Traditionally, koa was the most valued timber for the construction of Hawaiian wa`a and many other items, including 18' (5.5m) 150lb (68kg) surfboards. Two hundred years ago, koa trees were plentiful, but today like many other sought after trees, they are rare. The acacia koa tree is a timber not unlike mahogany. It is beautiful and incredibly strong, ideal for the rigours and demands of an ocean craft.

A koa wa`a is a functional object of beauty, transcending conventional notions of art. It is a manifestation of vision and purity of purpose. The creation of a single wa`a requires a time line of several hundred years from the time the tree starts to grow, matures, is selected, felled or falls, blessed, carved and finally named, to be reborn once again in what is considered a living entity - the wa`a.

Located high up on the mountain slopes, koa is today found largely on the island of *Hawai`i*, on *Mt Hualalai*, *Mauna Loa* and *Mauna Kea* at an elevation of 4-5,000ft (1,200–1,500m) where cool air and high rainfall suit these magnificent trees.

One massive log, split in two, forms the basis for two 'twin' hulls one to go to the island of Maui the other to remain on Hawai`i.

The natural environment in which they flourish often makes them inaccessible in soggy gullies, deep ravines and on steep slopes. An ideal wa`a tree must stand a straight 50ft (15.24m), have a diameter of 4ft (1.21m), and weigh as much as 20,000lbs (907kg), which makes felling and transportation an enormous task.

The selection of a koa tree, its felling, transportation from the mountain slopes and curing can cost as much as US$25,000. It can then take as long as seven months to complete the process of carving and construction. A wa`a sculptured from timber can be sold for as much as US$75,000.

Axe (Adze) marks reflect hours of initial work.

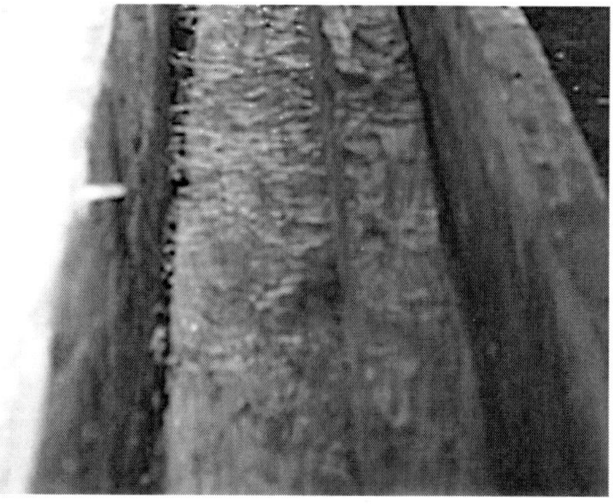

Koa Wa`a Ceremony

Such was the importance given to this entire process of tree selection that in ancient times the task was given to a *kahuna* priest. He would set out into the forests high up on the mountain slopes, committed to finding a suitable tree. He would spend many weeks, even months, observing the forest life, the birds and animals and their interaction with the trees. Most importantly, he would determine the *mana* (spirit, energy, life-force) that surrounded the tree, to assess its suitability.

The whole process was steeped in reverence. From the selection of the tree by the *kahuna*, the felling of the tree, the selection of the adze to be used, to the blessing and naming ceremony the wa`a would receive before it was finally ceremoniously launched. The day to day use of the koa wa`a still incorporates respect in its handling and storage, a practice maintained to this day amongst many clubs.

The Value of Club Ownership and Links with the Past

It is said that the koa wa`a instils a greater sense of respect in paddlers as a result of the handmade quality, the natural timbers and the knowledge that you are paddling one of Hawai`i's last remaining links with the past. Their remains a feeling amongst some clubs, that ownership of a koa wa`a is an essential requirement. It's mere presence is an object of beauty, which educates simply by being, and ownership provides the members with a deeper empathy for the culture and evolution of the wa`a. Throughout the Hawaiian Islands, there are approximately 100 koa wa`a in regular club use for regatta and sprint racing.

In 1995, I visited the club headquarters of *Kai E Hitu* on the island of Hawai`i, which has strong connections with the islands of Tahiti. Not a wealthy club by any means, they are however asset rich in the ownership of their koa Tahitian made va`a in which they take enormous pride.

Tahitian master carvers have had a very strong influence upon Hawaiian wa`a designs, which up until specification ruling were introduced spurned a strong synergy between Tahitian and Hawaiian craftsman.

Where membership is strongly indigenous, there seems to be greater emphasis on protocol, ritual, ceremony, food, music, family and of the koa wa`a and indeed less on the winning and more on the participation.

Restoration of Decaying Koa Wa`a and of Cultural Pride

In 1999, *Walter Guild* took me to visit a koa workshop located on *Sand Island, Honolulu*, founded by the late *Wright Bowman Jnr.* Managed by *Allan Dowsett* and run by brother *Jay*, the workshop undertakes vital restoration work to preserve koa wa`a of all types. The *State Harbours Division* provides the space, an enormous open shed, resembling a giant *halau*. Every available space is taken up with koa wa`a, rescued from backyards and beaches were they had been rotting.

Allan Dowsett **stands next to the *A`a* koa wa`a built in 1902 by *Henry Weeks* is for *Prince Kuhio*. Below; The *A`a* - a national treasure.**

At the time of my visit, *Allan* was working on possibly the most famous koa wa`a of them all, the *A`a* which was on loan from the *Bishop Museum*. It was considered to be the first known purpose built racing wa`a, commissioned by *Prince Kuhio* and built in 1902 by *Henry Weeks*. At the time it was the fastest wa`a in the Hawaiian Islands,

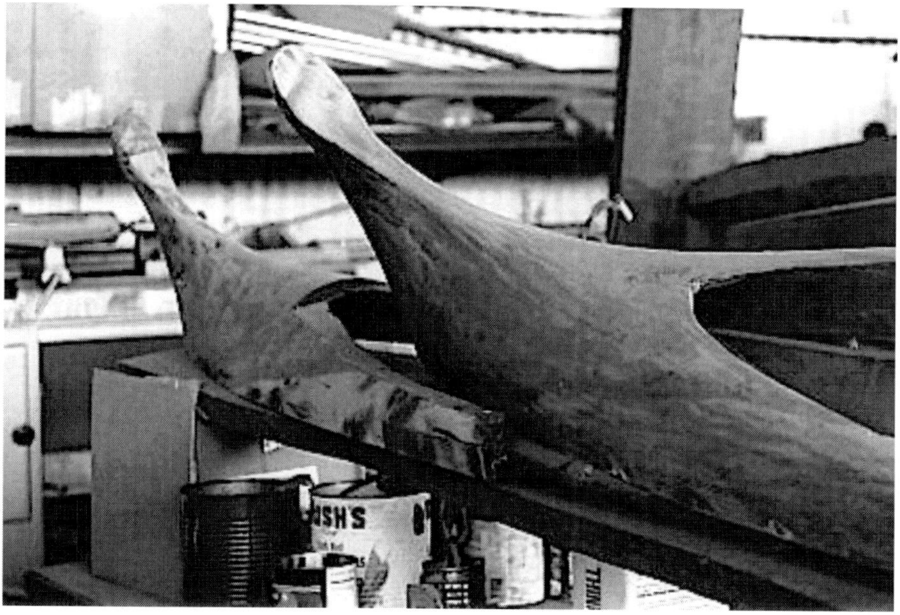

Koa bow cover one piece construction, *kupe`ulu*. Note wide spatula shaped manu extremity. Below a surfing wa`a which once surfed the breakers of Waikiki Beach awaits the final restoration touches. These Hawaiian icons, are priceless, beyond measure of mere dollar value, essential to the fabric of the Hawaiian Islands.

Hibiscus *Hau* ama of natural shape and curvature awaits the attention of craftsman.

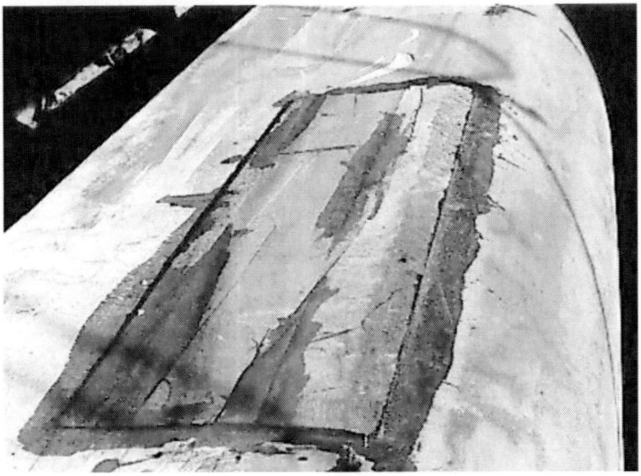

Patch work is the most common repair method used to repair damages which koa wa`a sustain.

On the island of Hawai`i, *Manny Vincent's* koa workshop overflows with repair work to be undertaken on koa wa`a.

crewed by a *Kona* crew to win a series of races from 1909-1910.

Allan recognised that with so many koa wa`a simply being allowed to decompose, with each loss, a unique piece of Hawaiian culture was being lost at the same time. Volunteers come together to work on the wa`a and gain a valuable lesson in an ancient craft. Restoration of the wa`a, encourages a restoration of cultural pride and therefore it is the perfect synergy with a very positive outcome. Specialised tools, educational programs and the learning of new skills have all been created as a result of the workshop.

Once a koa wa`a is restored, the difficulty is in knowing what to do with it. Historic value is priceless and the sentiment towards the wa`a are such that they are not sold, but loaned out to hotels and restaurants, where they are often suspended from ceilings, hung over bars or displayed in foyers. They are iconic in their very form, things of beauty and grace that both tourists and locals benefit from in the ambience they create.

Design Limits

The Severing of Tahitian and Hawaiian Design Alliances

Traditional Hawaiian Racing Wa`a?

In ancient times, no racing va`a of specific design existed within the geographical area of Oceania; at least most research would seem to imply this fact, yet va`a racing existed in isolated regions of the Pacific. The making of a va`a was a communal effort requiring the use of valuable raw materials. It was a utilitarian device of survival and great value, the notion of constructing a va`a simply for the purpose of racing would have been considered extravagant in the extreme. Consequently, va`a used for races were no more than fishing and trading craft.

Hawaiian traditional fishing wa`a. Often paddled to the fishing grounds early in the morning and sailed home on the afternoon trades. Honaunau, Hawai`i.

If such practice existed it would have ultimately been at the command of a chief or royalty. This was the case in 1902, with the making of the famous *A`a* koa wa`a in Hawai`i, built for *Prince Kuhio* specifically for the purpose of racing and the first in recorded history.

As the sport grew throughout the Hawaiian Islands, design specifications were introduced. Two major factors which lead to the introduction of the specifications were the influx of Tahitian designers into Hawai`i in the mid 1970s and the unprecedented 1976 victory of a Tahitian crew in Hawai`i's prestigious Moloka`i to O`ahu race. While some native Hawaiians were involved, the changes were primarily brought about by Anglo-Hawaiians, setting out in strict empirical terms what defined an 'Hawaiian' team racing wa`a.

The late Tommy Holmes in his book 'The Hawaiian Canoe' writes,
'Kaunakakai, Moloka`i October 1976 – the ocean is calm. A sleek, half-breed canoe explodes from the starting line and handily wins the Moloka`i - O'ahu Canoe Race. The impact of this victory continues to be felt. Made and paddled by Tahitians, the canoe was experimental, a marriage of Tahitian and Hawaiian design elements. It appeared to be faster than any existing 'traditional' Hawaiian racing canoe, at least under relatively flat-water conditions on that day. The following year, in response to this victory, specifications defining a 'Hawaiian canoe' were established to ensure that in future races, no canoe would have an unfair advantage.'

In short, the specifications created were determined by applying the 'law of averages', measuring the lengths, beams, draught, water line lengths and rocker line of existing competition koa racing wa`a, most built after 1930. Thus they arrived at a set of specifications, the limits of which, continue to this day to define what is or is not, an Hawaiian racing wa`a, be it koa or synthetic.

Arguably, to address the loss of this race on this particular day via the rulebook seems even today a knee jerk reaction, addressing what can only be described as a cultural juxtaposition. One could question whether this was actually about protecting tradition or because the Tahitians defeated the Hawaiians at their premier race. In addition, it also suggested that the Tahitian success was due entirely to their va`a, with little regard for the talents of the athletes themselves.

Notions of ensuring a singular wa`a (or va`a) *does not have an unfair advantage* because of a superior design, is a narrow view of competition. This is especially so when you consider the sport from the artisan's point of view throughout Polynesian and indeed Oceania. To be true to this virtue, the introduction of a *One-Design Class* as exists in yacht and dinghy racing is the only reasonable way to create neutrality between designs and therefore base results solely on the merits of the competitors.

The most compelling argument against the implementation of design rulings can be based on the very simple premise that there exists little or no evidence to support the notion that ancient Hawaiians designed purpose built racing wa`a. Therefore the manifestations of these rulings are entirely contemporary in concept and based upon no traditional virtue whatsoever.

Tommy Holmes in his book, *The Hawaiian Canoe* notes, *'After almost forty years of unquestioning reproduction of the Malia type Kona canoe, local Hawaiian canoeists, subsequent to exposure to Tahitian-type canoes, began experimenting in 1977 with some new designs. With few guidelines as to what defines a Hawaiian canoe, it has been difficult to say when certain racing canoes built in Hawai`i today depart from what is, or would have been considered Hawaiian.....regretfully the answers to these and other related questions do not exist.'*

Consequently, when you view this argument from the viewpoint of defining what is a traditional Hawaiian racing wa`a over that which is not, it soon becomes a moot

Fibreglass *Malia* wa`a designed 1933. Photo *Chris O'Kieffe*.

point. The Koa *Malia* shaped in 1933 could be considered contemporary as was the Tahitian-Hawaiian canoe raced in 1976. In view of these considerations, and as no rules existed at the time of their creation, we should consider the thought applied at that time, as contemporary, not traditional or ancient.

Billy Danford recounts,' *The koa canoe has its own spiritual presence and is the traditional canoe which provides the means to perform the rite of passage for all who have crossed the Kaiwi (Moloka`i) Channel in a Hawaiian Canoe. It is the purest form of a racing canoe or pre-contact canoe in limited edition. It is the ultimate spiritual crossing and remains more so today. Artisans of the twentieth century such as Weeks, Yamasaki, Takimoto, Grace, Mokuohai, and Henriques, were the traditionalists of koa craftsmanship. Their accomplishments have been well documented as have the innovative input of George Downing, Walley Froiseth, Rudy Choy and George Perry & Son and the renaissance canoe builders; Joe Quigg, Wright Bowman Jr. and Sonny Bradley.*

Possibly the greatest impact by any one group of craftsman has come from the Tahitians. Puaa Niho and several others from Tahiti, crafted koa va`a, using the traditional shallow draft 'V' shaped hull starting in 1975. In a very short time, the traditional values of Hawai`i were viewed as being 'compromised'. For the second time in seventeen years, innovative changes resulting in a new fleet of Tahitian designed va`a, forced the sports governing body, the Hawaiian Canoe Racing Association (HCRA) in 1977-78 to establish new rules governing the construction of 'new' traditional Hawaiian hybrid koa wa`a.

Consequently, future modifications to many of the existing Tahitian va`a would have to be made in order to protect the integrity of the traditional Hawaiian wa`a. All of the new artisans and other craftsmen over time have had a hand in melding the knowledge of wood and glass with the understanding of the ocean environment, to create new and improved hybrids of the Hawaiian koa and fibreglass racing wa`a.'

Tahitian shaped and inspired va`a on the island of Hawai`i.

Tahiti and Hawai`i Six Degrees of Separation

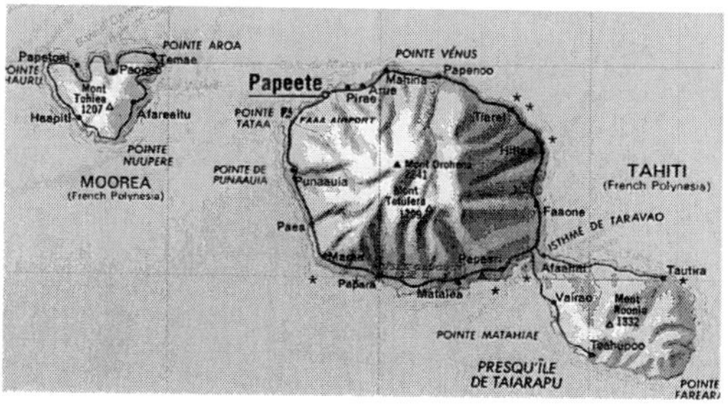

The islands of French Polynesian, sprinkled like emeralds across a vast expanse of the Pacific Ocean, are both isolated and remote in comparison to the relative notoriety of the Hawaiian Islands. While Hawai`i can take much credit for developing contemporary open ocean wa`a racing, it is the influence of the Tahitians which has profoundly influenced the evolution of va`a design and paddling technique across the Pacific and beyond, even to the extent of permeating the Hawaiian consciousness in the design of their own wa`a.

When you get down to the fundamentals, Hawai`i is culturally linked to Tahiti via ethnicity and origin causing the eventual introduction of design specifications to be considered by many Tahitians as a cultural slap in the face. It also ceased an ancient dissemination of knowledge between artisans from these two regions, at least in practical terms.

The rationale for creating design limits is thin when you consider that racing va`a in both Tahiti and Hawai`i at the time were being rationalised not on the basis of cultural narrow mindedness, but to create a faster va`a. There clearly existed a mutual cultural synergy; an open exchange of maritime architectural knowledge between artisans separated by distance, not culture, founded out of respect not the lack thereof.

If we concede that Hawai`i was settled by voyages from Tahiti and the Marquesas, the question must be asked, at what point did the Hawaiian wa`a evolve uniquely from that of the Tahitian va`a? And if this synergy of cultural exchange has been occurring since settlement, what genuine justification can be made for interfering with what was no more than a natural evolutionary process?

'*On June 25th 2005, Tahitian Carver Leon Teamo 'Fafa' Toofa aged 67 drowned when swept off rocks on the island of Maui. During his life on Maui, he crafted as many as 20 koa racing wa`a along with wa`a for hotels and restaurants.*' News items like this reinforce the Tahitians assimilation within the Hawaiian community as respected *kalai* wa`a.

There is a strong tribal notion running at the core of the sport. Pride and prejudice not withstanding, the sport is now larger than what one island group or culture can claim. Fundamentally, va`a racing and the craft itself, are the sum of the whole of all who have had influence on its conception over hundreds, if not thousands of years, and arguably should not be limited in its evolution.

The rules for French Polynesia read; *'There is no imposed shape. Wood, plastic or any other material may be used for the va`a or ama. The i`ato (i'ako) must be made of wood. 150kg is the minimum weight for the hull with spray cover accessories. 120kg is the minimum weight for the va`a without ballast. 30kg is maximum weight of the ballast. No water pumps, or foot chocks, drifters or keel to be added to the hull.'*

This is in stark contrast to almost every other Pacific Rim country, region, state and island group, which has chosen to align itself with the Hawaiian view of things and adopt their design limitations. While the USA, Canada and Australia, with eyes wide shut, have failed to consider the Tahitian factor or relevance, other regions have adopted for the Tahitian view or a blend of both, notably New Caledonia, Wallis Futuna and Southern France.

Established or emerging regions have tended to align either with the Hawaiian or Tahitian 'interpretation', with merits on both sides of the fence. However if you are interested in keeping the red tape to a minimum, together with the fundamental belief in the advancement of the craft itself (and the sport as a whole), then the Tahitian option is by far the better option.

Under such terms, va`a builders and artisans of French Polynesia are at liberty to advance va`a design. Those who implement and oversee va`a racing in these islands, acknowledge their fundamental right as Polynesians to continue the search and advancement of the va`a without restriction, thereby perpetuating their maritime heritage and honouring the skills of their ancestors.

From the mountainous Society Islands of Bora Bora, Tahaa, Raiate`a and Huahine and the principal islands of Tahiti and Moorea to the low lying Tuamotu Archipelago, Austral Islands and Mangareva and to the far flung reaches of the

Marquesas Islands, va`a artisans are free to act upon every instinct and implement this within va`a design as is their birth right without restriction or limit.

The Implications of Wa`a Specifications

Ceasing the evolution of the Hawaiian va`a, runs contrary to almost every notion of progressive thought amongst every culture. It seems an erroneous assumption to presume the Hawaiian wa`a had essentially reached a zenith and could no longer be made better, faster or more efficient. Was this not an insult to contemporary *kalai wa`a* indigenous to Hawai`i or were they too of the view that progress should cease? It would be hard to believe this was so.

If the purpose of introducing design limits was to specifically protect the integrity of the Hawaiian koa wa`a, then why did such specifications extend to include all 'fibreglass' wa`a, the legacy of which has served only to discourage the design of a superior wa`a. From retarded hull lines to the continued insistence of a minimum 400lb hull weight, a rule imposed in 1954, the ramifications have spread far and wide to every country and region having embraced these Hawaiian design limits.

From the outset, it seems the entire process was fundamentally flawed by a cultural juxtaposition with no place, nor rationale for Anglo-Hawaiian intervention. Hawaiian *kalai* wa`a were not working to any limitation of design, far from it. Natural instincts, inherent skills and an exchange of ideas determined the final design. There was no reason for a specific 'limited design' criteria as far as the *kalai wa`a* was concerned.

Doubtless the definition of what constitutes an 'outrigger canoe' is vital, yet there seems to have been an almost detrimental concern as to what specifically defines an 'Hawaiian' wa`a, above and beyond all other types, which came either before or after. Wa`a racing, is more often than not referred to as *Hawaiian Canoe Racing*, as if a stand alone sport; yet what of the Tahitians and every other Pacific Island region which now participates?

At the *Queen Lili`uokalani* race September 6, 2005, *Kai E Hitu Canoe Club's* open mens crew won the 18 mile iron race. However, they were second over the line by some way to *Lanakai,* disqualified for paddling a Tahitian designed va`a, which had been paid for by their sponsor, the *Ocean Club.* At a mere five inches over the maximum allowed length of 45', the va`a was defined as 'illegal'. When you reflect on the cultural logic of this, it makes no sense whatsoever. Ironically, *Kai E Hitu*'s strong Tahitian links makes the story all the more ironic.

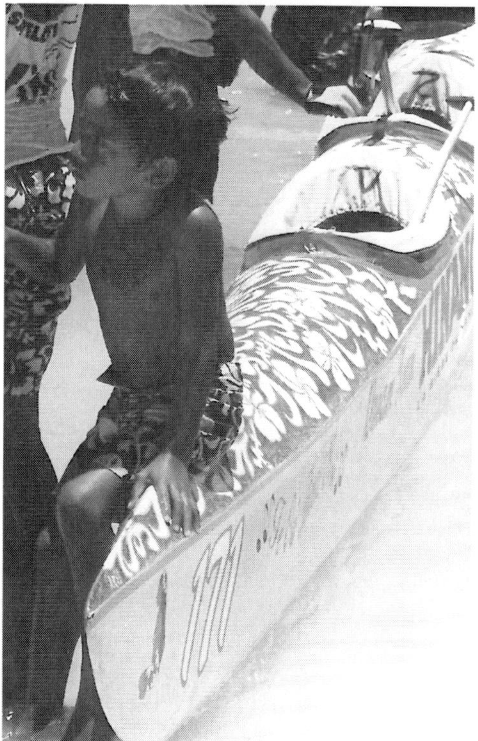

Implications of Design Limits for the Manufacturer

While specification limitations were ostensibly created to protect the integrity and originality of the Hawaiian koa racing wa`a, these mathematical scribblings went a long way towards serving the needs of the manufacturer of the fibreglass wa`a just as they were gaining momentum.

A cynic might argue that the implementation of design limits was no more than a smoke-screen protection mechanism, safeguarding the financial investment of manufactures of fibreglass wa`a, ousting limited one-off so called 'hybrids' which could potentially affect sales of any one particular synthetic racing wa`a design.

Manufacturers needed to feel protected through the mechanism of a defined set of specifications, as implemented by a governing association and more often than not influenced by the manufacturers themselves. Whenever the investment of money is involved and the return thereof, commercial considerations can affect people's values.

Ultimately this 'system' protects and permits the manufacturer to invest in research and development to create a wa`a within defined parameters and commit to producing wa`a in quantities for a period of time in order to recoup costs and profit. In French Polynesia, no such mechanism exists and consequently many va`a remain 'hand-made' one-off designs. With much secrecy and speculation regarding va`a design remaining open-ended, they allow the designs to evolve as a natural extension of the culture itself.

With the exception of the HCRA regatta season where koa wa`a are raced, no international teams compete. In the context of the Moloka`i to O`ahu International race, even as far back as the mid 1970s, fibreglass wa`a numbers were on the increase and koa numbers on the decrease, to the point that today, koa entries are few and far between.

Are we to assume the rule makers at this time could not see the future-trend and that in hindsight an 'open-class' of wa`a, as exists in the French Polynesia, would have been the best way forward in the context of open ocean racing?

Weight Issues

Throughout Hawai`i, the 400lb (181kg) rule has been applied to six person racing wa`a since 1954 and is still the oldest standing ruling imposed upon the Hawaiian wa`a. The weight was agreed upon as the average minimum weight that wa`a builders considered sufficient to ensure the structural integrity of the wa`a. If you attempt to shave down your koa wa`a too much, it's liable to break apart in rough water, and they still do at times, even at 400lbs plus. Realistically, without additional 'specific' requirements as to where the weight should be or how the wa`a should be constructed, it could just as easily weigh 600lb and fall apart, or 300 lbs and hold together.

Karel Tresnak of *Outrigger Connection* Hawai'i, regularly builds his *Mirage* wa`a to around 170kgs, 375lbs, which the clubs add weights to bring up to the 400lb limit. Over time, as the wa`a may gain some weight, the weights are removed accordingly. The Australian minimum weight is 330lbs or 150kg, whilst Canada and mainland USA adhere to the 181kg, 400lb ruling. Tahiti specifies a minimum of 330lbs, 150kgs 'hull only' weight complete with spray cover accessories, or 264lbs, 120kg without.

Forty years on from the first fibreglass wa`a and fifty years on from the establishment of the ruling and it's hardly surprising that there is pressure to lower the weight of team racing wa`a, as technology makes it possible, even affordable.

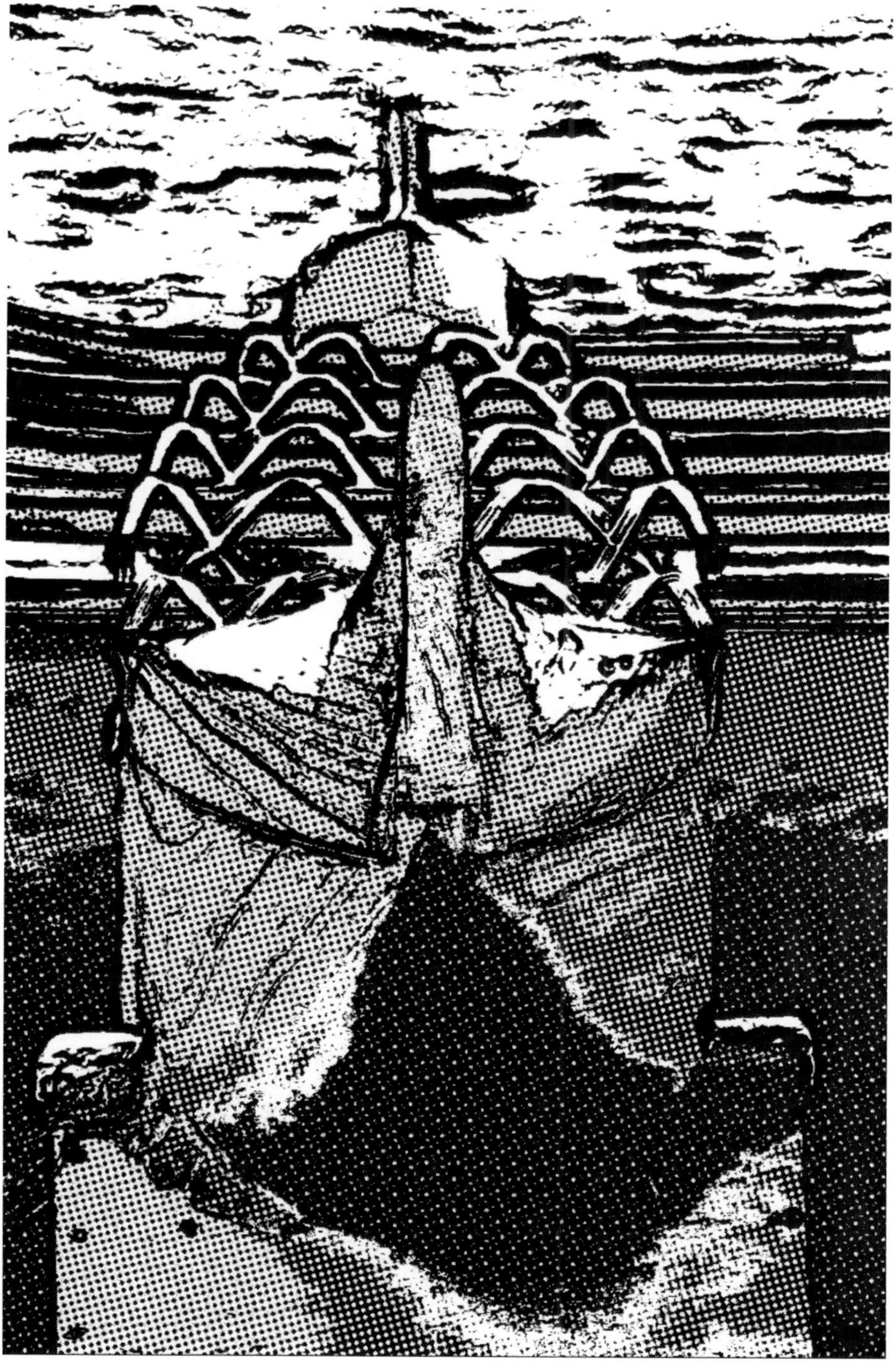

Paddlers naturally want to go faster, want to get more out of what they put in and inevitably there comes a time in every sports evolution, where the athlete demands more of their equipment than it is capable of delivering. This is especially true with team racing wa`a. Ordinarily this results in improvements and refinements so the athlete can continue their own development, thereby raising the bar on the sport as a whole. If we had decided that surfing was indeed a Hawaiian tradition practiced on 200lb koa surfboards and that's how it had to be, where would surfing be today - *Tom Blake's* radical 'paddleboard' of 1926 rejected in favour of continued use of 200lb surfboards for surfboard paddling . . .

Comparatively, ocean OC1's have constantly evolved and manufacturers enjoy pushing the envelope on all levels while paddlers have consequently reaped the rewards of being involved with a hi-tech paddle sport. As ocean athletes, they have not been 'held back' in terms of their athleticism and skill. As a follow on consequence, new and innovative OC1 events are being created, supported by sponsors, many of which offer monetary prizes.

If weight restrictions were relaxed, does this mean the use of exotics and high end manufacturing techniques would greatly increase the costs, creating a sport of elitism and one limited to the financially well off? Well, if you seriously believe that money is the relevant issue, consider that the cost of a koa log is around USD$35,000 even before the *kalai wa'a* has got his hands on it, once he has you can add another USD $25,000. This is huge money for a low-tech wa`a (no disrespect intended) and it takes every ounce of fund raising and skimping to raise the dollars to make this possible. Yet most Hawaiian clubs manage and its not just the more well off ones, but the more obscure ones as well, who remain faithful to the traditional koa wa`a.

Based on this, elitism in owning a synthetic made lightweight wa`a is a non-issue as the cost would be far less than that of a koa wa`a. Currently, one could argue elitism is in owning a koa wa`a. The argument that koa and fibreglass wa`a must be nearly the same weight to keep racing fair against each other, is a worn out moot point, as they simply don't race against each other, period. If they ever do so, side by side, they are in different divisions and as far as rough water races such as the Moloka`i to O`ahu are concerned, the number of koa wa`a entering the event has been dwindling for years.

80kg *Mirage*. Who wouldn't want to paddle one of these.

Karel Tresnak comments, *'It's a very sensitive issue. Traditionalists will tell you that you are jeopardising traditional koa canoes, if that's so, then anything constructed out of plastic is a threat to koa canoes, to tradition if you will. If you look at the Moloka`i to Oahu race, nobody is using koa canoes as they are so precious and clubs want to protect them. Also, from an environmental point of view, as the koa is now protected, it cannot be harvested and there is a massive shortage of raw material.*

If it wasn't for fibreglass, we wouldn't see the enormous growth of the sport. Every time I attach an ama on the left of the canoe, I honour the tradition of an ancient Polynesian design and I say this with a great deal of appreciation for this seaworthy, beautiful design. So from where I stand, what does it matter what it's made of?

If the ancient Hawaiians could have made their boats lighter, they would have, but unfortunately the trend is heading the other way. In 2002, the Canadian Association decided to bring all their OC6's up to 400lbs and demanded manufacturers make them to this weight on all club orders.'

As the sport has spread around the world, it seems the Hawaiian soothsayers have done a good job in convincing the rest of the world of the need to adhere to a weight ruling which is fundamentally no longer relevant. From the viewpoint of someone contacting the *International Va'a Federation* enquiring about starting the sport in their region, it would be interesting to hear what advice would be given regarding the choice, whether to go with the Tahitian or Hawaiian interpretation.

Expounding the virtues of safety as a basis for 'heavy' wa`a has also become irrelevant, since lightweight wa`a can be manufactured that are actually stronger than their heavier counterparts. They even last longer, so you get more value for your dollar. As time moves on and the sport spreads to more highly populated, affluent societies, the push for change will prevail. With these issues in consideration, it's a wonder more regions simply don't take more developmental issues into their own hands, while also being sensitive to the 'spirit of the sport'.

Without the benefit - or hindrance, of having one true unifying world body, the sport is open to a revolt. As more advanced designs, materials and manufacturing techniques of OC1s and OC2s are employed, it's only natural for the end user to question why they don't see this happening for team racing wa`a. The majority of paddlers want progress and mass consciousness generally wins out over the concerns of minorities who want to maintain the status quo even to the extent of questioning which traditions should remain and which should go.

'I made the carbon, lightweight Mirage, because it needed to be done and if paddlers could see it, carry it, paddle it and feel the difference - and there is a huge difference - they will ultimately pressure the Associations to change the rules. I saw the opportunity to do something unique and we took the chance. After the first one was made, I went on to make one for Canoe Camp Hawaii on Maui and one for New York.' Karel Tresnak.

In short it was not 'traditional' to build a 400lb wa`a, there just weren't many options in terms of raw materials. If a 'culture' can be defined by its 'people' then we can say with some certainty that all cultures have strived for advancement on one level or another.

During the thousands of years of maritime architectural evolution of the va`a, the Polynesians weren't limited by specifications of length, width, curvatures and weight, and only the 'village idiot' would have suggested such an imposition.

That paddlers and manufacturers want to advance the sport, embrace it, make it the best it can be, and raise it to new heights, is only natural. It should be seen as anything but disrespectful to the sport, indeed it is an indication of how much they value it and acknowledge the maritime skills and ingenuity of the ancient cultures of Oceania.

Evolution of the Fibreglass Hawaiian Racing Wa`a

By Bill Danford

'For the purposes of this chapter, the term 'wa`a' will refer to 'Hawaiian' not 'Polynesian' craft, but whether koa or fibreglass, they each evolved from the Polynesian Archipelago. The racing wa`a being discussed are of Hawaiian origin, though ultimately influenced by Tahitian artisans.'

The Californian *Balboa Bay Club Puamana*, a modified *Malia* in 1979, became one of the earliest composite wa`a constructed in synthetic materials, weighing 276lbs compared to the 400lb plus koa wa`a of Hawai`i.

Over the past forty years, without the actions of a few, the sport of Hawaiian wa`a racing may have entered the twenty first century from a completely different direction. Had wa`a officials in Hawai`i in the 50s listened more intently to *Louis Kahanamoku* and *'Toots' Minieville,* the introduction of the fibreglass Hawaiian wa`a may have developed more favourably and been accepted earlier than 1963. It is said that when *Duke Kahanamoku* was asked about the chance of the sport of Hawaiian wa`a racing taking roots on mainland USA, he voiced doubts as to whether it would gain any interest.

The koa wa`a has its own spiritual presence. It is the traditional wa`a which provides the means to perform the rite of passage for all who have crossed the Kaiwi Channel between the island of Moloka`i and O`ahu. It is the ultimate spiritual crossing and remains more so today. The koa wa`a entries have been diminishing as they age and because of the high financial burden on clubs in the event of damage or loss of the wa`a.

Artisans of the twentieth century such as *Weeks, Yamasaki, Takimoto, Grace, Mokuohai,* and *Henriques,* were the traditionalists of koa craftsmanship. Their accomplishments have been well documented as have the innovative input of *George Downing, Walley Froiseth, Rudy Choy* and *George Perry & Son* as well as the renaissance wa`a builders *Joe Quigg, Wright Bowman Jr.* and *Sonny Bradley.*

1933 | The *Malia* Wa`a

by Terry Wallace

The *Malia* has been the subject of fact, myth and legend throughout her illustrious lifetime. The blonde koa log used was about four hundred years old. It was felled and rough carved in 1933 above *Kailua Kona*, Hawai`i on the *Greenwell Estate*.

The *kahuna kalai wa'a* was *James Takeo Yamasaki.* The original 1933 length was 39'2" and in 1950 it was lengthened to 39'6" in 1973 further lengthened to 40'1".

In 1940, *Outrigger Canoe Club* commissioned *'Dad' Center* to purchase three wa`a at USD$200 each from the island of Hawai`i. He purchased the *Leilani* - sister wa`a of *Kakina* and *Malia*. The former wa`a were kept by the club, with *Dad* keeping the *Malia* for himself.

The *Malia* from which the first fibreglass wa`a were produced spurning expansion of the sport; and a new industry.

In 1948, the *Malia* was sold to *Waikiki Surf Club* for a whopping USD$2000. *Wally Froiseth* recounts, *'It was very expensive, but we needed a wa`a. It was either get our own or keep borrowing.' 'Dad' Center* received a USD$500 down payment, raised through a dance at the *Wai`alae Golf Course.* In 1950, *Wally Froiseth, George Downing* and *Rudy Choy* made changes to the bow design and in 1952, the *Malia* was used in the first Moloka`i to O`ahu Canoe Race, it came in second place.

Payments continued up until the second staging of the Moloka`i to O`ahu Canoe Race in 1953. The club finished as winners and collected a cheque for $500, as well as being runners up in the *Lanakila* for another $300. *'It was enough to pay the balance of the Malia'*, *Froiseth* recalls.

The *Malia* in the first Moloka`i to O`ahu Race. Photo *Wally Froiseth*.

Changes to the *Malia* were made for the race as *Wally Froiseth* recalls, *'We glassed a fin to the bottom of the ama, thinking this would give the canoe more stability, preventing too much leeway. What happened instead was that the ama turned out to be too effective. It put so much stress on the ama that it began to break the cords and also cut into the i`ako, making them loose, to the point where we had to jump into the water to fix it up.'* Though their dramas began eight miles from Diamond Head and despite being miles out front, the crew from Moloka`i eventually passed the disabled wa`a to win.

Between 1952 -'54, *Malia* won 14 straight Senior Men's races. In 1953 and between 1958 -'63, the *Malia* won the Moloka`i to O`ahu race and in 1959 won the inaugural Catalina Island to Newport, California race.

In 1960, the first fibreglass copy of *Malia*, named *Kawale`a*, a type of small fish, participated in the Moloka`i to O`ahu race, paddled by a crew from Newport OCC. During this race, another sister wa`a of *Malia*, *Malama* owned and paddled by *Waikiki Surf Club*, won the race in a record time of 5:24mins. This record stood until 1981, when it was broken by the Californian Club *Imua*. In 1961, the *Malia* won the Moloka`i to O`ahu race despite capsizing three times.

Between 1960 and 1978, fibreglass Malia wa`a participated in a separate Fibreglass Division of the Moloka`i to O`ahu race and in 1966, '69, '70, '72, '73 a fibreglass Malia won the event overall. In 1973, *Malia* was paddled 250miles, retracing the journey of *King Kamehameha's* invasion of O`ahu. In 1978 a Californian crew, *'Blazing*

Paddles' become the first 'foreigners' to win the Moloka`i to O`ahu race paddling a fibreglass *Malia*.

In 1978, a fibreglass *Malia, Wa`alele* crossed the English Channel in 4:15mins and was presented to the *Captain Cook Museum* in Middlesborough commemorating the 200th anniversary of Cook's landing in Hawai`i. Then in 1980, the *Malia Division* was founded by the *Kalifornia Outrigger Association* and in 1981 the first *Malia* wa`a were made in Australia.

1959 | Introduction of Wa`a Racing To Mainland America

In 1959, the first long distance mainland Hawaiian wa`a race took place in California between Catalina Island and Newport. Two koa wa`a, the legendary *Malia* crafted by *James Yamasaki* and the *Niuhi*, were transported by a *Matson Navigation Company* ship from Honolulu to the West Coast of California. There was to be a cultural exchange and race between a California crew in the *Niuhi* and a Hawai`i crew in the *Malia*, which won.

Niuhi, is the Hawaiian name given to man-eating sharks such as the Tiger and Great White. In old Hawai`i, catching the *Niuhi* was the game of chiefs, a dangerous sport for which special techniques were developed. The name *Malia* is hard to translate depending on the intent of whom ever named the wa`a. It could mean, 'To Flatter' or 'Perhaps' or 'To recollect' or be a women's name, *Mary*. It can also mean 'Calm' or 'Peaceful'.

'Toots' Minvielle, had fortuitously met with *Tommy Zahn* from Santa Monica who had just paddled the *Kaiwi Channel* on a surfboard. *Toots* asked *Tommy* would, 'outrigger canoeing' be embraced by Californians. *Tommy* subsequently set up a meeting in 1959 with *Tra David*, owner of the *Newport Dunes Resort, Sam Miller*, Commodore of *Balboa Bay Club* and *Al Oberg*, Harbour Master of Newport Beach. This meeting led

1973. The *Malia* retracing *King Kamehameha's* invasion of O`ahu.

Punching out through and English shorebreak

to the introduction of wa`a paddling and the founding of the Catalina to Newport *Dunes* Race – called at that time, the 'California Outrigger Classic'.

The event was won by *Toots' Hawaiian All-Star* team in 5hrs paddling the *Malia,* with the Californian team finishing just 11 minutes behind in *Niuhi*. Some of the Hawaiian crew included; *Chris Bodie, Blu Makua, Archie Kuana, Joe Gilman, Sonny Heniques,* and *Dougie Carr*. Californians included; *George Kopa, Tom Johnson, Dan Uadis, Frank Saddler, Mike Johnson, Dave Arne, Doug Wood, Ron Druman, Lorrin Harrison* and others.

Lorrin Harrison, the steerer for the *Niuhi* recalls, *'I had a dugout wa`a that I had built in 1950 and when I first heard about outrigger canoe racing coming to California, I was down in Doheny. Noah Kalama came by and asked if I could put a bunch of guys together to race against Hawaiians.'* A group of fifteen guys trained from the *Dunes* most nights until late for several months under *Lorrin's* guidance leading up to the race.

In historical terms, *Toots Minvielle* initiated Hawaiian wa`a racing on the mainland. His Californian counterparts started the first long distance marathon wa`a race and with it a long and fruitful beginning to the sport.

1959 | Californians Take Mould from Koa Wa`a, *Malia*

Of equal importance was the fact that this one event, now known as *'Catalina'*, spawned a new breed of innovative craftsmen and watermen. It also kindled an ongoing rivalry between two very similar coastal lifestyles and the development of the first fibreglass wa`a. Year after year this would be played out between California and Hawai`i in the Moloka`i Channel and Catalina races.

I think the individuals in California, who through their action of creating the first mould from a koa Hawaiian wa`a the *Malia*, permanently inscribed themselves into the sport's history. I can only surmise that California, as a leader in building boats and surfboards at that time, had the technological capability and the opportunity to make a fibreglass duplicate from one of Hawai`i's finest and most revered koa wa`a.

Classic Catalina. Below: Catalina Island.

I do not think that their acts were dishonest or unethical, for without this impulsive act, in all probability, the fibreglass racing wa`a would have taken years to develop. *Noah Kalama* and *Tom Johnson,* realising the development of wa`a racing off the California coastline would hinge upon California based wa`a, made a decision to make a mould. Pure and simple, the need to perpetuate the sport and manufacture a wa`a inexpensively and expediently, was basis enough at the time to act as they did.

Tom Johnson recalls that the *Malia* was placed in *Sea Scout Storage*, in the Newport facility, after completing of the Catalina race, awaiting shipment back to Hawai`i. Most of the *Hawaiian All Stars* equipment, shoes, paddles, cover, etc, were still packed in the hull which was sitting on the cradled trailer along with the *Niuhi.*

Tom Johnson had a working knowledge of moulds as well as newly fabricated glass and polyester products. He developed the first gun stock out of fibreglass for the *Armalite AR-15.* He also worked on the first fibreglass shell used for the helmets worn by jet pilots, fibreglass milk crates and tow targets for the Air Force, just to mention a few. He knew how to work with a mould, but building a mould was another matter.

Tom Johnson, now in his eighties and retired, recounted to me via telephone that initially he and several others involved in the early stages of wa`a paddling urged *Noah Kalama* to get permission to allow the *Balboa Outrigger Club* to use the *Malia* as a plug and create a mould. *Noah* was either reluctant or just hesitant about asking the *Surf Club* for permission *Tom* speculated, but said, '*... receiving no final answer from the Hawaiian club, they pointed out to Noah that being an officer of the club in Hawai`i and since no one had come back with an answer, he had the authority to give permission*'. Reluctantly and after much prodding, *Noah* with *Tom* and two Armalite workers took the *Malia,* still on the trailer to a boat manufacturer who made moulds.

They turned *Malia* upside down on the trailer, and cleaned and taped the hull. They then applied a parting agent to the entire hull and shot the hull with a black tooling gel coat. As the final step, they took a chopper gun and sprayed the gel coat with fibreglass and resin. In less then forty eight hours, they lifted the 3/8" plus thick shell, placed it on the top of a station wagon and returned the *Malia* to storage.

The shell was hidden on top of a building until the next spring when they turned the mould upright and built flanges for adapting the gunnels. The first *Malia Class Racer* out of the mould was the *Kawelea*. The effect on wa`a racing in California was instantaneous. This one act would clearly bring about dramatic changes and the rivalry between Hawai`i and California would instantly intensified.

In 1959, a Californian crew headed by *Tom Johnson* from *Balboa Outrigger Club* entered the Moloka`i Channel race as the first Californian or 'foreign entry'. Having just lost to the *Hawaii All Star Team* in Catalina, the *Balboa* crew was up for the challenge, but not the rough channel. They ended up capsizing in the koa *Niuhi*. After being towed close to shore, they re-entered the canoe and finished the race.

1960 | The First Fibreglass Wa`a Enters Moloka`i Race

Prior to 1978, the racecourse had changed at least five times over a span of twenty-five years. From 1978 to the present day, the course has been set; Hale O Lono, Moloka`i to Fort De Russey Beach, Honolulu, O`ahu, a distance of 48 miles.

In 1960, the first *Malia* fibreglass wa`a *Kawelea* was entered by the Californian club, *Balboa Outrigger Club* in the Kaiwi Channel competition. Since there was no classification other than koa, the *Balboa* fibreglass entry raced unofficially and was allowed to cross with the rest of the field.

Ironically, *Waikiki Surf Club* finished first overall in the koa *Malia* and set a new record 5:29mins, *Outrigger Canoe Club* was second in the sister koa wa`a *Leilani* at 5:32mins, *Lanikai* third in a koa, and *Santa Monica Life Guards* in the koa *Niuhi* came fourth. The fibreglass *Balboa* entry *Kawelea* was fifth and *Doheney* the fourth Californian crew in the koa *Hilo Boy* was ninth in 5:51mins.

I was paddling my first Moloka`i with *Outrigger Canoe Club* and I clearly remember how happy we were that we had beaten some very good athletes from Southern California, especially the professional life guards from Santa Monica.

Early days in California.

Because of the rumours which surrounded the development of the *Kawelea* and of the way it was introduced into competition, not much could be done to reverse the tide of resentment at that time. Sadly, the whole technological advancement and achievement were overlooked. The fibreglass wa`a became an instant threat to traditional wa`a values and it was perceived that the Californian crews were trying to break with tradition.

HCRA disallowed a fibreglass division over the next two years but the sport of wa`a racing, using fibreglass wa`a began to pick up interest along the California coastline.

Californian Wa`a Racing Grows

By 1961 eight clubs were firmly established and by 1963 the *Kalifornia Outrigger Association* or KOA was created to govern the sport. *Hawai`i All Stars* continued to win over the *californian boys* in the Catalina to Newport Canoe Race up to 1970. *Imua* of California with *Dennis Campbell* steering would win all long distance races along the California coastline until the Tahitians arrived in 1975 defeating them.

Tom Johnson, after paying off his partners for the original cost of the mould, went on to utilise his innovative fibreglass skills and continue to manufacturer the *Malia Class* from *Kern,* California. *Tom* was responsible for the first generation production of approximately 20 *Malia Class* wa`a, the *Kawelea* and the *Virginia* (after his wife) for the *Balboa Club,* the *Bella* (after *Noah Kalama's* wife) for the newly established Newport Club, the *Mamo Kai* for *Marina Del Rey,* one each for the *Santa Monica* and *Redondo Clubs* and fifteen to various Hawaiian clubs including the *Kawelea, Mahimahi* and one other used by *Balboa* in the 1962 Moloka`i. The *Kawelea,* was left with *Waikiki Surf Club* after the 1960 channel crossing and eventually purchased by the club. *Outrigger Canoe Club* purchased the two other *Malia* used by *Balboa* in the 1961 and 1962 Moloka`i crossings.

In 1968 *Bud Hoh* and *Mud Warner* developed the second generation *Malia* or *Balboa Mould* by using the *Oio,* the sixth wa`a out of the original mould as a plug. The plug was coated with black tooling gel and a flange was created to strengthen the hull and attach the gunnels to a new hull. Metal saddles were attached to the mould to jack rocker into a hull if desired as well as added leg supports to the mould. They went on to create ten of these wa`a financed by the *Balboa Club.* The mould was sold to *California Canoes Ltd*. at a later date.

In 1974, *Al Ching* bought the original 1959 mould and in 1976 left that mould with his brother *Roy Ching* in Northern California. A new fleet of racing wa`a were available as new clubs developed along the Northern California coastline.

Al Ching recounts, *'In 1974, as a young head coach of Lanakila OCC, I decided to track down the only outrigger mould in California. We were a four year old club and we needed canoes. No one at that time was mass-producing. I tracked down the owner of the Malia mould, Tom Johnson who lived in the mountains above Lake Isabella. He subsequently sold the mould to me for USD$600, along with a ton of advice. I kept the mould for several years, building a few canoes for the club and for a few others in Northern California and Hawai`i.*

We experimented with different hull configurations by laying up thinned skinned hulls and squeezing plywood frames inside the mould. We cut and reshaped the thin hulls using backsaw blades and shears. If it didn't work, we just broke it up and threw it out. Over time we concluded the hull needed greater rocker - curvature, for and aft to perform better in the ocean, increased length and proportionally narrowed, but the Malias were

Regatta day California

Californian Dreamin - Fibreglass *Malia* in the late 1970s on a glassy Californian Ocean. California's involvement with the sport pushed traditional values to the limit, but has done wonders for the common good and expansion of the sport.

restricted by rulings to 39'6". In 1976 I built the last two Malias for Okalani CC in Oakland, California and left the mould with my brother Roy. I never saw the mould again. A club borrowed it and never returned it.'

Many of the *Malia* in Northern California were purchased from Southern California Clubs who were upgrading. *Eddie Fonseca* built a lot of wa`a in the early 1980s. According to the late *Bob Steele* in Sacramento, California, there continued to be no commercial manufacturers of *Malia*. Occasionally, if a club was interested in building their own *Malia, O'Kalani OCC* of Alameda, California who had the mould, would rent it out to competent craftsmen.

Fibreglass Wa`a Manufacture in Hawai`i

By 1960, the Hawaiian *Malia* mould was being developed by *George Downing* in Hawai`i. *Tay Perry,* recalls that *George Downing* produced several of the wa`a himself utilising the skills of *George Caprivisa,* who worked with fibreglass at *Industrial Plastics. Caprivisa* would lay up the hulls at the old *Royal Brewery* on *Queen Street* on his own time.

Eventually, the manufacturing of the *Malia* mould fell to *George Perry* who continued to use *George Caprivisa* for the lay up work. *George* and his son *Tay* would finish off the wa`a using wood for the front and back manu. Californian made *Malia* wa`a had a separate mould for the glass *manu. Tay* also recalls that they produced approximately fifteen to twenty glass racers prior to 1975.

In 1971, *Sandy Stein* was paddling for the *Healani Canoe Club* on O`ahu. *Healani* had just won the Moloka`i to O`ahu race in the club's koa wa`a *Papaloa. Sandy* recalled to me from Maui, where he is still working hard building restaurants and other projects, that he and *Cappy Sheeley* started to manufacture fibreglass *Malia* on O`ahu around 1968. They used the wa`a *Oio* which was made from a California *Malia* that *Healani* had purchased from *Bud Hohl* (*Balboa* mould). This started them in the fibreglass business and eventually they founded *The Fiber Glass Shop* in Honolulu producing many *Malia* class racers.

Before *Sandy* sold the shop in 1977, *Brent Bixler* of Kailua started to work with him. *Brent* remembers that the mould was slightly twisted and crude. The hulls being finished were labour intensive needing to be cleaned up and the thirty foot wood gunnels had to be attached to the outside of the hull with adhesive and screws.

1963 | HCRA Includes Fibreglass Division to Moloka`i Hoe | Hui Wa`a Association Forms in the 1970s and Uses Fibreglass Wa`a Exclusively.

In 1963 HCRA incorporated the Fibreglass division in the Moloka`i Channel crossing. Throughout the 60s and 70s, the *Malia Class Racer* worked its way into various Hawaiian clubs. It became the workhorse for training new crews and allowed clubs to put their highly valued koa wa`a into storage until race day. Newly established clubs who did not have the financial support to have a koa wa`a would eventually start their own association, *Hui Wa`a*.

***Hui Wa'a* came into existence at this time and used only fibreglass wa`a in their new association. *Bob Crepes* was a real perfectionist and in 1976 made a new mould and implemented several innovative changes. There were uniform floatation tanks, the gunnel was now part of the mould which added symmetry and strength to the hull, along with an additional eight inches to the overall length of the wa`a. He then set up a refined system to manufacture the wa`a using more efficient techniques to handle the hundred or more orders which began to poor into the shop. Finally he purchased the shop and business in 1977.**

Brent remembers that, '*Our production of the Malia Class Racer brought about parity for at least five years to canoe racing in Hawai`i. All two hundred seventy plus canoes which we produced throughout Hawai`i were uniform after we remade the mould. All hulls were numbered and the list kept up to date with the Coast Guard until 1983.*'

The fibreglass wa`a was the racing vehicle of the association and in the 1970s put on a Kaiwi Channel race which excluded the traditional koa. The *Malia* is still used in our High School, Hawaiian wa`a racing venue and there are different *Malia* divisions in the *Queen Lili`uokalani* race in Kona, Hawai`i every Labor Day weekend and in California.

Outrigger Canoe Club won the first fibreglass division entry with its *Mahimahi* in the 1963 Moloka`i in 6:51mins. The late *Mike Tongg* of *Waikiki Surf Club* recalled that he was on the second crew which raced in the *Kawelea* and came in second in the fibreglass division. Once again the koa *Malia* placed first overall. For the next thirteen years the koa wa`a remained unbeatable and traditional values, rivalries and sportsmanship continued to flourish in the Moloka`i to O`ahu event.

1975 | Tahitian Paddlers Turn Up the Heat in California and Hawai`i.

The Catalina to Newport venue continued through the 1973 season but would not be re-established until 1979-1980 by *John Rader, Bud Hohl* and *Billy Whitford*. Long distance racing would continue in fibreglass wa`a along the coastline of California prior to the return of Catalina venue. California clubs such as *Santa Monica, Balboa, Newport, Doheney, Marina Del Ray, Redondo, Lanakila, Dana Point* and *Imu*a would continue the rivalry between Californian and Hawaiian crews until Tahiti made their first showing in the Moloka`i to O`ahu race of 1975.

In 1975, *Dennis Campbell* and *Imua* were poised to win their first Moloka`i. But at the end of the crossing *Outrigger Canoe Club* was first overall, with second going to *Maire Nui* of Tahiti, one of three Tahitian crews and third to *Imua*. This was not only a hard loss for *Imua*, but also a humbling experience, again creating another hotly contested rivalry to be fought in the channel between Tahiti, Hawai`i and California.

Ten Tahitian teams returned in 1976 with several newly designed koa va`a which were longer and had different water lines due to the V-shape of the hull, but they weighed 400 pounds. The outcome was an all Tahitian Fête. They took the first 4 places, as well as 7 out of the top 10 places, with only ten Tahitian crews out of a field of 35 teams. *Dennis Campbell* and the *Imua* team would place ninth overall. The Tahitians, in just one year, introduced the sleek Tahitian design and also a new paddling technique. They made their debut along the California Coastline in 1977 winning the fifty-two mile race from Marina Del Ray to Newport and again defeating Imua.

After the 1976 all Tahitian review in the channel, Tahitian crews were definitely the favoured teams in the 1977 crossing. *Outrigger Canoe Club* did the unforgivable. They won the overall in the fibreglass wa`a *Manu Ula*, Red Bird, and beat the highly favoured Tahitians in a time of 5:55mins. The Tahitians came in second in a time of 6:05mins and *Imua* of California third. *Manu Ula*, represented the first real 'Splash Off' of the fibreglass wa`a in Hawai`i as many of its properties came from the Tahitian design and not the traditional Hawaiian as did the *Malia class racer.* That the *Manu Ula*, had many design elements which were essentially considered Tahitian, is not insignificant.

Manu Ula had an overall length of 42' and was referred to as the *Rocket*. Each time HCRA would cite an infraction of a rule, *Tom Conners* would make the adjustment. First it was shortened after the 1977 Moloka`i to O`ahu race, then lengthened again to 45' in 1984 by *Joe Quigg*. *Joe* also made some changes to the bow and stern but never made the *Manu Ula* into a production wa`a. *Joe* had put a new moulded *manu* on the *Manu Ula* which would reappear on July 4th 1984.

Tahitian's Begin Making Va`a in Hawai`i

What is noteworthy at this time is that Tahiti brought over canoe artisan *Puaa Niho* to Kona and built several va`a in the traditional Tahitian design in koa. Many of the valuable koa logs shaped in this manner were later labelled illegal. Several remain today, classified as illegal under HCRA guidelines and are only used in the prestigious *Queen Lili`uokalani* race held annually along the coast of Kona, Hawai`i.

HCRA | Move to Protect 'Hawaiian' Design

As a result of this onslaught from Tahitian paddlers at the Moloka`i Hoe races and the arrival of Tahitian canoe artisans, HCRA immediately instituted new specification rules and between 1977 and 1978 the rules committee, headed by *George Downing* and *Dick Rhodes* along with *Walley Froiseth* and others, developed the first concise specifications using scientific calculations. What they did was to measure all registered koa racing wa`a in Hawai`i, take an average and set limitations for the water line and overall length of the wa`a.

A mission statement was introduced which would, '*protect the traditional integrity and identity of the Hawaiian koa wa`a.*' These rules and regulations are followed to this day, with some adjustments to the specifications.

(This decision, though justified on the basis of protecting the 'traditional integrity' of the Hawaiian wa`a, presumably on behalf of the Hawaiian people, the *kalai wa`a* and Hawaiian culture, failed to account for the fact that indigenous Hawaiians and Tahitians, not of Anglo decent, were simply rekindling their cultural ties in sharing maritime architectural skills in creating a faster craft. As a consequence of this move, the evolution of the Hawaiian racing wa`a has been retarded ever since, unlike the Tahitian va`a where the sport is representive now of its zenith.)

1978 | T-Grip Paddles Introduced to Wa`a Racing by Champion Californian Crew

In 1978, the California crew *Blazing Paddles* organised by *Pete Caroly* and steered by *Billy Whitford* in a *Malia* fibreglass wa`a, won California's first overall in 5:43:52. The Tahitians in a koa, were second with a time of 5:48:35. A green hull was popped out of *Bud Hohl's Malia* mould and additional rocker was added to the wa`a.

The wa`a stayed in Hawai`i with *Erval Kapua*. Not only did the *Californian All Star Team* win in a *Malia*, but they also introduced the first 'T' top paddles. This was highly contested because it was thought to be not traditionally Hawaiian. A picture from the *Bishop Museum* was produced which showed a Hawaiian paddle with a T-top, so it was allowed.

Modifications | Experimentation of Wa`a Designs Run Riot

In 1979, Outrigger CC would come back and win the Moloka`i Hoe in the re-designed *Manu Ula* which had been shortened, with California's *Balboa Bay* Club's modified *Malia* fibreglass wa`a *Puamana* taking second. In 1980, Outrigger would repeat this in a new fibreglass 'one-off', the 45 foot *Kaiulani*, a design taken from the *Manu Ula* - it later broke in half and was sold. *Balboa Canoe Club,* with *Billy Whitford* steering a stock *Malia* and *Kala Kukea* in another one-off named *Kaupiko*, were a close second and third. No koa wa`a raced that year.

1979 | The Californian Wa`a, *Puamana*

Eddie Frasier and *Howard Hamilan* had modified a *Malia* in 1979 to create the *Puamana*. *Eddie* took a second generation *Malia* mould in California and jacked a rocker into the hull giving the wa`a a banana shape and more shear line rocker in the hull. *Eddie's* initial lay up of the interior was comprised of a gel coat, two ounce aircraft cloth, eight ounce Kevlar and three eighth foam (Clega Cell) with coatings of *West System Epoxy* 105 and 201 instead of the standard polyester resin and glass cloth. The individual layers, with the exception of the gel coat, were vacuum bagged to thoroughly saturate the materials and any excess was removed.

The end result was a hull weighing 98lbs out of the mould. The wa`a gunnels were made of cedar, the seats made of foam and fibreglass, as were the front and back manu. Looking at the wa`a from the side, the gunnels followed the curve of the hull accentuating the banana effect. The gunnels flared out and the six seats were barely set below the top of the gunnel. This allowed the wa`a to be wider at the top than the bottom of the hull, creating more volume and buoyancy with a shorter water line.

Dressed hull weight was 276lbs so that 124lbs of lead had to be attached below Seat

#4 to bring the wa`a up to the 400lbs weight limit. The wa`a was shipped first to Kona for the *Queen Lili`uokalani* venue and then the *Balboa Bay Club*, with *Eddie Frasier, Bud Hohl, Craig Leaper, Billy Whitford* and the other crew members who took first overall.

The *Puamana* sustained some damage while being transported by a *Young Brothers Barge* and had to be repaired on Moloka`i prior to the start of the 1979 race. During the scheduled coaches meeting, many of the local club representatives claimed that the wa`a was not legal because it was in one individuals words, *'Made of Kryptonite!'*.

Passing specs for that year's Moloka`i, new weight distribution rules introduced by HCRA at the end of 1979 to control weight displacement eliminated the *Puamana*.

1981 | Californian's Win Moloka`i Hoe

The 1980 Moloka`i crossing had *Bud Hohl's* newly formed *Offshore Canoe Club* - using a stock *Malia* they borrowed from *Outrigger Canoe Club* - leading *Outrigger* in their new 45' *Kaiulani*, a one-off of the *Manu Ula*. *Offshore's* ama lashing stanchion broke and began to unravel, causing the ama and i`ako to separate. It took them five minutes to remedy the problem but by then they could not quite catch up to *Outrigger* who crossed the finish line just in front.

***Puamana*, Moloka`i 1979, awaiting repairs before Moloka`i Hoe, damaged en route from California.**

***Offshore California* founding photo.**

In 1981, *Offshore* finally got their first win in a borrowed stock *Malia* from the *Outrigger Canoe Club*, setting a record time of 5:25:07. They won again in 1982 using the koa *Malama* to win overall in the Moloka`i race. This was the first and last time, in the twentieth century, that a Californian club won Moloka`i in *Kapena, Whitford's* koa wa`a.

Two weeks earlier, the *Offshore* women's team had borrowed the *Malama* but were swamped in the crossing of the channel. Because of the extreme conditions and volume of water in the wa`a, the *Malama* began to break up from the number two seat to the front *manu*. *Bud Hohl* and *Billy Whitford* immediately jumped in the water, picked up the pieces and dragged the wa`a backwards for seven hours finally making it to Hawai`i Kai. They transported the *Malama* to Waianae and *Walley Forsieth, Kapena Whitford* and *Bud Hohl* worked on putting the *Malama* back together so that the *Offshore* men could race it in two weeks.

Californian's | Hints of Not Returning to Compete in the Moloka`i Hoe

Its important to point out that even though *Blazing Paddles*, *Balboa Bay Club* and *Imua* had been successful in placing second, third, fourth and winning the Moloka`i to O`ahu race over the last twenty-two years, *Billy Whitford* still felt that they were continually at a disadvantage. Availability of competitive canoes and rules affecting their own wa`a were a concern.

The cost involved in bringing together individuals who were highly successful National athletes from many different areas of America overshadowed their successes. He felt that some adjustments had to be made to allow these athletes and teams to continue to return to the venue,

'Offshore may never return to race Moloka'i because we have to race in what we can borrow. We're at a distinct disadvantage even with our top-notch Olympic athletes.' said *Whitford*. *Walter Guild* was sitting with *Billy, Bud Hohl, John Rader* and a few others and took *Billy Whitford's* concerns to heart and later talked to designer *Joe Quigg*.

1981 | Wa`a Racing Comes to Australia

During 1981, *Billy Whitford* (coach) and *John Rader* (president) of *Offshore Canoe Club* flew their women's team to Sydney, Australia. They took a *Malia* hull cut it in half to fit into the cargo portion of the *Continental Airline* Jet. *John Rader* arranged with *Continental* marketing and promotions to conduct the first instructional clinic on wa`a paddling techniques, rigging and racing.

They put on a promotional race between the Australian Men's *Surf Life Saving Team* from Newport Beach, in the Aussies traditional surf life saving boat and the *Offshore* women in the six person *Malia class* Hawaiian wa`a. Approximately one hundred boats of all sizes followed the event from Manly across Sydney Harbour to the

Sydney Opera House. This was the first fibreglass Californian made *Malia class* six person Hawaiian wa`a racer in Australia. It continued to be the workhorse for training crews. Most of the new clubs would use the *Malia* off-shoots produced from that wa`a.

Global Manufacture of the Fibreglass *Malia*

World-wide distribution of the fibreglass *Malia* wa`a by 1981 would include: Samoa, Australia, Great Britain, Japan, Canada, Hawai`i, U.S.A (California, Louisiana, Florida and New York) and Tahiti, as far as records show. It would be pretty hard to get an exact count on how many *Malia* fibreglass wa`a were produced because there were so many reproductions.

It should be mentioned that by 1984, the *Malia class racer* had done so much for Hawaiian wa`a racing, KOA made it a separate division in the Catalina venue. Until the Open Class fibreglass wa`a division made its way into California racing, the *Malia* had been the wa`a of the 1960s and 70s. New clubs could immediately get into the thick of things by picking up affordable used equipment.

California | Moves to Design its Own Wa`a

Still other limited, production fibreglass canoes such as the *Keoni* would be designed and built by *Mark Talbert* in Costa Mesa, California out of *Betty Cook's Kama Raci Manufacturing Plant. Betty* was a well known power boat racer, who loved the new sport of Hawaiian wa`a racing and not only supported the sport but also raced in many of the marathon races.

The *Keoni* was more of a flat-water wa`a and was developed to offset *Imua* and *Dennis Campbell's* earlier commissioned glass wa`a, the *Rhino*. It never made its way to Hawai`i but did make it up to Canada where a few were manufactured.

1983 | Hawaiians Continue to Experiment with new Hull Designs

Kirk Clarke developed the *Hawaiian Catamaran* in Hawai`i and *Hui Nalu* was the first crew to race it in the channel, coming in third in 1983. Years later, *Kirk's* wa`a would become the most popular hull for the sailing wa`a used to race across the channels and along the shores of Hawai`i. Then *Ernie Tanaka* built the *Tanaka*, another fibreglass wa`a which *Hui Nalu* tested in 1987-1988. But they found that it did not have the all-around characteristics needed for channel crossings and other races. Many of these types of wa`a had limited production.

1984 | Second Generation Production Wa`a, The *Hawaiian Class Racer*

In 1983, *Outrigger Canoe Club's* open men's team, in their koa *Leilani,* won first overall in the channel with *Offshore* and *Imua* of California placing second and third. The second generation fibreglass wa`a was on the drawing boards just before this time with *Joe Quigg,* the designer and *Diversified Glass* partners *Jeff Kissell, Hank Lass* and *Walter Guild* testing the *Hawaiian Class Racer.*

Joe, Walter and *Jeff* took two 1/4 scale models, the *Ula* and *Kea,* to the *Stevens Institute of Technology,* Hoboken, New Jersey, to be tank tested in November 1982. The tests did not prove anything more than to verify he had designed a wa`a which would accommodate most of what was needed for a production Hawaiian wa`a racer. The institute concluded, *'We do not have enough experience with such light, slender vessels to offer advice on what changes, if any, could improve performance in calm water, in waves and when manoeuvring.'*

Joe worked out the final specifications for the plug, which he produced from foam. *Brent Bixler* cleaned up the plug and took a one-off and then produced another plug which was tested during *Outrigger Canoe Club's* 4th of July Regatta at Waikiki Beach in the summer of 1984.

The plug was an instant success and *Brent* then went on to develop the mould for production, but before full production could be implemented, a second mould had to be made to correct a minor infraction which HCRA had detected prior to passing the specs of the wa`a. The *Hawaiian Class Racer* was just over 43' 3" long and its bow resembled the long and narrow lines of the *Manu Ula,* which *Joe* had previously remodelled. The sleek and subtle lines were a refreshing change, the overall effect, a wa`a which

***Walter Guild* with the 1/4 scale model of what was to become the *Hawaiian Class Racer* or '*Classic*' *OC6*.**

complemented traditional values of the Hawaiian and Tahitian wa`a.

The first *Hawaiian Class Racers* were in the 1984 Moloka`i crossing. *Keith Williams*, the first Australian entry, came in fourth overall, with the *Outrigger Canoe Club's* Masters crew in a revised *Manu Ula* placing third. *Outrigger Canoe Club's* open men were again winners overall in their other *koa wa`a Leilani*, in a record time of 5:19mins, followed by rivals *Offshore.*

Brent Bixler remembers fondly when *Waikiki Surf Club* purchased *Diversified Glass'* twentieth wa`a out of the mould and he invited *Joe Quigg* and many others to celebrate the event at the shop. *Brent*, *Joe* and others reminisced about the hours that went into creating the many innovations which made these technicians so uniquely different and essential to the development of the sport. This was their time.

What is not widely known, even among the membership of the *Outrigger Canoe Club,* is that the second model which *Joe Quigg* took back to New York, was what eventually became the design for the club's new koa wa`a *Kaoloa*. Both wa`a designs incorporated many of the same features and both have the same front and back manu.

Produced in 1984, the *Hawaiian Class Racer* was be the production model Hawaiian glass racing wa`a for the next ten

Hawaiian Class Racer completed in 1984 - a *Joe Quigg* inspired design. Below: Working on the *Keoni* a flat water wa`a designed in California, but it never became popular.

The foam plug of the *Hawaiian Class Racer*.

to twelve years. It was shipped to the mainland as early as 1985, to Australia in 1984 and would become the most prolific production wa`a to date. *Walter Guild* calculated that his production records alone account for almost 700 to 800 of the estimated 1000 *Hawaiian Class Racers* in the world.

I believe that the one shop production of the *Hawaiian Class Racer* gave all clubs an equal opportunity of winning the Moloka`i venue. It really was the 'User Friendly' wa`a. The Catalina mens and womens races, which were re-established in 1980 and the Queen *Lili`uokalani* in Kailua Kona, Hawai`i have the greatest diversification in fibreglass wa`a such as the *Rail, Rhino, Son of Rhino* and the *Pacific Islander,* the *Malia*, *Keoni* the *'IPCF'* and the *Hawaiian Class Racer* (and others since this time).

1985 | *Illinois Brigade* Win Moloka`i

In 1985, the *Illinois Brigade's Serge Corbin* and *Everet Croizer* borrowed the *Holomalea*, a new *Hawaiian Class Racer* from the *Outrigger Canoe Club* and won Moloka`i. *Illinois Brigade* had been paddling the channel since 1981 in borrowed *Malia* racers and had never done better then eighth, which they did in 1984. For the next four years, the *Hawaiian Class Racer* would dominate the channel. The *Outrigger Canoe Club* won in 1986 in the *Onipaa*, 1987 in the *Iwalani* - a foam core *Hawaiian Class Racer* - and set a new record in 1988 in the *Iwalani*, 5:08:11.

1989 | The Last Koa Wa`a To Win the Moloka`i Race Overall

Outrigger Canoe Club used their new koa wa`a *Kaoloa,* that was designed and personally crafted by *Joe Quigg.* The *Kaoloa* was the last koa wa`a to win the coveted Moloka`i Hoe Championship of the twentieth century. Had the head coach at *Outrigger* chosen to use the *Iwalani*, the *Hawaiian Class Racer* would have prevailed. *Billy Whitford*, who had been narrowly missing first overall, took the record to a new low of 5:06:29 in a *Hawaiian Class Racer*. *Hui Nalu* came in second setting the existing koa record of 5:11:38 in the *Maikai Roa*.

1991 | Aussies Win the Moloka`i Hoe

Outrigger Canoe Club Australia won Australia's first World Championship in the *Hawaiian Class Racer* provided by *Tim Guard* of Honolulu. Fellow countrymen, led by renowned aquatic talent, *Grant Kenny*, from *Panamuna Canoe Club* took second place in another *Hawaiian Class Racer*. The following year, *Panamuna* took home their first World Championship, ending the winning era for the *Hawaiian Class Racer* in the Moloka`i Channel, but not its winning way. From 1989 - 1997, the *Hawaiian Class Racer* was the racing wa`a of choice in Australia and the prestigious *Hamilton Cup*.

The Californian *Pacific Islander*, a large volume wa`a with similar hull lines to the *Bradley*. Exported to Australia for manufacture under license, the build quality resulted in poor sales. It was reborn some years later as the *Anderson*, its water line length increased by pulling down on the mould front and rear. Sales increased as the *Anderson* enjoyed some solid race results.

1984 | International Va`a Federation

Let me digress here a minute to talk briefly about the *International Va`a Federation* formerly known as the *International Polynesian Canoe Federation* or *IPCF*, the governing body for the World Sprints. The World Sprints were originally set in Long Beach, California in 1984. It was the hope of the *IPCF* that the *Olympic Committee* would embrace *Hawaiian Canoe Racing* and possibly add it to future Olympics as an event.

The *IPCF* decided to develop a fibreglass racing va`a, which would be manufactured by sponsors and used every two years at the chosen venue. It would ensure that all countries competing in the World Sprints would race with the same hull, eliminating any disadvantages. The Tahitians, under the tutelage of *Eduard Maa Maa Tua,* were responsible for several designs by 1988. But too many restrictions we forced on the designer and builder by the different associations, and the 'canoes' did not perform to the desired expectations.

The va`a referred to as the *IPCF Class* was finally completed by 1990, in time for the World Sprints in Sacramento, California. They were fast in the straight, but did not turn well and were less than efficient in variable ocean conditions. The *IPCF's* were used in Samoa in 1994 and last raced in New Caledonia in 1996. Many of the Sacramento *IPCF's* went out of the state to developing areas like Oregon, Washington, Canada and the East Coast.

The 1998 World Sprints in Fiji, switched to a fibreglass va`a designed by *Herb Kane,* locally called a *Takia,* but had not become a production design in Hawai`i. In 2000, the World Sprints were held in Australia. The Board of Directors changed the federation's name from *IPCF* to *International Va'a Federation (IVF)* and the wa`a used ('wa`a', because it was a Hawaiian 'canoe' not Tahitian) was the Hawaiian designed *Force Five.*

(The name change is culturally significant. The Micronesian and Melanesian participants could not accept the sport being limited to 'Polynesian'. The ultimate use of the Tahitian word 'va'a' was incorporated in the same way as the Inuit word 'kayak' is used to define the craft used an in respect of origin)

Fijian *Takia* designed by Hawaiian historian *Herb Kane.*

Credit is due to *Edwaard Maa Maa Tua* for his design of the *IPCF* wa`a and to *Herb Kane* for his design of the Fijian *Takia*. However, the reality of introducing flat water sprint/ lagoon canoes to many regions of the Pacific as a compulsory factor of winning the bid to host, proved ineffectual in allowing the sport to grow in any meaningful manner. Since the sport is open-ocean orientated, it would have been more expedient to have introduced ocean going va`a capable of going beyond the reef or harbour. Australia argued this point on the basis of financial suicide to do otherwise and won its case.

1987 | The *Bradley* Wa`a

As early as 1983, *Sonny Bradley* was becoming the koa craftsmen of the Hawaiian Islands but found himself caught between his love for wa`a racing, crafting the koa wa`a used for racing and making a living. So much of his life had gone into shaping a koa log into ocean going streamline racers that he finally found himself at an impasse. He had a difficult decision to make regarding his future in wa`a building and making a living.

A chance call in 1984 by *Calvin Hirahara*, who was then the coach of *Marina Del Rey Canoe* Club in Southern California, was instrumental in shifting *Sonny's* priorities to fibreglass design and manufacturing. *Sonny* has a koa wa`a, which even to this day he has not had the time to complete. It has a dramatically different design, not what you would consider traditional. *Sonny* integrated his conceptual ideas into the overall design where the widest part of the wa`a was moved towards the centre instead of the back one third of the wa`a. The front and the back of the wa`a were pinched.

The idea was to allow the wa`a to accelerate faster and surf better. The trade-off, which wasn't proved until later, was that it would take a very experienced steersman to control. This was all theory at the time because the wa`a had not been finished. *Sonny* put it to paper, I mean he literally put to full scale, the actual dimensions on butcher-like paper. *Eddie Frasier* came close to this concept when he produced the *Puamana* in 1979, but he did not take his idea to its fullest extent. Many articles have been written about *Sonny's* one week trek to Southern California where he was set up in a vacated *Hughes Aircraft* hanger with his set of designs. The actual prototype or foam plug was a patchwork of foam pieces glued together and shaped to his specifications. He completed the plug and had *Calvin* test and re-test the plug until finally a mould was developed.

Calvin Hirahara first had to get the wa`a certified by KOA before he could start to manufacture the _Bradley Racer_. His first attempt in 1986 would not pass KOA regulations. By 1987, a second mould was developed and KOA accepted it. The California production wa`a _Bradley Racer_, _Kaholo_, was a 44' 2" wide-bodied and high gunneled projectile. Eventually, the _Bradley Racer_ started to dominate the Catalina and California race circuit.

In 1989, the _Bradley Racer_ made its way to Hawai`i but not in time for that years Molokai`i to O`ahu race. HCRA first inspected the _Bradley Racer_ the following year and did not pass it then because the stern was found to be one sixteenth of an inch too small!

Sonny Bradley

1992 | A *Bradley* Wa`a Races Moloka`i

It was not passed until 1992, when *Waikiki Surf Club* ordered the *Ua Kani* which they had shipped to Hawai`i along with one other *Bradley Racer*. *Kala Kukea* would borrow the second *Bradley Racer* from *Waikiki Surf Club* and steer his young C-1 and K-1 *HCKT All Stars* to a second place behind *Panamuna,* Australia with *Waikiki Surf Club* coming in seventh.

1993 | A *Bradley Racer* and a Tahitian Team

Tommy Conner and the Tahitian team *Faa`a (Gabby Lou)* purchased their first *Bradley Racer* in time for the 1993 Bankoh Moloka`i Hoe. *Faa`a* rewrote racing history that day by shattering the course record and eclipsing *Offshore's* 1989 time by thirteen minutes in a time of 4:55:27.

This would be the first Moloka`i crossing under five hours since the course was established in 1981. In second place was *Panamuna* in a *Hawaiian Class Racer*, third was *Dana Point Canoe Club* in a *Bradley Racer*, fourth was *Lanikai* in a *Bradley Racer*, fifth was *Taniwa*, New Zealand in a Hawaiian Class Racer, sixth was *HCKT* in a *Bradley Racer*, seventh was *Waikiki Surf Club* in a *Bradley Racer*, eighth was *Outrigger Canoe Club* in a *Bradley Racer*, *Marina 1* of California was ninth in a *Bradley Racer* and tenth was *Outrigger Canoe Clubs* Masters in a *Hawaiian Class Racer*. Seven out of ten wa`a finishing in the top ten places were *Bradleys*.

Sonny redesigned the *Bradley* and released the *Bradley Striker* in the early part of 2000, adding greater rocker than the original *Bradley* and later went on to modify this further to create the *Bradley Racer*.

1993 | *Karel Tresnak* Begins Manufacture of the *Bradley* Wa`a and of his Own Designs

The *Bradley Racer* production demands were steaming ahead in Hawai`i. *Karel Tresnak* had started to manufacture the *Bradley Racer* in the Spring of 1993 out of his OC1 shop in Kailua and the landslide victory of the *Bradley Racer* in October only intensified the demand for them. *Karel* continued to manufacture the *Bradley* up until 1996. Over the next 3 years *Karel* developed his first team canoe called the *OC6*, for *Outrigger Connection*. For 3 years he tried to promote it and sold only eight wa`a.

Hawaiian Class Racer | Falls Out of Favour. The *Force Five* Wa`a is Created

Production of the *Hawaiian Class Racer* came to a screaming halt at years end and *Walter Guild* had to shift gears to keep abreast of the ever-changing market. B*rent Bixler* took a hull of the *Hawaiian Class Racer* and split the middle of the front and back manu 7' in from the bow and stern. He then, as he recalls, opened up the hull by no more than 1 ½ to 2" adding volume to the wa`a. He then secured the gunnels so that the wa`a would be rigid while he made small but necessary changes to the width of the hull. He turned the hull onto the gunnels and then painstakingly glassed the inside of the overturned hull for further support.

His next step was to place foam along the hull and shape it to enhance the rocker to amidships of the wa`a, but not quite centre. The hope was that the changes would be subtle and bring about a more efficient front and greater volume to the wa`a, without changing the entire integrity of the previous design.

Walter had first hand experience with the demands of having the first real production model *Hawaiian Class Racer* and so he was in no hurry to introduce the new prototype *Force Five* until he felt it had proven itself in the open ocean. All summer long, as head coach of *Outrigger Canoe Club,* he had his men's crews trade off between the *Bradley, Hawaiian Class Racer,* and his prototype *Force Five*. *Brent Bixler* remembers fondly how in control of the whole situation *Walter* was as head coach. He would conduct these tests between all three wa`a in varied weather and ocean conditions. This moment in time would be hard to duplicate today under such controlled circumstances.

1994 | *Force Five* 'Protype' Wa`a Wins Na Wahine O Ke Kai Race

***Walter Guild* made arrangements with *Billy Whitford*, coach of *Offshore* women's team to race the prototype *Force Five* wa`a in the Na Wahine O Ke Kai and they won. His men crossed in the 43' 5" prototype in the men's Moloka`i Hoe two weeks later and placed second to *Faa`a* in a *Bradley Racer*.**

Outrigger beat *Dana Point* in an outstanding finish that went right to the line. *Dana Point* was in a *Bradley Racer* as were eleven of the next finishers. By May of 1995 *Brent Bixler,* who was working for *Diversified Glass* before joining *Karel Tresnak's* shop, took the prototype which he had re-designed and made the mould. Production of the first *Force Five* wa`a came out of the mould in May of 1995 for the *Hui Nalu Canoe Club.*

By now *Diversified Glass* was owned outright by *Walter.* His shop's second generation Hawaiian fibreglass wa`a or *Force Five* is really a blown up version of the *Hawaiian Class Racer* and koa *Kaoloa*. It had a wider hull, higher gunnel and larger then life

Brent Bixler / Walter Guild* designed *Force Five.

front and back manu. The rocker was been moved forward but not quite as far amidships as the *Bradley*. Both the *Force Five* and the *Bradley Racer* are volume oriented and are fast to recover in large seas where they plunge into and across successive swells. Many people will describe the differences between the two as subtle, but I disagree.

1995 - 1999 | The *Bradley* Dominates

By 1995, the *Force Five* was in production and *Faa`a* chose to purchase one for the Channel crossing. They had won the two previous crossings in the *Bradley Racer* and had set a new record in 1993. *Tom Conner,* I am sure, thought that his veteran Tahitian crew could win in the new *Force Five,* but they were defeated by *Lanikai* in the *Bradley Racer*, eclipsing the *Faa`a* record by 2mins:24sec or 4:53:03.

This would be the year when other clubs who had previously raced in the *Bradley Racer* would try out the new production *Force Five*. *Outrigger Canoe Club* would come third in a *Force Five, Waikiki Surf Club* fourth in a *F-5, Outrigger Australia* fifth in a *Bradley Racer.* A total of four *Bradley Racers* and six *Force Fives* were in the top ten finishes. The year before there had been nine *Bradley Racers* and the *Force Five* prototype.

In 1996, *Lanikai* would do a repeat in slower conditions with five of the top finisher racing in the *Bradley Racer* and three out of the top tens in *Force Fives*. *Outrigger Australia* would win the channel for a second time in 1997 with the ocean being completely flat. Their time was exceptionally fast for flat conditions 4:57:45 with *Lanikai Canoe Club* three minutes behind. Most of the top ten canoes were *Bradley Racers* with the exception of the winners.

In 1998 and 1999, *Outrigger Canoe Club* won the Bankoh Moloka`i Hoe in their *Bradley Racer, Mamala*. Most of the ten top finishers were in *Bradley Racers* with one New Zealand team racing in the *OC6* out of *Karel Tresnak's* shop and produced by

Brent Bixler: The *OC6* placed third in 1998 and second in 1999 and was the newest production wa`a on the market at the time. *Steve Blythe* of Kona was producing a Hawaiian fibreglass racer but was not been widely used with the exception of Hilo or Kona, Hawai`i.

1996 | The Canadian *Advantage*.

In response to this 'logic', *Clipper Canoes* of Canada in 1996 embarked on a project to design a wa`a specifically to perform in moderate seas as experienced locally and elsewhere, as opposed to rough water, open ocean conditions. The project ultimately became a collaboration effort with Olympic kayak champion *Greg Barton*.

The *Advantage* was designed to meet 'Hawaiian Outrigger Specifications' using either the Hawaiian or California test methods. On April 18, 1998 a production wa`a was weighed, measured, and tested by *Bud Hohl* of California and certified race legal.

1997 | The Australian *Southern Spirit*

The Australian designed *Southern Spirit* was conceived in 1997 and created using computer cad software and the resources of *Bashfords International* yacht manufacturers and the design skills of 12m yachtsman *Iain Murray* and the impetus of *Harvie Allison*.

A closed deck configuration as used on the Tahitian va`a, was incorporated to improve longitudinal stiffness and to create a 'dryer' wa`a. The final result was a wa`a which by appearance alone was vastly different than that of Hawaiian designed wa`a such as the *Force Five* and *Hawaiian Class Racer* in use in Australia at the time.

It's performance qualities have been proven many times over in competition by a small band of converted believers in the design. Unreasonably, Australia's paddlers have responded for the most part unfavourably to this new design, falling victim to

the mindset, that if it's not Hawaiian, just how good could it be?

Cynicism aside, there were early manufacturing faults limiting sales. Ten years on, and the *Southern Spirit* is in the hands of an excellent manufacturer. In truth, this is an exceptional design ideally suited to a wide variety of general racing conditions. It's upwind/crosswind performance is outstanding, it's downwind performance, sound.

The *Southern Spirit* is now becoming the va`a of choice for the *Hamilton Cup* race in Australia, (Australia's Moloka`i in terms of status) being the winning va`a in 2008 and 2009, having taken a full ten years to gain acceptance from winning crews.

The *Southern Spirit* is a classic example of a 'sleeper'. Designed for Australian race conditions and waters, it's Hawaiian counterparts (*Force Five / Mirage*) found favour with winning Australian crews, until up and coming crews determined to think outside of conventional thought, used what is simply the best wa`a for the task at hand and improved their results to the point of winning, turning conventional thought on its head.

2000 | *Karel Tresnak* The *Mirage* Wa`a

Karel Tresnak of *Outrigger Connection* Hawai`i, had designed a racing wa`a called *OC6*. In 1998, New Zealand and Hawai`i finished 3rd and 2nd in the Moloka`i race, using this wa`a. But got no orders. When *Karel Jr* came back from the New Zealand Bay of Islands race, he and *Todd Bradley* brought pictures back from the *Americas Cup* race.

Karel took his inspiration from the rocker line he saw on a 12m NZ Yacht design, as had Australian *Iain Murray* during the design of the *Southern Spirit.* The tail rocker starts way forward and doesn't follow any curve line to the tail. Instead, it shoots straight to the aft end. *Karel* had always wanted to design a wide wa`a to gain more

buoyancy. Putting the parameters and specifications together he came up with the *Mirage* over a three month period creating a prototype.

'I took twelve guys and one Bradley canoe and we did the Makapuu to Outrigger Canoe Club run and we were switching entire crews. It became obvious that the Mirage surfed better than a Bradley and manoeuvres better in these conditions. We did that again after about a week or so and obtained similar results. We were on to something and I was very happy knowing that I could give Team NZ an edge for the Molo' race.'

Lanikai got word of the new wa`a and since *Karel Jr* was on their team they started to test the boat in every condition over a very long time and finally requested a *Mirage* for the 2000 Moloka`i race, which resulted in a custom *Mirage* being made on account of having no mould at this point.

Lanikai finished 1st with a new record and *Team NZ* second and those were the only two *Mirages* in the race. *Karel's* interpretation of the *Mirage's* design centres on predominently on improved rocker line and buoyancy.

'My theory on the improved performance goes like this. The wider canoe floats higher and has less wetted surface, resulting in less drag. Our draft is 7 1/2" compared to the Bradley's 8 3/4". The early beginning of the rear rocker provides percentually more hull surface in the release phase than the regular rocker. Last, but not least, the straight rear rocker is 'steersman friendly' and assists to glide the boat forward more than the curved one that tends to drive the boat to the oceans bottom.'

In the 2001 Moloka`i race 30 *Mirages* entered the race, 9 finished in the top 10.

2000 | Onwards

As the new millenium approached and as we pushed through it, it was evident that the sport of 'outrigger canoeing' was becoming big business in Hawai`i, in terms of generation of revenue from local events and the exportation and localised sales of product - from paddles to wa`a.

With the forming of crews such as *Team New Zealand / Hawai`i* who upset continuity of results between 2000-2005 and the coming of the Tahitian corporate crews over the past few years to the Moloka`i Hoe, it's apparent that *Sonny Bradley's, Bradley* wa`a reigns supreme - the Tahitians prefer it - and always have, and if we talk in terms of race records, the *Bradley* wa`a again takes the prize, while the success of the *Mirage* seems short lived in the face of choice. *Lanikai* ultimately reverted back to the *Bradley* and one could view *Team New Zealand / Hawai`i's* victories between 2000-2005 in the *Mirage*, merely coincidental to sponsorship from *Outrigger Connection Hawai`i.*

'Crews win races not canoes', would be a wonderful maxim to live by, but only truly applicable if we go down the path of strict 'class' racing - one wa`a design for all. Efficacy of choice is a wonderful thing, though reality dictates that even sponsorship clouds this notion. Just because you get to use it for free, does not make it necessarily the best per se. Ultimately free-will by top crews using exactly what they choose to, brings parity and purity to truly what is best in the absence of a third parties benevolence, strategic alliance and agenda.

The Rennaisance Men of Hawai`i

Sonny's* innovations are a direct reflection of his working knowledge of the wa`a. He has developed a sixth sense on how a wa`a should react to the ocean and he has done it on his own. *Walter Guild's Force Five* was an extension or a continuation of what *Joe Quigg* designed and *Brent Bixler* refined in the *Hawaiian Class Racer. Brent Bixler* learned the art of perfection and neatness from *Bob Crep* and *Joe Quigg.

Brent has become a master mould builder and tooler over the last twenty-five years. His moulding system is second to none when you consider that he has produced three exceptional moulds; the *Hawaiian Class Racer, Force Five* and *Karel Tresnak's OC6* - which never went to production. *Walter* and *Brent* both worked hand in hand to produce the *Force Five* and its development has again brought parity to *Hawaiian Racing*. Now the attention is focused back on the athlete and not the wa`a.

Fibreglass sailboats, fishing boats and surf canoes came on to the scene way before the racer in the 1950's. I only mention them because the materials and technology used in manufacturing them have been essential in the development of the fibreglass racer years later. Those craftsmen who began working with the polyester resins and ordinary fibreglass weave early on, made it possible for *Tom Johnson*, *Bob Cregs*, *Brent Bixler*, *Eddie Frasier*, *Tom Conners* and others to expand and create the prototypes of today's Hawaiian wa`a racers.

Bud Hohl, Dennis Campbell, Sonny Bradley and *Walter Guild* were instrumental in keeping the flow of new canoes and innovative ideas in the mainstream. Without the hybrids, Hawaiian wa`a racing would not be where it is today nor would the five hour mark have been shattered three times in one decade between Moloka`i and O`ahu.

End Note: From 1933 up to the present day, the Hawaiian islands remain for many outrigger paddling countries, more especially the Pacific Rim regions, the crystal ball of inspiration in terms of which wa`a are performing best and specifically in the context of the mens and womens Moloka`i races, as if no other event mattered.

It's important to be reminded, these wa`a, no matter how contemporary in design, are all fundamentally 'limited' by strict adherance to specification rulings, which only offer the designer limited room for performance improvement via design.

French Polynesia is littered with literally hundreds of differing va`a designs, where artisans are not limited by any 'anglo' constriction of the Polynesian way of things or the evolution of its maritime heritage. There are superior va`a designs throughout the island of French Polynesia - superior to that of Hawaiian by far.

Aotearoa Waka Ama New Zealand

'Tuituia nga t taura here waka
Kia kore ai e momotu
Nga taura hereanga tangata.

Thread together the ropes of waka
That they may not break and threaten
The links between our peoples.'

In 1884, *WH Skinner* wrote an article titled *'Surf-Riding by Canoe'* that was published in the Journal of the *Polynesian Society* [Vol XXX11.No1]. In it, he recounts a time when he was engaged in surveying work on the Taranaki Coast in New Zealand. He witnessed a man named *Te Rangi*, sixty years of age, *'surf-riding'* canoes within the area of a river mouth. Two waka were used of varying lengths and in each were two paddlers, the steersman and one in the prow.

'This canoe running had to be taken at a certain time of the tide…keeping just roughly a little short of its own length in advance of the wave, with a cascade of water thrown off from either side of the prow. Its expert helmsmen, as rigid as one cast in bronze, was intently watching the gradual curling of the roller (the bowman inactive, with paddle drawn in) until the moment he judges time has come. With a swift turn of his paddle, the canoe was turned sharply right, the wave breaking as it passed beneath its keel, and riding gracefully down the outer slope of the roller, turning seaward to repeat the manoeuvre. Had the steersman misjudged his time for turning by just a fraction, disaster would have followed, and herein lay the skill of the surf-canoer. The most lasting impression made on my mind in this surfing incident, was that of the poise and skill of Te Rangi Tuataka Takere, the high-born rangitara. As he sat statue-like, steering paddle firmly grasped, his fine muscular figure and clean cut tattooed features, reproducing, with the general surroundings, a grand picture of pure Maoridom as it had been for centuries prior to 1884. Alas! That we were to witness such a scene never again.'

New Zealand was one of the last areas to be settled by Polynesian voyageurs. The legend is told of a man named *Kupe*, who eloped with *Kuramarotini*, the wife of *Hoturapa*, owner of a great waka called of *Matahourua*. *Kupe*

murdered *Hoturapa* and they fled in *Matahourua* discovering a land he named *Aotearoa 'Land of the long-white-cloud'*. Exploring its coastline, he encountered and killed a sea monster called *Te Wheke-a-Muturangi,* finally returning to his homeland to spread news of his discovered land. Some tribes recount subsequent migrations to escape famine, over-population, and warfare, made in legendary canoes.

Archaeological and linguistic evidence supports a migration from Eastern Polynesia to New Zealand between 800 and 1300 AD. Maori oral history describes their ancestral homeland as Hawai`i. Astonishingly, though migration accounts vary among Maori tribes or *iwi,* these tribes can identify the name of the *waka* or *whakapapa* on which their forebears travelled and it is this link which makes their participation in the sport they call, *waka ama* so significant.

As with each successive discovery of new lands, the va`a became an integral part of ancient life. Historically, many waka (va`a) variations existed in Aotearoa, they were used for warfare, trading, voyaging and fishing. With an abundance of raw materials, the outrigger assembly itself was not as critical as it had been in many other island regions of the Pacific. Hulls could be built wide enough to create greater inherent stability and 'voyaging' was gradually coming to an end by this point in Polynesian history. Although waka with outrigger assemblies existed, they were ultimately not as prolific or produced with the same vigour as in tropical island regions.

In *Canoes of Oceania, Haddon and Hornell it is noted, 'At the time when Maoris made contact with Europeans, they were using double and single canoes and single outriggers. The outriggers appear to have been already rare and on the point of disappearance at that time and the double canoes followed them into oblivion in the early decades of the nineteenth century. By a curious mischance, no first-hand details of the construction of the Maori outrigger are on record.'* Ultimately, as throughout so many Pacific Islands, the European arrived and the waka culture died out.

'It is inevitable that as the canoe ceased to be a necessity in the changing life of the people, its production should also decrease until it reached the stage where the skilled canoe builders had no further call for their work. The craftsman laid aside their steel adzes, or turned them to more gainful use. The direct transmission of craftsmanship was broken, for the experts had no heart or incentive to teach their children a dead craft.' Sir Peter Buck, The Coming of the Maori, 1948.

Waka Taua

The Maori war canoe, *waka taua,* is the most revered Maori waka type due to its shear size, ornate design and creation process. There are strong parallels with the entire process from selection of a suitable *kauri* tree, its felling, shaping and launching with the Hawaiian process of koa wa`a creation. They are amazingly similar, yet not popularly known.Though waka ama is the common term applied to a contemporary waka with outrigger assembly in New Zealand, it is very much a derivation of Tahiti

and Hawai`i, not indigenous per-se. In the *Dictionary of the Maori Language* the word *'amatiatia'* means either the outrigger of a canoe, or a canoe with an outrigger, which raises questions, why was *'waka ama'* coined at the time of its reintroduction.

The most common and plentiful waka was the *waka tiwai* also called *waka kopapa*. Constructed of hollowed-out logs with no gunnels, carvings, thwarts, seats, bow or stern pieces, it was used for river, estuary and harbour work as the tribe's utilitarian beast of burden. In this respect, it was similar to the simple dug-outs of Africa's West Coast, Papua New Guinea and Fiji, which were recessive in design and simplicity.

In acknowledgement of this, the *Ngaruawaahia Waka Kopapa Regatta* was created, an annual two-day event at *Turangawaewae Marae*. This regatta is a celebration of the *waka kopapa* racing amongst primary, intermediate and secondary schools from the Waikato, Bay of Plenty and Manukau regions.

For the Maori of Aotearoa, the sport of waka ama has presented a life-line that stretches back to a forgotten heritage, ancestry, myth and legend. Like a chef who may describe in detail a delicious recipe, without the ingredients it can never be actually savoured. Stories of what once was, but was no more, were intangible until the resurgence of the waka in this land.

The poignantly powerful movie *Once Were Warriors* could just as well have been *Once Were Paddlers*, where misguided energies and a lack of connection or understanding of oneself lead to disassociation from life itself. The waka has given back purpose and direction for many, brought life to lifeless stories, and purpose to ceremony. It has also rekindled a connection that goes beyond ancestry with people such as those from the Cook Islands and Tahiti, Samoa and Tonga, where the sport is also practiced.

Waka Kopapa 1985.

You get the sense in this land, that waka ama racing is truly tribal, more so than anywhere else I have travelled and experienced the sport. Amongst the junior age groups, especially the teenagers, rivalry between clubs is intense. In vague terms, 'clubs' could be replaced with 'tribes'.

The Maori *haka* is an integral part of the sport of waka ama. It is common to have rival 'clubs' face-off, delivering a full blooded *haka* in a frightening display, intimidating the onlooker, and encapsulating an expression of the psychological using physical elements.

The History of Waka Ama in Aotearoa

by Kris Kjeldsen

'It is important to recognise and acknowledge the mana of Maoridom in Aotearoa where Maori people are the tangata whenua, the indigenous people of the land. The concepts that are inherent in a canoe culture belong to all peoples who understand and accept the special cultural perspectives of Maori and Polynesian people.' Tatou Hoe O Aetearoa constitution.

For the *tangata whenua* the Maori, the paddle symbolises a sense of purpose and direction while also affirming their cultural links with the waka. All individual Maori ancestry is linked with a particular waka, in which their forebears arrived on the shores of Aotearoa. This provides each person with an essential link back to Hawai`i and beyond, to creation itself.

Being one of the elders of outrigger canoe building in New Zealand and one of three people responsible

Kris Kjeldsen

for the revival of the sport here, I will tell our brief story of the history and growth of waka ama in Aotearoa.

Waka ama paddling was reintroduced in 1985 with the arrival of the *Hawaiki Nui*, the replica Polynesian voyaging waka built and sailed by *Matahi Whakataka* (master builder) *Brightwell* on an epic voyage from Tahiti to Aotearoa. *Matahi* spent four years in Tahiti building the *Hawaiki Nui*, during which time he became involved in va`a racing, the national sport of Tahiti. He recognised that this would be the very thing to help the youth of New Zealand regain some of their culture heritage and traditions.

Before coming to New Zealand, I had paddled for *Kai Nulu Canoe Club* in Southern California and was also involved for a short time in Hawai`i. So when I finally settled in the small Maori community of Pawarenga, in the far north of the North Island on the edge of Whangape Harbour, where I lived for about fifteen years, I wondered why there was no traditional Maori waka racing.

On reading in the newspaper about *Matahi's* intended voyage and his dream to rekindle racing of traditional waka, I knew it was time to do something about it, so I was on the beach at Okahu Bay, Auckland on the day the *Hawaiki Nui* arrived in December 1985. I met *Matahi* and told him of my plan to start waka ama paddling in

Hawaiki Nui, Tahiti, 1984.

the north and to start building waka. Matahi encouraged me and told me he wanted to do the same thing in the Gisborne/East Cape area.

With the high unemployment in both areas, especially amongst Maori people, we were able to take advantage of training schemes funded by the Government to start these projects. The people of Pawarenga got behind the project wholeheartedly and made it happen. By early 1987, we had a work-training scheme in place, building waka and paddles, and learning the art of paddling and handling them. Ocean knowledge, surf skills and swimming were very much a part of the programme.

Te Aurere – Waka Hourua **voyaging canoe has sailed from Aotearoa to Hawai`i, the Cook Islands, French Polynesia, New Caledonia and Norfolk Island and circumnavigated Te Ika a Maui - North Island, on several occasions. Built in 1991-92 in Northland from two giant kauri trees by** ***Hekenukumai Ngaiwi Puhipi Busby*** **and operating under the banner of** ***Te Tai Tokerau Tarai Waka Inc, Te Aurere*** **exists for the purpose of educating on many different cultural and skill based levels.**

About this time, I met a Samoan named *Pili Muaulu* who lived on the coast near Whangarei. He told me of his father's dream to find a suitable log to carve into a traditional Samoan *Pao Pao*, a small two person fishing canoe. Coincidentally, I had a friend who had a suitable log on his property; I managed to talk him into donating it. As a result, our trainees, *Pili* and his family built the first traditional Samoan *Pao Pao* in New Zealand.

The training scheme in Pawarenga eventually evolved into, *Nga Hoe Horo o Pawarenga*, 'The fast paddles of Pawarenga'. *Matahi's* group in Gisborne became, *Mareikura Canoe Club*. *Pili's* extended family formed a club called, *Mitamitaga Ole Pasefica Va'a Alo*, 'Pride of the Pacific' canoe club of Ngunguru. These three clubs along with one other in Okahu, Auckland represented the original four clubs of New Zealand.

In May 1987, at the launching of our first waka ama in Pawarenga, a meeting was held to form a national waka ama association. The three founding members of the association named, *Tatou Hoe o Aotearoa*, 'All the paddlers of Aotearoa', were, *Nga Hoe Horo o Pawarena, Mitamitaga Ole Pasefica Va'a Alo* of Ngunguru and *Mareikura* of Gisborne.

Immediately we started plans to bid for the 1990 IPCF World Outrigger Canoe Sprints. In July 1987, a team of New Zealand paddlers, *Matahi* and myself travelled to Tahiti to participate in the *Turai Festival* races. On this trip we gained a lot of experience in paddling and racing Polynesian canoes. In June 1987, *Pili* and I

Mitimitago O le Pasifika* mens crew 1989, *Sa Feetau, Ropati Siasosi, Pili Muaulu* and *Maui Kjeldsen.

attended the first international regatta held in Apia, Western Samoa. While there, we spoke of our newly formed association and our wish to host the 1990 World Sprints.

When we returned, we formally adopted a constitution and elected officers for the *NZ Maori Polynesian Canoe Sporting Federation, Tatou Hoe O Aotearoa*, 'All the Paddler's of Aotearoa', in July 1988. *Matahi* was elected as president, *Pili* as vice president and I was the executive committee. In August of the same year, teams for *Mareikura* and *Nga Hoe Horo* travelled to Hawai`i to participate in the world sprints at Keehi Lagoon, Honolulu, with one men's crew and one women's crew. While there, we put in our bid for the 1990 titles and we won the honour.

Much had to be done, including the building of a fleet of waka ama, this was left to me - sixteen, six-person waka ama. We were supposed to build the newly adopted IPCF va`a hull, but we had problems getting it and were instructed by the late *Mary Jane Kahanamoku* to do the best we could with what we had.

New Zealand has one of the broadest age divisions, ranging from Midgets 7 - 10 Intermediate 11 - 13, Junior [16] 14 – 16, Junior [19] 17 – 19, Junior [23] 20 – 23, Open 24+, Master Women 35+, Master Men 40+, Senior Master Women 45+, Senior Master Men 50+ years. Pictured are 'Midgets' who must be steered by an adult. Sprint / Regatta racing is extremely popular in New Zealand.

New Zealand's Hauraki Hoe race which leaves from Auckland harbour is one of its premier 'change-over' distance races.

Matahi Whakataka Brightwell in his President's message wrote, *'In 1981 I was on Huahine Island, French Polynesia, not long after Dr Sinoto excavated Maori artefacts and canoe parts which were found to be over one thousand years old. There I was asked, "You Maori people have no canoe, yet you are known here as a once great canoe people." When I revived waka ama (amatiatia) in 1985 and when the Hawaiki Nui canoe arrived in Aotearoa, Maori people were saying these were not our canoes. Yet Captain Cook reported seeing many in Hauraki and Mahia. A waka found at Te Horo near Katahika gives us an indication that waka ama were very much part of our history. Waka ama brings dimensions few other sports offer; a Polynesian cultural expression, encompassing waka architecture, marine skills and the traditional song, dance and poetry of our ancestors. Maui, Hiro, Rata and Tamatea-pokai-whenua, who were all canoe heroes, handed down to us all the skill, health, fitness and radiant physical prowess. Canoe culture gives to us a jewel in an ocean sky, where Pacific origins, old and new, meet through our Tipuna, our illustrious ancestors.'*

***Ngai Tahu*, New Zealand's South Island tribe on a 20 day voyage to places of cultural significance. 14 tribal members tramped, ran, sailed and paddled waka ama across the island. Here seen paddling towards their sacred mountain *Aoraki*, New Zealand's highest peak, the first time a waka ama had been paddled on an alpine lake. Photo *Eruera Tarena*.**

The 1990 Waka

We had begun waka ama with two Tahitian style canoes, which were given to *Matahi* by *Edward Mamaatua*. The hull was altered to be as close to the IPCF va`a while keeping in mind New Zealand's ocean conditions. New decks and ama were designed and made.

In redesigning and building the 1990 waka, the overriding idea was to build it for New Zealand conditions, so that the waka would subsequently be useable for both offshore racing and flat water sprints. These waka became the nucleus fleet for waka ama sport in Aotearoa. We built them to last and perform, and they have.

The vast majority of W6 canoes in New Zealand are the 1990 design. Their one fault was that they were a little hard to turn. By putting a little more rocker in later models, the turning improved. As a result of the world sprints held in Orakei Basin, Auckland, which were a resounding success, waka ama was finally and really running. Since then, waka ama sport in New Zealand has enjoyed phenomenal success.

1999 Onwards

The *MahiMahi* was designed by *Maui Kjeldsen* in 1999 as an improvement over the 1990 model, particularly in rough seas. It incorporated design ideas from Hawai`i and Tahiti. The *MahiMahi* has a higher volume hull and is more manoeuvrable, turning faster than other New Zealand designs. The hull shape makes it easy to catch steep ocean swells as well as smaller bumps, taking advantage of every lift the ocean offers.

From humble beginnings, the sport has grown rapidly and by 1995/96 the sport had grown to the point that a review was made of its constitution and structure. The name was changed to *Nga Kaihoe O Aoteoroa*, a new regional structure was set up and is the basis of the sport as it exists today. In 2003, New Zealand's administrative structure included 6 regions, 53 clubs and over 3,000 active paddlers. In 2006, Aotearoa held its second World Sprints under the banner of the *International Va`a Federation*, which had also made a name change from the last time they held the event in 1990, under the name of the *International Polynesian Canoe Federation.*

With a handful of hardcore paddling expatriates, who formed part of the nucleus of the highly accomplished Team New Zealand / Hawai`i team, New Zealand's reputation for producing world class waka paddlers has been cemented in contemporary history. Members of that team included; *Rob Kaiwi, Maui Kjeldsen, Woogie Marsh, Bo Herbert* and the likes of *Andrew Penny, Rick Nu`u and Gavin Clarke.*

One anomaly regarding the growth of the sport in New Zealand is why, with such strong cultural ties to French Polynesia, was it decided to follow the path of Hawai`i in relation to specification rulings. It would seem that the idea of embracing the 'any design' goes policy as is prevalent in French Polynesia, would have been the clear and obvious path to take, yet it was not. In the case of sprint / regatta racing there are always sound reasons for uniformity of equipment, if not identical 'class' orientated, but to extend this to the creation of a better waka for open ocean paddling, seems incredulous.

***MahiMahi* waka ama in the Marquesas.**

The rules state that after measuring a waka for conformity, they have the right to withdraw any waka from competition, which they deem to have an unfair advantage. An 'advantage' as a result of improved design seems logical, rationale, evolutionary and to the benefit of all who paddle. What is 'unfair' is surely the lack of vision or scope for improvement of the waka within the bounds of cultural acceptance.

Kanu Types

Terminology

It is incorrect to use the term 'outrigging' or 'outriggering' or to say 'I am an outrigger', yet they are not uncommon. 'Outrigger canoeing' or 'outrigger canoeist', 'outrigger canoe paddler' are all correct terms. While we have 'anglocised' the following; kayak, kayaks, kayaked, kayaking, kayaker, canoe, canoes, canoed, canoeing, canoeists, the adaption of either 'wa`a' or 'va`a' is problematic.

Could a paddler be referred to as a 'va`aer', a 'va`aist' and could one go 'va`aing' - doubtful. In French Polynesia, it is common to be simply called a 'rameur', from the French word for paddle - rame. Realistically, one is a 'wa`a' or 'va`a' paddler, who goes 'va`a paddling' in one's 'wa`a'or 'va`a' and in New Zealand one would be a 'waka ama' or 'waka' paddler and would go 'waka ama' or 'waka' paddling.

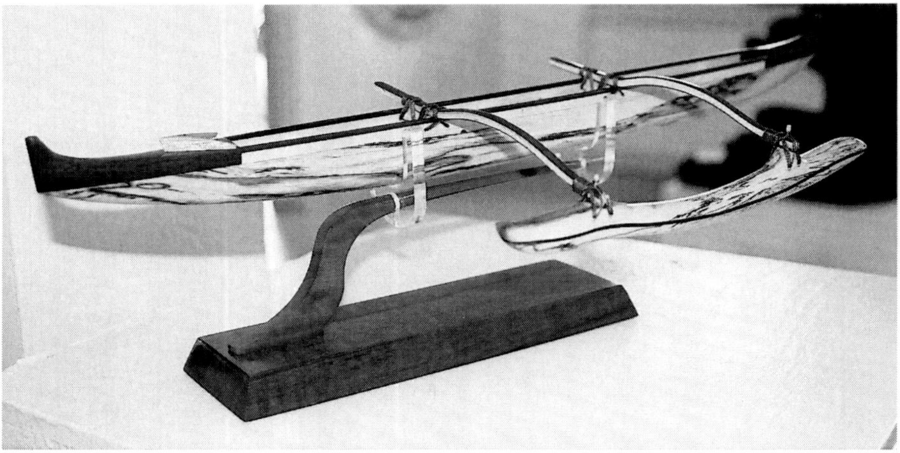

Above: The classic Hawaiian Wa`a lovingly hand crafted in model form.
Below: An ocean racing OC1 whose evolutionary peak is now closer to that of a surf ski than of its original inspiration, the rudderless Tahitian Va`a - V1.

Common Geographical Names Outrigger Canoe

Hawai`i / USA / Canada / Australia / UK / Hong Kong/ England

OC1, OC2, OC3, OC4, OC6, OC12 / DC12 (x2 OC6 joined – Double Canoe)

A set of specifications derived from 'averaged' measurements taken in Hawai`i 1976 defines today's 'Hawaiian' outrigger canoe, which has become the anglo-pacific nomenclature, particularly in Pacific Rim countries and Hawai`i itself.

Wa`a

Hawai`i

W1, W2, W3, W4, W6, W12

Not in common use, though correct in terms of tradition.

Euro-centric researchers and those who assisted in the development of the sport of wa`a racing, ignored the use of 'wa`a' in preference for 'outrigger canoe', perpetuating a disregard for the Hawaiian language and ultimately for the wa`a itself. The term 'Hawaiian' outrigger canoe suggests there was but one single type of wa`a in use in ancient Hawai`i. In fact there was a broad and varied range of wa`a types, essentially originating from the Marquesas and Tahiti, modified to suit Hawaiian waters.

'I think we need to remember that outrigger canoes are not only from Hawai`i, but the whole of Polynesia. Our club, Imua here in California, is influenced more by Tahiti than Hawai`i and as such our vocabulary includes some Tahitian.' Colby Vose.

This is indeed the belief in areas such as Southern France, Wallis Futuna, New Caledonia, Fiji, Cook Islands and New Zealand, where they have been strongly influenced by Tahitian values and va`a designs.

Va`a / Pirogue

French Polynesia / New Caledonia / Wallis Futuna / South America / France / Samoa / Marquesas

V1, V3, V6, V12 [x2 V6 joined] V8, V16 - x2 V8 joined

Wherever there has been a prominent 'Tahitian' influence

Vaka

Marquesas / Cook Islands / Rapa Nui

V1, V3, V6, V12 - x2 V6 joined

As for Tahiti with the omission of V8 and therefore V16.

Both island groups are strongly 'Tahitian' influenced.

Waka Ama

New Zealand (Aotearoa)

W1, W2, W4, W6, W12 - x2 W6 joined

New Zealand's reintroduction to the sport was and remains 'Tahitian' influenced.

***Stingray* OC2**

OC1 / OC2

Solo and duo sit on top, rudder steered craft. They include adjustable or moulded seating, mechanical rigging and are generally designed for open ocean paddling.

The design originated in Hawaii but were derived from Tahitian lagoon solo va`a. Some limited designs exist for flat water / sprint use.

OC3/ OC4 Surfing Wa`a

OC3 and OC4 relate primarily to a wa`a designed for surfing, though some OC4 are rigged for sailing. OC4 surfing wa`a are in the order of 21-24' and include added rocker (hull curvature fore and aft) some smaller 15' OC3 'junior' sized surfing wa`a are also in use. **Interestingly, surfing wa`a were manufactured in fibreglass during the 1950s in Hawai`i, long before any team racing wa`a.**

Canoe surfing competitions are popular on the island of O`ahu. Points are awarded for the best wave ridden and also for tricks performed. The most famous canoe surfing contest is the *Buffalo Surfing Classic* held in Makaha, founded in 1977 by *Richard Kalolookalani 'Buffalo' Keaulana.*

'My intent in bringing back this older form of riding waves is to perpetuate our Hawaiian surfing heritage, much as we have done with long-boarding, paipo boarding, tandem surfing and canoe surfing.'

His inspiration came in 1977 on his return to Makaha from sailing the Polynesian voyaging canoe *Hokule`a* on its maiden voyage to Tahiti. He realised that there was a need to reawaken Hawaiian surfing heritage together with an attitude that stressed fun and camaraderie in surfing contests.

Walter Guild's Fibreglass Shop in Hawai`i manufactured two variations of surfing wa`a; a 22' surf class and a 15' junior class surf series, originally shaped in the 70s. In 1999, the renamed *CanoeSports Hawai`i* merged with *Karel Tresnak's Outrigger Connection,* and they embarked on a project to produce a high performance OC4 surfing wa`a.

With input from *Mel Pu'u, Brian Keaulana (Buffalo Keaulana's* son and an excellent waterman), *Teene Forsyth*, and steersman *Todd Bradley,* the *Makaha* was created, using the lines of a *Mirage* OC6, modified for the 23' OC4.

Makaha has added rocker so it stays on the face of the wave and doesn't run in front of it; higher gunnels so it is dryer in the waves; greater buoyancy; and a 23" wide hull on the bottom while the gunnels are still only 1 inches wide.

Makaha OC4. *Chris Miller, Jimmy Boy Austin, Todd Bradley, Mel Pu'u* steering. OC4. Photo by *JOSS.*

The ama is 13" wide and high to provide the wa`a with the support it needs, especially in the wave when only portions of the ama is in the water. The ama size also improves the bailing of the wa`a, because its floatation helps the crew to lift the wa`a above the surface to get the water out of the hull.

Team Racing Wa`a and Va`a (OC6/ W6/V6)

The six person team va`a is the craft used most predominantly for racing. The Hawaiian wa`a is, for the most part, designed as an open decked craft, its design limited by specifications. Hawaiian (fibreglass) wa`a designers and builders have learned that a wa`a that wins in the Moloka`i to O`ahu race is a saleable commodity, not just in Hawai`i but wherever Hawaiian specifications have been adopted. Designs are therefore biased towards the conditions of the Kaiwi Channel which separates the island of Moloka`i and O`ahu; suited to rough water, down wind conditions, not flat water.

OC3 Surfing wa`a. Photo by *JOSS.*

This has been true of the *Malia, Hawaiian Class Racer, Bradley, Force Five* and today the *Mirage* as it is true of ruddered sit on top OC1s and OC2s.. It must be stated that the sum of the whole of this sport, especially

in terms of design, cannot be encapsulated by the virtues of one race alone, across one stretch of water. However this attitude seems to have come to dominate both the economic successes and virtues of designs almost as far back as the race's inception in 1953.

An OC12 / DC 12 is simply 2 OC6s joined. Photo *Daphne Hougard*

Wa`a

Hawai`i - While this is the traditional name, it is used only among traditionalists and a few grass-roots clubs. This reflects a degradation of the everyday use of the Hawaiian language and yet it is the appropriate term to use. It is somewhat ironic that in most other Pacific island regions, the appropriate traditional names are used, but in Hawai`i this is not generally the case. Ironically *Hui Wa`a* formed in the 1970s on the basis of wanting to use only fibreglass wa`a, counter to the traditional use of koa wa`a of the time, adopted the traditional nomenclature - wa`a.

Va`a

V1 are designed for lagoon or open ocean paddling. In either case, both are paddle steered in the absence of a rudder and include a cockpit in which the paddler sits which distinguishes this craft from its Hawaiian counterpart, the OC1.

No V2s are currently in popular use. V3 racing va`a were introduced in the 1980s and embraced intermittently. A new V3 race between the islands of Moorea and Tahiti is currently being developed.

There are many variations of the Tahitian V6 because there are no restrictions or design limits. They are collectively very different from the Hawaiian wa`a and

Va`a rack Bora Bora with a variety of lagoon and ocean va`a.

include marked differences such as a preference for a semi-closed deck design, narrow sterns, reverse transoms, raised stantions for rigging i`ato to va`a and the seat placements are closer together.

Tahitian va`a design exudes a level of maritime architecture in a symmetry and form which is both evocative and provocative. Every line and curve emanates purpose. With so many different va`a designs in this region, on a percentage basis only, many of these va`a designs are uniquely superior to Hawaiian designs which are constrained by limitations. Note closed deck configuration.

Overall, the differences are so varied that the two craft are often dissimilar in every way. Open specifications nurtures vision and freedom to express creativity.

On a small beach, va`a are placed gunnel to gunnel, they are brightly coloured and posses the most beautiful shapes and forms; each sporting different graphics and motifs, blended with the traditional feel of timber.
Like hotrods or streetcars lovingly polished and buffed, artistically airbrushed and presented, these va`a have a personality of their own, brazen and purposeful, with design lines emanating freedom of expression and creativity without limits. Ocean craft with attitude. Va`a on Huahine Island, French Polynesia.

V3 in Papeete. A very demanding form of racing.

French Polynesia has a huge array of different racing va`a designs, far more so than anywhere else on the planet. They have va`a for every occasion, every condition and are not limited by a 'mass-production' mindset.

Consequently, va`a designs here are varied, exciting, unique and often brilliant. Many are purpose built, for flat water, some for rough, but no single va'a design dominates for long, because there are no rulings on specifications, secrecy in creating a better va`a and an insatiable need to pursue their cultural right in producing an ever evolving va`a.

Below: One of French Polynesia's most successful va`a designs by *Raymond Ah-tak* from the island of Huahine. This va`a has uniquely different lines, more like that of a submarine than a conventional 'boat' which rides on top of the water. This is an acknowledgement that a portion of the hull spends all of its time in the water while the rest, on occasion, is also totally submerged and therefore it too must be efficient in shedding water.

Rounded hull, strip plank construction.

Therefore, there are marked differences in va`a designs between these two dominating forces. To what extent the sport can continue to be marketed as 'Hawaiian canoe racing' is an interesting consideration, when so much influence has been embraced on many levels from the Tahitian way of thinking. Va'a racing would seem a far more culturally encompassing term.

New Zealand has aligned itself with Tahiti since the 1980s, with the use of paddle steered, sit inside cockpits, but this is changing. The W2 generally includes a rudder. The W4 is used for surfing and the W6 and W12 are similar to the Tahitian configuration.

Two V8s are joined to form a V16 which are used exclusively for the *Bastille Festival* held in July in Papeete Harbour. They are unique to the region.

Components and Accessories

For the purpose of this work, we are primarily concerned with today's racing va`a, the likes of which are strongly influenced by Hawaiian and Tahitian artisans. While you could be forgiven for believing Hawai`i is the leader and dominate force in this unique paddle sport, the fact is, Tahitian influence is omnipresent. From these isolated exotic isles, a veritable plethora of knowledge and talent, serves as an aspirational chalice from which the rest of the world sips, but rarely gulps. This is due to the fact that the Tahitians are overshadowed by Hawaii's ties and association with America to the extent that the notion of Hawai`i being a mythical isle, and a part of Polynesia, seems but a romantic notion long since forgotten.

The Outrigger Assembly

The 'Hawaiian' outrigger canoe is but one of hundreds of va`a types across the region of Oceania, which encompasses Melanesia, Micronesia and Polynesia. Construction variances of the outrigger frame across Oceania gave rise to unique styles of outrigger assemblies. Va`a hulls are also different, but it is the outrigger itself which highlights the different approaches to a maritime technological problem; devising a means of stabilising the dugout hull which led to the development of the outrigger framework in its various forms.

Traditionally, the outrigger frame has always been fitted on the left side of the va`a. No definitive reason for this seems to exist and interestingly the Polynesian name of *ama,* (ah-mah) given to the outrigger float, is derived from the word *hema* meaning left or south side of the va`a.

The outrigger assembly consists of two i`ako (ee-a-koo) or booms (spars) rigged out on the left side of the wa`a and attached to an ama or float, which functions as

a counterpoise in stabilising the wa`a. The entire framework is lashed inboard across and onto the wa`a by the two spreader bars or thwarts. These are spaced appropriately apart according to the wa`a design and function, and attached using an intricate weave which provides flexibility and rigidity to the outrigger assembly. The i`ako is interchangeable and on surfing wa`a it is often placed on the right.

Tahitian Interpretations

The ama is considered 'female' because of its size, smooth curved lines and its function in providing balance to it's larger, stronger male counterpart. The hull or va`a, is considered to be the *tino* or body (Tahiti / Samoa). The female ama and male va`a are joined by the i`ato, which is flexible and moves in harmony with both bodies and the ocean.

Outrigger Boom

i`ako (ee-a-koo, Hawai`i); i`ato (ee-a-toe French Polynesia); kiato (kee-a-toe New Zealand); muku (Hawaii) short overhang; kapua`i (Hawaii) long overhang.

Contemporary racing wa`a include two i`ako, rigged traditionally on the left side and attached inboard by means of a traditional lashing technique using cordage. Other

Tahitian i`ato, aerodynamically shaped and exquisitely laminated, reinforces the Tahitians high level of craftsmanship, passion for the va`a and pursuit of the notion of form and function as a maxim in honouring their culture.

I`ako on this Hawaiian wa`a are traditional single lengths of hau timber cured and fashioned to fit. Commonly the front and rear lengths are more or less straight, with neither being more 'raised' then the other.

popular materials include rubber inner-tube, or mechanical ratchet tie downs - snap lashes, the outer ends of which are lashed directly to the ama, using cordage.

There are differences in the number of i`ako used throughout Oceania. Some use one, two, three or more and there are differences in the way in which they were attached to the ama. Throughout Oceania, i`ako were generally straight for lagoon work.

During the late seventeenth century, Hawaiian double wa`a builders began to incorporate the curved i`ako, lifting it above the water level to allow them to attach a deck platform between two wa`a hulls. This then became a design applied to single wa`a designs which minimised the contact the i`ako had with the water, permitting on-coming waves to pass under them rather than crashing into and over them. Curved i`ako, however, were already in common use in other areas of the Pacific in various forms, including Tahiti.

The i`ako sit flush across the wae wa`a spreader simplify lashing while outboard they tend to rise in a flat arch marginally above the level of the wa`a gunnel, before curving down to roughly the level of the gunnel, attaching to the ama. The forward i`ako generally has a greater amount of curvature than the rear. This is to compensate for the raised curvature of the ama or lupe, so the i`ako meets at the correct height, though this is not always true with all designs. Some straight i`ako are still in common use.

Hau `iako, extremely strong and flexible due to its fibre structure, were considered ideal by the ancient Hawaiians.

Throughout Oceania, different methods were used to attach the i`ako to the ama and they were often attached indirectly, with the use of vertical stick connectors. Direct attachment of the i`ako to the ama became a traditional feature of the Hawaiian canoe for added security in rough waters but was also a feature of the outrigger canoes of Samoa, Marquesas, Tahiti and the Ellis Islands.

The wa`a builders of Hawai`i had the ideal raw material for i`ako making; *hibiscus tiliaceus* commonly called *hau,* which grows with a natural curve to allow the i`ako to be fashioned. It has properties which suit the demands made on it and the environment in which it was used. It is lightweight and strong, yet flexible enough to give under pressure. Once selected and cut, they were then immersed in saltwater for several months and then cured in the sun to kill borers and other infestations.

The length of i`ako varies in relation to the size of wa`a. However, using the laws of leverage, it can be assumed that the greater the length of the *kapua`i* - long overhang, out from the side of the wa`a to the ama, the greater the stabilising effect, which could vary from 5-12'. The negative effect of this is greater drag as the ama sits deeper in the water.

Among the islands of French Polynesia, i`ato (Tahitian) designs are quite unique and often aerodynamic in profile. Since they attach to raised stanchions, often high above the level of the gunnel, they are commonly straight and often show an extremely high level of craftsmanship.

Float

ama (ah-mah); lupe, fore-end; kanaka, aft-end.

The floatation device attached to the extremity of the i`ako acts as a counterpoise (counterbalance) of equivalent force to stabilise the wa`a hull.

Tahitian style, note Dolphin head.

The traditional selection of an ama was of great importance because its characteristics determined, to a great extent, the handling of the wa`a at sea. It is believed that the crafting of the ama was performed by separate craftsmen each having access to the correct tree type and the inherited skills of ama shaping.

An acutely curved ama is very stable, sitting deep on its mid section. It has a very defined pivot point which assists the steerer when turning. In open water, this ama does not track, potentially allowing greater manoeuvrability. For wa`a surfing, this older, traditional style ama is still preferred.

Due to excessive drag caused by the ama shape and the resulting pull on the wa`a to the left, the ama is traditionally rigged toed-in. This means that it is set closer-in, between 2-5cm (3/4–2"), towards the wa`a hull at the *lupe* fore-end. Skill and understanding of the water conditions and nuances of each individual wa`a determines the amount of toe-in applied during rigging.

The long gradual fore to aft ama curvature is somewhat unique to Hawai`i. It is attributed to the Hawaiian's maritime design ingenuity for improving the stability of the wa`a on rough and chaotic waters.

The curvature which runs the length of the ama prevents the ama nose diving beneath oncoming waves, as well as reducing the amount of surface area of the ama in direct contact with the water. While it is the purpose of the ama to function as a counterpoise, this does not mean that an undue amount of its surface area should be in constant a contact with the water, as this would create more drag and a reduction in speed.

Therefore, the ama is deliberately shaped so that the lupe and *kanaka* (stern) remain clear of the water. The lupe was traditionally, and still is today, shaped in a unique way, almost head-like, thought to represent the head of a lizard.

Traditionally curved ama, affectionately known as an 'elephant tusk' or 'banana' ama.

A well curved ama, traditionally called an *ama kaka,* will stay in contact with rough water more readily than an ama with less curvature. It will always appear to be in contact with the water at some point along its length, resisting the tendency to break free entirely and putting the wa`a at risk of capsize. Traditionally, it was not uncommon for wa`a owners to have several different ama, which can be selected and attached according to the expected sea conditions.

When the ama lifts in response to an oncoming swell and the wa`a movements, its contact with the water is progressively reduced due to its curvature. Likewise, in returning to a level position in the water, the ama offers a gradual increase and decrease in resistance to the forward motion of the wa`a and the amount of strain transferred along the i`ako to the attachment point at the spreaders.

This effect is directly related to the degree of curve of the ama. In the case of a straight ama, its release and re-entry with the water is immediate and not at all progressive. For many traditional wa`a designs this would have been highly undesirable, especially in rough water, as it creates instability and greater shock on the entire outrigger frame on its re-entry.

Contemporary Ama Design and Development

It was not until the mid 80s as high performance, extreme paddling began to evolve, that ama designs began to move away from the radical curve. Original racing designs were low in volume and tended to bury badly with heavy crews and in big seas. The desire was to create an ama which rides more 'on top of' the water rather than 'below it' incorporating long straight sections, higher volumes and longer water line lengths

Tahitian art form.

and streamlining. At speed and particularly when paddling in a following sea, the surface area or 'footprint' of the ama is reduced and therefore so is the drag.

One of the first of the new generation ama was the *Moby Dick*, designed by *Tom Conners* of Hawai`i, with the input of *Joe Quigg* and *Walter Guild*. It was so named because of its high volume and shape when compared to the traditional ama of the time.

'Tom Conner built an ama that we used and won in the 1986 Moloka`i Channel race. It was a departure from the traditional banana shaped ama, it had a flatter bottom, large volume, lashing holes and raised platforms for `iako attachment.

Some of the design remained similar on future models. A longer water line, flatter bottom, higher front neck, a pedestal at the back to get the rear `iako up and away from the water, with holes through that for lashing, though the front was still lashed right *around under the ama. It was the beginning of a realisation that there was something faster than the banana ama.*

We learned some things with that ama, using it in the Moloka`i in 1986 and 1987 and winning both years. Hank Lass, our partner here at the Fibreglass Shop at the time, contracted Joe Quigg to build a prototype of his idea of a new ama and Joe came up with the Channel Master ama. Hank, at the time, was paddling Senior Masters at the Outrigger. They paddled with it for awhile, then gave it to me to try. I realised it was exceptional, way better than the production ama of the time.

So we went ahead and Brent Bixler built the mould, incorporating all hole-tied lashing points front and rear so all the cordage would be free of the water. That ama did really, really well – paddlers seemed to like it as an all around ama. This became the standard ama supplied with Force Five canoes.

We will see increasingly more ama designs being tried. It is very difficult to design an ama and a hull both in the development stage at the same time. The ama is a very important factor, more so than many have thought. We look at them as separate hulls. Either one can limit your potential. You can have a great primary hull with a lousy ama and you're not going to reach your full potential.

Therefore, what we would do is develop a constant at one end, for instance the ama, and to test hull design, have the same ama used on two different hulls. Once we establish that this is the best we can do with the hull, then we go back and keep the hull constant while we change the ama.

***Tom Conner's, Moby Dick* ama of 1986. A catalyst for new thinking on ama design on many levels, from attachment to issues of performance requirements given varying sea conditions.**

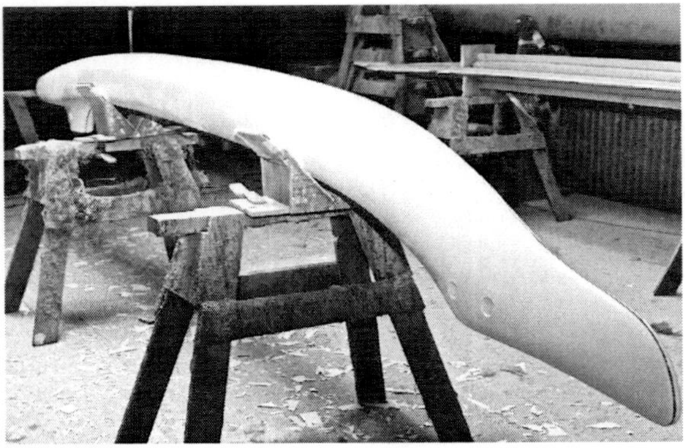

We really learned a great deal about the importance of ama design when designing solo canoes. It didn't become that evident until we started our testing with ama for the Kaiwi Challenger – Ocean Master (Australia), one of the earliest commercially available ruddered OC1's. We were amazed at how much faster we could go with the ama in the air. That told us that the way in which the ama makes contact with the water and the way in which it's rigged and sits on the water is critical to hull speed.' Walter Guild.

From the top:
The *Channel Master* ama designed by *Joe Quigg* and detailed by *Brent Bixler* became the first production ama to deviate away from the traditional *Elephant Tusk* designs.

The *Tahitian* ama, a modified version of the *Channel Master* ama.

The *Wizard* ama designed by Australian *Ian Rawlings* in 1997.

The *Catamaran* ama developed by *Offshore California Canoe Club* by *Billy Whitford* and *Bud Hohl.* Based on the *Hobie Cat* hull shape, the idea was to develop an ama better suited to Californian conditions.

With the design of larger, straighter, high volume ama, paddlers began to rig the ama parallel to the hull without toe-in because the drag was less. The Tahitians later modified the *Channel Master* into a slightly more refined shape suitable for Tahitian waters, which became known as the *Tahitian* ama, from which subsequent designs have been created.

Significantly in 1997, Australian paddler, fibre-glasser and designer, *Ian Rawlings* designed an ama named the *Wizard* which played an important role in ama development.

'My crew, Outrigger Australia had an accident during the Gold Coast Cup, resulting in a hole in our ama which then sunk. I went on to design and construct a polystyrene foam/epoxy/glass ama which we used with a Force 5 canoe to win the 1997 Moloka`i to O`ahu race.

After the race, I made 3 moulds of the foam plug. The first was sent to Walter Guild in Hawai`i and was provided with the Force 5s manufactured by Canoe Sports Hawaii. Karel Tresnak, also offered it with his new OC6 and it is still

The *Axe* ama supplied with Australia's *Southern Spirit* wa`a is truly a monster. It is based on catamaran hull concepts and designed to suit 'average' Australian race conditions.

Two different Tahitian ama. There are as many variations of ama in Tahiti as there are va`a, if not more. Ama supplied with Californian designed *Pacific Islander* wa`a.

available as an option for the Mirage. The second mould went to Canoe Sports Australia on the Sunshine Coast and the ama is offered with all Force 5s in Australia. The third mould went to California and was made by Calvin Hirahara for the Californian Bradley canoes.'

The *Puffy* ama as supplied with the current *Mirage* wa`a. It is large in volume and is designed, when paddling downwind, to have only its rear quarter in contact with the water. A rounded under surface prevents 'tracking' thus increasing manoeuvrability and a distinct curved flange has been added along this rear quarter, where the hull meets the top-side, to reduce the potential for submersion. Below: A *Brent Bixler* designed ama, without lashing holes, but a single large space with 3 separate ridges which permit the lashing to conform.

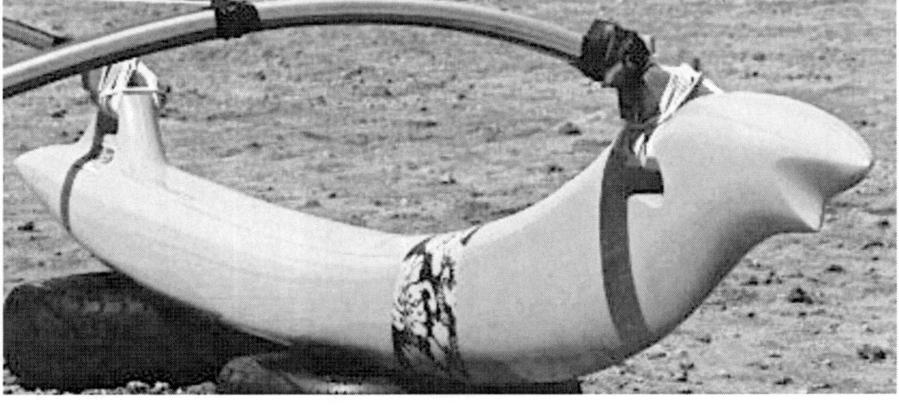

Wa`a Spreaders

wae wa'a

The *wae wa`a* - spreaders, have two vital functions. Their primary role is as the point where the i`ako is attached to the wa`a hull, with a variety of lashing techniques. Their secondary roll is as braces or thwarts, much like the seats, however they are of extremely strong construction and positioned level with the top of the gunnel.

Functioning as the two connection points between the wa`a and outrigger assembly, no other point of the wa`a comes under the same amount of strain and stress as the i`ako is constantly tensioning under the pressures of the wave and swell action.

Hawaiian wa`a builders fashioned U-shaped wae from the root of a special tree, which had a natural curve and possessed incredible strength. That U-shaped sections were chosen exemplifies an understanding of engineering and the inherent strength in such a curve. Today's modern fibreglass wa`a generally incorporate a block section of timber, laminated with fibreglass, which is positioned level to the gunnel, permitting the i`ako to run flush from gunnel to gunnel.

This adjustable wae is rarely incorporated and yet affords flexibility in its positioning. The entire outrigger assembly can be moved fore or aft and ama of differing lengths can be used. The wae itself is a traditional Hawaiian shape.

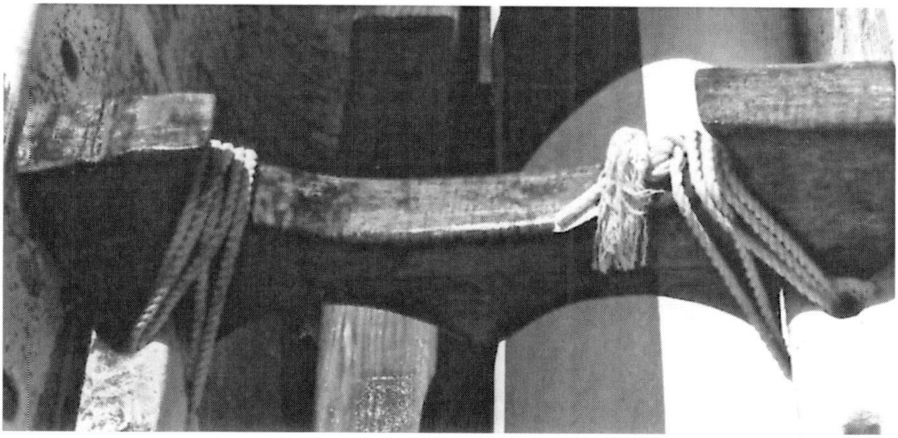

In contrast, the va`a of Tahiti and her islands use raised stanchions carved from solid timber and sometimes laminated, which attach to a strong cross-member and sit high above the level of the gunnel. This alters the dynamic of the va`a and raises the height of the i`ato outboard.

From a purely logical standpoint, this system seems preferable for several reasons. The 'rigging' process is easier because it is above the level of the gunnel and not within the va`a. The rigging is visible at all times. Tensioning adjustments can be

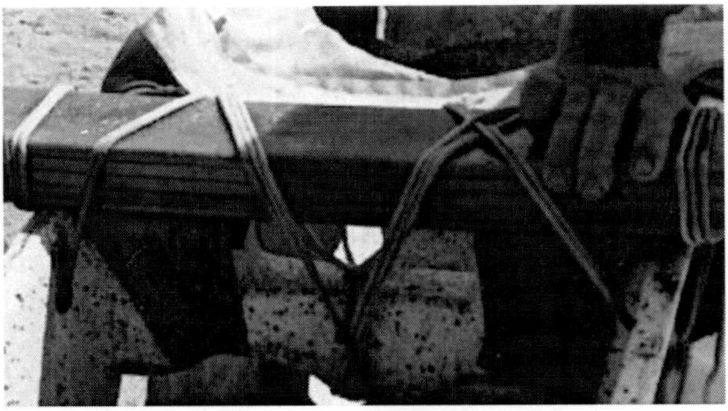

Above: Wae wa`a on a Hawaiian wa`a.
Below: This Tahitian made koa va`a in Hawai`i incorporates both the U-shaped wae and a raised platform. The difference in this case is that the va`a is completely open decked, but the rigging remains above the level of the gunnel and the covers wrap around the lower portion.

Raised timber spreader on a Tahitian va`a. The two approaches are markedly different.

managed with relative ease. There are no covers obscuring the rigging and covers can be fitted better. The added height of the i`ato from the water, improves the safety of incoming paddlers during change-overs. The engineering dynamics of how the va`a responds with a raised rigging point in rough water, is beyond the scope of the author. But suffice it to say, Tahitian paddlers have mastered its nuances.

Gunnel

Mo`o gunnel; niao gunnel

The *mo`o* - gunnel, runs along the upper edge of the wa`a hull. Its function is to provide longitudinal strength at the upper edges and to protect the thinner edge of the wa`a hull.

A strong mo`o is important in supporting the weight and stresses exerted by the i`ako, which rests across the *niao* - gunnel edge and wa`e wa`a.

Racing covers are attached along the underside of the mo`o by either an aluminium track or moulding within the hull.

Manu

manu ihu - bow end piece; kupe ihu - bow cover; manu hope - stern end piece; kupe hope - stern cover

Manu ihu ocean facing. Moloka`i.

The manu are the distinctly shaped end pieces, curving elegantly upwards at the extremities of the bow and stern. On occasions the *manu ihu* - bow end piece, is raised higher than that of the *manu hope* - stern end piece. First thought of as purely decorative, the manu function as wave breakers and give added buoyancy to the bow and stern when submerged, encouraging lift. The strong construction of the manu gives it impact strength in the event of a head on collision. Much of the 'character' of the wa`a is defined by the shape and form given to the manu.

These sections were originally made as 'pieces', separate items carved from timber. Today's modern fibreglass wa`a moulds create the complete section as one unit.

Tahitian va`a invariably do not incorporate forward or rear manu into their designs due to their preference for reverse transoms and slender conventional bow shapes.

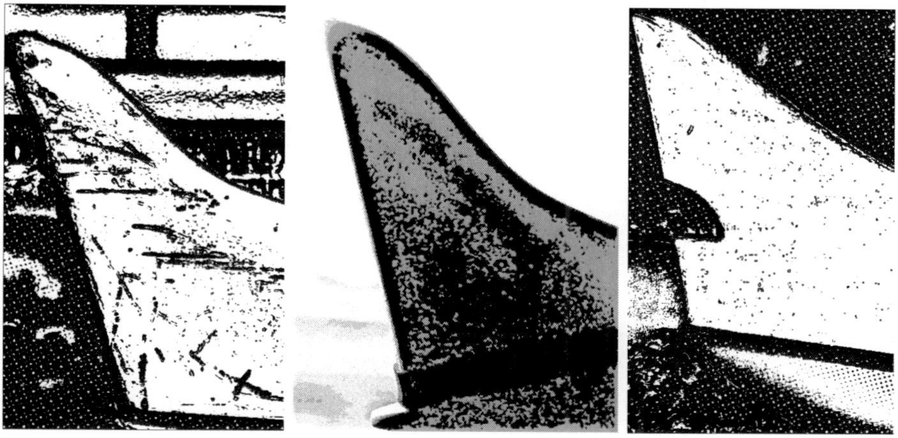

Manu Hope - ***Hawaiian Class Racer - Pacific Islander - Classic Force Five***

The spatula-shaped manu were traditionally exaggerated in size and in the case of ceremonial wa`a decorated. End pieces add to the elegance and grace of the wa`a. The *kupe ihu* - bow cover, and *kupe hope* stern cover, are essentially an extension of the manu and reduce the amount of water that would enter the wa`a when a wave broaches. These are marginally convex in shape and truncated in modern wa`a by a watertight bulkhead.

Koa bow covers, Sand Island O`ahu, Hawai`i.

Know your Manu

by Terry Wallace

The term *manu* throughout much of Polynesia, means, 'bird'. The two projections on either end of a wa`a, are called *manu* (ma-noo). These projections are functional as well as traditional and in some cases religious. In some parts of the Pacific, the manu is minimal and in others, they rise several feet.

'Winged' manu hope illustrating the translation of manu to 'bird'.

Most sea-going vessels through the ages have had some kind of up-swept bow and stern. Viking ships used end-pieces with God-like manifestations on either end. All sea going vessels in Polynesia and throughout the rest of the Pacific, fashioned up-swept end pieces. Some are fancier than others. Lagoon and river wa`a seldom add it, as they were not functional in this environment.

The purpose of the *manu mua* (moo-uh) or *ihu* (ee-hu) both meaning forward, was as a cutwater when ploughing through waves. If a wave came over, its power was minimised and cut also by the *pale ka*i (pahlay-kaee) splashboard.

The purpose of the *manu hope* (ho-pay) rear, was to prevent or minimise a following sea from coming over the stern. Why the term manu is used is a little harder to explain. The sea can be a scary place. *Moana,* the *Great Ocean* simply does not care one whit about the people who ride on her skin.

Because you want your wa`a to ride on the sea not in it, giving this design the name *bird*, makes sense. Polynesians held much significance for birds, which they considered as a manifestation of the human spirit, leaving earth and going to heaven. The name *`Iolani*, one of the many names of *Liholiho* or *Kamehameha II*, means the *Hawk of Heaven* or *Royal Hawk*, used because of its high flight in the heavens.

Birds were also observed to flow on the wind currents when at sea, having the ability to ride over the waves, without touching the water. If one observes a wa`a, using a little imagination, a bird is visible; Manu ihu, the beak, *mo`o* (moh-oh) or gunnel being the wings held back in a gliding position and manu hope, the tail feathers.

By employing bird symbols, both visibly and in the mind, it was hoped that a sea-going wa`a would symbolically ride the air currents over the dangerous seas.

Moamoa

by Terry Wallace

A curious design feature, where the *kupe hope* and *manu hope* terminate a few inches short of the wa`a hull. The *moamoa* seems to have always been a feature of the Hawaiian wa`a.

Variation of a theme Kona Coast, Hawai'i. Tahitian va`a with a figure which, in strict terms, is not a manu, but more of an adornment.

The moamoa or momoa has no function or does it? *Na Maoli,* the original people of what is now called the State of Hawai`i, were not known for decorating functional tools. Unlike the Maori of New Zealand, wa`a were not usually intricately carved or decorated. Everything was functional.

Parts were tied together by different systems, some being quite elaborate, but function was the main element. *'Any non-essential ornamental design feature either structurally weakened a canoe or resulted in a canoe that was less rugged than a simpler and cleaner craft. To survive the pummelling surf and raging channels of Hawai`i, every design feature, every component, every inch of the Hawaiian canoe had to be functional and rugged.'*
Tommy Holmes - The Hawaiian Canoe.

So it was with the momoa. Looking at the extreme aft end ka hope, you should find a small flat spot. As if the manufacturer had not quite affixed the kupe hope to the *ka`ele* (hull) correctly, leaving a small projection about 1-1.5" or so of the top hull visible. '*What was this for? Fastening covers? Tying the ama to the manu in heavy seas to prevent excessive movement? `Aole – no! It's where your, "wa`a `akua' " rides to protect you while at sea - your personal spirit.*'

About seven hundred years ago, the religious *kahuna, Pa`ao*, went to *Kahiki* to find new blood for a king. He finally selected *Pili Ka`aiea* and asked him to come to Hawai`i. As they sailed from Rai`atea, heading back to the island of Hawai`i, the *Tahunga* priest *Makuakaumana* cried out from the cliff that he had been left behind. *Pili* replied that the wa`a was full, but if you leap from the cliff, you can ride here, on the *momoa.*

Waka ama manu, New Zealand.
Tahitian manu

***Makuakaumana* leapt from the cliff and flew toward the wa`a, meanwhile changing from a man into a spirit so he could ride on that small place. From then on, *momoa* was considered an essential part of any wa`a.**

Historian *Herb Kane* comments, *'Perhaps the only distinctive feature of Hawaiian canoes that may be considered non-functional (depending on how you think about ancestral spirits) is the slight projection of the hull from under the manu at the stern, called the momoa. That projection has become traditional in Hawaiian canoes, some say as a place where an invisible but benevolent ancestral aumaku spirit can ride.'*

Since the advent of fibreglass wa`a and the story of the momoa has been misplaced, many manufacturers and carvers have either moved, redesigned or forgotten the momoa.

Floatation Tanks

The floatation tanks are located at the front and rear of the wa`a, providing buoyancy in the event of a swamping or capsize. A bulkhead is added to the bow and stern covers to create a water tight seal. This is a modern development and not present on traditional wa`a, including koa wa`a.

Some tanks include a bung, while others do not. Wa`a with bungs can present some problems. If the tank develops a hole, as long as the bung

is watertight, only a small amount of water will enter. If, however, there is more than one hole, then air will escape as water enters and the tank could fill to capacity which is extremely dangerous in the event of a capsize.

Ensure your bungs are not worn and that water does not flow out from the *pikaos* hole when you release the bung. Ideally, they should remain dry at all times. To avoid unnecessary stress on the tanks through extreme expansion and contraction in hot and cold weather, the following procedure should be adopted. It is are particularly important in tropical and sub-tropical environments.

When you finish paddling, always release the bungs fore and aft for storage on land. This will prevent excessive internal air expansion and structural stress being created as air heats up within the tanks during the day. If, when you release the bung, air rushes out, this is due to warm expanded air inside caused naturally by the warmth of the sun.

Splashboard

pale kai - breakwater, weather board

Fitted towards the rear of the kupe ihu, the *pale kai* - splashboard is an essential fitting that is extremely effective in providing a barrier to water entering the wa`a. It is usually triangular and with a curved top lip.

Tahitian designers have a different view regarding splashboards. While some may say this has to do with prevailing ocean conditions, in reality, they feel that it slows the va`a when nose diving.

Tahitian va`a splashboards tend to be much smaller in size and on some va`a are not present. Theories behind this are varied, but in essence the Tahitian va`a will often have added volume in the bow section and some designers think the splashboard increases drag when the bow is submerged.

Seating / Deck Configuration

noho `ana wa`a

Seating is more than just a place for the paddlers to sit. Importantly, the seating provides effective braces or thwarts which support the upper sides of the wa`a hull preventing warping and twisting.

The seating arrangement differs markedly between Hawaiian wa`a and Tahitian va`a since the Hawaiian design are open decked and the Tahitian are closed.

In reality, the Tahitian design reflects an evolution of the open deck va`a, in order to increase hull stiffness and reduce water intake.

Open decked Hawaiian wa`a.

Australia's *Southern Spirit* closed deck configuration.
Tahitian closed deck va`a.

Rigging Materials

When it comes to selecting a suitable lashing material for rigging, it is necessary to consider the alternatives. Each type of fibre performs differently under stress, especially when wet and in a marine environment. Ideally, you do not want the lashing material used to be overly rigid or too flexible, it is the balance between these two qualities which form part of the art of *`aha hoa wa`a* or wa`a rigging.

Rough water paddling requires some give and take in the rigging.

A balanced 'give and take' dynamic constitutes effective, safe rigging. Too much rigidity can compromise the structural integrity while too much movement can lead to the dismantling of the outrigger framework. Overly rigid attachment of i`ako to wae wa`a, or i`ako to ama, creates a 'stiff' wa`a, that is sensitive to every movement throughout the outrigger framework and failing to absorb some of the ocean's irregularities.

High tensile, pre-stretched cordage is not suitable, as it presents a danger to the structural integrity of the wa`a and outrigger assembly, lacking spring and flex, and even the opportunity to break under extreme load and torque. It's better for the lashing to snap than a structural component of the wa`a.

Therefore, it is desirable to have some flexibility at the point where the i`ako attaches inboard to the wae wa`a. This allows the outrigger framework's movements, originating at the ama, to be transferred back along the i`ako and absorbed by some 'give' in the lashing. Herein lies the skill of wa`a rigging and the selection of suitable material.

Preparing rigging cord.

Notes Regarding Cordage and Rope

Cordage and Rope

The point of difference between rope and cord is the diameter. Rope, by definition, has a circumference of 1" or more, which equates to an 8mm diameter. A size less than this is, by definition, cordage.

Static and Dynamic

Cordage and rope can be classified as either 'static' or 'dynamic', which takes into account the amount they stretch under load. Static cordage stretches very little under normal load, if at all. While dynamic cordage will stretch to a greater extent under an equal load. Dynamic cord is required for rigging a wa`a.

Elongation Percentage

The amount the rope or cord stretches just prior to reaching its breaking load -point. A good example is Cotton which tends to stretch 5-10% when dry prior to breaking.

Laid Construction

Usually consists of three separate strands that are wound around one another (twisted fibres). It is generally stronger than braided or plaited types, and tends to be a little stiffer and harder to handle. All natural fibre rope and cord as well as some synthetic fibre types are of laid construction. Laid cord and rope are made by twisting together yarns to form strands. They are susceptible to abrasion and other types of physical damage as all load-bearing strands are exposed at various points along the length. Hard-laid cord and rope is twisted tightly to form a stiffer, more abrasion resistant rope however, it is difficult to form knots and hitches. Soft-laid, which is not twisted as tight, is softer, more easily tied and somewhat stronger.

Braided

Some braided ropes and cord are made from natural fibres but most are synthetic, they are constructed by uniformly intertwining strands together. A braided rope has no outer sheath or core and is susceptible to abrasion and damage.

Braid on Braid

A 'jacketed' rope or cord constructed with a braided core and braided sheath. It is very strong, but does not resist abrasion and has a problem with the outer sheath sliding along the inner core.

Kernmantle

Jacketed rope and cord are made of a braided covering (mantle) over the main load bearing strands (kern). They may be twisted or braided and have good stretch resistance and load characteristics. The kern is made of high strength fibres, which account for 3/4 of the total strength. The sheath is designed to absorb most of the abrasion and protects the load-bearing core. Kernmantle can be dynamic or static; dynamic kernmantle is used as a sport rope for rock or ice climbing, while static is used for rescue rope.

Natural Fibres

Natural fibre cordage is made from several fibre types and given the general classification of being either 'hard' or 'soft'. Two common examples of hard fibre cordages are those made from Sisal and Manila while Cotton is, by comparison, a soft fibre cordage.

Hard and soft relate in part to the feel and flexibility of the fibre - hard fibre ropes are generally course and prickly as opposed to soft fibre ropes, such as cotton. Both hard and soft natural fibre ropes tend to be hard wearing with low stretch characteristics. Neither though, is as strong as its equivalent size in synthetic fibre ropes.

A characteristic of natural fibre is that 'creaks' under pressure, particularly after some time has been spent exposed to the elements when the oil has leeched from the fibres. You can hear it when it is at breaking point. Natural fibre ropes do not resist damp or saltwater particularly well and therefore need to dry out after use - sennet being the exception. They do not melt when subjected to frictional heat.

Some natural fibre ropes perform well as lashing cordage. It's preferable not to use synthetic rope with a greater breaking strain and more stretch than natural because in heavy seas the canoe gunnel, spreader or i`ako, could well break prior to the cordage 'giving'.

Sisal, Jute and Hemp are unsuitable lashing materials, while Manila also has its drawbacks, even though it is commonly used in a marine environment. Sennet remains an excellent traditional natural lashing fibre but unfortunately it is available only from specialists, is expensive and the flat braided variety is very hard to find.

Cotton braid is ultimately the only natural fibre cordage readily available that is inexpensive and suitable for outrigger canoe lashings.

Sennet

The cultures of Oceania mastered the art of rigging a va`a using lashing techniques with cordage made by weaving coir (koy-er), the fibres found between the husks and the outer shell of the coconut. Commonly called sennet (`aha - Hawai`i) it provides ideal binding and lashing for va`a as well as rigging masts, sails and many other things. Production of sennet cordage was reserved for special groups of people and was usually the domain of women.

Two basic varieties were made, 'flat' and 'square'. The flat variety was favoured for wa`a rigging as it tightens over itself more efficiently, providing a firmer lashing.

Being practically impervious to the degrading effects of sunlight and salt water, as well as its remarkable ability to shrink when wet, sennet is perfect for wa`a rigging and use in a marine environment. Sennet has one third to one quarter the breaking strength capacity of Manila. And while resistant to salt water and ultra violet light, it soon rots in fresh water. Today the use of sennet has largely been replaced by synthetic cordage, cotton braid and manila. Still used in marine applications for mooring and towing lines, it is hard to come by and expensive.

Traditional use of sennet cord for binding and lashing. *Captain Cook Museum* Auckland, New Zealand.

Manila

Produced from the fibres of the wild banana plant and grown in the Philippines, Manilla was originally available in a variety of grades, but is now limited to one. Manila is the strongest of the natural fibres, and is hard wearing. It has low stretch and because of its reasonable resistance to weathering, is the most commonly used natural fibre in a marine environment - though it will rot if left damp for long periods of time.

Manila is marginally reduced in strength when wet and ruptures with 13% dry stretch and 15% wet. It does stretch when wet, which is a definite disadvantage. Many brands are lightly oiled making handling and cinching difficult, causing it to loose up to 1/2 of its tensile strength when wet.

Cotton

Lightweight, flexible, inexpensive, readily available and attractive in appearance, cotton is defined as a soft fibre and is possibly the best known of the natural fibres. It

Pre-stretching 'new' cotton before rigging is a must in order to avoid stretching during rigging or worse, stretching and loosening of the rigging while paddling.

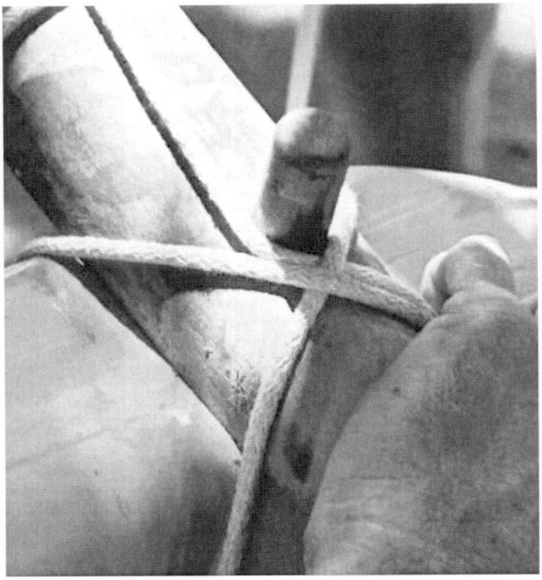

Solid braided cotton being used for lashing i`ako to ama.

is still popular where a soft pliable rope is preferred and is used for dinghy and yacht sheets, warps, lacings and dinghy fenders. It is flexible when dry, when wet it tends to become hard and stiff. Not as strong as manila, it is particularly sensitive to sunlight degradation.

Cotton elongates 5-10% before rupturing and is the only natural fibre which increases in strength marginally when wet. Suitable for applications where low strength and elongation are required, it has excellent abrasion and resistance to wear. With these qualities it is an excellent choice for lashing and the most commonly used today.

Three strand twisted cotton, is a popular rigging material for its added strength as expected from laid rope and cord. It is not as 'soft' or pliable as solid braided cotton, which cinches down on itself more effectively, thereby binding to itself.

Relative Tensile Strengths of Cotton and Manila

6mm Cotton
with reinforced-core
250lbs/114kgs

6mm Manilla
540lbs/245kgs

Manila however, looses 1/2 its strength when wet.
Cotton is manufactured in two primary forms braided and in a laid construction, such as Three Strand Twisted Cotton.

Cotton Diamond Braid is used in many applications where superior knot holding is required. This braid is used extensively as awning cord, traverse cord, clotheslines, and drawstring cord. Diamond braid cords are constructed of 8, 12, 16 or 32 strands, braided in an 'over and under' pattern giving the cord a diamond pattern, noticeable on the outside. Diamond braids can be made with a core of varying fibres, or can be coreless. Braids without a core are easily spliced; commonly referred to as 'hollow braid'.

Cotton Solid Braid is commonly referred to as 'sash cord' and includes a synthetic core for added strength and comes with or without a polished finish. Its uses include window sash cord, awning cord, halyard, and general utility cord. Solid braid is constructed from 9 or 12 interwoven strands. It has a smooth surface, holds its shape under load and also knots well.

Hollow 'coreless' braided cotton is not as strong as solid cotton braid. Hollow braided cotton has much greater stretch and a lower break point, however it's ability to stretch makes it superior to cotton sash cord for rigging which tends to 'snap' without warning and quite readily.

Synthetic Fibres

Man-made fibres in most marine applications have largely superseded the use of natural fibre rope. Four common synthetic fibres are presently used for rope, cord and net manufacture; nylon, polyester, polypropylene and polyethylene, all are derivatives of coal or oil. The physical and chemical characteristics vary between them, thus offering the user a choice of properties to suit each particular application.

Nylon

This is one of the strongest of the man-made fibres. With an elongation percentage of 23-42% dry and 27-34% wet, nylon has a high-energy absorption capacity and exceptional ability to sustain repeated shock loads. It is the only synthetic fibre that reduces in strength when wet by approximately 10%.

Nylon is commonly used as a tow rope because of its high degree of stretch and ability to absorb large amounts of repeated shock loads. Polyester rope is also used extensively for towing in a marine environment since it floats, but does not stretch to the same degree as nylon.

Nylon makes a suitable towing rope; however it does not float which can be a real problem. Realistically, it is impractical to attach the 'desired' length of tow rope because of its bulkiness. However, aim for at least 70' (32m) to ensure a safe distance from the towing vessel and so the shock back to the wa`a can be dissipated (See towing and rescue).

One inherent danger with nylon is that it has a powerful recoil if it does break that could cause the lashing to unravel quickly or perhaps even harm a paddler.

Nylon is affected by prolonged exposure to sunlight. Because of its rather slippery plastic coating, it is difficult to create a firm and reliable lashing as it is inclined to slide over itself. It loses between 10-20% of its strength when wet, but is technically the strongest of the synthetic cordages. It is overly strong and elastic for lashing and not recommended.

If it is the only available cord, you can apply a thin coating of surfboard wax to give it grip. This should be only done as a last resort, as sand and debris can get stuck on the waxed cord and cause abrasion and scratching.

Polyester

Polyester is the second strongest of the synthetic fibres. Size for size it is heavier than nylon, but has a lower breaking point. It has excellent abrasion resistance and a reasonably high elasticity and spring. With an elongation percentage of 30-35% at break point wet or dry, polyester also has the greatest resistance of all the synthetic fibres to ultra-violet degradation.

Its ability to stretch and spring back to shape ensures that the canoe structure is protected from stress, but could cause the lashed equipment to work loose. Not recommended for lashing.

Looks nice and is certainly stronger and longer lasting than a natural fibre. But the issue is that synthetic fibres are overly strong and in time cut into the timber i`ako and ultimately fail to safe-guard the structural integrity of the wa`a.

Polypropylene

Polypropylene is the lightest man-made fibre and popular when cost is the most important consideration. It has equal strength when wet or dry and an elongation percentage of 25-35%, giving it the lowest stretch properties of all the synthetic fibres. Polypropylene has proved to be the most popular replacement for natural fibre cordage largely because of its low cost.

Of all the synthetic fibres, polypropylene is the least resistant to sunlight, which results in reduced strength, but it is generally treated. It is however very 'slippery' and unsuitable for rigging as it does not cinch well.

Polyethylene

Often called silver rope, it has the hairy appearance of a natural fibre and a smooth, silky feel. This is not in its favour as this allows it to slip over itself when lashed. It does have a good recovery after stretching and an elongation percentage of 35%. Even though it has excellent abrasion resistance and flexibility, it is not recommended for outrigger lashing.

I`ako to Wae Wa`a - Spreader

For single cordage lashing using a modified diamond weave, it is common practice to take five full wraps around the centre of the i`ako and wae wa`a incorporating, five passes out through the lashing holes around the i`ako and back inboard. You will need approximately 60ft (18m) of a 6mm cordage, depending on the height of any blocks used under the i`ako. This is the same for front and rear.

I`ako to Ama

It is common practice to take four full wraps through the ama lashing holes and around the i`ako, using approximately 50ft -15, of 4mm cordage.

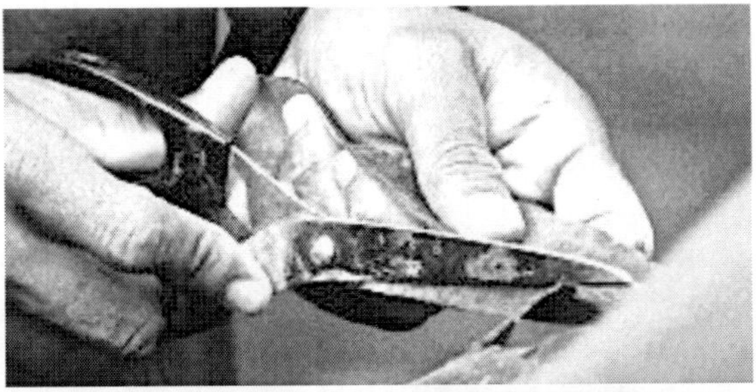

Cutting inner-tube for rigging i`ako to wae. DC12 rigged using rubber. The added flex protects the structural integrity of the wa`a lashing points in particular. Tahitian va`a are regularly rigged with rubber.

The ugly side of rubber's degradation by UV exposure and degradation from salt water. Vigilant checking is required.

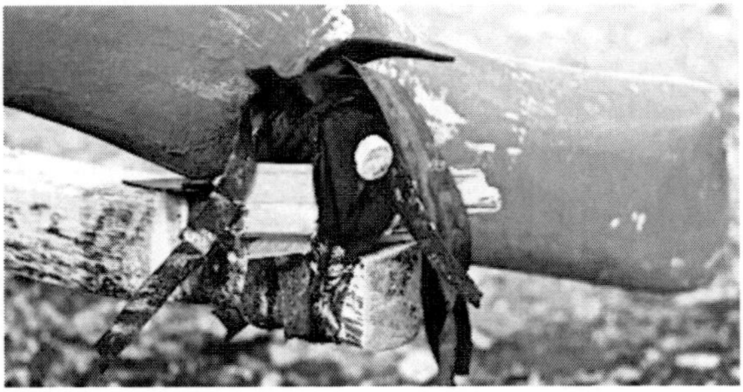

Rubber

The use of rubber inner-tube is popular in many regions of the Pacific; Tahiti, New Caledonia, Fiji, Wallis Futuna, and New Zealand to name a few. It is also used almost exclusively on surfing wa`a in Hawai`i and elsewhere.

Rubber is often a preferred material when rigging two Hawaiian wa`a hulls together to make a DC12 (double wa`a) in order to ensure some flex and movement between the hulls.

It's obvious merit is that it's a cheap, cut into lengths from 'used' tyre inner-tubes. Pre-cut commercially purchased rubber lengths are expensive by comparison.

Rubber is strong, flexible and offers excellent qualities, its downfall is that it perishes quickly in strong sunlight and in the event of a breakage, it tends to unravel.

Ideal sizes are 1.5mm – 2mm thickness, (inner tube) pre-cut in 5cm (2") wide strips. For i`ako to wae wa`a attachment there are a number of variations of wraps to use.

1. Single continuous wrap, beginning from the non-ama side, each wrap overlapping by one-half its width, which requires a 20ft continuous length.

2. 3 lengths wraps, 1 to each outer side and 1 in the middle of 15' lengths.

3. 2 lengths wrapped from the outer edges towards the middle, of 15' each.

For i`ako to ama lashing, it is advisable to only use cord.

Snap-Lashes | Mechanical Ratchet Systems

Snap-lashes were introduced to the sport in 1998 by *Dick Michelson, Walter Guild* and *Ted Perry* and first used in the Moloka`i Hoe in that same year by the *Outrigger Canoe Club* of Hawai`i. The idea originated from the East Coast of America, not Hawai`i, with people seeking a way to create a quick-rig system for those who often had to rig and de-rig their wa`a. They also unwittingly helped those who did not know how to rig in the traditional manner with cord. The introduction of these snap-lash systems dispenses with the need to rope-rig altogether, accept for the `iako to ama attachment.

Various models were experimented with until a secure and reliable system was finally arrived at, constructed of marine grade stainless steel and high tension webbing. The system was reliable by most accounts, however due to costs and problems of supply, clubs began to purchase 'trucking' tie town straps, with wider webbed ratchet systems.

Clubs have saved money buying the non-genuine article however the most notable problem that has arisen is the compression fractures caused to the wa'e or spreader by over-tightening. The force exerted by the ratchet is excessive and over-tensioning is common as you hear the glass being crashed down on the timber thwart or foam.

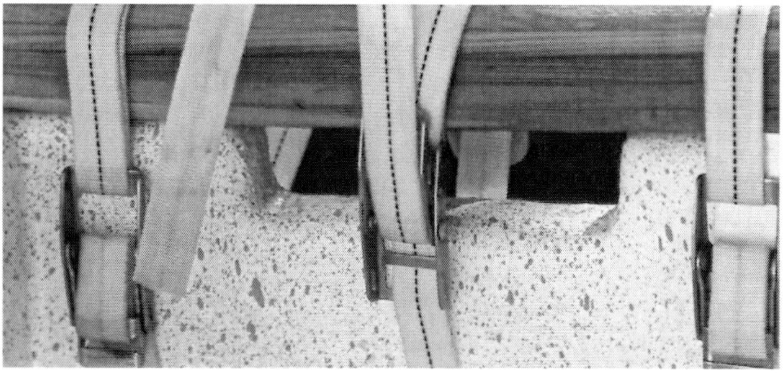

This is a set of original 'snap-lashes'. These were soon replaced by even more powerful 'ratchet' tie downs as used for securing loads on trucks. Snap-lashes were only marginally mechanical, when compared to ratchet systems. Erroneously, early pioneers failed to use the lashing holes, which failed to negate any transverse movement of the outrigger assembly or spread the 'load'. This was initially compensated for by lashing a 1m length of cotton cord through the lashing holes, around the gunnel and i`ako, both inward and outward. Snap-lash webbing was ultimately lengthened so a wrap through the lashing holes could be incorporated.

While the use of straps speeds up the process, you have to wonder if it's worth the expense of damaging the structural integrity of one of primary load points of the wa`a. It is also a concern that if the ratchet were to fail and release, the rigging would quickly disintegrate as there is no cinching, weave or interlock to prevent the weave from losing tension.

Traditional lashing techniques will soon be a thing of the past if this quick fix solution becomes endemic. Perhaps some races should insist on traditional lashing to stem the flow of reliance on such a practice and to ensure the continued teaching of traditional methods.

'I don't know how dangerous they really are but I would have to say that they have the potential to place unwitting and careless crews in questionable situations. Here on the East Coast of the United States, the quick straps have been very popular amongst clubs within ECORA (East Coast Outrigger Racing Association). These straps (including their recent upgrades and modification) have been quick and easy to use, especially for crews who either do not know or are not proficient at traditional lashing methods with cotton cord or temporary rigs with rubber. Quick release straps have contributed to stress fractures and (seemingly) excess wear on the wae. Quite simply, this is due to the fact that cotton cord or rubber allows a certain amount of flex and impact absorption, while the quick straps transmit that shock directly to the canoe.

This has led me to believe that the possibility exists that excess shock from rough conditions (and possibly "regular" use over a period of time) can lead to the total separation of the wae from the gunnels and the rest of the wa`a. This leaves the possibility that a crew may be overwhelmed in rougher conditions due to a catastrophic failure of the wae. As a member of ECORA, I am starting to feel that while these quick straps are convenient, they also pose a possible safety problem that sanctioning bodies should examine.' Jay Caragay, ECORA

'After development and modification of these snap-lashes over the past few years, I agree with Jay Caragay's assessment of the potential danger these devices pose to the integrity of the wa`a, but only if applied in the traditional way of ratcheting down the i`ako to the wae.

A compromise, use of a single snap-lash and two outer wraps of rubber inner-tube. Less 'stressful' than the snap-lash only method, when lashing holes are not used.

Ted Perry, co-designer of the Snap Lash has developed a way of lashing the i`ako to the wae that encompasses the use of the puka (holes) in the gunnels. Because the lashing goes through the holes, the stress is transferred from the wae to the outrigger itself, as it should be. The process still offers significant savings of time when compared to rope lashing. Though I find this method quick, in rough conditions I would always revert to the lashing of the outrigger with the appropriate cotton rope.' Blake Conant, ECORA

'As a canoe manufacturer, I must agree with the concerns regarding the safety and stress put on the wae when using snap-lashes. We did have some cracking of the wae attachment point when the holes in the gunnels were not being used to pick up the load as with traditional lashing. We redesigned the snap-lashes, and on all early testing on the water, I find there is considerably less stress on the wae, the strap and buckle. For racing and for paddling in rough conditions, I still recommend lashing traditionally with cord. Sometimes one cannot forget tradition.' Ted Perry

While the idea was sound, the need to learn any form of traditional lashing of i`ako to wa`a was made redundant overnight, which should have raised questions regarding its authenticity, but practicality and a euro-centric mindset overwhelmingly won out. Today, clubs worldwide, use all manner of readily available ratchet tie down systems.

Conclusion

Which cordage to use for rigging today comes down to a question of which physical characteristics are suitable. Sennet is traditionally considered to be an ideal fibre for the purpose. Based on the advantages of sennet, we can conclude that the best lashing material would have the following characteristics:

Low stretch - but not pre-stretch, so the i`ako do not progressively work loose.
Relatively low breaking strain, so fibre ruptures before wa`a or components.
Ease of handling; soft, flexible and tightens down on itself without slippage.
Some degree of resistance to prolonged exposure to sunlight / salt water.
Some degree of recoil / memory so that it holds its original shape.

Cotton braid cordage is the best alternative; it is inexpensive and readily available. It's also easy to handle, hard wearing, has low stretch and low breaking strain.

When rigging with cotton braid some suggest that you soak the cordage in water for at least twenty minutes so that it absorbs water and is allowed to expand to its maximum. This is totally incorrect. Cotton, once wet, becomes stiff and difficult to manage as well as increasing in strength. Pre-stretch to some degree by tensioning and pulling around a fixed item when new and then apply dry.

Cotton, as with all natural fibres, should be rinsed well with fresh water after paddling. Exposure to sunlight will help dry it out and prevent mildew, but the sunlight itself will be the real enemy. Covering with duct-tape or something similar can prevent the cotton from drying out but the adhesive promotes degradation.

Lashing Maintenance

Regular inspection of cotton cordage must be made, both externally and internally. Remove the lashings and check for internal damage (common where cordage is under stress when wet) every 300mm or so by carefully opening up the strands and looking for signs of excessive looseness of the yarns and strands.

Check for 'powdering' (caused by repeated stretching), looking for small grains of powder and flattened fibres. Check externally for abrasions usually at the point where the lashing wrap around the i`ako and also where it passes through the lashing holes. Look also for signs of permanent stretch. Once it has lost its ability to stretch and spring back, the flexibility is lost from the overall rigging and it should be replaced. Permanent stretch is liable to be localised, ie in certain areas and not throughout its length. It is visible by flattened sections and torn fibres. Synthetic fibres will, like natural fibres, bleach in the sunlight. So check for deterioration by comparing the colour of outer and inner fibres.

In the case of rubber, check for splits and UV deterioration in particular. If using snap-lash devices, check for damage to the wa`a and the attachment points as these are more susceptible to damage than the webbing or ratchet.

Rigging Know How
Hawaiian Wa`a

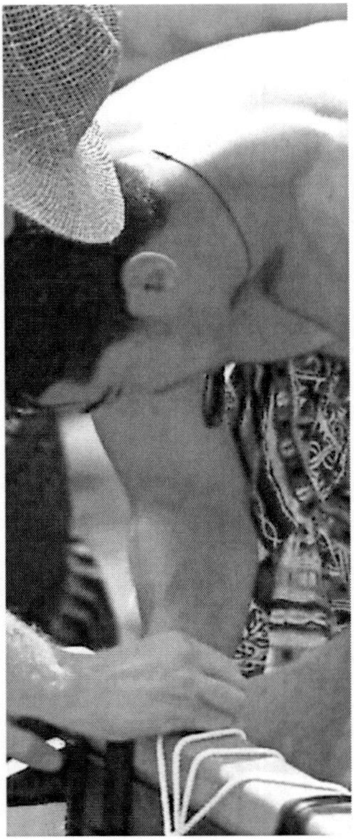

If you paddle a team wa`a, then you better know how it all fits together. If you were a sailor, you would need to know how to rig your yacht, dinghy or windsurfer, so why should this be any different? Not only will it allow you to check your rigging before setting off, but you will also be able to re-rig slack rigging or replace it where necessary.

Rigging per se relates directly to lashing the outrigger assembly together then attaching it to the wa`a. However, rigging can be extended to the practical skills needed to carry out minor repairs and maintenance on the wa`a including; replacing and checking bungs, repairing cracks to seats and wae, attaching bailer hooks and hoop retainers, and taking care of all the details to ensure your wa`a is seaworthy and sound.

Rigging allows a bond between paddler and wa`a to be formed, one built on trust. The rigger's energy and attention to detail is returned by the assurance the wa`a is safely and soundly 'put together'.

Learning how to rig should form part of the learning process, part of the initiation of wa`a paddling. In terms of safety, being able to rig is just another part of good risk management and duty of care. Ultimately, you will feel more of a 'complete' paddler in learning the skill.

Invariably, rigging is left to a few 'riggers' who take on the responsibility. These guys tend to be at regattas early to make sure the wa`a are rigged and ready to go, irrespective of whether they are first up on the water or not. Those who rig the wa`a take their task very seriously and are often guarded about the responsibility they have taken on. In some regards, those who know how to rig seem to have a higher status within the club. There is also a male/female thing going on in some clubs with some men guarding their knowledge from the women. There is a myth at work which suggests that a wa`a rigged by women, will fall apart. You don't need to be really strong to rig, but you do need to have good attention to detail. In Oceania, tasks which required attention to detail like basket weaving, rope making and sail making were all handled by the women.

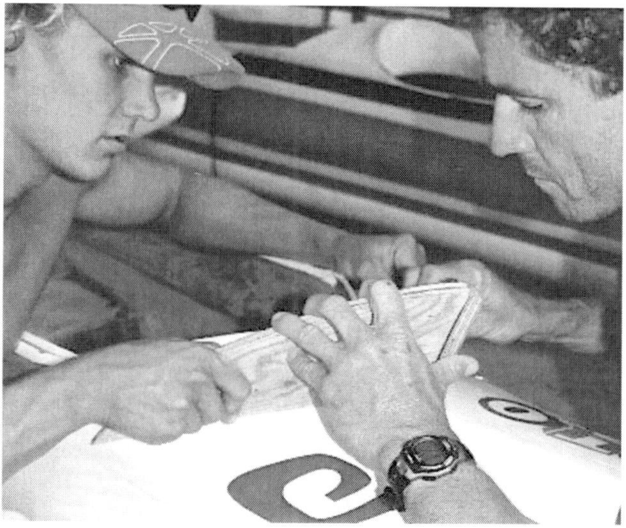

Marquesas road trip. On inspecting their va`a, the lack of splashguard prompted Australia's *Chris Maynard* and *Jamie Mitchell* to knock-up a make shift splash guard with what was on hand.

Unfortunately, many paddlers, both male and female, remain in the dark, not acknowledging that the art and skill of lashing the outrigger assembly to a wa`a is a fundamental part of being a capable wa`a paddler. From a safety point of view, being aware of the mechanics behind the rigging, encourages checking and maintenance of lashings each time the wa`a is paddled. More importantly, knowledge of the process enables the creation of makeshift rigging in case lashings unbind or break.

Rigging sessions should be a part of every club's training regime, a skill handed-down to all new participants from the beginning, male and female from all age divisions This important undertaking encourages a feeling of being a more complete paddler and consequently more confident in ones abilities. Quintessentially, rigging should represent an initiation process.

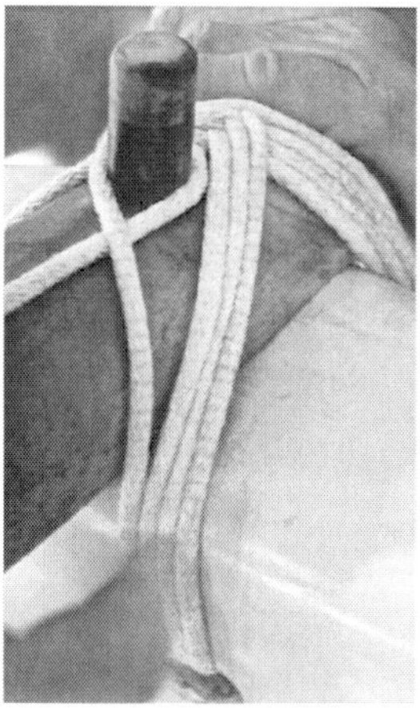

These ama lashing-pegs (common on many va`a) were found to be rotten. The solution was to knock them out and lash the regular way through the lashing holes. Improvisation often constitutes good rigging skills.

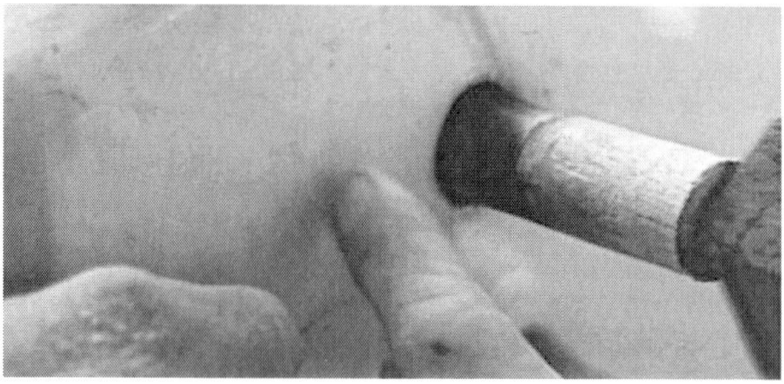

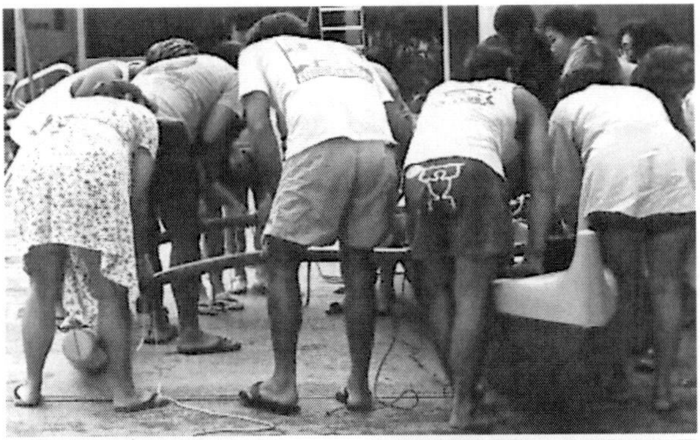

Putting all the bits together.

Rigging

Rigging consists, in its most basic form, of attaching the two i`ako (spars) to the wa`a hull across the canoe spreaders – wae wa`a – then attaching the ama to the i`ako. Beyond this, attaching accessories such as bailers, covers, spare paddles, and water systems should also be considered part of the rigging and preparation process.

In rigging the wa`a, consideration must be given to a variety of ways in which the rigging can be attached and fine tuned. In order to 'put all the bits together' to create a functional assembly, it is necessary to consider the essential function of the outrigger assembly.

Rigging should ultimately be a 'team' effort, not left to a few individuals, with the 'know-how'. There's a task for everyone and everyone should know all the tasks.

As described by *Haddon and Hornell's, Canoes of Oceania,* the outrigger assembly acts as a 'counter-poise', defined by the Oxford Dictionary as, *'a counterbalancing weight, thing of equivalent force on opposite side'.*

Why Steerers Need to Know How to Rig

Of all the positions in the wa`a, the steerer is the one who will feel the effects of a poorly rigged wa`a more than any other. Therefore, knowing how to rig is an essential requirement of being a steerer, so you can take an active role in the rigging process and ultimately 'fine tune' the wa`a to your liking.

A well 'trimmed' rig will ensure optimal performance for the wa`a, the crew and lessen the work load for the steerer who can focus more on steering and less upon keeping the wa`a upright and on course.

Learning how to fine tune your wa`a is something of a skill which requires that you understand some of the objectives of good rigging so you can get the optimum performance out of the wa`a and your crew. This will help make your job of steering as comfortable and trouble free as possible.

A well rigged wa`a will be; responsive to your steering, stable without 'lolling' too far left and compressing the ama, hold a relatively straight course without pulling too hard left or right, and the ama will not cause excessive drag or pull, exhibiting clean entry and release.

As weight is added to the wa`a, both the hull and ama sink deeper into the water, increasing the 'wetted surface area', increasing the drag and therefore resistance. When rigging, your aim is to ensure that the ama is trimmed appropriately and that the wa`a is not leaning in excessively towards the ama which just compresses it and sinks it more than necessary.

The Ama

The ama acts as a secondary hull, which, because of its contact with the water, creates drag in addition to the primary hull. Ideally, we aim to keep this contact with the water to a minimum, so hull speed is maximised and the power required to push the wa`a through the water, reduced. This has the net effect of reducing fatigue on the paddlers and in the long term, increases endurance and potential hull speed.

'The closer the ama is attached to the hull, the more the canoe behaves like a single hull, being faster and more responsive.' Walter Guild.

The ama; a secondary hull.

This is also countered by the relative angle of the i`ako as they leave the wa`a gunnel, altered sometimes by the use of wooden chocks, which ultimately affects the trim of the ama in regards to its water line length, 'footprint', compression, entry and exit at bow and stern.

On the one hand, there is a desire to minimise ama contact with the water to reduce drag, balanced with the need for stability – providing enough for a crew to feel comfortable and secure given their level of experience.

Rigging Determinants

Having a wa`a rigged up on a semi-permanent basis for general club use, means that it will be used for a variety of levels of experience, water conditions, and training purposes.

While it is possible to rig your wa`a in many different ways for a variety of scenarios, ultimately it pays to rig your club wa`a the same way every time, for training and or racing. Any radical deviation from the 'norm' requires practice and a universal agreement that the 'changes' are ultimately beneficial.

Quantifying the merits of altered rigging 'set-ups' is generally a matter of subjectivity and intuition, as it's all about the 'feel' and the 'run'. Validating one 'set-up' over another can sometimes be hard to prove or disprove without long-term practice and refinement in a host of different ocean conditions.

If your club includes juniors, women and men of all ages and ability you should create an environment where no matter which wa`a they take, the 'feel' will be more or less the same – a feel which all will become used to. As long as the manner in which the wa`a is rigged provides a safe, stable and optimally efficient craft, all paddlers will benefit. Radical rigging alterations on race day will tend to alter the nuances and handling of the wa`a, often resulting in more negatives than positives.

The advice here is 'Rig for racing as you do for training' and don't get too stressed out about the variables you can add. Each year at major events, especially rough or big water events, you see the pained look of confusion on the faces of the inexperienced as they observe others rigging and tweaking things differently. The need to try something different creeps in and confusion often sets in.

Wa`a race ready at Hamilton Island, Australia.

Club wa`a of similar design for training should be rigged more or less identically so the handling characteristics are the same for all. No matter what level crew jumps paddles, the nuances remain the same. Provided that the ama and i`ako are the same, this is achievable.

***Chris Maynard*, Steerer for *Outrigger Australia* tells a great story of a similar scenario. *Grant Kenny's* crew, racing under the Hamilton Island banner, were up against *Outrigger Australia* at the 1991 Moloka`i to O`ahu race.**

'Prior to the race at Hale O Lano, the Hamilton Island guys came over to measure our canoe to see how wide we had rigged our ama. That night we talked (quite loud) about how we had "moved it in" to 64" and they began to panic because they had rigged at 68", so they stressed all night before the race. This was a tactic put in place by John Doak. At the end of the race, Channel 2 approached Dwayne Thuys and asked him about the epic race and Dwayne replied, that they had a lot to learn and that they had rigged their canoe at 68", 4-6" more than Outrigger Australia. We heard this and knew at this point that our little psychological trick had worked.'

Issues you should consider when rigging include; crew experience, expected water conditions, and the length of the race, ie sprint race or long distance. Then consider the physical properties of the ama, i`ako and wa`a and how to ensure optimum synergy between each when rigged. In the case of wa`a surfing, you should consider surf size, direction of break and again all other relevant determinants listed.

Race Day Rigging

When rigging the canoe on race day, the following considerations apply if you feel the need for change. Ultimately, don't do anything radically different to what you have trained with.

Different Crews Paddling One Wa`a
If the wa`a is to be used by a variety of crews during the course of a race day, it would be best if the crews had a similar level of expertise. Setting the wa`a up for an experienced crew who then hands over to an inexperienced one could result in disaster, particularly if the wa`a is rigged with light compression on the ama. Often there is no time to make adjustments to the lashing between races. If an experienced crew must share with a less experienced one, then there needs to be a compromise in the rigging.

Experienced vs Novice Paddlers
The fundamental difference between rigging for an experienced crew as opposed to a novice one is the position of the ama. The experienced crew will generally want the

Race rigging day, Rio Va`a, Brazil.

Rigging day on Moloka`i. Crews are particularly meticulous regarding their rigging, with much testing and adjusting to suit their needs and the conditions.

ama closer to the wa`a and or 'choked' so the compression on the ama is minimal. This reduces the amount of weight pushing down on the ama, reduces drag and increases potential speed. This also allows the ama to fly periodically and respond better in swell and surf conditions. While this is fine for experienced crews, novice crews would find that the unstable nature of the wa`a could (will) cause feelings of insecurity and anxiety.

Heavy vs Light Crew

This is a complex factor yet a significant one. Experience suggests that a heavy crew makes the wa`a more stable, while a light crew, especially in rough water, is more vulnerable to capsize. This is due to the fact that a light crew is less likely to create the force which exceeds the total counterpoise force of the ama and i`ako.

A heavy crew ultimately, compresses the ama to a greater degree than a light-weight crew. In the event of a capsize, the light crew would struggle more to 'save' the wa`a in negating the 'heeling moment', whereas a heavier crews combined weight would make it easier to negate the continuation of a capsize.

What this all means is that in rough water, a light crew require the wa`a to be rigged to be very stable, whereas the heavier crew can get away with a 'lighter' rig.

Crew Height

A taller crew will have a centre of gravity that is higher relative to the wa`a than a shorter crew, which could increase the capsize potential. However, while this is generally offset by increased body weight bearing down on the wa`a, it does suggest that in rough water and in strong head winds, taller paddlers should aim to lower their centre of gravity by assuming a lower paddling posture.

Steerer Experience

It must be appreciated that the steerer has a very strong bearing on the general stability of the wa`a and is more often than not, largely responsible for a capsize.

In rough conditions, an inexperienced steerer can make what should be a stable wa`a seem like a roller coaster ride. A constantly lifting ama creates instability and raises the anxiety levels of the paddlers. Poking and paddling on the non-ama side of the wa`a at inappropriate times will make any canoe twitchy, even if rigged out wide and choked appropriately.

Therefore, if the conditions are rough, consideration must be given to the level of experience of the steerer. An experienced crew, who looses their regular steerer and has to call on one with less experience, should consider changing their usual set-up.

Ama Design and Weight

Since there are a variety of ama available and in use, you need to consider weight and design suitability in relation to the conditions. This requires special knowledge. Some ama are better suited to downwind paddling (often large volume ama), while others are better suited to choppy or flat water.

Time on the Water – Changing Conditions

The more time spent on the water, the greater the chance that conditions will change. It is common to start in the morning with glassy water and not a breath of breeze. Two hours later when the race starts, the breeze is picking up and another two hours into the race its blowing hard. The rule on this one is: 'Don't rig for now, rig for later as well!' Weigh up predicted current and conditions.

'In the Blue'. Marquesas Islands.

Preparing the va`a for an 11 hour paddle between the atoll of Ouvéa to Poindimie, New Caledonia, approximately 130km. Serious stuff.

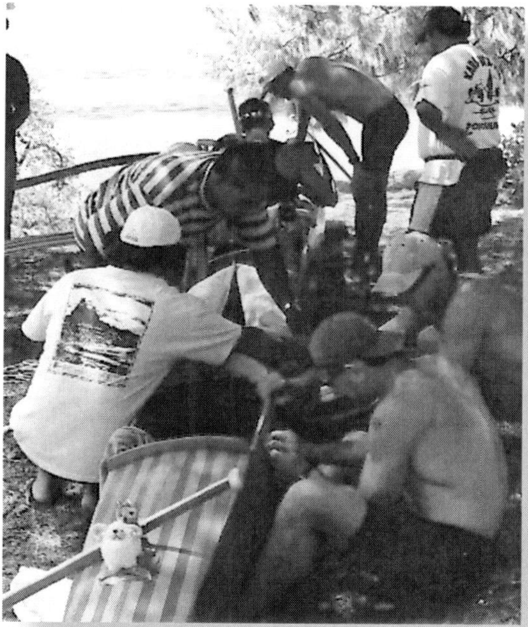

Expected Conditions and Forecast

Crucial for race and training days. Do some research and get informed, rig accordingly. In the case of training days, it may be easier to take a different course to avoid re-rigging.

Sprints or Distance

Whether the race is a sprint (regatta) or distance will have a bearing on the way you rig. In flat water sprint races the ama should be lashed in closer than for open water paddling. This will reduce the turning radius of the wa`a and increase responsiveness, while also giving the ama the potential to float higher with less drag. Speed around the buoys is crucial to winning sprint races and therefore practicing turns while rigged in tight is crucial.

In distance paddling you have more options and as already outlined, your choice to rig wide or close will be dictated by; water conditions (now and later), the forecast, the crew, and the steerer's level of experience.

Downwind or a Variety of Points on a Course

Careful consideration of conditions including the swell, wind direction and course, will help determine how you rig your wa`a. Different angles of the wa`a hull, relative to wave and swell action, will determine the ability of the wa`a to cope with those forces. The wa`a is at its most vulnerable when the wave and swell action travels across its aft beam or quarter from the ama side. This tends to lift the wa`a and ama, causing the craft to twist as the wave or swell travels underneath

A beam sea onto the ama side can cause a feeling of tippiness, but a good steerer can easily flip the wa`a with a strong poke or stroke on the non-ama side.

Beam on from the non-ama side generally presents little problem, but in big seas remember the ama and rigging will be under enormous stress as the ama buries itself frequently. An 'ama under' capsize is potentially very dangerous.

A wa`a is the most stable with a following sea, as long as it is being steered correctly. With inertia from the wave and swell, and little or no sideways torque, the wa`a and the lashings are under minimal stress. This is true as long as the steerer avoids

broaching - allowing the wa`a to turn sideways, so it gets hit side on by oncoming wave and swell.

Hamilton Island provides all kinds of conditions over its course. Rigging securely and conservatively is the smart option.

Generally speaking, it is not the size of the swell that poses the greatest threat to capsize, but the sea that goes with it, in the form of chop and short standing waves, which cause the ama to bounce violently. Another issue is that many crews in a 'sea-state', tend to lose their rhythm and smooth technical style, which contributes to instability.

Additional Considerations

Armed with all these considerations you would be right in thinking that much of the art of *`aha hoa wa`a* is based on expertise and experience. A competent 'rigger' will have intimate knowledge of the wa`a and how it behaves in a variety of conditions, as well as an understanding of the crew and their paddling and ocean skills.

But do not let this deter you from learning the basic skills. Listen to and watch those who have knowledge to share and make an effort

Above: *Outrigger Australia* steered by *Chris Maynard* hit hard sideways. Below: Polishing, measuring, aligning, cutting, pontificating, all part of the big build up to race day. It can make you can feel as if you are practically building the entire wa`a with spare parts from the ground up.

to inform yourself about the science behind outrigger canoe rigging. This way you can gather your own personal experience and learn to apply your intuition.

When we think of rigging, we should also remember that the process includes a host of other things. These should become a natural extension of involvement in rigging and can include the following:

Covers (*Pa`u*)

The ancient Hawaiians realized the benefits of covering the wa`a hull to minimize taking water on board, much like the *Eskimos* in their *kayaks*. *Pa`u* covers were woven from pandanus into mats of various dimensions to accommodate any individual wa`a. They were then attached to the wa`a by passing cord through them and holes made along the length of the *mo`o* gunnel, which criss-crossed over the cover along its length to hold it in place. As with today's racing covers, a hole was made to allow a paddler to sit at their seat and be securely surrounded at the waist. Unlike most sea kayak cockpit covers, in the event of a capsize, the paddler must be able to fall free of the covers.

Spray covers are an essential accessory. Note the zipper curves towards the left gunnel, designed for change-over events, for paddlers exiting - right, and entering-left. Separate pouch - seat 6, for steerer to include drink and supplements during longer races. Covers slide through a track just below the gunnel - on older designs within a aluminium track, more recently within a moulded grove.

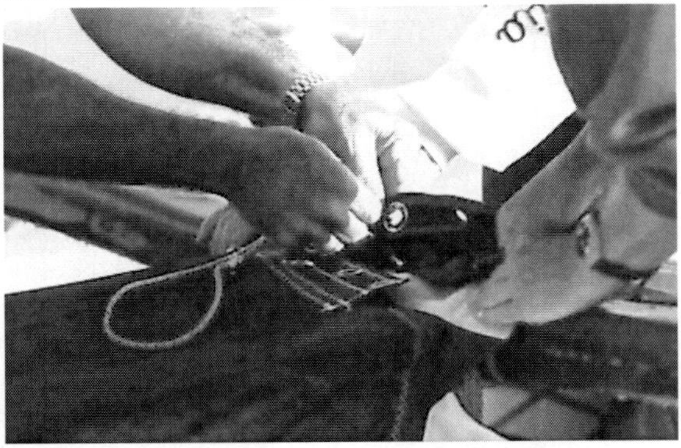

Front and rear covers join the middle cover at the wae, using a variety of methods including lacing, Velcro, and or buckles It's critical that the join is sound and watertight. Below: Foreground Tahitian va`a uses three separate covers to cover each third of the seating as opposed to a separate cover per seat / cockpit.

Because the Tahitian va`a incorporates a semi closed deck hull - cockpits, and the Hawaiian wa`a an open decked design, the covers are markedly different.

The Tahitian design generally requires six individual smaller covers, one for each cockpit. Some will use 3 sections as per the Hawaiian wa`a, but they are considerably smaller in area than their Hawaiian counter-part. The Hawaiian wa`a ordinarily uses three separate sections, to fit the front, middle and rear thirds of the wa`a.

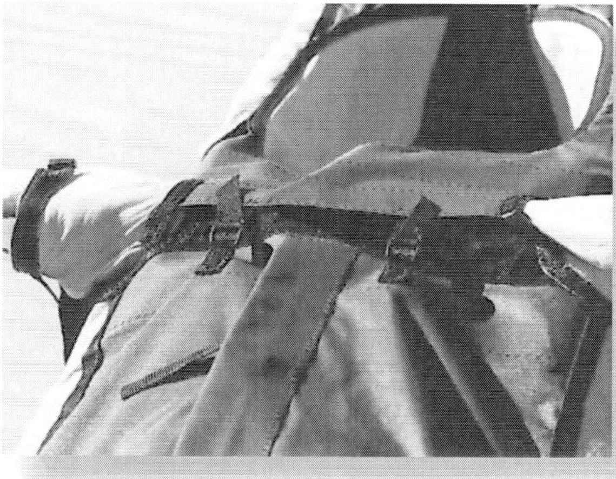

The open decked wa`a requires 'hoops' providing support for the material to prevent water 'pooling' and creating a depression in the surface. This requires the fitting of a set of 'hoop-brackets' placed in front of each paddler. They are usually made from plastic or aluminium.

Hoops generally include a 'paddle-bracket' or 'clip' positioned at its apex so a paddle can be secured around its mid shaft. This is necessary for change-over races where the paddlers exit but leave the paddle for the next paddler.

Today's modern racing covers have evolved greatly. They are fashioned from water proof synthetics, often include water proof zippers, neoprene and draw strings, and are attached to the wa`a by moulded tracks along the gunnel. The fitting of covers is meticulous and requires adjustment. Older style covers can be difficult to slide along

Above: Tahitian va`a seating arrangement. Note paddle-bracket, padded side-walls of hull, water-bottle holder, raised splashguard on each cockpit, as well as Velcro and push stud clip to accommodate covers. Below: Like the exposed ribs of a sea creature, hoops have been custom fitted forward of each seat. These will be removed before sliding the covers on, then refitted. Right: Open decked Hawaiian wa`a, note hoop-bracket holders on the side of the hull. This is markedly different from the Tahitian va`a.

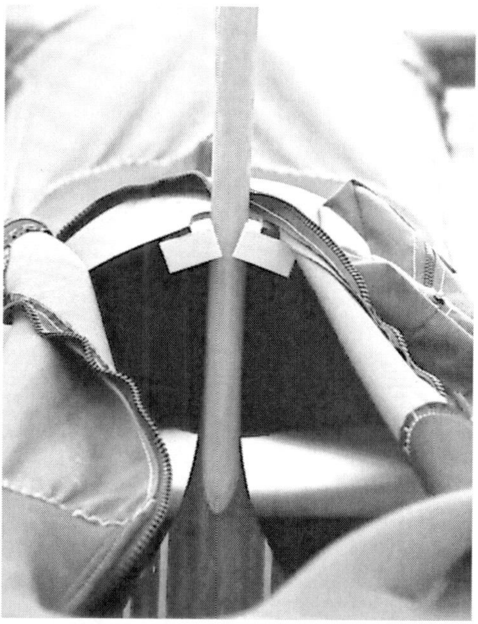

Tahitian va`a, note the timber seat and backing. Top Right: Paddle holder fitted into aluminium hoop. Right: A beautifully carved paddle-bracket on a Tahitian va`a formed with the cowling. Below: Modern racing covers fitted to an open decked Hawaiian designed *Mirage* wa`a. Below Right: A Tahitian va`a paddle-bracket attached directly to the bow-cover.

Cover fitted over splashguard. This often lets water in underneath in extreme conditions or can even be pulled off. Lots of duct-tape is often used to prevent this. Below: In an effort to prevent water 'ripping' the covers over the splashguard, this design extends the aluminium track beyond the level of the splashguard. Recent design improvements, include fitting the forward cover rear of the bow cover and not over the splashguard.

the aluminium rails, try some spray or cooking oil to improve the glide.

Work continues in creating the perfect covers. Some are incorporating technology such as inflatable ribbed sections to replace traditional fibreglass or plastic hoops which prevent the covers from sagging and allowing water to 'pool'. Making efficient lightweight covers is something of an art.

Seat Padding | Repairs

Comfort is king! Some commercially available detachable seat covers are available secured by buckles or Velcro.

Bailers

Checking zip function and placement of bailer-brackets, paddle-brackets should all be fine tuned pre-race, not during.

Spare Paddles

No matter what the distance or nature of the race, a spare steering paddle and a regular paddle should be lashed to the i`ako – regular paddle to the front i`ako, steering to the rear. In sprint events, the steerer can place a spare steering paddle behind their seat. The i`ako mounted paddles must be within reach and able to be pulled free quickly. Securing with Duct Tape is not advisable. Use rubber and tuck the end under inboard, using a quick release loop.

Sling Shots

Line attached between the *manu ihu* - front and forward i`ako / ama. Nylon rope is preferable due to its stretch and recoil qualities. They are commonly attached to surfing wa`a to prevent the outrigger assembly from moving aft in the event of impact.

A seat in need of attention. Sharp edges were removed, seat 'glassed' to hull for added strength and padding added. Pre-race work is essential - especially on occasion when loaned a va`a when racing overseas. Feel the difference!

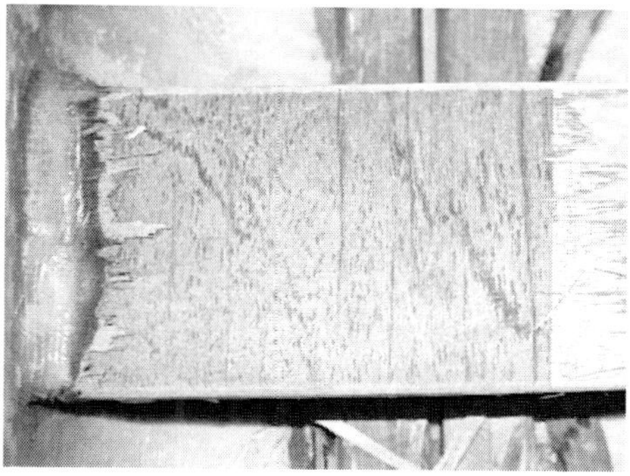

Spare paddle secured with rubber inner-tube, grip in towards the wa`a. Standing spare paddle behind steerer, may be fine for training days, but not when racing.

Below: Elastic bungee type cord with clips. Below Right: A set of plastic or aluminium clips screwed into the i`ako is the most effective, neat way to secure a spare paddle, seen here on this Tahitian va`a.

Australian rules make it compulsory to have a tow-line attached during ocean races. While considered 'safe-practice' in real terms it is impractical to attach an 'adequate' length because of the amount of space it would take up. At 45' a ratio of 3:1 would be desirable or 135' - 61m.

Left: Tipping string.

Tipping String

Attach approximately 1.5m from the side of the wa`a to either i`ako and ensure there is adequate tension. The string is used as a brace against which the paddlers in seats 3 and 4 can press with their paddles in case of a potential capsize. Consider using a turnbuckle for added tension.

Tow Rope See 'Rigging Materials' and 'Towing'.

Rigging Box

Every club needs a 'rigging box' containing the essentials required for rigging, often the responsiblity of the club captain. Consider assigning one rigging box per wa`a. Don't allow rigging kits to become denuded and a shambles. A rigging box will include a sufficient lashing material, and will include but not be restricted to:

Duct tape (heavy duty), to securing and repair all manner of thiings, tape measure, cordless drill, fibreglass repair kit, spirit level , spray oil (for zippers), material patches for covers, contact adhesive, screwdriver, leather gloves for rigging, dive weights for weighting ama, timber wedges for chocking i`ako, silicone for bung holes, water proof spray for covers, board-wax for hull floor, screws, bailers, knife, sand paper, spare bungs, spare seat coverings (foam), rubber, cotton cord, bungy cord, snap lashes.

The Value of Note Taking

It's a good idea to make a note of how you set up your wa`a when it is rigged optimally; distance of ama from primary hull; chocks used; their size and placement so you can repeat in the future given the same style of wa`a, ama and i`ako. Ideally, 'pair-up' all elements for each wa`a and use exclusively.

The Rigging Process
Hawaiian Wa`a

The ancient Hawaiians used many different lashing configurations to secure the i`ako to the ama and the i`ako to the wa`a. However, today's rigging process has been diluted to only a few lashing configurations, especially using cord. Whether rubber, cotton or webbing is used, the primary objective remains the same, to keep it all together. Each configuration performs uniquely and if a failure occurs, there are substantial differences.

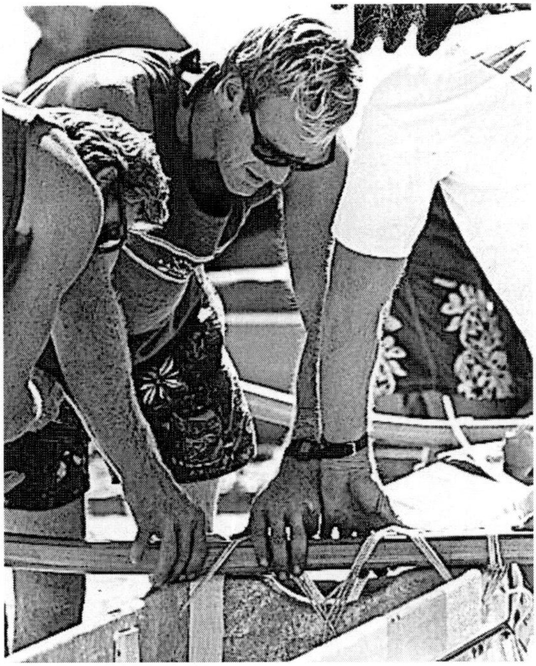

'Indeed, lashings were regarded very critically. As with the canoe, the whole concept of lashing bespoke a very sophisticated understanding of naval architecture, physics and ocean dynamics. The most seaworthy, well-built canoe in the world was worthless, and a potential coffin, if its lashings were not adequate for the given seas'. **Holmes, Tommy. *The Hawaiian Canoe*. Honolulu, Editions Limited 1981.**

It has also been noted by Holmes, that while the Hawaiian wa`a was comparatively 'devoid of ornamentation', their lashing configurations were often ornate and aesthetically intricate without sacrifice to their intrinsic function. With the erosion of value and the well worn justification of 'evolution', this notion has essentially been eliminated as rapidly as the sport has grown over recent years.

While certain evolutionary issues are justifiable from the perspective of nurturing the growth of the sport without undermining essential values (use of fibreglass, lowering of weight limits, relaxation of defined racing wa`a specifications), the loss of this simple skill in lashing with cord is akin to scout groups eliminating ropes and knots from their programs.

It is my firm belief that associations world wide have been neglectful in the overwhelming acceptance of 'quick fix' alternatives. This also extends to the race organisers who are in a position to make rigging with cord a compulsory condition of entry. Ironically, while the use of webbing and metal fasteners may have originated on the East Coast of America, they were road-tested and given the stamp of approval by Anglo-Hawaiian paddlers. This is the very same group who is totally strung out over weight rulings and wa`a specifications, apparently this sanctity of the craft does not extend to how it is rigged.

Notes on Lashing with Cotton Cord

Lashing with cotton cord is by far the best way to 'rig' a wa`a. Not only is it the strongest method but, more importantly, it provides 'give and take' at the appropriate time, absorbing load and torque without compromise of the structural integrity of the wa`a. Where interlacing and frapping are used, if a breakage does occur, the lashing will remain intact without unravelling. Few of these qualities can be said of either webbing or rubber, but these values have apparently become redundant and meaningless.

Based on the rigging faults seen on the vast majority of contemporary racing wa`a and va`a Pacific-wide, it seems that there are few true 'master riggers' left. Cord erroneously layered on top of itself, i`ako lashing pegs used as strong points, and wraps not made parallel, are all reminders that while this was once an art, it has now become something much less.

There is also a growing unfounded obsession with the need to over-tighten and use pre-stretched high tensile materials. The reality is, this is overkill and may actually be damaging the structural integrity of the hardware components themselves. Lashing techniques and materials which serve to ultimately damage or cripple your wa`a and its components under stress is hardly a measure of good rigging.

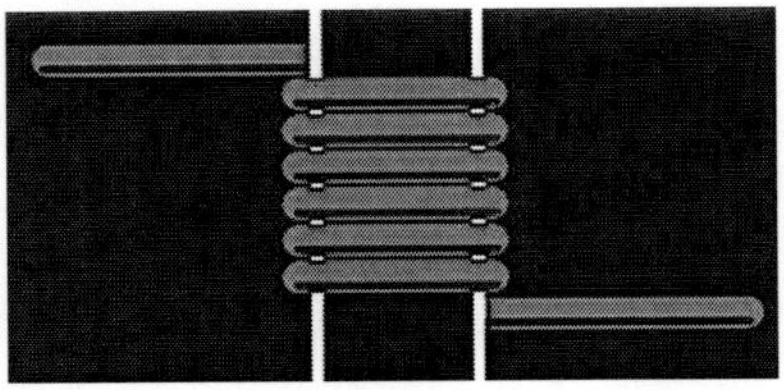

Wrap
To wind cord around an object, such as a pole or spar.

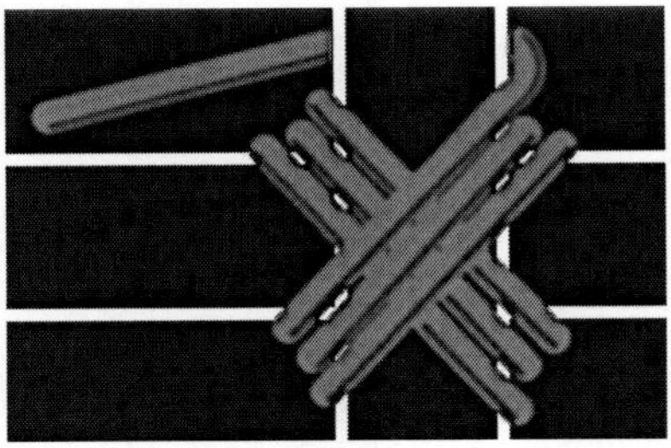

Diagonal Lashing
A lashing knot of diagonal configuration used to bind two spars together.

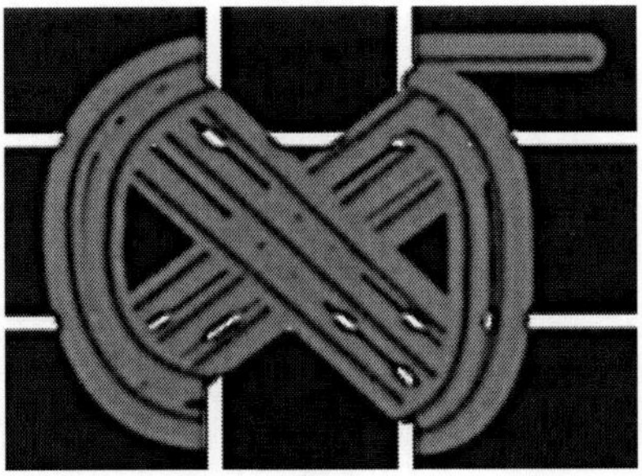

Frap
A lashing, binding a thing tightly or binding things together.

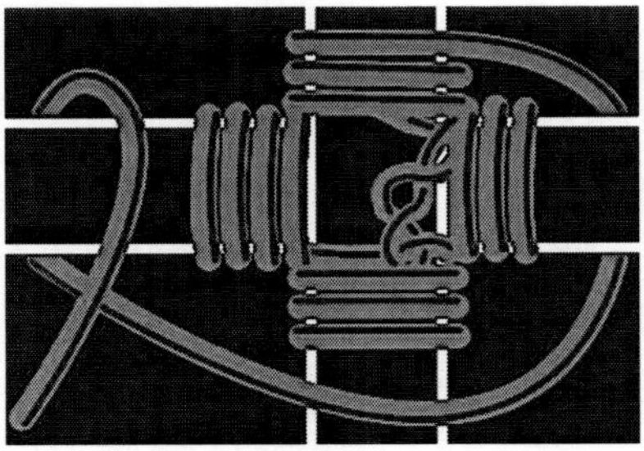

Square Lashing
A lashing knot of square configuration used to bind two spars together.

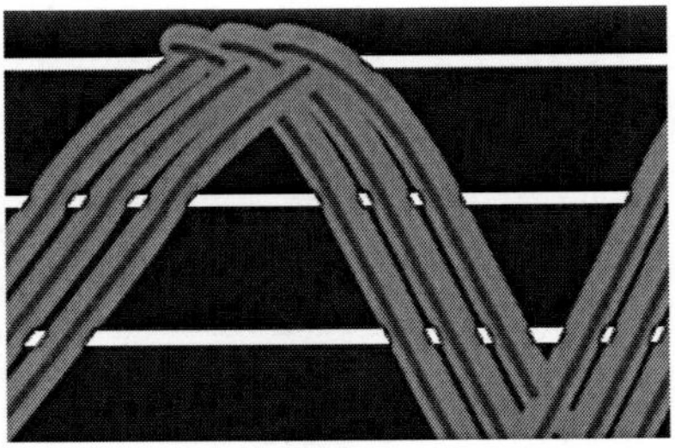

Oblique
Having a slanting or sloping direction.

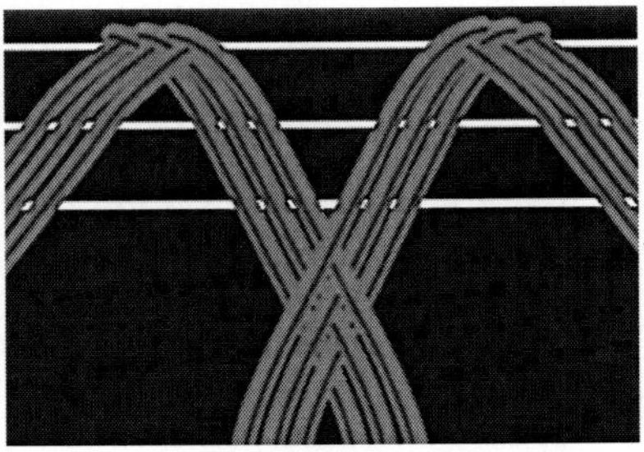

Diamond Weave
Interwoven diagonal lashing used to bind i`ako to wae wa`a.

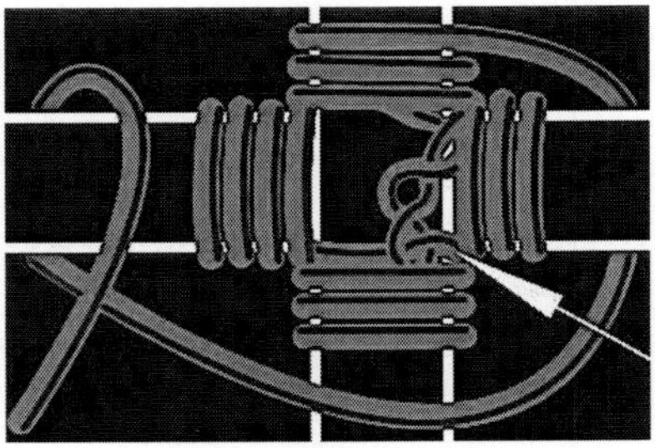

Standing End
Static end of cord made secure at beginning of lashing.

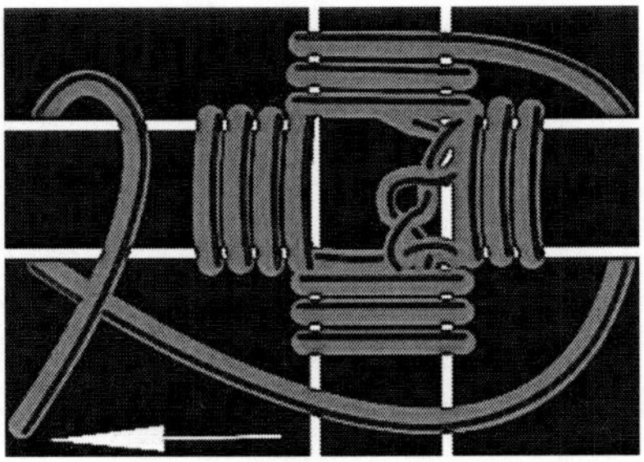

Running End
Dynamic end of cord used to make lashing.

Some Definitions

Strength is improved if care is taken to lay rope 'wraps' and 'fraps' parallel with a minimum of crossings thus, ensuring the cord has maximum contact with the i`ako and ama, or the i`ako and wae wa`a.

Unfortunately, many 'riggers' are clearly unaware of the fundamental principles of lashing, reinforcing the reality that it is for the most part, a lost art while justifying the use of webbing and mechanical ratchet systems.

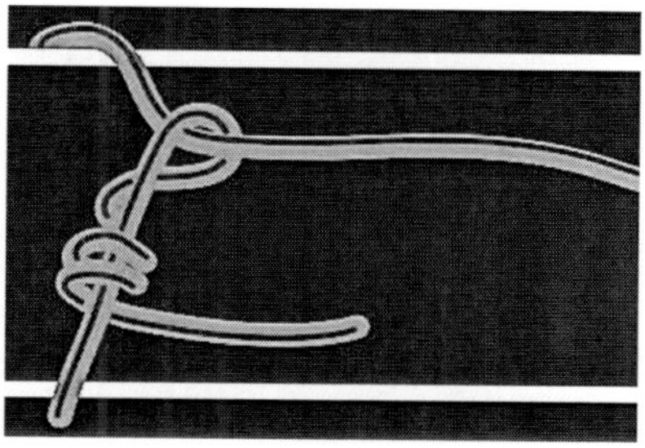

Timber Hitch Knot
used to secure the standing end of cord to i`ako.

Get Supported

Ensure your wa`a is off the ground, level and secure. The most common supports are used tyres. While these work well, they can badly mark the underside of the wa`a. Ideally, custom made padded wooden supports should be used, with the ama supports at an optimum height relative to the hull.

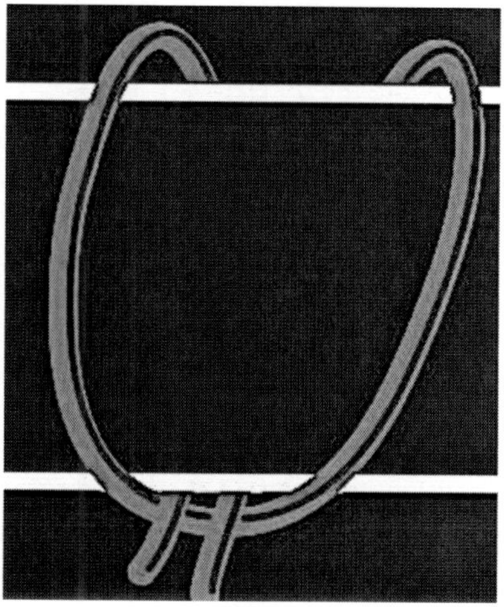

Girth Hitch
Knot used to secure rigging cord to wae wa`a.

Levelling the Wa`a

The wa`a needs to be level when you begin with no loll, use a spirit level. This will help you determine the degree to which you want the wa`a to be rigged relative to the ama.

Use a spirit level to ensure wa`a is level prior to attaching i`ako as this will visibly show how level the wa`a is relative to the ama. Place equidistant between the wae.

Double Fisherman's Bend
Knot used to secure standing and running ends of cord.

For sprint racing, you will want the hull absolutely level. For open ocean distance paddling, there is the option of lolling the wa`a inward towards the ama, actively putting additional downward compression on the ama. The downside of this set up is additional drag and therefore a loss of overall

potential hull speed. Near level is preferable in most conditions. If loll is to be included, it should only be marginal.

Rigging Distance Ama to Hull

Measuring from I`ako Lashing Peg to Wa`a Gunnel

The generally accepted distance measured from the edge of the wa`a gunnel to the centre of the i`ako peg ranges from 68" - 1727mm to 72" - 1828mm, with a variation of 4" - 101mm. A common setting is just under 72" or 1820mm.

Measuring from the gunnel side wall to the i`ako peg will include any varying hull widths at these points, we only need to work with what is relative to the centre of the hull. Measure wae widths and allow for any variation.

Provided the spreaders are the same width front and rear, your measurements from gunnel to the centre of the peg, should be

Tyres are commonly used to support and protect the wa`a and ama during the rigging process. Below - Custom made wa`a supports –traditionally known in Hawai`i as *Lono*.

equidistant front and rear and create a 'square rig'. If there is a difference in the widths of the spreader and you measure equal distances from the gunnel to the centre of the peg, then there will be an equivalent variation. This will create a rhombus and the ama will not be running parallel to the keel line of the hull. To ensure the rig is 'square' and true, measure the spreader and recalculate distances by adding/ subtracting to arrive at equivalent measurements.

Measuring from centre of peg to the gunnel and below, determine centre hull keel line by running a length of cord between front and rear manu. Ensure enough tension to keep the cord straight.

Measuring from I`ako Lashing Peg to Hull Keel Line

One of the primary determining factors of accurate rigging is judged by how closely both ama and hull keel line are to parallel or offset with accuracy, as required. Consequently, the only accurate way of achieving this is too use the hull keel line and not the gunnel as a point of reference. The hull keel line can be determined using a length of tightly pulled cord, running between manu ihu and manu hope.

Ideally, if you use an identical or similar set of i`ako with a wa`a, you can make permanent markings on the i`ako where the lash to the wae goes. This will save time and ensure accuracy.

Toe In

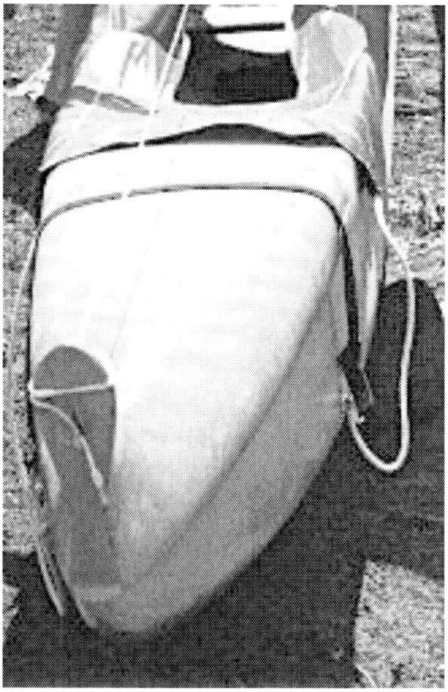

While still practised by some crews toe-in, has become a rarity. When acutely curved ama affectionately known as the *Elephant Tusk* were used, drag caused by the ama sitting deep in the water at its mid point caused excessive pull to the left. As a consequence, the ama was 'toed in' at the front by approximately a 1/2 to 1" relative to the rear, to counter the affects of the pull left. Since ama designs have become 'straighter', with less curvature and greater volume, the trend is now to rig the ama parallel to the hull.

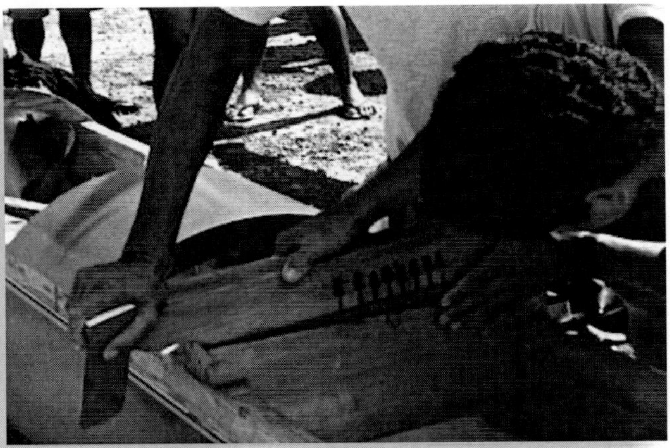

Pre-marked i`ato on this Tahitian va`a make rigging a breeze and more recordable in terms of performance.

Adding I`ako Wedges

If you need to add wedges at this point, do so. Otherwise, they can be positioned when the final 'trim' of the wa`a is made, during the final lashing process. The primary means of fine-tuning the stability of the wa`a is the use of wedges, or not as the case may be. Placing wedges between the i`ako and spreader at any one of the four corners, or in combination, will alter the wa`a 'loll' inward or outward towards the ama. Additionally and importantly, it also alters the trim of the ama.

Back Right Wedge
Causes canoe to loll away from the ama. Front of the ama is raised, riding further back along its leading edge, while the stern rides lower.

Front Right Wedge
Causes canoe to loll away from the ama. The ama rides closer towards its bow, while the stern rides higher.

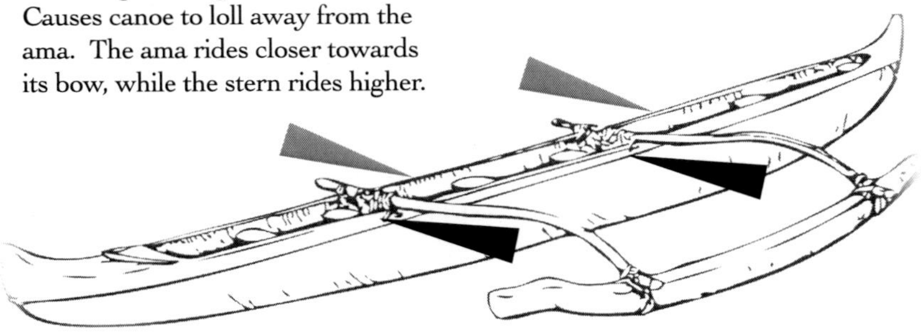

Front Left Wedge
Causes canoe to loll towards the ama. Front of the ama is raised, riding further back along its leading edge, while the stern rides lower. A thin wedge of timber, positioned at the edge of the gunnel, between the spreader and the i`ako. The thick end of the wedge varys from a .25"- 2".

Back Left Wedge
Causes the canoe to loll towards ama. The ama rides closer towards its bow, while the stern rides higher.

By carefully placing the wedges, you can 'fine-tune' not only the trim of the ama, (secondary hull) but the wa`a itself (primary hull). The relationship between the hull and ama is critical in creating a 'well mannered', stable, responsive wa`a. As a whole, the wa`a is strongly influenced by the i`ako and how they are connected with the wae and ama. The rigging distance of the ama to hull is often given greater consideration as a factor of stability, when indeed the relative angles of the i`ako are more relevant and often overlooked.

You want to use the minimum amount of wedges, keeping in mind that the cantilevered affect will apply. For every 1" of 'chock', you can expect approximately 4" of rise, or fall if reversed, outward to where the i`ako meets the ama rigging platform.

String Test Ama Level

On a Hawaiian wa`a, if you wish to check the position of the ama to the wa`a hull in relation to its forward elevation; working from the front of the ama.

1. Have your partner firmly hold a length of cord at one end, at the gunnel level on the non-ama side.
2. On the ama side, pull the cord tight and lower it until the cord touches both gunnels with equal pressure, i.e. the cord is level.
3. Crouching down level to the ama, the lashing holes should be approximately 6 - 8" above the level of the string. Any substantial variation, adjust by adding or adjusting wedge.

You do not want the bow of the ama to be pushing water, just as you do not want the stern end of the ama to be buried, you want the water to 'release' to minimise the drag. The ama tail should not be in contact with the water to its extremity, but should release 3-6" before. You can judge this during the 'float test' in flat water.

Temporarily Attach I`ako to Wae

Initially, you can temporarily secure the i`ako to the wae using lengths of rubber or webbing once the distance has been established. Ensure you select appropriate front and rear i`ako; forward i`ako tends to have greater upward curve. Secure temporary wraps of rubber or webbing to the outside edge of the right side of the wae and i`ako, then on the left side.

Why Temporarily Attach I`ako to Wae?

Fine-tuning a wa`a depends on the relationship of the i`ako with the wae wa`a and the distance of the ama from the hull. Therefore, attaching the i`ako to the ama permanently and then adjusting at the wae until satisfied, before permanent connection, is logical. In this context, the basic sequence for the Hawaiian wa`a.

1. Level the canoe.
2. Establish distance from the centre of the i`ako lashing peg to the centre of hull.
3. Temporarily secure the i`ako to the wae wa`a, adding wedges if required.
4. 'Permanently' secure the i`ako to the ama.
5. Float test the wa`a.
6. Adjust at the wae if required (add or adjust wedges)
7. Re-float.
8. 'Permanently' secure the i`ako to the wae wa`a.

'Floating' the wa`a is optional. It is more common for longer, rough water races. If you know your wa`a well and rig consistently with the same i`ako and ama, chances are you will have pre-determined distances and wedges. This will allows you to move directly to the permanent rigging stage and dispense with the float test, as long as you are confident of achieving a consistent result.

'Riggers' and 'Tailors' | Rigging Partners

Pairing up with a partner to work each rigging point together is ideal; i`ako to spreader (left and right), ama to i`ako (front and rear), making a total of four pairs.

When working as a pair, one person is 'rigging' while the other is 'tailoring'. The person rigging is taking care of the actual lashing configuration, while the partner takes care of 'tailoring' excess cord, i.e. one feeds, while the other pulls.

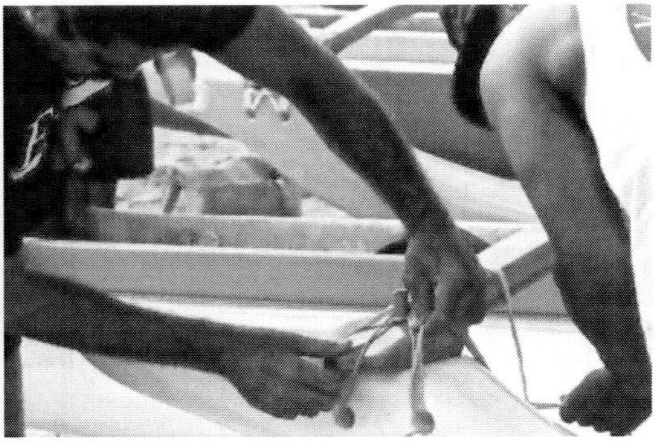

When rigging the i`ako to the spreader, with a rigger and tailor on the left and right side (it may only be a rigger either side), it's important that the lashing process is performed sequentially, so a balanced 'weave' can be made. When rigging near wet sand or dirt, keep rigging material from contacting the ground.

Rigging of I`ako to Ama

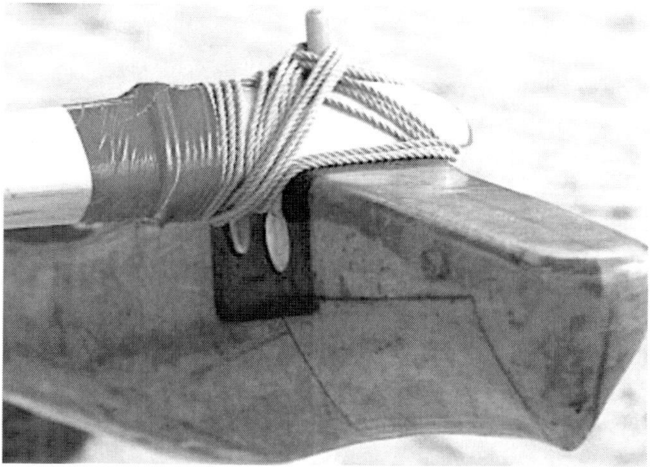

The 'head' of the ama is said to represent that of a lizard. From this angle you can see clearly see this – it is traditionally called a lupe.

No temporary rigging is required here, so you move straight to a permanent rig, whether using rubber or cord. There are different designs of i`ako and ama mounting points to consider. Some ama don't have lashing holes and therefore, you will need to wrap cord / rubber completely around the ama (common on surfing wa`a).

Classic surfing wa`a rig. Rubber used for the i`ako to wae for added flex in dangerous surf and cord rigged fully around the ama. Note also the 'sling-shot' line running from the manu to the ama to the i`ako lashing mount.

Over recent years, manufacturers have devised a number of methods for attaching the i`ako to the ama - a peg on the underside of the i`ako which slots into the ama mounting platform. Some i`ako have 2 lashing pegs one behind the other, others have a dove tail cut into the i`ako extremity. Whether these are actual improvements is questionable as the process is unnecessarily more complex with few gains in security. For the purposes of learning, we will assume simplicity. Once you have a basic knowledge of the process, you can improvise and work with a variety of i`ako to ama lashing configurations.

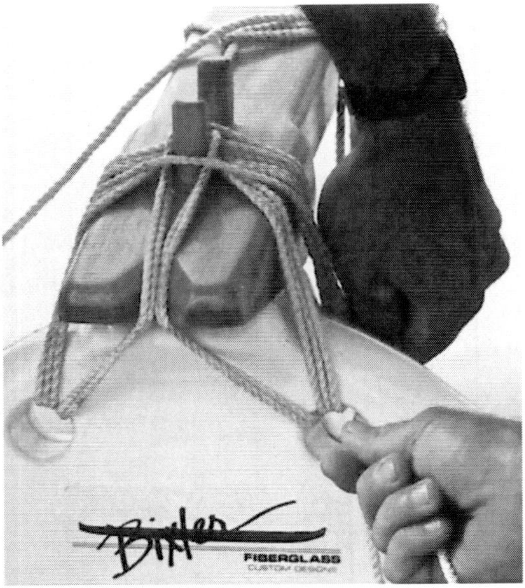

Note the guide peg on the i`ako which slots into a corresponding hole in the i`ako mounting point on the ama. Rear mounts. *Brent Bixler* remains one of Hawai`i's most influential designers of contemporary wa`a.

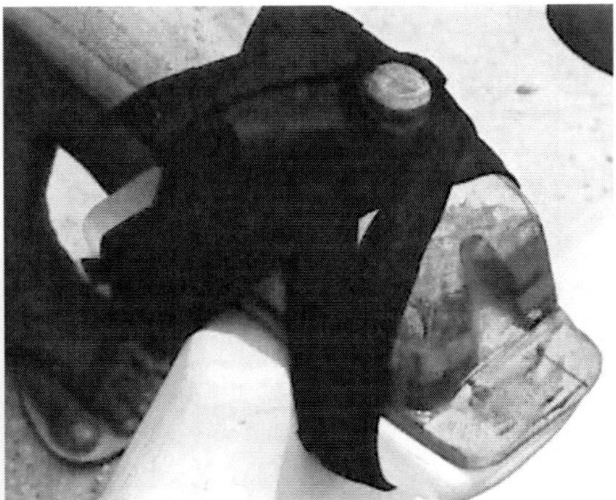

Dovetail end, single peg i`ako. Tahitian ama without lashing holes but extra wide i`ato platform, permitting rubber to be wound around.

There are different schools of thought on the lashing configuration of the i`ako peg. The cord can be woven on both sides of it or simply behind it, but it should never be woven only in the front. With the lashing on both sides of the peg, the wa`a is more protected if it is hit side on by a large swell.

The most common misconception regarding the i`ako lashing peg or pegs is that they are strong point to which the lashing is secured. The peg is a 'guide only' and cord should not be wrapped either around or up it. If the ama were to experience extreme force on its beam, the peg runs the risk of literally snapping off and significantly compromising the lashing. Always rig for the possibility of the peg to snapping off and ensure the lashing would remain in-situ and continue to function. Lashing which uses the available surfaces to spread the load is preferred to 'layering' the cord upon itself.

The i`ako to ama is ideally lashed with cord, not rubber. As with any weaving process, use a simple repetitive pattern – the key is knowing the pattern once-around, then after that it's easy.

I`ako to Ama Lashing - Using Cord

The ama to i`ako lashing knot combines a variance of square lashing, commonly used to bind two poles together and diagonal lashing. It also incorporates frapping turns around the first set of wraps which traverse both the i`ako and ama -usually 4 or 5, in order to bind together the lashing, and increase pressure and tension between all the elements. A timber hitch is used to secure the standing end to the i`ako and a Double Fisherman's Bend or whipping incorporated to secure the final wrap.

I`ako Lashing - Behind Peg

Many rough water paddlers regard the use of cotton cord to lash the i`ako to ama as the most reliable lashing. While you can pass lashing either side of the i`ako lashing peg, it is a guide only. This particular method safeguards the peg in the event of the ama rolling inwards if it is hit side on violently. It has certainly proved its worth.

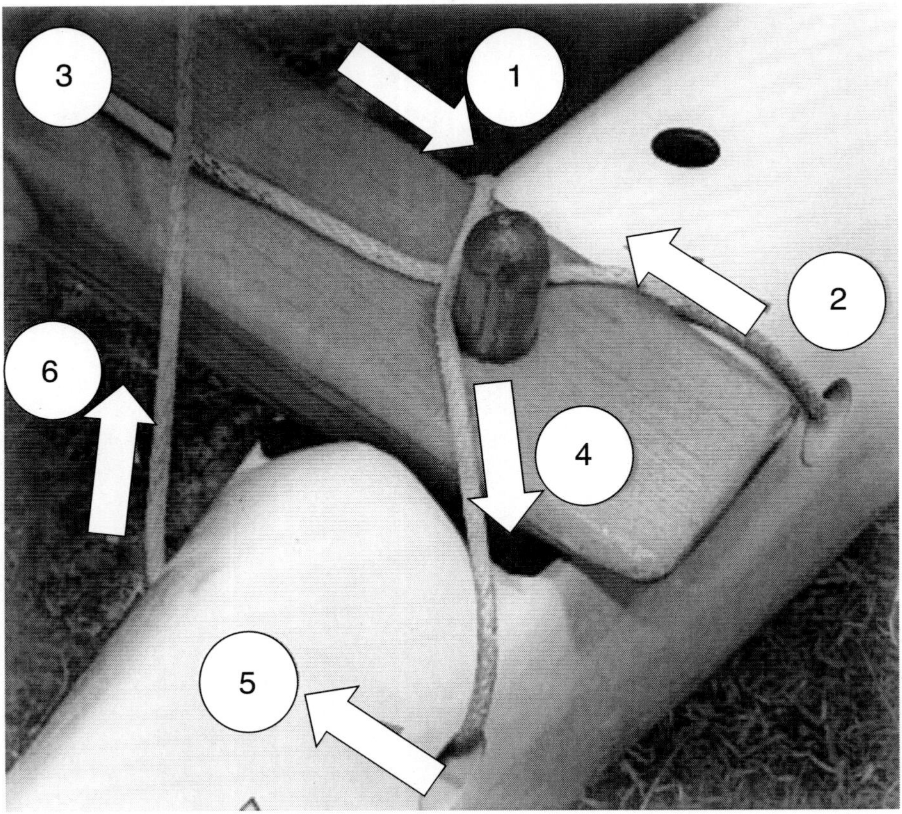

1. Pass the short end of the cord through the inner rear ama lashing hole (1) and pull through enough cord so there is approximately 30cm (12") of cord travel back along i`ako towards the wa`a (2). Secure standing end (3) around i`ako using a timber hitch. This then becomes the tied off standing end.

2. Pass the cord behind i`ako peg, diagonally (4) to meet the forward outer ama lashing hole, and pass the running end through the lashing hole (5) and tailor slack cord through the forward inner ama lashing hole (6) and pull until under reasonable tension. Ensure tension is maintained.

3. Cross over diagonally behind i`ako lashing peg, ensuring cord is parallel with first wrap and pass end through the rear outer ama lashing hole (7) tailoring the slack cord through rear inner ama lashing hole (8) and pull until under tension. Pulling in an upward direction, ensure tension, this completes one full wrap. Repeat process following the path of 9,10,11 and repeat pattern.

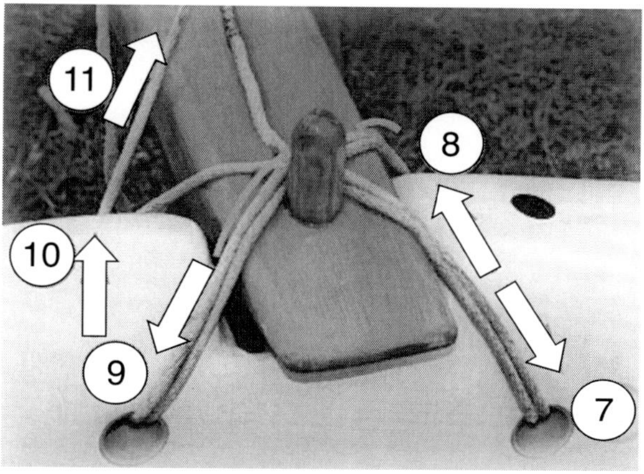

Make 4 to 5 wraps, last wrap ends under tension from inner forward ama lashing hole.

5. Once completed you will now Frap the cord pulling it together. From the forward inner lashing hole, pass cord directly over ama (12) outward then around the over hang (13) then up and back over the ama (14). Pass cord under the i`ako and wrap around and repeat. Make 4 frapping turns where the i`ako and ama join at the i`ako platform, ensuring even tension. Each frapping turn must run parallel to one another, not on top.

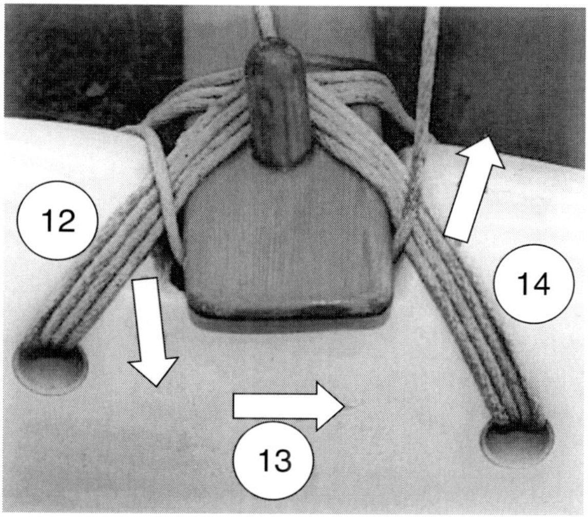

Important Note: All subsequent wraps through the outer ama lashing holes must be laid to the outer edge of the one before. However, as the cord is pulled through the inner ama lashing hole it must be crossed over, as the inner wraps must work inwards. This insures wraps made over the i`ako are as close to the peg as possible with minimum deviation. Looking within the lashing hole, you will see this cross-over of the cord. Ensure with each wrap to lay the cord parallel, butted up to the former.

Strength is improved if care is taken to lay rope 'wraps' and 'fraps' parallel with a minimum of crossing and ensure maximum contact between the i`ako, ama and cord. Cord layered on top of itself in a vertical manner fails to spread the load efficiently and if it falls free, will loosen the lashing.

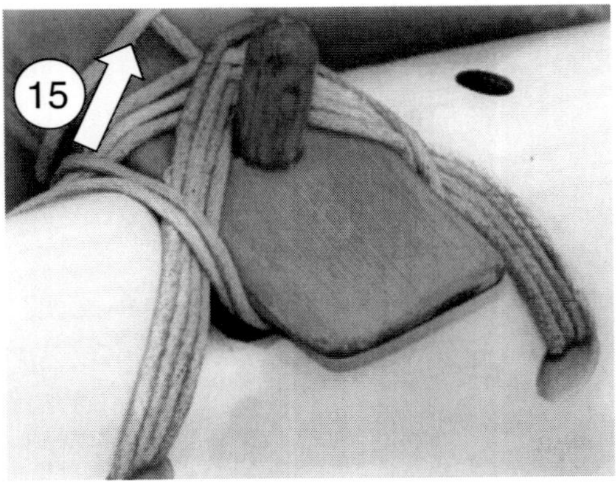

Finishing Off

6. Your last frap will end having passed the running end over the rear topside of the ama. The original securing timber hitch tied around the i`ako can be slackened and the cord run along the length of the i`ako towards the wa`a. Take round-turns of the running end under and over the i`ako, laying cord parallel and working towards the wa`a. Make as many wraps as required to come to the end of the cord or to where it meets the standing end and tie off with double fisherman's bend. Secure with duct tape, wrapping it around the i`ako and knot.

7. Whipping. Alternatively, secure ends using a simple whip. Before taking round turns around the i`ako, double back over the standing end of cord towards the i`ako peg so it forms a loop. Make wraps around the i`ako close to the diagonal lashing near i`ako peg and wrap towards the wa`a, keeping doubled over cord in the middle of the i`ako. When at the end of the double-overed cord, pass running end through the loop, then pull the standing end which will pull loop and running end of rigging under the i`ako wraps. Pull mid-way, then finish off by cutting off excess or secure with duct tape.

Here we see the beginning of setting up the wraps.

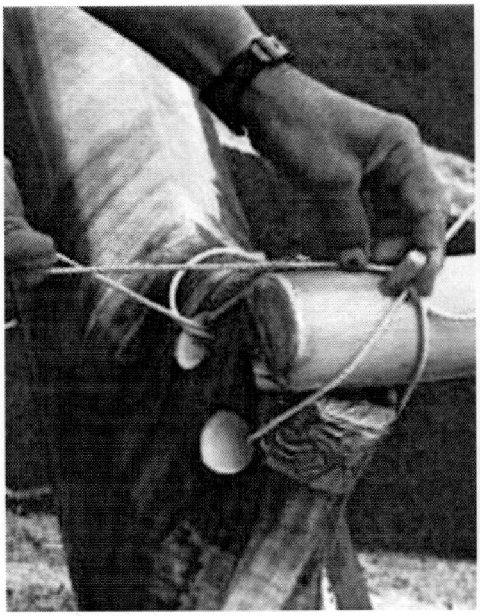

Frapping the cords tightly together towards the end of the finishing off process.

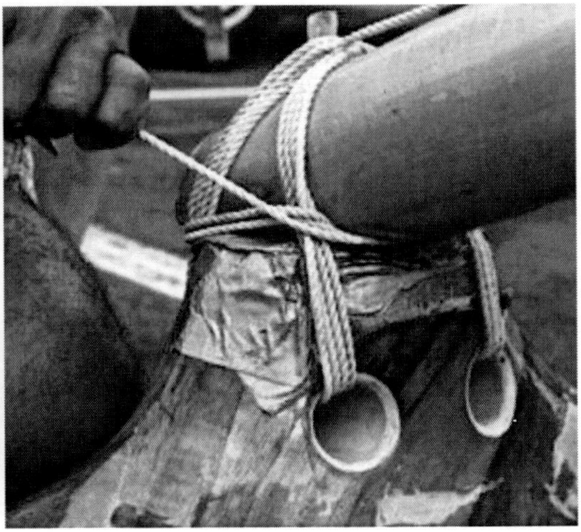

Lashing Behind and In Front of Peg: The simplest method is to lash as for behind the peg, making 3-4 complete wraps, then on the forth wrap, pass the cord in front of the peg and proceed for 3-4 more wraps. Finish with frapping and tie off around the i`ako as outlined.

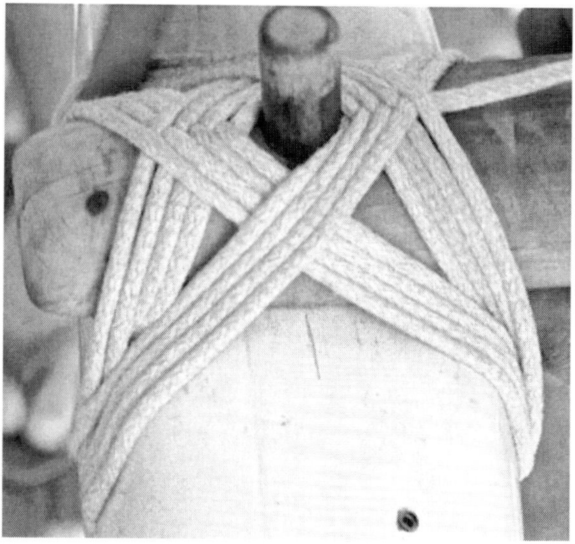

Note: It is important to be neat and constantly aligning cord as it crosses over so each wrap lays parallel and is butted up against the other. Ensure ama remains upright and parallel during the rigging process.

Absence of Ama Lashing Holes.

Lashing in the absence of lashing holes, necessitates that the cord wraps around the ama. Each successive wrap lays outside of the next, forming a secure point to butt up against. The essential lashing knot is similar without the need to alter the direction of travel of the cord as it wraps underneath the ama.

Test Float Wa`a Before Final Rigging

(This is optional) Carry your wa`a to calm water, float and observe the trim and loll of the wa`a and ama. Use a spirit level across the gunnel - it should only have marginal loll to the left. If the 'bubble' is in the middle of the spirit level, the wa`a is rigged level, but will no doubt feel 'tippy' with a crew added. Add the crew, check spirit level again and assess the stability and trim of the wa`a. Make adjustments as required by adjusting, adding or removing wedges.

Floating the wa`a to check how level it is. Perform also with crew seated to see how it varies once loaded. In the absence of crew members, you can part fill the hull with water to see how the level alters.

Below this, adjustment being made to a koa wa`a rigging while on the water.

Based on your assessment of the way in which the wa`a is rigged, use the wedges to fine tune the rigging. Once satisfied, rig the i`ako to the wa`a firmly using rubber, cord or webbing, as preferred. If the i`ako wedges require adjustment in order to fine tune the wa`a trim, loosen the rubber and add or remove wedges, then re-tension, checking measurements, and float again.

I`ako to Wae Lashing - *kua`iako*

Published in 1957, *Sir Peter Buck's Arts and Crafts of Hawai`i* by *Bishop Museum Press*, describes, *'A pattern of oblique crossing turns is used in the Kamehameha V canoe'.* Contemporary Hawaiian racing wa`a paddlers largely use similar lashing configurations on Hawaiian designed wa`a. An illustration of the lashing used on a wa`a which belonged to *Kamehameha V* also appears in *Haddon and Hornell's, Canoes of Oceania.* This has become the popular lashing knot used on contemporary Hawaiian racing wa`a and is known as a diamond weave.

Merits of an Ancient Lashing Knot

The i`ako to wae lashing is essentially a diagonal lashing, with the added variance that the lashing at the point where the i`ako meets the wae crosses alternately, interlacing and creating tension down upon each other. The outboard lashing incorporates a round turn around the outboard `iako overhang, before passing back

Using 'tension-toggles' to pull the cord tight. Simply use two short bits of timber, square edged will ensure less slip. Take a wrap of cord and pull. They can save your hands from blisters!

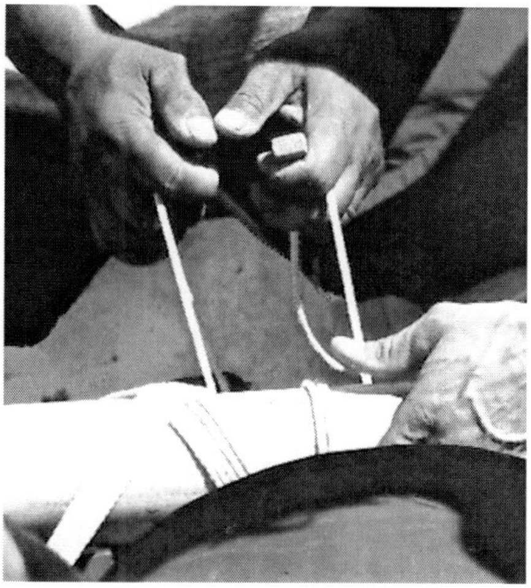

inboard through the lashing holes along the gunnel. The lashing consists of a single length of cord which begins in the centre of the wae wa`a. Pass the cord outside of the wa`a hull through the lashing holes made in the gunnel and make round-turns around the i`ako before passing back inboard through an adjacent hole on the other side of the i`ako. This reduces the chance of slip in the event of a break in the cord, while transverse movement of the outrigger assembly is also minimised. The use of cotton supports the i`ako better when they are pulled down fast on the gunnel and gives it the added opportunity to flex under pressure if required.

The skill employed during the woven lashing technique ensures that the cord is often passed over itself in several uniform areas to tighten down on itself and create a slip-free effect in the event of a break. Various forms of lashing are used today for racing outrigger canoes, all of which relate back to a more or less traditional lashing style.

Using 1, 2 or 3 Lengths of Lashing Material

Predominantly, if rigging with cord, a single length is used for the wae to i`ako connection. If using webbing, use 2 lengths. Rubber can be used in 1, 2 or 3 separate lengths.

Preliminary Connection To Wae Wa`a

Pre-stretch cotton. Simply loop around fixed object and pull. Do not wet the cotton, rig dry. Ensure correct length. See 'Rigging Material'

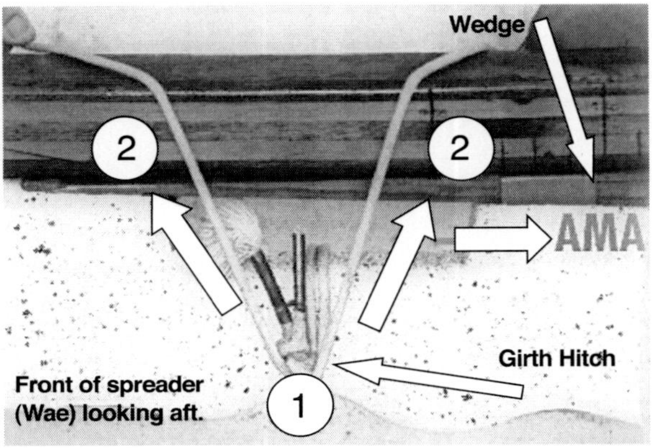

Begin by bringing the running ends together to form a loop and wrap middle hooped end around the centre of the wae (1) or over the i`ako and wae (depending on design), then pass the running ends through the loop to form a girth hitch, tailor slack until under tension.

Separate (2) so one cord travels left and the other right. Ensure girth hitch is at lower extremity of the wae. Take the running end and pass it obliquely forward and upward, then back over the i`ako towards the rear inner i`ako lashing hole (3).

Pass cord through the lashing hole and tailor all slack cord. Pass running end under the i`ako (4) and pull directly upward and make a full round-turn (5) anti-clockwise around the i`ako, then pass the running end through the outer forward i`ako lashing hole so the cord comes back inboard (6). Pull through and tailor until under tension.

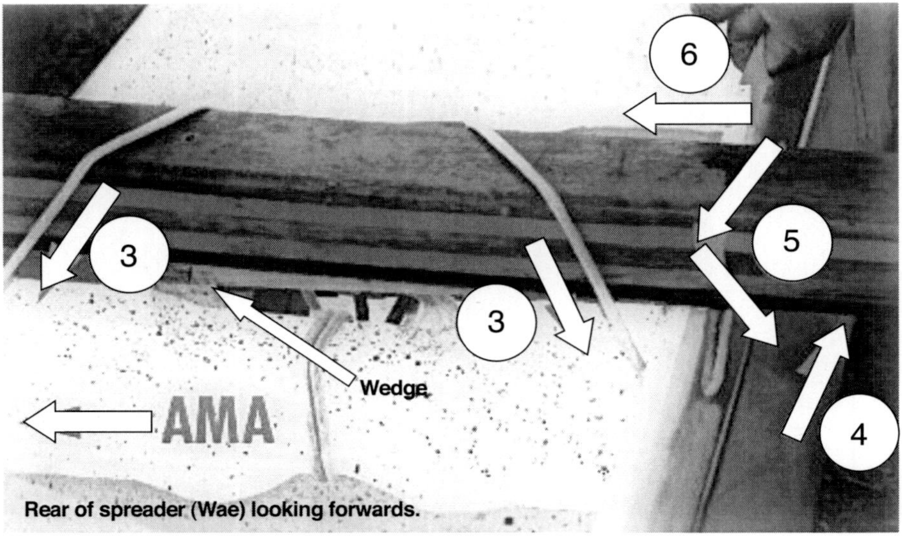

Maintaining tension, the running end then travels upward and inward diagonally back over the i`ako then down (7) to pass underneath the wae wa`a on the opposite side of the initial connecting loop made around the wae wa`a (8). Ensure that where the cord crosses the i`ako, it is central to the first wrap.

The running end then travels back upward on the opposite side (9) and crosses diagonally back over the i`ako (10) ensure cord is parallel and on the inside of the first wrap. It then travels out through the rear i`ako lashing hole (11) and is wrapped around the `iako as per step

These wraps work progressively inward towards the middle (12) of the i`ako. The wraps on the overhang, outwards (13) the wraps under the spreader (14), outwards. This completes one full wrap.

Repeat to complete either 4 or 5 wraps ending once cord is tailored and under tension from the middle of the wae.

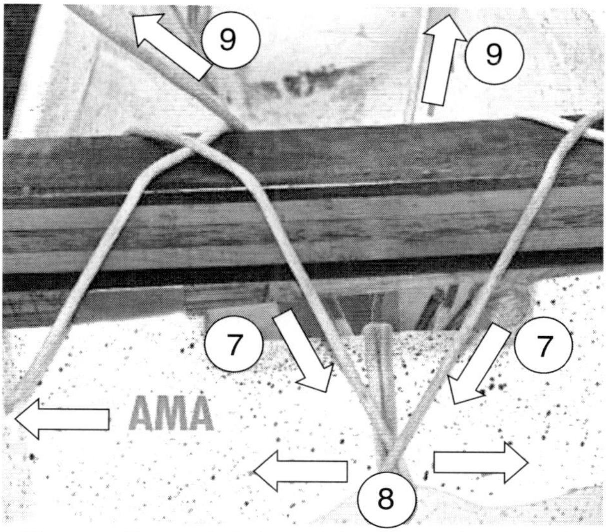

Wherever the cords interlock (cross-over) ensure they do in sequence ie under the spreader (8) and on the i`ako (9,10).

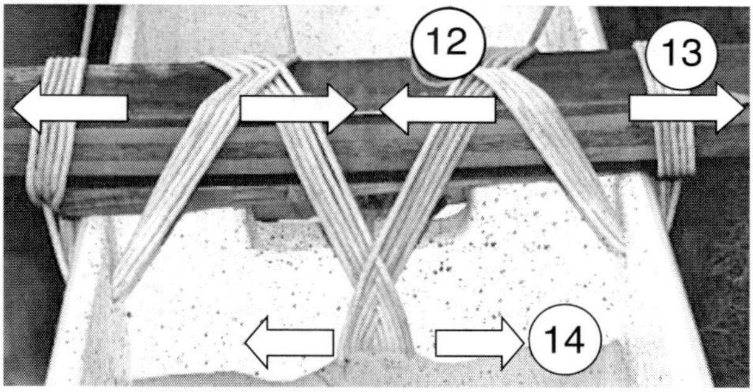

Note: Ensure a sequential left over right pattern when rigging in this manner and ensure wraps lay parallel and are butted up against each other. If one rigger gets ahead of another, the pattern is lost. The cord must be wrapped in sequence, left, right, left, right or visa versa.

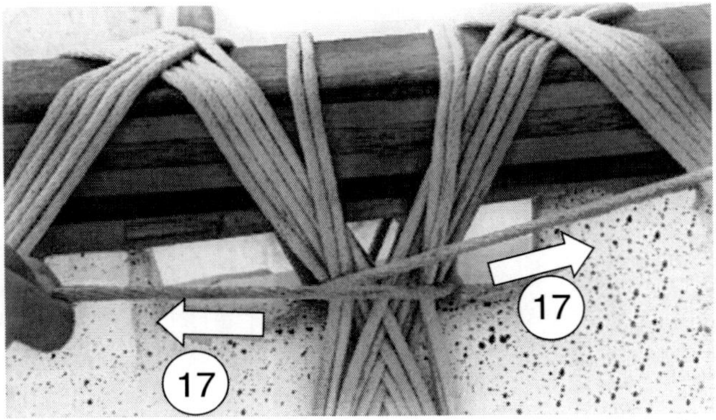

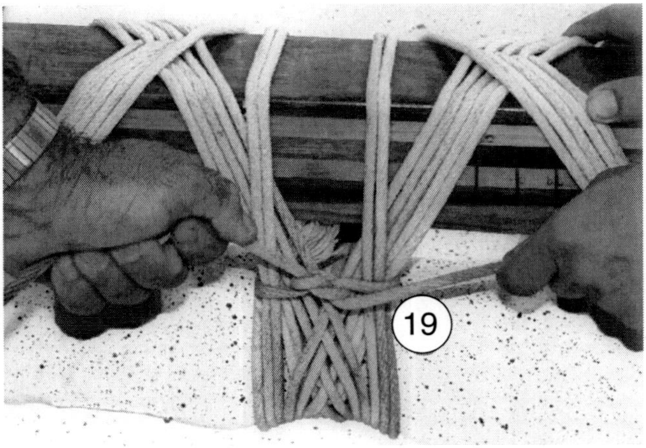

Finishing Off

How you finish will depend on the design of the wae. If there is a gap between the i`ako and wae, you can take frapping turns around the cord (17) to tighten and finish off. Pass between the i`ako and wae wa`a on the outside of the inner lashing (18) and pull tight to frap the lashing. Make several turns and tie off the two running ends (19).

Lashing with Rubber

Tahiti

Raised stanchioned spreaders as seen on va`a in Tahiti are almost exclusively rigged with rubber, more from necessity than design. Stanchioned spreaders means that no lashing is secured to the gunnel. The philosophy behind rigging in Tahiti is as different as the craft they paddle and design. Here, the understanding of 'give and take' and protection of the va`a and its components is understood. Simple overlapping round-turns are made to secure the i`ato to the spreader, usually with a single length or, on occasion, 2 lengths.

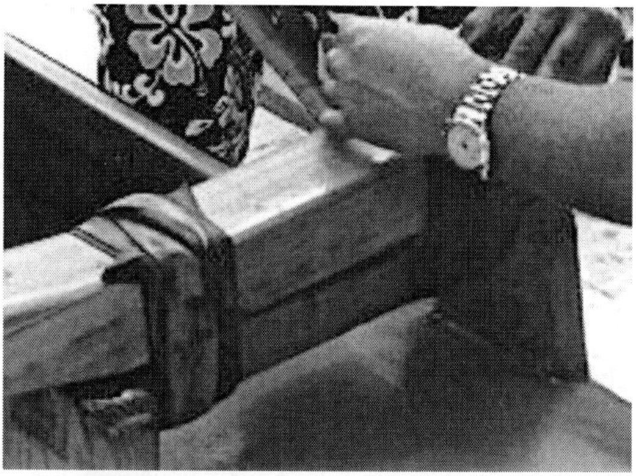

Typical stanchioned spreader as seen on Tahitian va`a, where lashing with rubber is almost exclusively used. Here they are using 2 lengths, one at either side of the spreader.

A popular method is to use a single length wrapped continuously from right to left, though 2 or 3 lengths are sometimes used.

Rubber is also predominantly used for the i`ato and ama lashing where some designers have created i`ato mounting platforms on their ama to accommodate rubber lashing in a more secure manner. The inclusion of two aluminium or wooden horizontal lashing pegs are a common feature on the ama, so the rubber can be pulled tight and tensioned around these extensions. Traditionally, this design was commonplace, but cord was used for lashing.

Note horizontal lashing pegs for the i`ato to ama attachment.

Hawai`i

When rigging a Hawaiian wa`a with rubber at the wae, it is not uncommon to omit passing the rubber through the gunnel lashing holes. You can use a 4' (1.25m) length of cord through each lashing hole, using a diagonal lashing to prevent any lateral movement of the assembly.

Options Include:

1 continuous length, which begins on the outer right hand side and progressively travels left to the opposite side of the wae.
2 single lengths positioned on the outer left and right sides of the wae.
3 separate lengths, positioned left, middle, right.

Begin by making the first wrap completely over itself to secure the rubber. Ensure strong and constant pressure. Wrap so that each one covers one half of the proceeding wrap. Finish by tucking the running end in on itself.

Two *Hawaiian Class Racers* ready for rigging. Begin lashing outer edges of wae to support i`ako. Rubber lashing with 2 single lengths per i`ako to wae.

While more complex patterns can be implemented using rubber to secure the i`ako to wae, it tends to perform best if used in a simple pattern rather than in any complex diagonal direction. If there was a better way, the Tahitians would have long since discovered it because of their near exclusive use of the material.

For the most part, the i`ako to ama are rigged using cord, especially with the ama which include lashing holes. In the absence of lashing holes, the rubber is wrapped fully under the ama.

Double Wa`a

***by Ted Ralston, Kahakai OCC*, California**

In Long Beach California, we use a nominal 36" clear between the hulls, with a toe in of 1-1/2" on the forward section of the i`ako. This spacing is consistent with historical measurements proportioned to our length.

This tight spacing puts minimum loads on the lashings

and wae when angling over swells or in chop or anytime there is unsymmetrical power in the two hulls. Traditional doubles had multiple i`ako, perhaps 10, which distributed the load more uniformly than two i`ako that DC12s are rigged with. Loads do need to be considered.

The tight spacing we use results in a fairly well built-up bow wave trapped between the hulls, which can reduce freeboard in the middle seats. The double is always markedly faster than the single, even if paddlers in the double are not as proficient.

Toe in is added, to prevent the two hulls actively being 'pulled' apart by the on flow of water. Rubber provides adequate flex to protect the wae from failure.

'Quick Lashes' and 'Snap Lashes'

'Snap Lashes' have now become part of the esoteric language among wa`a paddlers. Quick Straps are associated with 'ratchet' operated straps. While Snap Lashes refer to the older original design, which relies on partially pre-tensioning the strap, then folding the clamp over with pressure from the palm of your hand to create tension.

Ratchet tensioned straps have the potential to damage the wae wa`a, i`ako lashing holes and i`ako if over-tensioned. Snap Lashes, while capable of being over tensioned, are less likely to cause structural damage. Damage can occur during the 'tensioning' process, but also while the wa`a is in use. Adverse pressure from wave and swell action can contribute to structural damage if over-tensioning has removed the ability of the assembly to 'give'. The issue here is, avoid over-tensioning.

With the introduction of mechanical snap-lashes, there has been a period of time where crews have experimented to arrive at the best possible configuration. Originally, it was common practice to use two snap-lashes, wrapped around the i`ako and spreader at either extremity, without passing the webbing through the gunnel lashing holes.

While this is effective, the configuration fails to prevent lateral movement of the entire outrigger assembly, as the lashing does not extend to the i`ako overhang through the gunnel lashing holes. Consequently, it is necessary to use a separate length of 2m (6') cord. This is wrapped around the inboard section of the i`ako, then passed through the lashing hole, under and around the outboard section of the i`ako (a round-turn), then passed back through the alternate lashing hole – repeated four times or so. This configuration, secures the rigging laterally.

Webbing, when used with a ratchet tensioner, is exceptionally strong. However, a weak-spot is effectively created where the webbing tightens over the i`ako. It is preferable to use 2 lengths beginning at either side of the wae to spread the load and tension. A diagonal lashing pattern can be used in order to achieve this, incorporating the lashing holes.

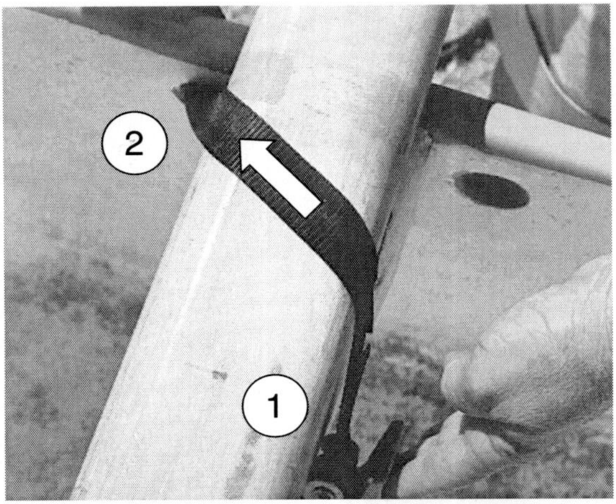

Ensure webbing lies flat and there are no twists within the gunnel lashing holes. Use 2 straps per i`ako to wae attachment, beginning at either extremity.

Position ratchet on the back face of the wae (1) close to centre, with the webbing at the top, keeping it diagonally aligned. Pass running end of webbing up and over i`ako, feeding through forward inner lashing hole (2).

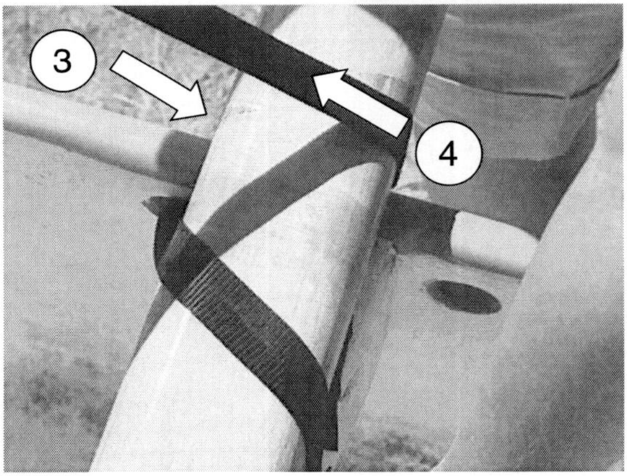

Pass running end under the i`ako (3) then cross diagonally back inboard over the i`ako (4) crossing over the first lashing turn at (5). Continue (6) under wae then back over i`ako (7) crossing centrally back over the lashing (8).

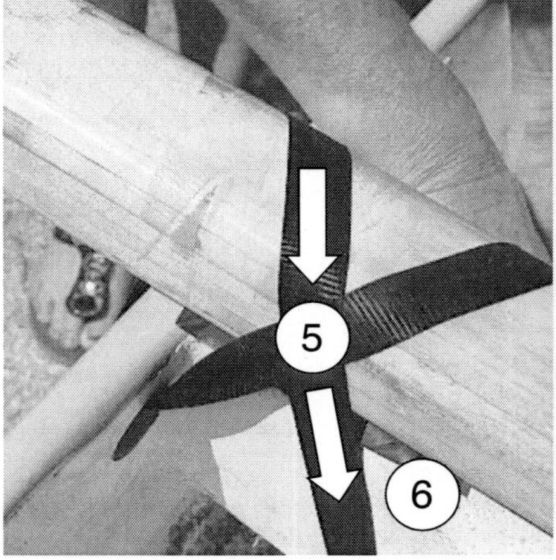

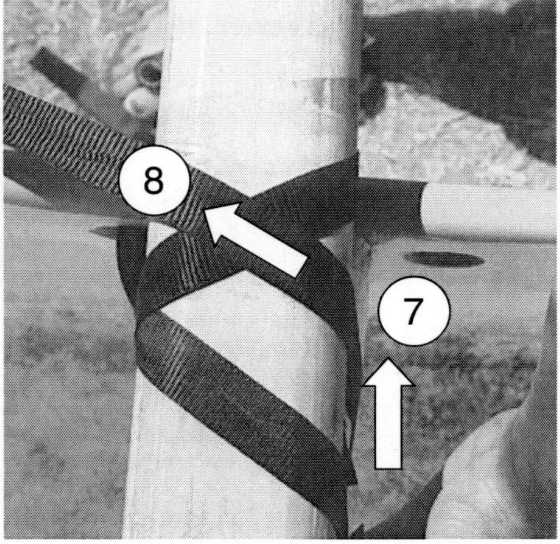

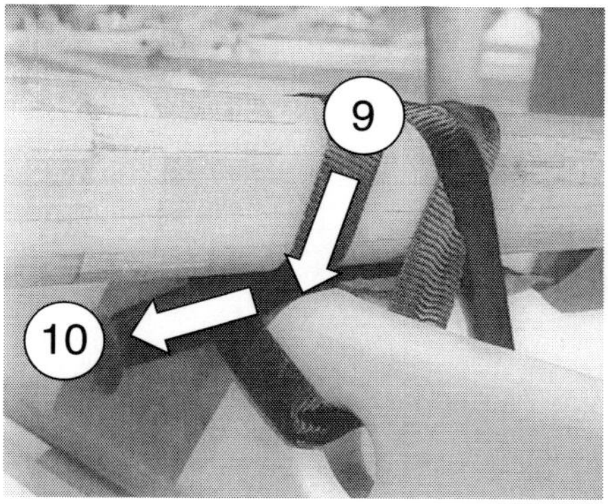

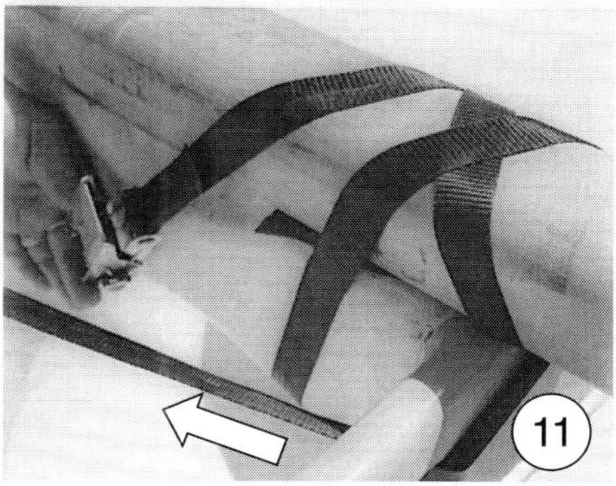

Pass runing end outboard(9) under the i`ako (10) then back inboard via the rear lashing hole (11). Thread running end under previous wrap (12) and cross obliquely up and over i`ako, then downwards towards the middle of the wae, thread running end through ratchet and tension (12). Repeat on other side.

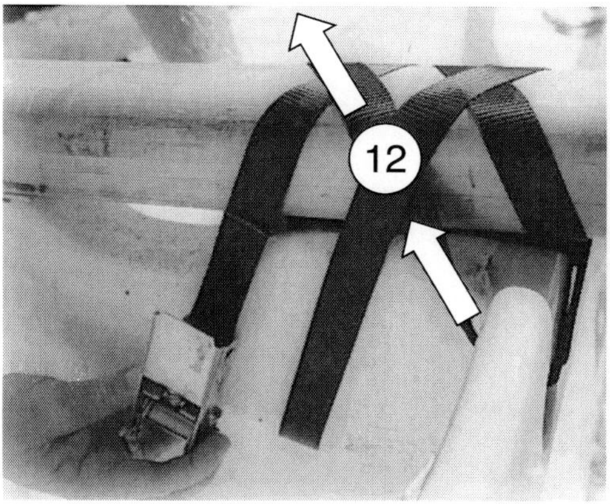

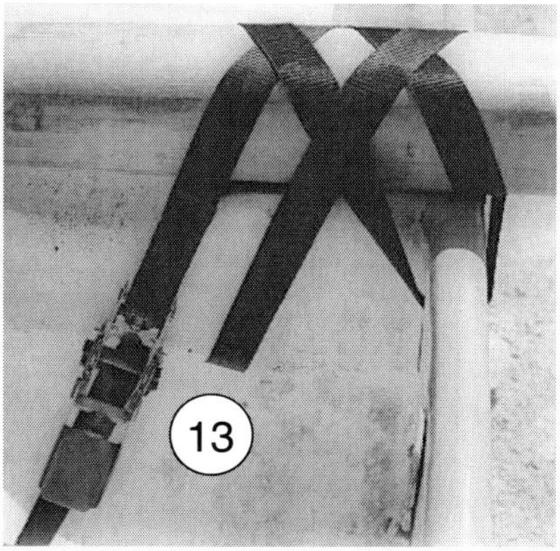

Rear of wae after completion

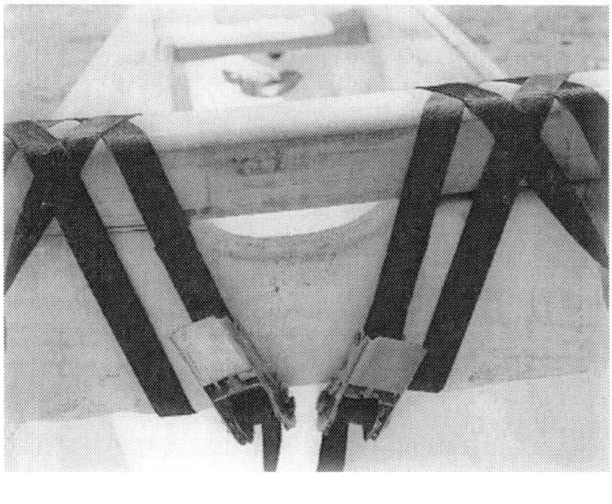

Front of wae after completion

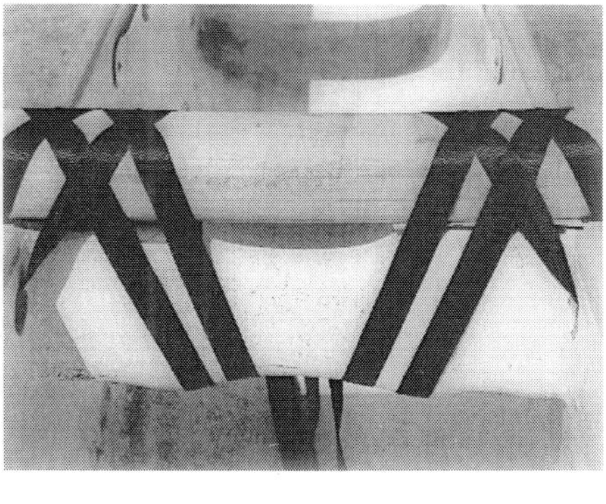

Adding Weight to Ama

If you feel the need, you can add a 'dive weight' to the extremity of the rear i`ako using duct tape. This can provide some added security and prevent the ama lifting radically. While this can help, for every reaction there is always an equal and opposite reaction. If the wa`a is about to capsize, the added weight can ultimately contribute to the capsize. It is best to rig properly and avoid having to use added weight.

Paddles

'A man feels at home with a paddle in his hand, its as natural and indigenous as a bow or a spear. When he swings through a stroke and the canoe moves forward, he sets in motion long-forgotten reflexes, stirs up ancient sensations deep within his subconscious. When a man is part of his canoe, he is part of all that canoes have ever known.'

Sigurd Olson - The Singing Wilderness.

Lewis Laughlin **Team** ***Rai*****, Hawaiki Nui Va`a.**

A well designed, handcrafted timber paddle is surely a work of art. Beautiful in form, soft to the touch, the va`a paddle represents to the paddler, the most important and expensive accessory they will purchase. More than just a handy implement for propulsion, the paddle has taken on powerful symbolism throughout many canoe-cultures. Its form has been revered in sculpture, jewellery and drawings. Even with the march of progress, whether all wood, carbon or a mix of materials, a well crafted paddle is the pinnacle of art, form and function.

Lovingly hand drawn adornment over timber, Kona, Hawai`i.

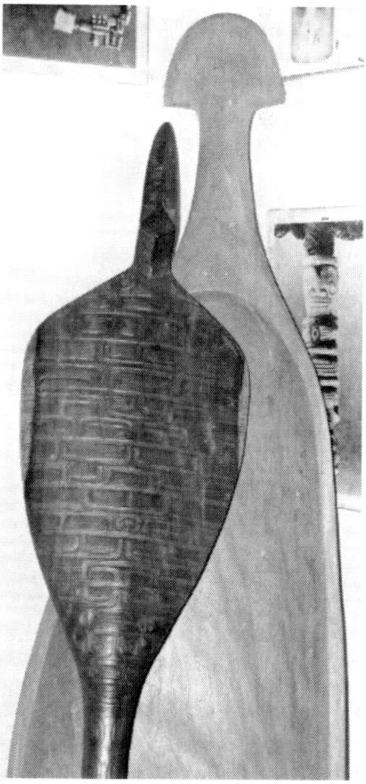

Left: Paddles in Auckland's *Captain Cook Museum* collected from around the Pacific, display spear-like qualities. Right: Ancient Marquesan paddles displaying weapon-like features; clubbed grips and thick heavy shafts, sturdy blade faces, some with extensions capable of clubbing or stabbing opponents, some ornately carved.

Its simple form evokes in the paddler an empathy for what it represents; a way of propelling yourself over the water, symbolising freedom from constraint, recreation, a good time and ultimately what you would rather be doing.

In ancient times throughout the Pacific, the paddle was in the context of warfare, both a means of propulsion and a weapon. The blade face was often used to shield and protect the warrior's face and body from thrown objects. The blade edge was used to chop down and cut at their opponents, while the shaft end was often used as a staff or long-bo as used in martial arts. Some designs from around the Pacific could have doubled as spears, with razor-sharp blade tips and edges.

With the passing of time, the form of the paddle has narrowed down to one primary concern, efficiency as a tool of propulsion over water. In this respect, the changes have been enormous and exhaustive in every single facet of their creation. Once carved from a single solid slab of timber, today's paddles are largely constructed from a variety of timber types and synthetics, positioned within shaft and blade with careful consideration and precision.

A collection of Hawaiian Hoe belonging to the late *Mike Tongg*, which would have been phased out of use progressively through the 1970s. They have solid shafts and weigh in at well over 3lbs, each.

Without exception, paddles used today for va`a paddling are only vaguely 'traditional' by any standard. In many regards, many of their contemporary design elements are due to the advancement of Native American open canoe (river) paddle designs fostered by Euro-American and European racers and shapers. In the quest to develop an efficient, ergonomic paddle, traditional values and virtues have all but been disregarded.

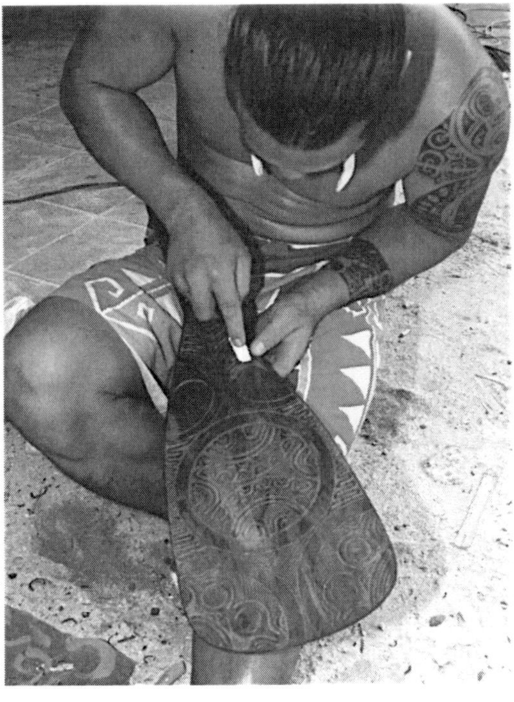

Ornamental paddle carver *Huahine*, French Polynesia. Paddles such as this can fetch over USD$700, in Hawai`i an ornamental koa paddle with stand can set you back USD$1000. In reality, most commercially made racing paddles are grossly undervalued when you factor in the labour and skill involved in their creation and there are few in 'the business' who would disagree with this.

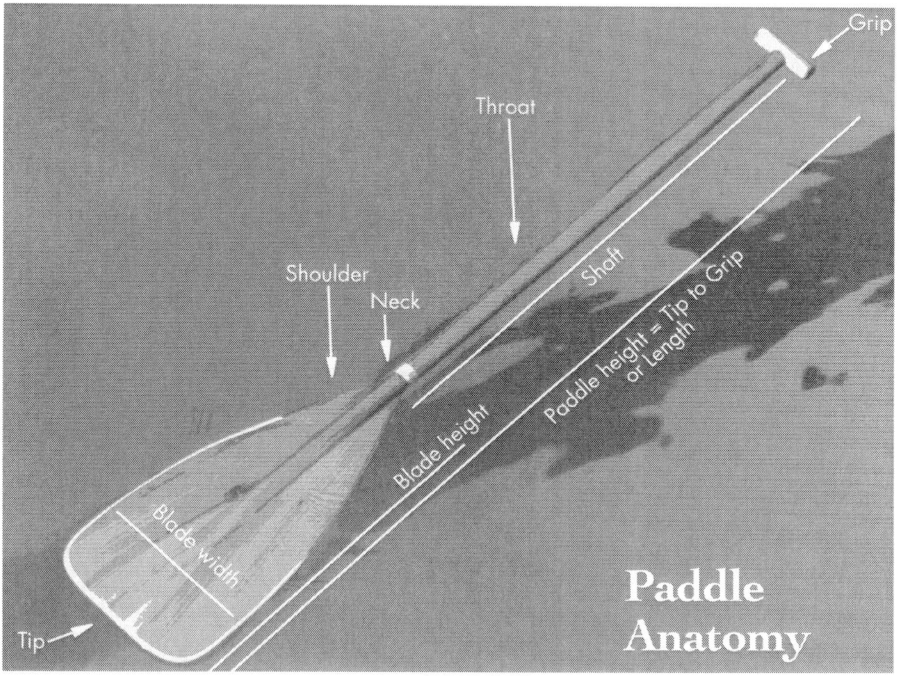

Paddle Anatomy

The edges constitute the extremities of the blade. Grip circumference is the measurement taken around the throat - important that this is suited to your hand and finger dimensions. Too narrow and you will have to squeeze hard to gain control which can stress your forearms, too wide and you will struggle to gain any control.

Grips from left: Palm / Pear Grip, Hammerhead or J-Grip, T– Grip. The palm grip is the least suited to va`a paddling as it does not provide a firm, positive grip in rough water.

The power-face of the blade is the surface which grips and is pulled against the water, in contrast to the back of the blade.

Long, solid timber, heavy, straight shafted, paddle without hand grip as used by one of the first Tahitian crews to compete in the Moloka`i to O`ahu race in the late 1970s next to a paddle of the mid 90s; shorter, single-bend, laminated, lightweight, with T-Grip handle.

The shaft has two sides. The back is the 'compression' side and the front is the 'flex' side. Some makers add a 'compression-strip' of a specific timber such as Ash to absorb the continual 'crushing' of the timber fibres. This is the side which often get stress fractures and ultimately fails. Stress fractures often appear as small dark creases or fissures on the surface of the timber on the compression side.

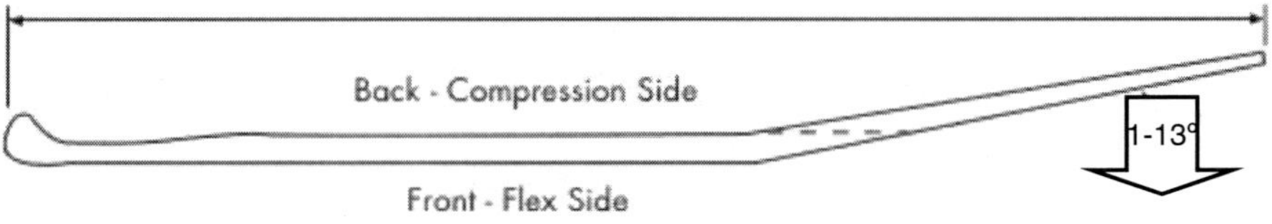

Blade Design Performance Requirements

Blades are assessed on their four main areas of performance which are entry, grip, exit and air transfer. This directly translates into the various phases of the paddle stroke.

Entry

As the blade enters the water, it should do so in a way that minimises energy waste; splash and excessive bubbles of air around the blade. Clean entry is vital. Air tends to be dragged down with the blade as it is pushed into the water, especially along the back-face of the paddle. Excessive air drawn down the blade greatly reduces the paddle's efficiency, leads to cavitation and reduces its grip on the water. While the paddler is largely responsible for 'clean placement', the blade design can either hinder or assist in this respect.

In the past, when blade faces where larger and tips thicker, flat (straight) tipped blades would sometimes create a noticeable 'plopping' sound. This was both annoying and inefficient as it was a sure sign that air was being drawn down the back of the paddle on entry. A 1-2" curved lip was added to the blade tip by some manufacturers, angled back toward the blade face marginally so that on entry, the lip entered vertically rather than 45°.

This may have resolved some entry issues but can cause problems at the exit, where water can be 'trapped' and 'scooped' by the lip, creating drag. As blade areas have reduced, edges thinned, and paddling 'styles' changed, this issue has diminished and the curved lip is seldom seen on va`a paddles out of the USA, Hawai`i, Australia, Canada. However, they are still prevalent in Tahiti where blade areas remain somewhat larger with longer blade lengths. In Tahiti, paddling technique and styles are somewhat unique and there is still a preference for double-bend paddles.

Poor paddling technique will often allow air to be drawn down with the blade as it enters the water. Developing a smooth entry technique is essential.

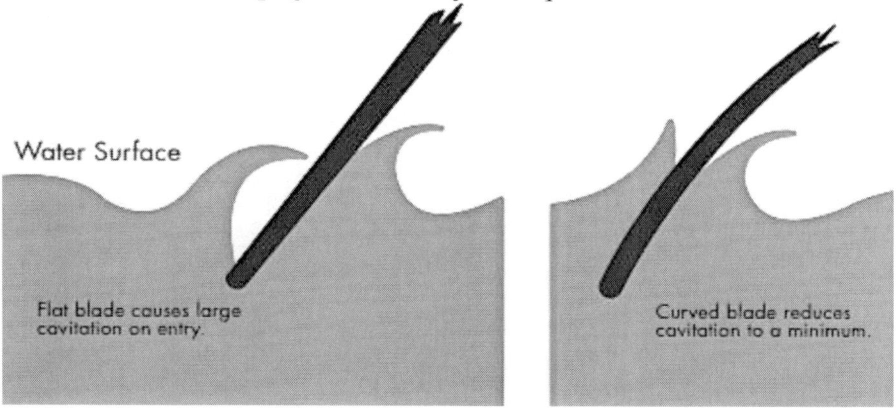
Water Surface
Flat blade causes large cavitation on entry.
Curved blade reduces cavitation to a minimum.

Grip

The paddle must 'grip' the water so an effective pull can be generated. This has led to the analogy of a paddle acting as an anchor; the paddle remains anchored or fixed as the canoe is pulled up to its level through the water.

The degree of grip or resistance relates to the surface area of the blade. There must be enough area to provide grip, but not so much to create undue resistance and drag.

Blade areas have greatly reduced since the mid 90s, moving away from the 'bigger must be better' theory. Smaller blade areas have led to slightly more 'aggressive' paddling techniques and styles, with higher stroke rates to accommodate. Some paddlers, as they age, move back to a wider, larger blade area, preferring a slower stroke rate.

While more blade area equates to more grip, there is also more drag to contend with at the exit phase of the stroke and more weight in the paddle.

***Offshore* California's women's crew using giant sized paddles in 1996. Photo *Daphne Houghard. Lanikai CC* 2001 paddling with much smaller blade area 'hybrids', Heemoana Va`a race Tahiti, lower left.**

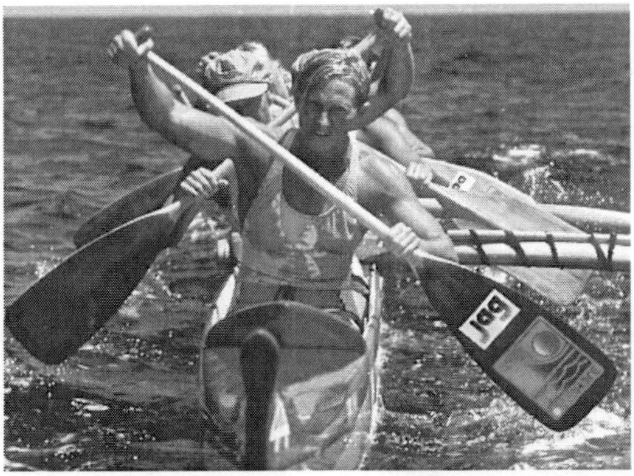

A 12" water-whacker, it's maximum blade width is nearly three-quarters down the face.

***Kialoa E-10* Paddle, popular from 1991-1997, long blade height, near straight shoulders.**

From an evolutionary stand point. *Kialoa* paddles mirror the changing needs and wants of some of the top level paddlers throughout the Pacific having worked closely with many of the top crews in Hawai`i and California. From left a late 90s *Wiley Coyote* with cut-away shoulders, borrowed from river racing canoes, to conform to the curvature of the hull of the wa`a and to give a low centre of effort on the blade face; a *K-9* with longer shoulders; and an older original *E-10* which clearly has a much larger surface area, phased out in 1997.

Flutter

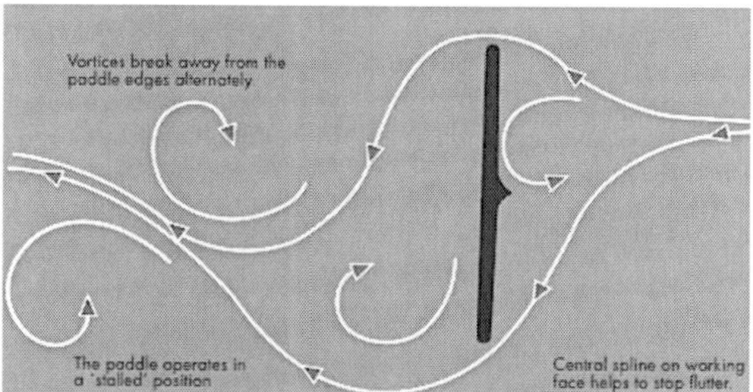

Flutter is caused by water under pressure, leaving the blade face at random points on its edges, causing shifts in the forces acting against the blade. The inclusion of a spline or raised dihedral from the neck to a quarter or two thirds down the centre of the power face of the blade, helps provide some balance and reduced flutter.

Flutter is a problem associated with large surface area, flat faced blades. It occurs when the blade tends to 'wander' from side to side as you make the pull. The larger the surface area of the blade, the greater the effort required to prevent flutter, though it may not be consciously felt by the paddler, particularly strong paddlers. Weaker paddlers will be far more aware of this happening.

Since the late 90s, there has been a move to greatly reduce the surface area on paddle designs. This is partly a result of rethinking the paddle's function; ie, that its surface area only has to be large enough to anchor itself. Surface

Late 1990s *Xylo Bladz*, Australian designs are evolving. Two very different blade shapes.

area beyond this optimum size adds extra weight and ineffectual surface area which translates into unnecessary resistance and drag, particularly during the exit phase of the stroke. Paddles with less surface area suffer much less from flutter. With diminishing blade areas over recent times, the spline has essentially disappeared from va`a paddles.

Exit

When you remove the blade from the water, you want to minimise energy loss by both the paddler and paddle. This is achieved by exiting the blade from the water at the earliest opportunity after the power-phase of the stroke, even if some of the propulsive power is lost from the end of the stroke.

Left: Typical contemporary Tahitian paddles. This shape still remains popular due to their preference for double-bend paddles and the availability of materials which governs what a designer can shape and create.

If you pull the blade too far past your body, it slows your potential stroke rate down and uses unnecessary energy, as the critical and most powerful part of your stroke has already been made. Once the blade passes your hip, your pull becomes a push; a much less effective use of both blade and body. This relates only to team va`a technique, not too solo and duo craft, where some 'push' is an advantage as used in marathon canoe river paddling.

The larger the surface area of the paddle, the greater the drag or resistance will be during the exit part of the stroke. The solution for this is to reduce the surface area of the blade, particularly its length. A short blade length; 18" (45.72cms) measured from the tip to the neck of the shaft, will mean that the blade is not buried so deep in the water and can be exit-ed and re-entered with smaller movements and with less energy expenditure.

The inclusion of concaves or scoops within the blade face can actually 'hold' water at the power phase of the stroke. However, there is a distinct disadvantage at the end of the stroke as the water fails to release from the blade face. The blade must be released very early at the hip and 'lifted' to allow the water to 'spill' from the face of the blade. Excessive drag at the exit phase will lead to early fatigue, slower stroke rates and often a 'pull down' effect acting on the va`a.

Design and Suitability

Outrigger paddling is an endurance sport and it is essential that you can manage your paddle efficiently for long periods of time, in a way that is comfortable and effective, avoiding undue fatigue and a reduction in performance.

When selecting a paddle, you need to take into account your individual requirements which are determined by your physical attributes, your paddling style and the type of va`a you are paddling. A poor paddle design or even a good one that is not suited to you or your team's style of paddling will mean that you will fail to reach your full potential.

The va`a will only ever be as good as its least effective paddler. Remember, your paddle is what provides the essential link between your energy expenditure and the effectiveness of your stroke. How many paddlers are using paddles completely unsuited to their physical and technical needs?

Over the years, paddle designs have changed in an effort to increase comfort and reduce fatigue while improving it's over all efficiency. How much of this is simply a smart commercial move in order to offer something different or is a genuine attempt to improve comfort and efficiency while reducing fatigue is uncertain. The design features undoubtedly have merits, some paddlers like them, others do not, ultimately it's a matter of personal preference. It is worthwhile to try as many different designs as possible, then make an assessment of what works best for you.

Sizing a Paddle

When choosing a paddle, its size, the overall length from tip to grip, is possibly the single most important issue you need to consider. Unfortunately, it is far from being a perfect science, and we have a range of theories which are worthy of note, more to exemplify why they are not suitable methods of selection rather than why they are.

The problem with most theories is that they fail to account for the height of the va`a seat relative to the level of water, while others fail to take into account the length of your arm.

The following are examples of methods that claim to determine the correct paddle length for any individual. 1 - 4 are examples of what to avoid. Number 5 offers the best solution.

1. When standing, the paddle should reach your chin. **This measures your leg and trunk length but fails to take into account the length of your arms, the canoe's depth or the seat height.**

2. A paddle shaft should be 6 to 8" (15.24cm to 20.32cm) longer than your arm from armpit to the tips of your extended fingers. **This still fails to take into account the characteristics of the va`a.**

3. When standing, the grip of the paddle should fit snugly up into your armpit with the blade level on the ground. **This fails to take into account the length of your arm and again the characteristics of the va`a.**

4. The paddle shaft should be as long as the distance from the top of your shoulder to the ground when you are sitting on the ground, plus the height of the va`a seat from the bottom of the va`a. **This fails to take into account your arm length.**

Clearly all these theories end up with a variety of so called 'ideal' lengths which are confusing. Here is the best method, it is simple and worth the effort.

5. When the blade is fully immersed at the mid-point - (vertical phase) of the power phase of the stroke, your grip - (top hand) should be level with your eyes or the tip of your nose.

This may sound simplistic – but it does ultimately take into account the va`a specifications as well as the paddler's physical and biomechanical make up. Following on from this, we could conclude that the most accurate method of sizing a paddle removes leg length from the equation. Remember, this is based on exercising good technique.

One of the simplest methods endorsed by *ZRE* paddles in the USA suggests sitting in a chair and measuring the distance from the chair seat to the bridge of your nose or eye-level. This equates to the length of your required shaft from neck to top of the grip. From here, add the blade length of the paddle model you prefer, in order to obtain the total paddle length from tip to grip.

Carbon paddles often come supplied at one length, 54" or greater. The grip is not glued so the shaft can be cut to length.

Paddle manufacturers have a variety of formulae that they use, but even these will not always guarantee that you will end up with the correct length for you or your craft. *Kialoa* in the USA uses the following simple recommendations;

Your Height	**Length**
5'0"-5'2"	46"-47"
5'3"-5'5"	47"-49"
5'6"-5'8"	49"-51"
5'9"-5'11"	51"-52"
6'0"-6'2"	52"-53"
6'3"-6'5"	54"-56"

Australia 1995. Take a careful look and consider how many of these paddlers are using paddles too long? Top hand way above the level of the head, driving downwards, can cause painful shoulder problems. The view that longer and bigger is best is the thinking of neolithic primates, negating any rationale that technique 'also' matters. Many of these paddlers would struggle to find good form, simply because their weapon of choice is more of a liability than an asset.

1. If you have broader than average shoulders, go to the high end of the range.

2. If you have a long torso relative to your height, go to the high end of the range.

3. When ordering a paddle to be used with a one or two person canoe, go to the middle or low end of the range.

Over time, paddle lengths have been shortening. For example, even a paddler who is 6'6" can be found using a 52" paddle. The most popular lengths for a wide variety of heights seem to fall between 50-52" which is only a small variation. Lengths 1" below this length are rare and beyond that, rarer again.

Cautionary Note: An overly long paddle can and probably will, over time, cause rotator cuff - shoulder, damage because you are applying power to the stroke with your upper arm raised well above the level of your shoulder. Better to use a paddle marginally too short than too long.

Because of the obvious physical differences in the heights of the seat in an OC6 and OC1, paddlers need a different paddle for each craft. The difference in length can be up to 1" - 2.5 cm, in general terms.

Grip Circumference

The circumference of the shaft at the throat is important for both comfort and control of the blade. How much attention has been given to this in the manufacture of outrigger paddles is a little hazy. It is fair to say though that most men's grips are larger in diameter than the women's. However, paddles generally come standard, with no allowance for women. This could be a distinct disadvantaged if the diameter of the grip is too large.

When you grasp a paddle, your thumbnail should be level with or slightly overlap the line of your fingernails. A larger diameter than this will cause unnecessary fatigue, as you will need to 'squeeze' the grip more to control the blade. This can lead to elbow and wrist injuries as well as cramps in your forearms. The shape of the shaft makes a big difference in comfort and control. Some are almost perfectly round while others are more oval in shape. Personal preference plays a large part in selection.

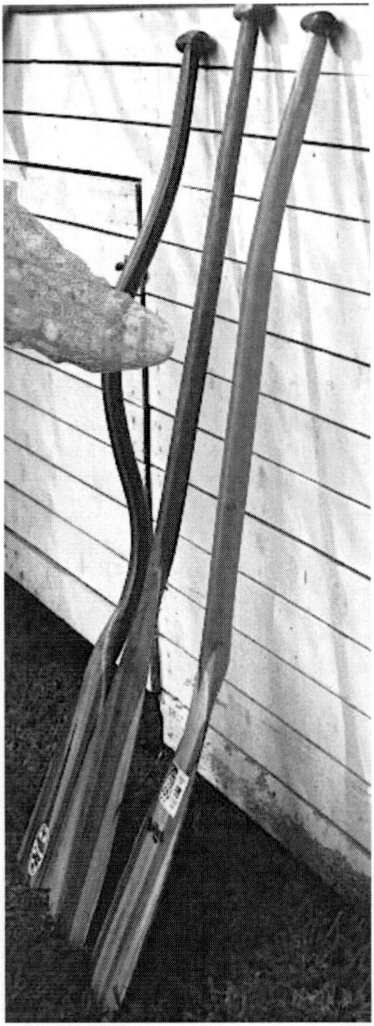

Shaft Types

Paddle shafts fall into three basic categories – single bend, double-bend and straight.

Shafts with bends are also referred to as 'cranked'. *Sawyer Paddles* of the USA produced a 'Quad' paddle, which took the added mechanical and ergonomical advantages of bends added within the shaft to new heights. However, it never caught on with va`a paddlers.

From left, Quad-Bend, Straight Shaft and Double-bend.

A degree of flex or spring in the shaft is preferred. Stiff shafts increase the chance of shoulder injuries. Spring gives the paddler a more encouraging, relaxing feel to the paddle stroke and in this respect, timber shafts are far superior to synthetics. However, advances in synthetic construction, largely carbon fibre, now allows for varying amounts of flex to be built in.

Bent Shaft | Cranked Shaft, Crooked Paddle, Single Bend

Beyond specific blade shapes, there are also differences in the profiles of paddle shafts. The origin of the bent shaft paddle does not lie in Oceania. It was originally developed in 1948 for the sport of canoe racing, made popular by *Eugene Jensen* in 1971 and introduced into va`a racing at the 1978 Moloka'i to O`ahu race by a mainland American team. They went on to win and in doing so, created great interest in their paddles. These paddles also included a T-Grip, which at the time, was not in popular use in va`a paddling. Since this paddle design was introduced to the sport, it has become a catalyst for the development of va`a paddles.

In 1994, we saw some radical adaptations of the outrigger paddle, specifically a reduction in blade width and height, but the blade still angled away from the shaft, averaging 10–13°. Steering paddles also became narrower and taller, from tip to shoulder, with an angle nearing 5 degrees relative to the shaft.

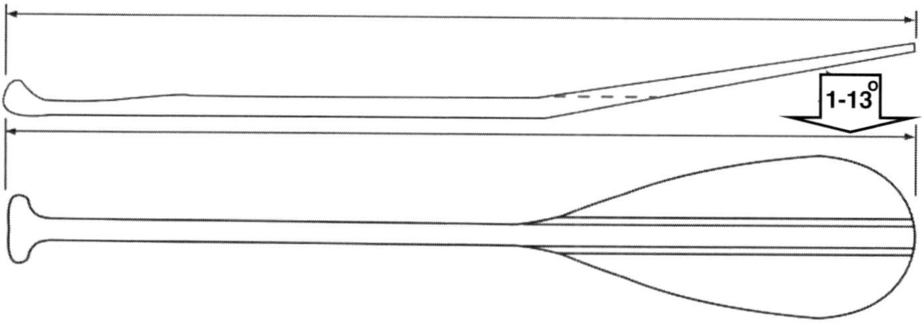

The benefits of the bent shaft paddle;

1. The blade maintains less angle in the water during the latter part of the stroke.
2. Thrust is maintained along the side of the va`a over a greater distance.
3. The tendency to lift water during the exit phase of the stroke is reduced.
4. The paddle reaches farther forward during the catch phase of the stroke.
5. It has a natural tendency to 'feather' (turn outwards) when it leaves the water.

These points are based on the assumption of the use of sound technique.

Double-Bend Shaft Paddles

This is a variation of the bent shaft paddle in an attempt to go one better. Its design concept aims at reducing fatigue and wrist strain and makes good sense when you consider its design elements. Unlike the single-bend paddle shaft where the bend originates at the neck of the paddle, the double-bend shaft has a bend in both the upper and lower shaft.

Curved

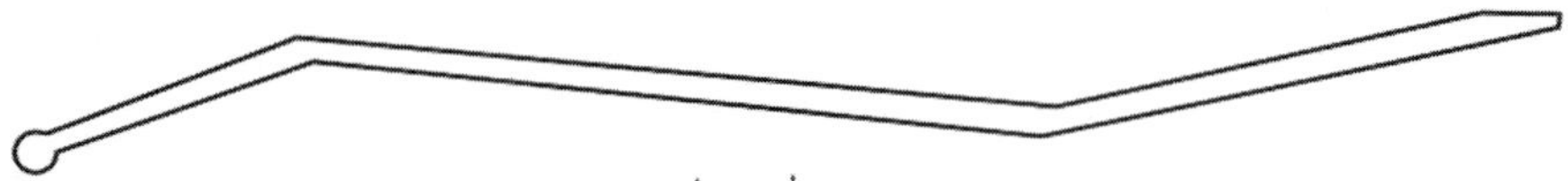

Angular

The benefits of the double-bend shaft paddle;

1. The upper angle brings the grip back towards the driving hand, so that the paddler's shoulder and arm extension is lessened, reducing fatigue.

2. The lower shaft angles towards the paddler so that the wrist is naturally aligned with the shaft at an angle reducing wrist strain and fatigue.

Double bend paddles specific to va`a paddling come in two distinct types. The curious issue here is whether this developed from different approaches to construction or genuine thought regarding performance. The top paddle, is essentially a series of 'curves' and more often than not laminated in a 'jig'; timbers bent and glued to conform to the jig's shape. Conversely, the double bend below is far more angular and often made as a straight shaft, then the last third or so of the shaft is 'scarfed' - cut diagonally, reversed and laminated back on to be angled away. This is common to Tahitian paddles.

Double-bend paddle ready to be finished.

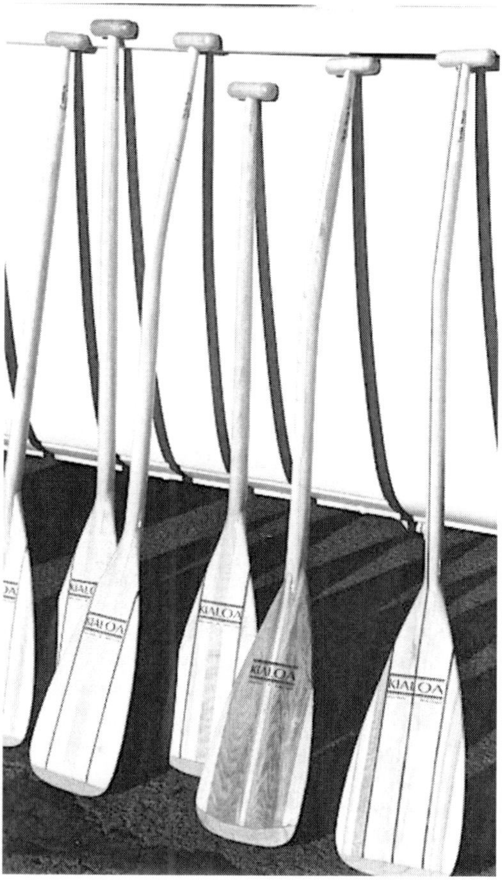

The soft 'S' shaped double bend provides less mechanical advantage as the pivotal point is less acute than with the more angular shaft. Tahitian paddlers use this mechanical advantage by pushing forward with the top arm when the blade is vertical, during the power phase, and their concern is far from one of ergonomics, which seems to be the primary selling point for many manufacturers.

A mixture of single and double-bend paddles, note added 'kink' in the top third of the upper shaft. This brings the grip closer to the paddler so the top arm is further back during the set up and entry phase of the stroke. While initial designs were thought to be purely ergonomic, the Tahitian paddlers in particular have adjusted their paddling technique in order to use the mechanical advantage inherent in the additional upper bend in the shaft.

Straight Shaft (near straight) - Steering Paddles

The steerer is continually using their paddle to make directional adjustments to a craft that is more than 40' long, weighs over 680kgs (1,500lbs) with crew and this requires, at times, enormous effort. Add to this the abrasive and leverage stresses that are put on the shaft of the paddle as it is used against the side of the canoe in executing a pry or rudder stroke and you can see why a steering paddle must be tough.

Two different sized steering paddles, the larger for big seas/rough water, the other for more moderate conditions.

Steering paddles need to be considerably stronger than standard paddling blades because of the great stresses that are put upon them. They tend to be marginally heavier because of the selection of timbers used to make them more robust. The steerer has a specialised position in the canoe which holds much responsibility and demands the use of a special paddle. It would be tempting fate to use a regular paddle for steering, not one designed to take the load. It's a sickening feeling when your paddle buckles in your hands – even repaired, it won't be the same.

Steering paddles generally range between 0 and 5° bend at the shaft. Because the paddle is used by the steerer much like a rudder, it naturally performs and handles better being straight or nearly straight shafted.

Certain rules do apply. In the case of canoe surfing and sailing, the steering paddle is generally straight and of a heavy duty construction. These paddles are under a great deal of pressure and designed to do one thing well; act as a rudder. A steering blade for the most part is used for both paddling and steering. In flatter seas and sprint racing, the steering paddles can be one which is more suited to a balance of paddling and steering. It can be closer in design to the crew's paddles. In rougher and larger the seas, the paddle will need to be more 'steering specific' as the steerer will be steering more than paddling.

Timber Paddle Construction

Many paddles out of Tahiti may seem 'rustic' when compared to the paddles of Hawai'i, USA, Canada or Australia. In these locations, the paddler's demand a highly polished, well-finished implement built to out-live the paddler's life expectancy.

Yet, in the remote islands of French Polynesia, the art of paddle making is as revered as the design and creation of the va`a itself. Limited to tropical timbers and an economy that must allow anyone be able to afford it, the paddle is considered more of a consumable than a permanent item. As such, this keeps the flow of ideas constant.

Here, the premise is that the paddle must blend with the paddler's technique not the other way around. They are, in short, demanding of and not subservient to the paddle or the paddle maker. It's not uncommon for crews in French Polynesia to begin a race with one particular paddle shape, then at an appropriate time, dispense with these and replace them with a completely different paddle to suit the changed conditions. This level of thinking is unique in the paddling world.

Traditional paddles were simply carved from solid lengths of timber. Contemporary paddles use a well known manufacturing procedure called 'laminating'. The laminating or layering together of woods by gluing them, adds to the uniform strength of the paddle. Another advantage is the creation of a lighter paddle by combining light and heavy timbers, rather than just being limited to one type for strength.

The workshop of *Tahiti Rame,* Papeete one of the most prolific makers of va`a paddles in the region, churn out a staggering number of paddles, the vast majority of are double-bend shafts.

***Tahiti Rame* paddles drying after having been sealed with epoxy.**

Laminations

Weight versus strength is the eternal quest, as strong as possible, as light as possible. These requirements are in the hands of the craftsperson, whose skill lies in the careful and skilful selection of the timber and with meticulous laminating, which determines the paddle's durability.

Once timber is selected for the blade, they can be cut into varying widths. A template shape is drawn then laminates glued, cured and shaped.

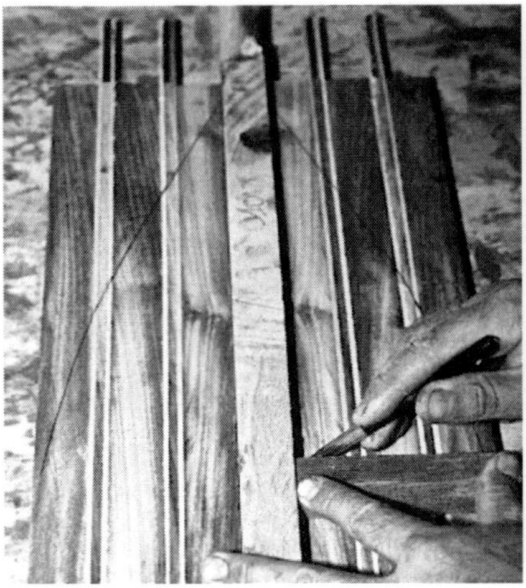

Laminations - thin strips of timber which are joined and glued together, often using a mix of hard and soft timbers. This can often create a visually appealing result, especially in the creation of ornamental paddles. Laminations can be used in both the blade and the shaft, or one and not the other.

Assessing a Timber Paddle

Very thin glue lines between laminates will indicate a stronger finish.

Wide gaps between laminates will indicate that the timbers have not been butted up hard against each other during curing. Adhesion between timbers is essential.

The greater the number of laminations, the stronger the paddle will be.

Check for wood defects such as knots, resin pockets, short grain shakes and warping. All of these will cause weak-spots which will be prone to breakage.

Look for a well-made, long tapering splice on the shaft. This will ensure good shaft strength in a uniform length from the neck to the grip.

Check the quality of the varnish and the lay-up of the glass on the blade. Check for air pockets. Pay close attention to the edging and blade tip regarding the seal and finish. Is the edging synthetic (resin) or fibreglassed hardwood, and is it sufficient protection for the blade?

Hardwoods - Softwoods

Hardwoods include all the broad-leafed groups of tree species; eucalypts, oaks, meranti etc. Softwoods include all the cone bearing species (conifers) pine, spruce and fir trees. Hardwoods are not necessarily hard or softwoods, soft. These general terms are *biological classifications* and are given to describe the general qualities of the wood and in particular its resistance to impact. However, do not put too much faith in this, as Balsa wood, one of the softest and lightest of timbers, is classified as a hardwood!

The thin laminate strips of timber are rough cut to a template shape.
Using a belt sander, the blade is smoothed over. Once the shaping is completed, the paddle is hand sanded with a block. Almost ready to have the final sealing coats of epoxy or varnish.

In this process, the quality of the water-proof glue is essential for ensuring the longevity of the paddle. The quality of the join or laminating performed by the craftsperson is also critical. Many paddle manufacturers use a combination of hard and soft woods, primarily to keep the weight to a minimum while relying on the strength of the lamination and the hardwoods to provide strength.

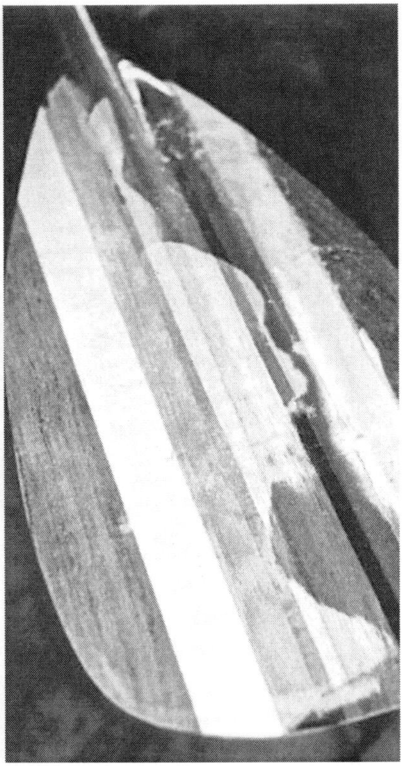

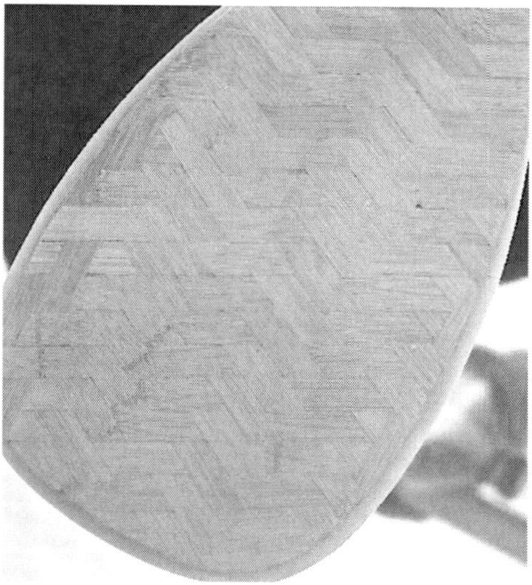

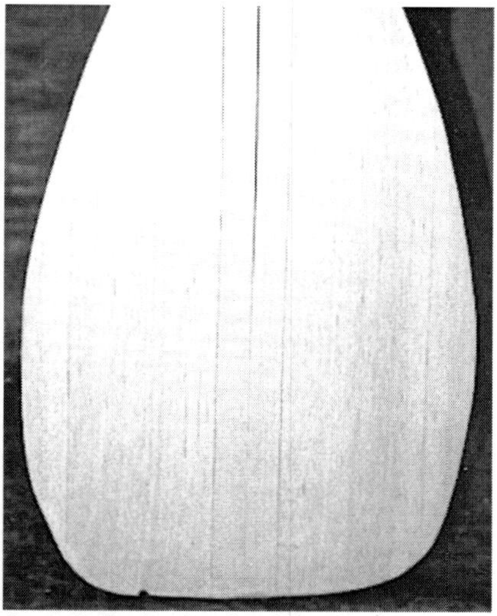

Laminated Bamboo paddle. Balsa blade, hardword shaft of ash with a carbon stringer dividing the laminates. Balsa is a hardwood, but you would never guess it. Hard to work with it, but lightweight, it is often laminated with carbon fibre and epoxy. Below: Cook Island mangrove paddle using different 'shades'. Mangroves grow not only beside the ocean but also thrive inland and even at elevation. 'Green' mangrove tend to be heavier, grow near the water and have higher water content. 'Silver' mangrove tend to be lighter, grow away from the ocean and have less water, sometimes laminated together, green for shaft and silver for the blade. Tahitian paddle made from mangrove; lightweight, fibrous, strong and flexible.

***Bob Zaveral* from East Coast USA, *ZRE* all carbon paddles, some of the finest made. Note the different widths. The paddle on the right includes an inlay of screen printed silk.**

All Carbon Paddles

Carbon paddles began their push onto paddle sports in a meaningful way during the mid 1980s. However, it wasn't until the mid to late 90s, when the popularity of the sport increased in Canada and the East Coast of America, did the notion of using all carbon paddles in team outrigger canoes take on any real consideration. This was due in part to the large number of river marathon paddlers entering the sport, bringing with them their views on the way things should be. This ultimately created a mild clash of cultural standpoints. *Walter Guild* commented, '*If they want to sign up for this sport, that's great, but not if they're here to change it. If they see something they don't like, then they have the option to not be a part of it.*'

The benefits of all carbon paddles are simply stiffness and lightness. At the low end of the scale, a carbon paddle can weigh in at a mere 9oz and be as rigid as an iron bar. Arguments for the use of these paddles are largely a matter of personal choice over preferred 'feel', some measured performance improvement (but not always) and budget. For the most part, the carbon paddles are more expensive than their timber counterparts.

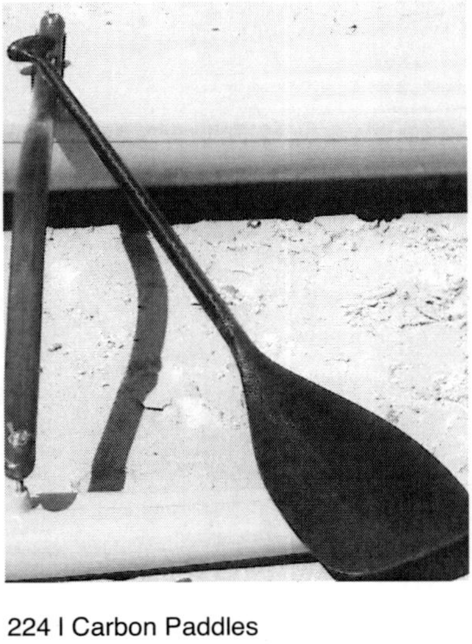

A *Black Bart* carbon paddle; another East Coast USA. Ironically, one of the biggest contributions the elite carbon paddle makers of East Coast USA made to the sport of va`a racing, was in providing new ideas on blade shapes and refined designs in general, which in time were adopted by many timber va`a paddle makers.

The notion of using carbon paddles for ruddered solo wa`a was a popular consideration during the formative days of their development in the mid 1990s (supplied predominantly by East Coast manufacturers *ZRE* and *Barton*). But the Hawaiians resisted the temptation to move quickly to use them within team wa`a on the grounds of 'tradition'.

Carbon paddles were quickly embraced by OC1 and OC2 paddlers. Kailua-Kona 1995.

Rules relating to the materials permitted in the construction of paddles vary around the world, though for the most part, anything goes. Initial reactions included the HCRA in 1998, passing a 'Wood Only' policy for the State of Hawai`i, which related to their regatta events where koa wa`a are used. This raised some interesting anomalies due in part to the fact that synthetic glues, edges and neck reinforcing were commonplace. The O`ahu Hawaiian Canoe Racing Association moved to implement a '51%' ruling, which stated that 51% of the paddle must be constructed from wood.

The 2004 OHCRA and HCRA race rules stated; *'Paddles must be single bladed and shaped of wood only. However, the paddle used for racing may have a protective or supportive (strengthening) covering which may be fibrous, kevlar, carbon fibre, etc. The paddle may have an edging or prosthesis for protection on the bottom or sides. The paddle may have laminated (horizontally or vertically) synthetic materials (kevlar, etc.) for strength and support.'*

Though Australia, in 1996 moved to allow the use of all carbon paddles, teams continued to favour the use of timber and hybrid composite paddles. The use of a carbon paddle for solo or duo outrigger craft is easily justified; however their virtues are somewhat less valid in terms of use within a team wa`a.

California, East Coast America and Canada permit the use of synthetic paddles. However, composite or all light-weight all timber paddles remain the favoured construction because of the added 'flex' in the timber shaft and the greater resistance to breaking when in contact with the wa`a.

'In my opinion the weight of the canoe and load on the paddler is a very serious consideration regarding which paddle material to pick. Remember that along with being light, carbon paddles are extremely stiff. If the shaft of a carbon paddle cannot flex, then the load from the blade is transferred further up the system, to you. Your body's joints, first your wrist, then elbow and shoulder, can be stressed and injured. It is very important not to use a blade that is too big for you when using stiffer shafts, especially if loads will be varying on the paddle such as open ocean, up wind, sprint turns, starts etc.

You may find that you can offset the strain of stiffer paddles by reducing the blade size and actually get the paddle deeper in the water. I personally prefer wood in the six man canoes. With the added weight of the canoe, it allows for a certain amount of flex in the shaft to take place and relieve some stress on the body.

There are some disadvantages to light paddles and also in ultra-stiff paddles. I have used them all, but would not make a blanket statement like "The lighter the better; always" not that light and stiff aren't great, there's more to it than that.' Walter Guild.

Carbon paddles being used by *Team Hawai`i* Hamilton Island 1997. At the end of the race they concluded that they were ultimately too 'hard' on the body and hands in the context of team wa`a racing.

So far as team wa`a racing is concerned, I am yet to be convinced that super lightweight, super stiff carbon paddles are superior to the light weight, timber paddle whose shaft has a reasonable degree of flex, especially over the virtues of a hybrid paddle. No world-class wa`a team uses all carbon paddles, period. Therefore, to argue for their choice is to fly in the face of expert opinion.

In 1995, *Greg Barton* predicted that, *'If the rules do change and allow carbon fibre paddles in all OC-6 races, I will switch over immediately. I predict that all the top teams would switch to carbon within a few years.'* This has not been the case even where carbon paddles are permitted.

The argument that light has to be superior, always, has been discounted by most of the best paddlers, who genuinely prefer some discernable weight to give the paddle a degree of inertia during the recovery phase. The notion of zero shaft flex is also considered a negative, giving the paddle a lifeless feeling with no recoil at the exit phase of the stroke when load is released from the blade.

Where paddlers predominantly train and race in 'flat' water conditions by virtue of where they live, they have nurtured the use of carbon paddles. Directly opposed

to this, rough water ocean paddlers almost without exception have reverted back to all timber or hybrid paddles. The argument about which is better comes down to a preference for using the right tool for the right job. Supply and demand being what it is, the vast majority of smaller Pacific islands do not use carbon paddles, period. In short, their use is confined to the more affluent areas of the world where river canoe racing and flatter conditions are prevalent.

'It's okay to advertise the merits of an ultra light paddle, but to imply that reduced weight will save energy channelled into paddling harder or efficiently is incorrect. I have an uncomfortable feeling about the reasoning. Many paddlers prefer a little heavier paddle in ocean swells and wind. The weight helps their swing and thus the rhythm.'
Al Ching.

Flex Appeal

It was concluded towards the end of the 1990s, that the ideal va`a paddle should have a super stiff blade and neck area to prevent 'flex' and morphing of the blade shape, and that the shaft should have a degree of inherent flex. Hence the creation of 'hybrid' paddles.

There are two critical stress areas where flex can occur on a paddle, at the neck and further up the shaft, particularly just below the point where the lower hand grips. If the neck and shaft flex as you apply pressure during your 'pull', it's like compressing a spring and this energy will remain stored in the paddle, until you release it when the pull is relaxed.

Essentially you've redirected and reduced the torque in the most powerful and efficient phase of your stroke, the pull, only to release that torque in the exit phase where it's all wasted energy.

Todd Bradley **and** ***Ron Grabbe*** **using** ***ZRE's*** **in Hawai`i 1996 on** ***Kaiwi Challenger*** **OC1s.** ***Ron*** **at 6'7" has a visible bend in the top third of the paddle's shaft despite the carbon.**

Some paddlers notice a 'snappier' movement of their solo or duo wa`a as a result of using a carbon paddle, because of the added stiffness. A flexing blade creates an inefficient shape on the blade face which allows water to slip away and creates a fluctuation in the pressure/vacuum ratio between the front and rear faces of the blade. This causes the blade to flutter. While a stiff paddle is best for energy transfer, a paddle whose shaft has a slight amount of flex is easier on the body.

'When I used a pure carbon, I used to have pain in my joints at night, even when I wasn't on the water,' said Mike Judd. 'Since I changed to a paddle with a wood shaft, I haven't had any pain.' Walter Guild expressed a similar opinion.*'The biggest thing about these paddles is the flex of the wood shaft with the efficient entry and exit of a very thin blade.'*

Taken to extremes, many islands of Oceania construct paddles from mangrove, which is flexible and strong. The paddlers of Tahiti and her islands use this timber extensively, though they do use a small quantity of other timbers such as *Western Red Cedar, Mango,* and *Monkey Pod* to add some variety to their appearance and performance.

The added flex within the shaft, suits the Tahitian style of paddling, thereby cushioning the joints in particular, especially over the super long-distances for which they are renowned.

***Dave Chun's*, *Dave's 99 Hybrid* the 'original' *hybrid* model which went into production in June of 2001. *Dave's* pioneering work with *hybrid paddles* provided the missing link between too soft and too stiff in terms of paddle feel. He has combined a super stiff blade face and neck area with a shaft which provided a comfortable level of flex and at a weight which provided enough inertia in the recovery without being too light or too heavy.**

Wood Composite Paddles – Hybrids

Advances in materials and construction techniques have led to the development of 'hybrid' paddles, which use a mix of timber and synthetic materials. They are now used by many of the top crews. *Walter Guild* describes wood composite paddles as, *'The next generation or level of paddles in outrigger.'* Wood composites are similar to traditional all wood paddles in that both have solid wood blades and sometimes shafts.

Where the two construction methods differ is in the use of reinforcing composite skins such as fibreglass, kevlar, or carbon fibre on the blade. The combination of the lightweight core and composite skin allows the builders to use lightweight woods, usually Balsa, as the core of the blade. The combination of a light weight core and composite skin produces paddles which are lighter, stronger and more durable than traditional wood paddles.

To a large extent, wa`a paddle manufacturers were motivated to start building wood composites because of requests from their sponsored athletes.

'We wanted light paddles, because little things count when you are battling with another crew', said *Mike Judd* of *Lanikai. 'The real light, all wood paddles were for race day only, and weren't very durable even with limited use. It seemed like a waste to throw away a paddle after only a few uses. So we asked the Hawaiian builders if they could come up with something light, yet durable enough for everyday use. We felt strongly that we wanted to develop something with our builders, rather than look outside the sport.'*

The Weight Game

'After five hours on the water, you want something light'. Kai Opua steers women Jackie Taylor. Wood composites generally weigh between 14-18oz, depending on the blade surface area, overall length, and the particulars of the manufacturer's construction method. Weight reductions of 25% are common when compared to similar size wood paddles.

'They are light enough. They aren't as light as a full carbon, but lighter than a woodie. They are right in the middle. The extra weight can be user friendly into the wind. They have just enough weight to keep them on track. The carbons sometimes fly around.' Jim Foti Lanikai.

Dave Chun **finishing of a** ***hybrid blade*** **which has just come out of the 'mould'.**

Paddlers often guess the weight of their wood composites as much lower than they actually are. Most of the weight reduction comes from the blade portion of these paddles. Typically, they are blade light, meaning the blade weighs less than the shaft. Traditional wood paddles tend to be blade heavy, unless they have a small blade surface. Blade light paddles have a quick, balanced feel to them. Compared to a blade heavy paddle of the exact same weight, most people will guess that the blade light paddle is lower in weight.

Durability

With its composite skin and synthetic edge around the blade, wood composite paddles are generally more durable than all wood paddles. The use of epoxy resins and aerospace skin allows the paddle manufacturers to utilise high performance technology from other applications such as auto racing, airplanes, and space travel.

Les Look from *Makana Alii* said, *'It's been a long road experimenting with our Ultra-Lite paddles. I spent a lot of time talking with surfboard makers, boat builders, etc., about the characteristics of composite material and epoxy.' Les* estimates that it takes about 40% more time and twice the material to build one of his Ultra-Lites.

Static load testing at the *Kialoa* shop has yielded data which suggest that their *Hybrid blades* are up to 25% stronger under compression loads than their wood paddles.

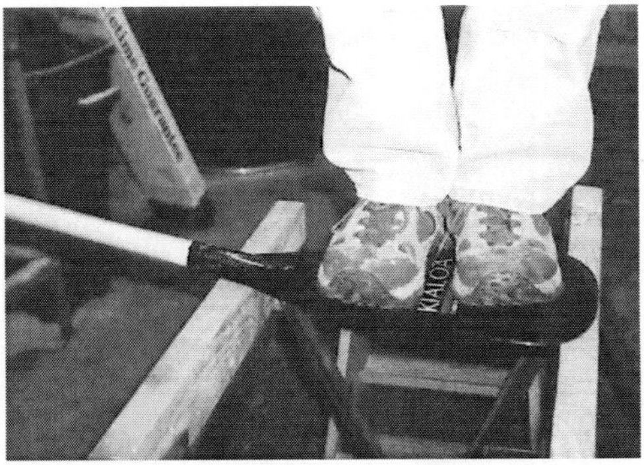

Hanging weights from the tips of their blades, a typical wood paddle failed at around 76lbs (34kg). *Hybrids* were able to handle weights of 108lbs (49kg), at which point the wood shafts began to fail. While it is difficult to translate this data into real world paddling, in the test environment, wood composites are proving to be stronger than traditional paddles.

Dave 'stress tests' a kialoa hybrid. 'Our methods were rather crude. Load a bucket full of weights and see when it breaks, drop the blade edges on a cement floor, swing the blade into a wooden post, shovel snow! We found that our Hybrids were at least 30% stronger than our all-wood. blades.'

Will They Make You Faster?

Data to support the claim that a certain paddle or characteristic of a paddle, makes a paddler faster is difficult to substantiate. Variables such as effort of the paddler, water conditions, wind direction, or duration of the event make it difficult to control and say that the paddle is the sole reason for any speed difference.

Testing by *Kialoa* in sections ranging from 1 to 20 minutes yielded data, which suggested that with paddles ranging in weight between 10-24oz, weight did not make a significant difference in speed. The surface area and/or design of the blade seemed to be a more significant contributor to speed changes than the weight of the paddle.

So will a lightweight wood composite paddle make you faster? Probably not. However, when the difference between first and second place in a 40.8 mile race is decided by a mere two seconds, the top racers want to know that their paddles are as light as those of their competitors.

The Evolution of Paddling Techniques

1820-Missionary Intervention. Purity and Parity Remain in Tahiti But not Hawai`i.

Prior to the arrival of the missionaries in the Hawaiian Islands in 1820, Hawaiians clearly had their own defined paddling style. For over fifty years however, when there was an effective ban on paddling, the intricate nuances of the Hawaiian paddling style were partially lost. Hawaiian wa`a paddling technique was introduced back into Hawai`i not through written text, but ideas passed down orally - a tribal dissemination of knowledge. It has been suggested that the so called 'Hawaiian Style' of paddling that was reintroduced, was not an accurate copy of the original, given that most of the elders had past on.

In contrast, on the islands of French Polynesia a ban was never imposed, so their technique and style remained true. However, in Tahiti the process kept evolving and there was less adherence to tradition. In this sense, two major style of paddling have been created from the two va`a cultures.

So, you know what perfect paddling technique is. You've read the books, seen the video, listened to the flat water paddlers, had the dragon-boaters set you straight on a few pointers, you're good to go. Now, sit on mechanical rodeo bull in a wind tunnel, hang on by the skin of your butt and have your buddies throw buckets of cold water at you. Now, start paddling. Hopefully some of what you've been told will come in handy. *Outrigger Australia*, Hamilton Island, a better rough water crew you will not find – watermen to the core, surfers, paddle boarders, bodysurfers, ski paddlers, lifeguards, they can do it all.

This is a legacy which remains to this day, with an ever continuing melding of styles from many different cultures including Hawaiian, Tahitian and European.

In the early 1880's, va`a racing was introduced to the July 14th *Bastille Day* events in Tahiti, however lagoon va`a racing had been a way of life prior to this. Until 1976, this was the only official va`a race in the region. From 1945 to 1965, there was a gradual increase in the development of organised va`a racing with the creation of ten new clubs on the island of Tahiti. During the early 70s, the sport grew rapidly and the *Ligue des Pirogues* was established in 1973 to formerly administer the growth of the sport.

Ultimately, no reasonable discussion regarding va`a paddling technique and style can be complete without some understanding of its evolution and acknowledgment of key events and interventions. For the most part, so called 'experts' often take a far too narrow view of the issue; micro-managing the various phases of the stroke, seeking perfection while often missing the big picture and what make some crews 'elite' over others.

Many, if not most, of the world-class, rough water, ocean crews have had little or no 'technique' training. Their skills are largely self taught and honed through a way of life dedicated to ocean paddling. This is often in stark contrast to the flat-water kayak paddler, who emanates from a culture obsessed with technique, style and the science of paddling. This is not to suggest that the analysis of sound va`a paddling technique and styles have not been considered – far from it, but there is also a great deal of intuition involved.

Yardsticks | Moloka`i to O`ahu

A simple yardstick we can use to illustrate the evolution of the finer points of the sport of wa`a is the Moloka`i to O`ahu race in Hawai`i. If we look at the results, we can see some of the significant advancements and trends.

1952 -1973 *Waikiki Surf*

Between 1952 and 1963 *Waikiki Surf club* won the Moloka`i to O`ahu eight times and were the dominate influential force in Hawaiian wa`a racing. *Waikiki Surf* was beaten in 1964 by *Kailua Civic CC* and *Outrigger CC* in 1965. They won again in 1966 in huge seas and *Outrigger CC* won in

***Waikiki Surf* 1996 2nd place finishers.**

1967-68. 1969-1973 *Waikiki Surf* and *Healani* were overall winners of the Moloka`i to O`ahu race and both were dominate influential forces in Hawai`i.

This ended a period of older traditional paddling techniques, paddles and wa`a styles as things were about to alter radically.

1974-1994 *Outrigger Canoe Club* Dominate But Tahitians Make Their Move

This twenty-year span produced the most significant changes the sport had ever experienced. The period was dominated by *Outrigger Canoe Club* of Hawai`i but for the first time, overseas and mainland USA teams also won.

Outrigger Canoe Club's 10 year dominance of the Moloka`i Hoe between 1974 and 1994 - *Lanikai* in 1974, was subjected to critical 'local' analysis, which concluded that their success was due to their 'money and equipment'. *Walter Guild* retorted that the equipment was available to anyone, and *'...if you think Outrigger will win due to these tangibles, they will win...it's the intangibles that fuel a winning team; commitment, tradition and expectations; goals in common; and homogeneity in background and motivation. These are open to any club.'*

Dominance by a Hawaiian club was one issue, but it was the 10 Moloka`i open mens line honours won by crews from Tahiti, California, Australia and Illinois - more if you include koa division wins, which hurt the most. The following rationalisations were used to lessen the pain; Australians were 'all ironman water athletes', the crews from California and Illinois were 'Olympic calibre athletes and all-star teams', and the Tahitians were 'heavily subsidised by the government where paddling is a paid vocation'.

The last five years of the 1970s saw some of the most significant and contentious changes to va`a paddling technique and equipment. Hawaiian paddlers were confronted with the Tahitians joining the world stage for the first time at the Moloka`i Hoe of 1975. Over the course of the next four years, their participation and successes shook the foundations of a sport Hawaiians considered their own. For all that is good and noble regarding 'traditional' Hawaiian wa`a paddling techniques, it took other regions of the world, less constrained by tradition and more concerned with speed to break the mold.

At the start of the 1975 Moloka`i to O`ahu canoe race, three Tahitian teams took on the Hawaiians in their prestigious event. *Fred Hemmings* who at the time was steering the *Outrigger Canoe Club* team recalls, '*Three Tahitian teams blew off the line in a sprint with a stroke count of what must have been 65-70 strokes per minute. We were sprinting too, our stroke count went from the "traditional" 42 strokes a minute up to what was the incredible pace of about 48-50 strokes per minute. By Lauu Point, the three Tahitian teams had at least a 300 yard lead...we eventually ran them down in the Channel. The*

Tahitians spawned great revelations in canoe paddling. Hawaiian 'tradition' was replaced with innovation and new techniques.'

1975 *Maire Nui* Tahiti (foreground) take on the Hawaiians for the first time at the Moloka`i Hoe.

This was the first time Tahitian teams had entered the Moloka`i to O`ahu race and in doing so the legacy and legend of the Tahitian paddler was born. *Maire Nui* won the fibreglass division in 5:47:33 and their win was far from 'lucky', they had already been famous throughout French Polynesia since the club's founding in 1948. Not only did they win in their first attempt in the fibreglass division, but they also went on to win again in 76, 77 and 78 in the koa division.

Another Tahitian crew, *Te Oropaa*, won the fibreglass division in 76, in 7:54:40 ahead of *Maire Nui*. To add insult to cultural injury, this year's course was the longest ever run, 55.6 miles. Putting their success into greater perspective, at this time no formalised ocean distance racing existed in Tahiti. It was not until 1978 that a formalised distance race was run between the island of Tahiti and Moorea and back.

How did these paddlers train, what paddles did they use, what was their paddling technique, how did they go so fast? Consequently, a great deal analysis and melding of ideas between Hawaiian and Tahitian paddlers followed. These years were the most significant and affected the consciousness of every wa`a paddler throughout the Hawaiian Islands.

The Tahitians presented to the Hawaiians a paddling stroke which required less body motion, less reach out in front and less pull back past the hip. In addition, their stroke rates were way beyond that of any Hawaiian team and they used paddles that were uniquely teardrop in shape, with smaller blade area. If this wasn't enough, they introduced new, sleeker racing va`a, shaped by Tahitians living in Hawai`i, which in time would effectively be banned by Hawaiian rulings.

Fundamentally, these wins hit the Hawaiians right where their pride resided; ocean skills, athleticism and knowledge of what was 'their' sport. Yet if we go back to *Walter Guild's* comments regarding the intangibles, narrowing excellence down to one factor is to have little or no understanding of what it takes to win. Credit should be given to whoever wins for whatever reason, provided it is in keeping with the sport and within the bounds of the rules.

Racing in Papeete during the July Festivals.

From paddle to va`a design, through to the act of paddling itself, the paddlers of French Polynesia together with their coaches, mentors and artisans, have elevated the sport of the va`a to a level of technical excellence and obsession. All other regions of the Pacific can only marvel and learn. While for many of us the sport is a part of our lifestyle, for the paddlers of this region it is more a 'way of life' that carries with it much greater levels of meaning and *raison d'etre*.

'In no other country in the world is outrigger canoe paddling, or any other sport, as important as it is in the Tahitian Archipelago. We cannot yet ask why this is. Yet we should revel in the fact that it is so, and be inspired.' Dr Hugh Fisher.

Maire Nui

The Legend of *Maire Nui*

Located in the village of Tautira on the island of Tahiti, *Maire Nui* had dominated va`a racing in Tahiti since 1948 and was undefeated in the V6 division for roughly thirty years. As a consequence of *Maire Nui's* brazen onslaught in Hawaiian waters between 1975 and 1978 - and *Te Oropaa* in 76, in Hawai`i there was an inevitable feeling of respect and admiration mixed with resentment and disbelief.

Walter Guild once commented, *'No team can come here and in their first attempt expect to win Molokai, unless you're from Tahiti.'* These Tahitian successes can be considered on several levels. Significantly, the Hawaiian stroke was uniquely and fundamentally bound up by tradition with paddle designs. Alteration of either was to question the elders, tradition and all that is Hawaiian wa`a paddling. The 'how to' aspects of paddling were something of a taboo, not to be messed with.

Tahitian Paddlers - Hawaiian Steerers

Tahiti had used Hawaiian steerers over time and as a consequence lost respect from some. They formed the opinion that the Tahitians were not good rough water paddlers and didn't have steerers with enough skill to deal with the conditions. However, having a 'local' steerer familiar with 'local' conditions and the necessary skills is universally accepted as advantageous and many crews have taken this same approach over the years, especially overseas crews.

In more recent years, in 2003, the *Honolulu Advertiser* following *Tahiti's Rai* 2002 win, commented, *'Conditions for last year's race (2002) were considered to be relatively flat, something that may have worked to the Tahitians advantage.' Lewis Laughlin's* response confirmed the belief, *'I don't know if it's a tradition, but people like to say that it has to be flat for Tahiti to win.' Tom Conner*, a veteran Hawaiian steersman, who steered Tahiti's *Faa`a* in the Moloka`i Hoe victories of 1993 and '94 commented, *'If it's rough, only one guy needs to know how to surf, that's the steersman and Lewis knows how to surf. The other five can just go and go.' Conner's* involvement in steering *Faa`a* after having been a loyal steerer for *Outrigger Canoe Club* Hawai`i, was justifiable as he had married into a Tahitian family. This practice has now stopped and the Tahitians continue to dominate the Moloka`i race.

Californian Impact of 1978

As if the Tahitian wins were not contentious enough, the participation and success of a team of canoe and kayak paddlers from mainland USA in 1978 created more issues. They challenged the sport from a variety of angles including paddle design, fitness levels and the notion of professionalism. For all that is good and noble regarding 'traditional' Hawaiian paddling techniques, it took other regions of the world, less constrained by tradition, to create a shift in thinking.

Billy Whitford is one of the sports true 'off island' legends. His lateral thinking contributed greatly to making the sport more ergonomic, the introduction of 'canoe' paddles and new paddling techniques. He was also extraordinarily supportive in mentoring and coaching the most successful women's crew in the history of the sport, _Offshore California._

In 1978, while the Tahitians won the koa division of the Moloka`i Hoe, the fibreglass division was won by *Blazing Paddles*, a Californian team who used what were considered to be very radical paddles at the time. The paddles were lightweight, short, had smaller blade areas and single bends with 'T' grips that were borrowed from Olympic class canoes. Attempts were made to ban this type of paddle. They were abandoned when it was discovered that the *Bishop Museum* in Honolulu had drawings and artefacts which included T-Grip paddles.

The Californian's technique was considered an 'Olympic Technique' where the blade is placed close to the wa`a and enters and exits vertically. The power was generated by vertical downward power, a technique which was adopted from marathon river canoe paddling. At this time, the blade areas were smaller, had a square rather than tear drop shape and included lay back - a bend in the shaft. They did however, still pull the blade past the level of the hip, so the handle would be level with the stomach as recounted by _Billy Whitford_ and their stroke rate was marginally less than 60/min. Over 60/min he believed at that time, was excessive, labelling it 'Slippy Dippy' paddling with all elbows and wrist - the paddles merely churning the water.

1980s Hawaiians Begin Radical Change

At this point, Tahitian, Mainland American and Hawaiian paddling techniques were all very different from each other, each one based on a different theory and belief. The Tahitians were going purely on instinct and evolving their technique naturally. Mainland Americans were considering what they had learned through Olympic canoeing and river canoe marathon paddling. While the Hawaiians continued to hold on to their traditional techniques and paddles.

Traditional Hawaiian notions of paddling technique were being challenged head on and not within Hawai`i, but from regions where tradition was not going to stand in the way of speed. By the early 1980s the Hawaiians, under siege since the mid 70s, had little option but to rethink everything they knew about the wa`a stroke and the paddles they used.

The 1988 winning Molokai Hoe crew *Outrigger Canoe Club* Hawai`i. They set a new record time of 5:08:11 in relatively calm channel seas. They beat the 1984 record by more than 10 minutes, also set by *Outrigger*. Coach *Steve Scott* remains as one of the clubs most successful coaches. The crew included, *Kainoa Downing, Marc Haine, Bruce Black, Mark Rigg, Scott Rolles, Tom Conner, Chris Kincaid, Walter Guild* and *Keone Downing.*

For the most part, the Tahitian style of paddling dominated the minds of paddlers, as teams moved towards higher stroke rates and even consider the use of double bends as favoured by Tahitians. Clearly adopting any one particular style of paddling, makes it necessary to consider the entire package. Look at your paddling technique and style holistically. Paddle, paddler and paddling technique - and canoe/va'a, must all be suited to ensure the absolute best performance.

However, it wasn't until 1981 that Hawaiian teams began serious experimentation with the open river canoe paddle designs as introduced by the Californians. Gradually at first, then in a sudden a dramatic shift, traditional designs were cast aside in favour of what amounted to a far superior design; lighter, more efficient and ergonomically pleasing to use. The issue now became one of blending these paddles with paddling technique.

1990s - Aussie Men Make Their Mark Using a Fast, Aggressive Hybrid Stroke

The Australian's win in the Moloka`i Hoe races of 1991 *Outrigger Australia* and 1992 *Panamuna,* once again raised questions regarding technique, but also levels of physical fitness and professionalism. The sport had only been in Australia since 1978, they were using a couple of imported Hawaiian 4 person surfing wa`a and the *Malia* imported in 1981.

Australia's *Panamuna* men led by *Grant Kenny* on the way to Waikiki and the finishing line in 1992.

Australian's initial interest was purely that it is an ocean sport and they would love to compete in Hawai`i and ultimately win this prestigious event. There were no limits of traditional 'does and don'ts' and no cultural affinity with the wa`a whatsoever for these brazen 'Aussies'. In many ways, this allowed them to start with a blank slate as they took paddling technique to another level.

Both *Outrigger Australia* and *Panamuna* crews were comprised of elite surf ski and kayak paddlers, who brought with them unique ocean skills and levels of fitness rarely seen at the event. It was yet another cultural wake up call for the Hawaiians and indeed the Tahitians. Such was the physical prowess and ocean skills of these athletes, technique and style seemed almost a secondary factor in their ability to make a wa`a move so fast. Though their sense of 'timing' was less than impeccable, their technique was aggressive, explosive and ultimately unique to the sport. In addition, they used a fast stroke rate of upwards of 70 strokes per minute, faster than the Tahitian crews of the time. They used paddles similar to those favoured by the Californians and a variation of the Olympic style paddling technique incorporating greater elements of surf ski twist and rotation.

A magazine article following the 1992 Australian victory quoted, *'Then in 1991, the Outrigger Canoe Club of Australia won, broadening the competitive horizon by a few thousand miles. "Aussies are year-round professionals,"* says *Kaakuahiwi. 'To me, that's taken away from what the local people have been used to. For us, paddling is a lifetime thing, not something so painful that after a couple of years, you don't want to do it anymore. We have family programs. But the way the best crews train is so advanced now that if we (Native Hawaiians) want to win again, we'll have to start looking for thinner boys and thinner girls. And there goes our tradition. You don't see too many thin Hawaiians.'*

Putting the wins of the Australians into some perspective, most crew members, especially those from *Panamuna* had barely spent any time whatsoever paddling a wa`a. Some had as little as 12 months experience, while others had at most 3 years, pitted against paddlers with 20 years plus wa`a experience. You have to ask yourself, why did they go so fast? Experience in a wa`a or just the experience of a lifetime of being on the ocean and making a wide variety of paddlecraft move quickly?

Greater body rotation as used by surf ski and kayak paddlers was beginning to make inroads into outrigger wa`a paddling. Much of the emphasis centred on reach and power at the front of the stroke, with an early exit at the hip. This allowed for the generation of power from the larger muscle groups by rotating around the spine, with less emphasis on the downward drive as promoted in river paddling.

Faa`a Tahiti Learn from Australians

As a result of *Outrigger* Australia's win in 1991, *Gabby Lou* - father of *Lewis Laughlin*, of the *Faa`a Canoe Club* of Tahiti at the time, took notes and studied the Australian paddling style. He then blended this with the Tahitian style to create a winning technique which would help them win the Moloka`i Hoe in 1993 and 1994.

Lewis Laughlin is one of the world's finest contemporary va`a paddlers. His status in Tahiti is one of a true champion amongst champions. He is a master of rudderless va`a hoe paddling and a multiple winner of the country's toughest race the _Super Aito_ between Moorea and Tahiti, and a multiple Moloka`i Hoe winner having also won the solo surf ski event. He brings with him to any va`a team, experience, professionalism and confidence.

In 1993, for the first time in the history of the event, the time went below the 5hr mark with a crossing in 4:55:27 setting a new record. The crew included; *Tuura Mairao, Armand Tavaotaha, Lewis Laughlin, Milton Laughlin, Yannick Aaama, Karyl Maoni, Jean-Pierre Barff, Ralph Teariki* and Hawaiian steerer, *Tom Conner*. They paddled a *Bradley* wa`a built and designed by *Sonny Bradley*. *Tom Conner* was a 9 time winner prior to this and record holder, as steerer for *Outrigger Canoe Club* Hawai`i. Within French Polynesia, *Faa`a* dominated during the late 1980s and through to the mid 1990s.

Pirae Va`a Mobil and *Maitai Shell* Tahiti

Pirae Va`a Mobil* supported by *President Gaston Floss* dominated the late 1990s locally, with *Fare Ara* from the Island of Huahine also winning several major events. *Lewis Laughlin,* a team member during those *Faa`a victories, had a short stretch with *Maitai Shell,* then returned in 2002 with his three-year-old team *Rai,* to win the Molokai Hoe with an all-Tahitian team. *Matai Shell* renewed their dominance mid 2000 and continue to do so.

Tuura Mairao – not Tahitian but from one of the outer lying archipelagos (The Austral Islands) fabled for its warriors. _Mairao_ was a crew member with _Pirae_ after paddling with _Faa`a._ He is the stuff of myths in French Polynesia.

***Pirae Va`a Mobil*. Supported by *President Gaston Floss*, *Pirae* dominated va`a racing for a five year period during the latter part of the 90s and early into 2000.**

Top: Pirae Va`a and below, *Team Shell*. A young wahine paddles her va`a, testimony to being a natural extension of the Tahitian way of life for so many. Bora Bora.

Teams such as *Maitai Shell* are in direct competition to the *Mobil* sponsored *Pirae club.* They have waged their own war on domination of the Tahitian racing scene and certainly did so during parts of early 2000. In 2004 *Shell* spent roughly AUD $70,000 to participate at Australia's Hamilton Cup, but struggled with the unfamiliar conditions. Back home, by 2006 they had regained their dominance and have remained so to the present day, including a record breaking Moloka`i Hoe race time.

Throughout French Polynesia, the sport has grown in prominence into a fully-fledged national sport. The involvement of the government, major corporate companies and sponsors has helped it reach new levels of professionalism and excellence.

Other Factors

In *Canoe Racing and Paddling in Hawai`i* composed by *Annette Kau Summerlin, University of Hawai`i* May 1994, California's *Billy Whiford* said *'We use the cheapest paddles because moving a boat goes back to the engine, the machine. Basically we use a 9.5" blade. The handle top should come to the sternum.'* This seems a little dismissive of the importance of the paddle, yet *Billy's* crew in 1978 introduced the single bend, 'T' gripped blade which was a critical element of their success. He made this comment while coach for *Offshore California* women's crew, who since 1986 has won 8 Na Wahine O Ke Kai, Moloka`i races.

Around the same time, *Annette Summerlin* interviewed *Rockne Freitas* of *Waikiki Surf Club*, Hawai`i. Incredulously he commented, *'We use the modified Tahitian-Hawaiian style stroke with a simultaneous entry, 12" of pull and 60 strokes per minute - racing stroke, 74 strokes per minute - power tens, and 80 strokes per minute -sprint rate. We use 10.5" blade with a straight handle- shaft, and a T-Top. The objective is to use the widest blade possible, eventually a 12.5" blade. The stroke technique is push, pull like a bench press, the power curve using your chest to exert power to bury the paddle deep vertically, then pulling with the latissimus dorsi, the large back muscles.'*

This was contrary to the way paddle design was headed. Not withstanding the calibre of athlete of *Offshore California's* crews, this was a surprisingly irreverent attitude, given that in 1978 the significance of the paddles used by *Blazing Paddles* was critical.

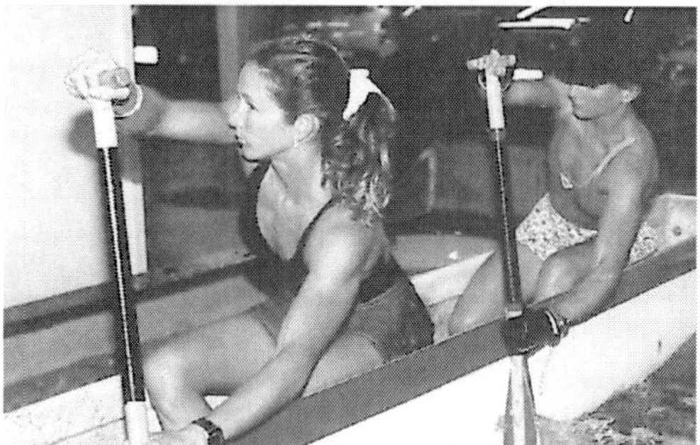

1995 Coach *Steve Scott*, *Outrigger CC* Hawai`i, puts his ladies through a tank training session. The mirror allows paddlers to 'mirror' image each other. Very clearly, by the mid 90s, the old Hawaiian style of paddling and paddle was out of favour if you wanted to go fast for long periods of time, though there was still emphasis on twist and getting low to the gunnel during the entry phase.

Other Paddle Sports

Many factors have acted upon the evolution of the va`a paddling stroke and none more so than its ever widening global participation. A proliferation of dragon boat paddlers entering the sport over the past fifteen years has seen a change of what they construe as a modification of their own unique technique to suit the va`a. Additionally, North Americans and Canadians who hail from Canadian canoeing backgrounds, have brought their own interpretation of the ideal va`a stroke.

What can be said of both dragon boat and Canadian canoeing is that both are predominantly flat water (sprint) sports, while va`a paddling is primarily an ocean endurance paddle sport. To what extent this matter is debatable, but as previously mentioned, you need more than just good technique to deal with the dynamics of the ocean.

Rough water paddling requires you 'switch-off' to external discomforts and keep swinging away, constantly adjusting each and every stroke to the nuances of the wa`a and the ocean. Ultimately it's a state of mind to which you either concede to or triumph over and no amount of theory will help you.

From 1995-2005 there has been a gradual refinement of paddles and of paddling techniques. Paddler makers are working with paddlers as shapers would work with surfers. Hawaiian paddlers and others are rising to the challenge by improving their fitness levels and improving their skill based by cross-training and racing solo wa`a. Subsequently, things learned racing alone can be brought back into the team wa`a. In some regards, paddler's are more accountable then ever before and whereas the 'team' was the critical issue in the past, there is more emphasis on the 'individual' having what it takes to make a wa`a go fast.

Lanikai Canoe Club 1995-2005

Lanikai CC were winners of the Moloka`i Hoe in 95, 96, 00, 04, 05 setting a new record of 4:54:05 in 2000. Their close relationship with Tahiti and regular visits to compete has put their reputation on the line many times, in a way that no other Hawaiian club has dared attempt. What they have learned, they have brought back to Hawai`i and vice-versa. This willingness to venture to Tahiti has earned them enormous respect among their peers in this region. *Jim Foti* in particular seems to have been one of the primary driving forces of the club together with brother, *John.*

The *Team New Zealand* - *Hawai`i* Factor

Team New Zealand was founded in 1998. By 2000 it became Team *New Zealand Hawai`i* and was a somewhat eclectic group of talented individuals who served to upset continuity between 2001 and 2005. They won in '01 by a mere 2 seconds ahead of *Lanikai* in 5:02:27 and took line honours again in '03. Their contribution can be measured in terms of a common purpose, significant sponsorship dollars and equipment support in a way which eclipsed most other crews, certainly *Lanikai CC*. However their level of athleticism and ocean skills are beyond reproach and in this sense they have reinforced the theory that team work is one thing, but individual talent is also critical.

Brothers *John* (left) and *Jim Foti* are amongst a small band of contemporary paddling icons who, over the past fifteen years in particular, have stamped their influence on the Hawaiian way of things. *Lanikai CC* located in Kailua, *O`ahu*, holds the three fastest ever recorded times for crossing the Kaiwi Channel since 1995. *Jim* steered all three and *John* was a crew member on each occasion. Also *Mike Pedersen*. Below Aussie Style *Outrigger Australia* Hamilton Is.

In Conclusion

The Hawaiian stroke was altered as a result of Tahitian influence and further modified by the incoming marathon river paddlers, the use of radically different paddles and a technique more conservative in its motion but more efficient.

This was subsequently improved again by the Australians and their aggressive, surf ski stroke which incorporated greater body rotation and

power generated through the torso. This being said, the Tahitian style remains fundamentally unique as a result of a reliance on the double-bend paddle in particular – though not always.

Added to this mix we have two distinct paddling styles, 'dynamic' and 'static' the latter more closely associated with some merits of the original Hawaiian style of paddling; hyper-extension, lowering of the torso to the gunnel during entry phase and use of body weight; 'static' more associated with power generated from powerful torso-rotation and a more upright position during the entry phase of the stroke.

Historically, the 2006 Moloka`i to O`ahu race, will long be remembered for the Tahitians domination of the event. They took out the top three positions with the winning crew, *Shell Va`a*, winning in a record time of 4:46:04, bettering *Lanakai* Canoe Clubs 2000 time of 4:50:31. This was a crushing victory and a smashing of the record, defeating the second Tahitian team of *Hititoa/Erai* by 14 minutes and 23 seconds. This is the largest winning margin since 1962 when *Waikiki Surf Club* finished ahead of *Lanikai* by 15 minutes. Using double bend paddles, 'typical' Tahitian paddling technique and rating at times in the high 70 strokes per minute in the hot, flat conditions, *Shell's* performance was supreme. Taken a step further, they were paddling a *Bradley* wa`a restricted to Hawaiian design specifications with which the crew was unfamiliar. The question should be asked, just how fast could their crossing have been if they were paddling a Tahitian va`a better suited to the days conditions?

Members of the winning crew were *Heiarii Mama, Karyl Maoni, Jason Ori, Jimmy Pirato, Lucien Tara, Vatea Taraufau, Bruno Tauhiro, Roland Teahui* and *David Tepava*. *'We don't go out to break records, we just try to go as fast as we can," Shell Va'a* coach *Gerard Teiva said. "But today, I guess God gave us the strength to get the record.'*

In 2005, *Shell Va`a* did not enter the Moloka`i Hoe, but set a record in the *Hawaiki Nui Va`a*. *'We won the big races in Tahiti, but we knew we had to win Moloka`i to prove we were the best,' Shell Va`a president Richel Moux* said.

Despite their record breaking time, the old adage of being 'professional' paddlers and that the conditions suited them were used dismissively to account for their achievement by some. Excuses for wins or losses are moot points when in the scheme of things, since the later part of the 1970s, the Tahitians have had to reluctantly conform to Hawaiian specifications. As a consequence they have had to race predominantly in unfamiliar Hawaiian wa`a and contend with numerous inconveniences, unfamiliarities, expenses, language barriers, xenophobia and prejudice by some of their counterparts. *Shell* went on to win again in 2007, 2008 and 2009. Just how much convincing some Hawaiian paddlers need that Tahitian paddlers are at the top of this sport baffles the mind.

The Moloka`i Hoe and Na Wahine O Ke Kai at days end are but 'local' races for every Hawaiian crew. For others, it's a logistic mine field full of adversity to be overcome even before the starting gun signals the start of the race. For every excuse made to account for such a victory, there are half a dozen more which could be presented to account for a loss.

Perplexingly, it is worth asking why the Tahitian way of paddling, whilst intriguing is all but ignored by Hawaiians, Australians, Californians and others, when they consistently prove their abilities over distance or short course events. Their achievements are often marvelled at; but rarely analysed or embraced by others.

Wahine Influence 1984 - 1996 *Offshore Cal*

No discussion regarding the influences on wa`a paddling would be complete without mention of the women's contribution and particularly the *Offshore California's* women's crews. Between 1984 and 1996, they won 10 Na Wahine O Ke Kai Moloka`i races. In the final winning streak race of 1996, considered their toughest, team members included, *Cathy Whitford, Honolulu, Hawai`i. Gina Aubrey, San Clemente, CA. Julie Wolfe, Lancaster, CA. Vicki Mills, San Clemente, CA. Donna Meyer, Honolulu, Hawai`i. Anna Olsson, Karlstad, Sweden. Sharon Attelsey, Newport Beach, CA. Dru Van Hengal, Santa Barbara, CA. JoJo Toeppner and Mindy Clark, Big Bear, CA.*

***Offshore California* 1996**

***JoJo Toeppner*, training on Lake Tahoe 1995. Photo *Daphne Hougard*.**

Criticised for being 'professional' athletes and 'kayakers' with only a passing interest in outrigger canoeing, the reaction to their wins among many Hawaiians was about as positive as America's *Lance Armstrong's* Tour de France wins among the French. Yet, the paddlers will tell you that although many did paddle kayaks, their passion was with outrigger canoeing. *JoJo Toeppner* would travel eight hours from her home in Lake Tahoe to make training sessions. A passing interest, it was not. With 10 Molokai wins this was dedication personified.

Much of their success is attributed to the coaching of *Billy Whitford* and the shear athleticism and competitive spirit with which a succession of crews paddled. As their results clearly illustrated, on many levels they were clearly in a league of their own.

1997 Aussie Women Make Their Mark

It ultimately it took another powerhouse women's crew to rob them of their crown. In 1997, Australia's *Panamuna OCC,* led by *Lisa Curry-Kenny* and overseen by husband *Grant Kenny* with mentor and coach *Danny Sheard* announced their arrival on the world scene.

Traci Phillips of *Outrigger CC Hawai`i* and former US Olympic kayaker commented after the race, *'This was a muscle race all the way. The Aussie paddlers were big and strong, several were even world-class. No local club of part-time athletes is going to win a muscle race against this powerful crew,'* she said. Charging into the lead from the Moloka`i start, *Panamuna* never let up until arriving at the *Waikiki Beach* finish, 41 miles and 5 hours, 35 minutes and 17 seconds later. It was the second-fastest time in

Australia's *Panamuna* 1997, *Jasmin Kelly, Amanda Rankin, Robyn Singh,* Brooke *Harris, Cassandra Sedgeman, Katrin Borchet, Kirsty Holmes, Jane Hall, Yanda Nossiter.*

Not from the same club, the women hailed predominantly from the Sunshine and Gold Coasts as

the history of the race. *Offshore* set the record of 5:24:32 in 1995. *Offshore Canoe Club* of California, *Na Wahine's* four-time defending champ and winner of 10 of the past 11 events, still finished a distant second in 5:40:34.

Lisa Curry-Kenny's crew returned in 1998 as the *Riggeroos* to win the event for a second year running. In 1999, they were unable to attend the race due to Olympic paddling commitments by several team members, which was probably just as well given that some crew members were at their peak of fitness. Between 2000 and 2002 Hawai'i's *Kai Opua* enjoyed 3 straight wins coached by *Beanie Heen*, which for locals was a welcome return to form.

Moving to Mooloolaba OCC, *Lisa* returned in 2002 with a crew she was rebuilding which finished 3rd. Disappointed she vowed to return to win the title which she did with formidable crews in 2003 and 2004, lowering the record to 5:22 in 2004. Much of their winning ways can be attributed to a high level of single-mindedness, organisation, fitness, athleticism, individual talents and support. Emulating their paddling 'style' is somewhat problematic for most female crews who simply do not have the same level of strength, fitness or dedication.

Mooloolaba's 2004 record breaking crew, *Jasmin Cohen, Cassandra Sedgemen, Sonia Adams, Kirsty Holmes, Cheryl Skribe, Lisa Curry-Kenny, Robyn Saultry, Danielle Lindsay, Leigh Townsend* and *Andrea Polkinghorne.*

I believe it is a curious anomaly that after speaking with coaches and in observing - without the benefit of data, Pacific wide, men's crews have over time become lighter, leaner and 'keener' while successful women's crews have always been more 'physical' than their opponents. This is a sweeping observation, but nevertheless worthy of consideration.

Wa`a Paddling for the Physically, Economically or Socially Challenged, and as a means of Rehabilitation.

***Jill Atkinson*, a Rehabilitation specialist at *Rochester Rehabilitation Centre* USA, lowering a paraplegic paddler into the wa`a using a purpose made hoist permanently bolted to the decking. Photo *John Court*.**

Special mention should be made of the sport's unique potential in providing for people in the community who may have special physical or social needs.

On the physical level, with some modification to the seating arrangement and the rigging in order to further reduce the risk of capsize, the biomechanical action of paddling can bring a great sense of freedom, achievement, invigoration and therapeutic benefits to the disabled or for those in need of rehabilitation. One of the leaders in this field has been the *Rochester Rehabilitation Centre,* in New York, USA, under the watchful eye of *Jan Whitaker*.

Modifications can be made such as lowering the seats, the addition of a backrest, or use of a commercially made postural support system or material camp chair with backrest, and the attachment of a secondary ama on the opposite side to the primary. By doing this, wa`a paddling has been made accessible to many who otherwise could not participate in a paddle sports.

For the socially or economically disadvantaged, wa`a paddling has already had an impact in various island groups of the Pacific. Critically a loss of cultural identity, disempowerment, sense of purpose and direction has to varying degrees impacted on many peoples of the Pacific region.

In some ways, throughout Tahiti and her islands, embracing the wa`a so fully and completely has nurtured a social reform and ensured that cultural pride, physical prowess and purpose are maintained. The magnitude of the social and economical importance of the wa`a in this part of the world, is not insignificant.

A paddler with multiple sclerosis being assisted into the wa`a. Note the high backed material seat which has been attached to the regular flat seat. Back rests are of particular importance for stability.

In some regions, the va`a sport has become a central vehicle through which many individuals connect and identify with their Pacific cultures. Indirectly, consciously or otherwise, government support of the sport of va`a throughout the island of Tahiti, has very possibly prevented many greater social problems on both a collective and individual level.

Speculation suggests that similar results could be achieved with indigenous Hawaiians, if they were provided the same measure of incentive and financial support through government. Regrettably, euro-centric sports or at least anglo-American sports dominate the consciousness of those in power and the media.

In an unlikely region of the world, the *Rio Va`a Club*, Latin America's pioneering va`a club (founded in 1999) is developing the *Rio Canoa social Project*. The *Canoa Rio* paddling program is aimed at educating kids from low-income families through the practice of the ancient team sport of va`a. Through the *Canoa Rio* project, educators are able to pass on values such as team spirit, respect of authority and environmental awareness that may help give 13-18 year old kids from low income communities a broader approach to citizenship as well as opportunities in sports or activities related to tourism.

Kelvin Ho of Kauai runs a similar program on the Hawaiian island of Kauai, working with kids who have had problems fitting in with a changed society and with the education system. In New Zealand thorugh a variety of Maori trust funds, waka ama is used as a means of binding communities together and in educating children of their Polynesian heritage.

In Tonga, New Caledonia and Samoa and to some extent Fiji, the va`a has been reintroduced as a platform of learning and continuity.

Cultural Preferences for Single or Double Bend Paddles

The decision to use either a single or double-bend paddle is, for many paddlers, a decision based on ergonomics and how comfortable the paddle 'feels'. However, we need to take this 'feeling' one step further. Through constant use of one type of paddle over another, techniques have been unintentionally developed that have subtle yet different paddling styles. Switching from a single to double-bend or vice versus, is not just a matter of a different paddle, but one of a different technique also.

When adopting one particular style of paddling, it is necessary to consider the entire package and look at your paddling technique and style holistically; paddle, paddler, paddling technique and va`a must all be taken into account to ensure the absolute best performance.

From a cultural standpoint, there are preferences for one style of paddle over the other Pacific-wide. Both single and double bend va`a paddles are used extensively within va`a paddling, with some regions having greater preference for one type over another. French Polynesia almost exclusively uses double-bends, as do many of the smaller island regions of Oceania, especially those influenced by French Polynesia. While paddlers in the Hawaiian Islands, California, Australia and Mainland USA, have a preference for single-bend paddles.

I have always been intrigued by the technical differences you can see while observing the top level Hawaiian, Australian, Californian, New Zealand or Tahitian crews. But you cannot successfully do this or come to any firm conclusions about their 'technique' without considering the paddle type they are using, as this dictates many aspects of the stroke itself.

Naturally, paddle makers strive to keep up with supply and demand, and to some degree there is a cross-flow of influence between paddler and paddle maker. But for the most part, paddlers dictate to the makers what it is that they like in a paddle.

Some paddle makers claim that there is no 'real' difference between the double and single bend in their usage and that they have little effect on dictating paddling technique, beyond the advantages of improved angle of the wrist relative to the blade angle and in moving the grip further back towards the top shoulder. This is simply not the case.

Single bend paddles are for the most part popular with male and female paddlers in Australia, Hawai`i, California and New Zealand. Double bends are universally popular throughout French Polynesia and wherever they have had influence. Tahitian women's crews on the other hand, often use single bend paddles and there are sound

Single and Double Bend Paddles Require Differing Techniques

Any coach or individual seriously interested in different paddling techniques displayed by top level crews must take into consideration the paddles being used. If they don't, then they are only getting half of the equation. Without question, excellence in paddling comes down to a mix of dynamics and not just one simple factor. Universally, world-class crews will use either all single or all double bend paddles but never a mix of both.

The initial design alteration away from a straight shaft paddle to a single-bend was to eliminate fatigue in the wrists and arms, and to improve the ergonomics of

the paddle. There are unintentional benefits including increased potential for extra reach, keeping the blade vertical for longer during the power phase of the stroke, and preventing excessive drag at the end of the stroke.

With the introduction of the double-bend shaft, to further improve comfort, more unintentional benefits were inherent in the design. Through many hours of observation and discussion, there is no question that top level crews apply a different technique when using either single or double-bend paddles. Less knowledgeable paddlers, or coaches often don't realise such a notion exists and a mix of single and double paddles will prevail in the one crew.

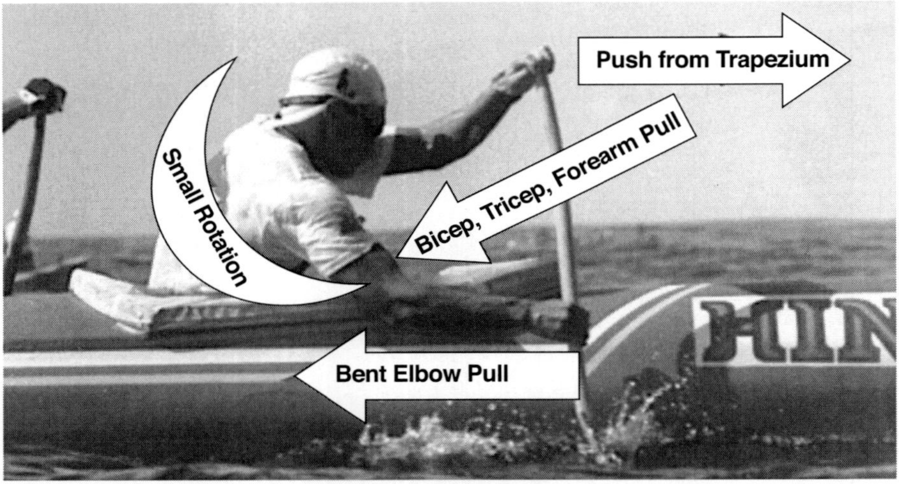

Comparisons between double bend (above) and single bend techniques

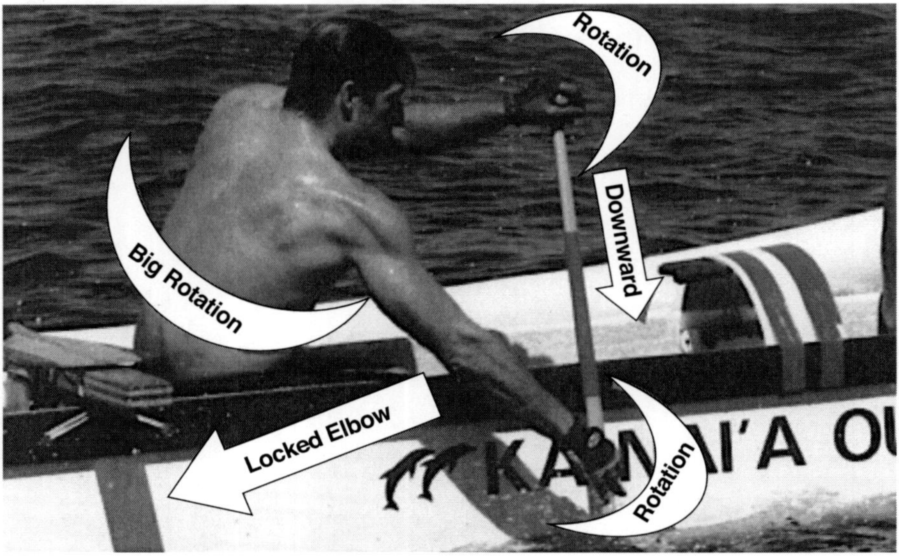

The bend that exists in the double bends shaft, three quarters the way up or so, is often referred to as a 'crank' and with good reason, because in real terms that's exactly what it can be for the paddler. Provided it is a well designed double bend, this crank or fulcrum point can act as an addition lever in providing drive and power to the blade. What started out as a means of producing a more ergonomically pleasing paddle, has now been mastered so as its inherent design features can be used to maximum effect.

Double Bend Technique

The Tahitian stroke, which uses the double-bend paddle, is the most definitive example to use as our yardstick. It is one of the few regions of the Pacific which uses this style of paddle, not just for comfort, but also because it suites their preferred technique. Historically, Tahitians have been radically modifying their paddling techniques, paddle choice and design, in sync with the Hawaiian development, through the 80s and 90s. The outcome was that the Tahitians preferred the double-bend over the single and a paddle that has more flex than the Hawaiians single-bend. These factors have helped define the contemporary difference between Tahitian and Hawaiian paddling techniques.

While using the double-bend paddle, there is more emphasis on pull generated from the lower arm and mid-way through the power phase, the paddler pushes forwards with the top arm, when the blade is near vertical. A short, powerful push forwards using the trapezium and triceps muscles can generate a powerful force,

***Hanz Salmon* was one of *Pirae's* finest strokers during the years in which they dominated. Classic use of the double bend paddle; top arm bent downwards at the elbow, poised to push forward when the shaft is vertical, lower arm is bent and already pulling as body unwinds.**

at a point where many paddlers are inclined to back off. This is combined with a powerful pull of the lower arm using the smaller forearm and bicep muscles. The stroke ends abruptly near the hip and the blade is carried out marginally away from the va`a then lifted in an upward manner to avoid 'push' and drag at the end of the stroke and carried forward to the point of entry.

There was a time when one of the key identifying factors of the Tahitian stroke was their style of exiting and recovery. It differed from the Hawaiian style by the blade slicing away from the va`a, the top arm coming down across the gunnel, sweeping the feathered blade forward in a low arch.

This has modified with the use of the double-bend paddles in recent years as the recovery incorporates less feathering and a squarer recovery motion. Oddly, the Hawaiian stroke now incorporates greater feathering and a lower arched recovery. There is a suggestion that this was once traditional practice which had over time moved to a more direct lift and squarer motion back to the entry.

One very important and often overlooked fact is that most Tahitian paddles are made with quite a bit of natural 'spring' or 'flex' due to type of the timbers used. Nevertheless, these paddles work very well. The 'whippy' feeling they provide assists with quick recovery rates and provides the paddler with a very pleasant, encouraging 'feel' during the power phase which enhances a feeling of rhythm and timing.

In rough water, especially downwind paddling, Tahitian teams occasionally use single bend paddles. This could imply that single bend paddles are easier to manage and more effective in such conditions, though there would need to be some modification of technique which downwind paddling often demands.

Single Bend Technique

There are essential differences regarding the entry and power phase of a stroke with a single-bend as opposed to a double-bend paddle. There is emphasis on downwards drive - push, as the paddle enters, followed by rotation around the spine. At the mid-point of the power phase, when the blade is vertical and at is most efficient, the paddler aims to keep the top and lower hand, hand-over-hand, arms locked briefly as the body continues to rotate. It is important to keep the blade vertical for as long a possible, before the lower arm bends and the paddle is moved through to the exit phase of the stroke.

When the blade face is nearly vertical, the paddler reduces the downwards drive and continues to rotate the body around the spine, the lower arm ultimately bending radically when it reaches a point where it naturally looses its ability to remain locked. At this point, the paddle moves through to the exit phase of the stroke and the paddler removes the paddle from the water by relaxing the wrist, lower shoulder and elbow, and moves on to feather the blade. The paddler then swings in a long arch through the recovery phase back to the set-up phase of the stroke. At the end or exit phase, the paddler remains marginally leaning forwards.

The single-bend paddle stroke appears longer in reach out front and in push behind. Stroke rates are generally slower and there is generally more body lean and body movement as a whole. From a technical point of view, the single bend paddle and technique can be considered easier to use than the double. There is, if you like, less to think about and do. However, rotation and the lack of it during the set-up phase and over rotation at the exit phase of the stroke are all common problems, in combination with pushing the top arm forwards at the catch / pull phase causing the blade to pass through vertical prematurely permitting water to spill off the blade face.

Crews Mixing Single and Double Bend Paddles in the Same Va`a

Why do some crews, mix single and double-bend paddles among crew members? Is this OK? If it's fair to say that there is a difference between double and single-bend technique, wouldn't this mean that there would be a lack of uniformity of paddling technique and power applications within the va`a. Worse still, are paddlers, using single bend paddling techniques whilst using their double bend paddles, because they don't know any better.

Many coaches advocate and teach just one particular technique and not a variety to suit single and/or double-bend paddles. But you certainly can't have it both ways. Your crew should only be using either single or double-bend paddles. Regrettably, some paddle makers continue to be diametrically at odds with this notion, which makes life challenging for the coach and the paddler alike. There is no 'I' in 'Team' as they say, and paddler's and crews alike should agree on what stick to use, could you imagine a rowing-eight using a variety of oars out of 'individual' preference?

If a crew is fortunate enough to have a coach, shouldn't the coach make the decision about the nature of the paddles that will be used collectively based on the technique they will teach? It may be that the coach believes in using the top arm to push forward to create some drive. In this case they should consider using double-bends. What started out as a means of producing a more ergonomically pleasing paddle has now been mastered so that its inherent design features can be used to maximum effect.

Different Strokes for Different Folks

In a rapidly changing sport, the wa`a racing paddler is increasingly concerned with perfecting a personal paddling style. While we may define a particular paddling technique as 'best' for a given paddle craft, we must remember that there is no one style that is best for all paddlers. Technique is essentially a defined how-to. Style is inherent to (and often limited by) the biomechanical and physiological make-up of the paddler. What suits the individual 'best' is what tends to work best.

If we can think of ourselves as machines providing power to drive the wa`a through the water, each paddler is essentially a different engine type attempting to achieve a similar goal. Biomechanically, we all operate in a more or less similar fashion, but 'more or less' means a lot in regard to the different ways we apply and move our bodies to create the most efficient pulling of the wa`a up to the blade.

The Hawaiian Stroke

The 'traditional' Hawaiian Stroke was very long - from entry to exit, coupled with exaggerated body movement and lunging forward, so the ribs almost touch the canoe gunnel. All this contributed to a much slower potential stroke rate - as low as 45 strokes/minute. The stroke was slow, long and deliberate, with emphasis on the pull at the front and the push at the rear of the stroke, and the paddle exiting at the back of the paddler's seat. Power was achieved by incorporating the body weight behind and over the stroke.

Little body rotation was used in the stroke. From the side it looked like the paddlers were attempting to 'dig' a hole in the water and then throw what they had 'scooped' up, out the back. The recovery of the paddle involved little or no 'feathering' of the blade and moving through the 'recovery phase' was a long, lopping movement, perfected with the use of traditional paddles. Much of this paddling style was due to the nature of the super long, heavy, straight shafted, large blade area paddles. It was a style which had to change as paddles evolved and as the need for speed grew ever more urgent.

This technique is associated with using much longer, large blade areas, straight shafted paddles without a handle. Logically, as we have moved away from traditional va`a paddles, paddling technique and styles have naturally evolved to suit. They now permit the paddler to move in a way which is bio-mechanically more efficient, free-flowing and energy efficient. Today's shorter paddle with handle, single or double-bend and smaller blade area, has encouraged the evolution of wa`a paddling technique, turning the sport into a far more aerobic pursuit. Stroke rates have increased dramatically, into the mid and high 60s, as a base rate. While the introduction of these contemporary paddles was quick, the evolution of a new paddling technique to suit was not

The traditional Hawaiian stroke was replaced with a more upright technique, rotating around the spine, leading shoulder forward, top arm back and entry achieved by dropping the shoulder to drive the paddle downward for the entry, rather than allowing the entire body to drop to gunnel level. The emphasis is now upon rotation of the body around the spine, careful paddle placement and keeping much of the emphasis of the stroke, the power-phase, 'up front', then during the 'vertical' phase, pulling the blade out early at the hip. This allows the crew to maintain higher stroke rates and enables the wa`a to 'run'.

New Paddles, New Technique

Many wa`a paddlers and designers clung to 'traditional' ideas into the early 80s and even as late as the mid 90s. In Hawai`i especially, the thought was that 'bigger must be better' as far as blade area was concerned. The biggest issue was modifying paddling technique to suit the smaller blade areas and therefore validate their use.

Paddle maker *Brad Gillespie* commented in *Canoe and Kayak Racing News* January 1990. '*When I first began racing canoes, a sort of primitive logic existed regarding the size of the blades. We simply figured that a bigger blade meant better. If we used larger blades, we would push more water and go faster. Time and experience modified our views considerably and over the years we reduced the size to just a smidgen over 8". This was a comfortable width, although at this time I couldn't define precisely why we were successful with these smaller blades. Our stroke seemed smoother, we could sink the blade without a lot of splashing and we found a cadence that was efficient for longer distances.*'

As with any evolutionary process, paddlers clung onto certain design concepts for a while, more importantly the large blade area in the belief that more must be better. Stroke rates remained relatively low, in the low to mid 50/minute. Paddling techniques in Hawai`i remained relatively unchanged for sometime after the introduction of these new generation paddles, with big lunging movements and emphasis on hyper-extension, driving downwards using some degree of body weight.

It was not surprising that it took some time to alter paddling technique to suit the new style of paddle, a style which had been learned over thousands of years throughout the Pacific Islands. Historical research makes the comparison between what has become termed as the Tahitian and Hawaiian paddling styles and the influence they have had on va`a paddling technique across the Pacific. These have now blended with European ideas learned from Olympic canoe paddling and general recreational open canoe river paddling - Native American Indian.

***Lanikai Hawaiki Nui Va`a*, old style Hawaiian paddling stroke long gone. Below *Outrigger Canoe Club*, Hawai`i, 1996.**

The Tahitian Stroke

Traditional Tahitian lagoon va`a have much less freeboard than their Hawaiian counterparts. Therefore, the need for smoothness, without lunging, was an absolute necessity in order to avoid swamping the canoes. This was taught from an early age and has perhaps helped to shape the Tahitian stroke.

The Tahitian stroke is easily identifiable as having a high rating (70+) consisting of a quick, short, powerful stroke with minimal body movement, less emphasis on rotation, and the exit of the paddle around the level of the hip. The arms, shoulders and upper torso of the paddler play a major role in applying power to the stroke. Because the stroke is short, timing must be absolutely precise. There is little room for error, it must be executed with smoothness and minimal movement of the paddler's body, permitting the va`a to travel smoothly forward. Paddlers at the exit phase of the stroke are nearly upright and the paddle tends to be 'lifted' more directly upwards and moved squarely back during the recovery phase, with only marginal 'feathering' of the blade.

Good timing and rhythm are things the Tahitians have in abundance; after all, music and dance play a big part in their culture. This natural sense of rhythm is a huge advantage. Smooth, explosive power in the stroke is key. There is a rule of thumb which states, 'the recovery phase of the stroke is nearly twice that of the actual stroke itself'. This rule varies depending on which style you develop, as the Tahitian style using the double-bend often appears closer to equal proportions as opposed to the single-bend technique which is closer to the 1:2 ratio.

Tahitian style paddling has been referred to as *Chilli Dipping* by the Hawaiians. They say it looks like someone dipping a corn chip into the dip. Today these crews have only marginal body movement in the va`a, except for some body rotation and arm movement. When you observe a top level crew, it appears as if the stroke is effortless, with the set up and entry phase of the stroke appearing to have less emphasis on downward drive.

***Team Rai*, Tahiti using double-bend teardrop shaped blades.**

The Tahitian stroke is in fact, quite static in its application (see 'Static' technique) when using the double-bend paddles. This is especially true when compared to some Hawaiian paddling techniques with single-bend paddles, where driving down hard at the entry is encouraged.

Tahitian paddlers are extremely technical in their approach to all facets of the sport. Two distinct paddling strokes where traditionally used; the *Huti* and *Pine* strokes. The *huti* is a relative slow, deep, long stroke used for long distance paddling in flat water and with between 60-64 strokes/minute. The *pine* stroke is a quicker, lighter, choppy, shallow stroke, used in sprint racing, off the start and for bursts of speed with a rating which may exceed 80 strokes/minute.

This paddling stroke technique is noted in *Jeff Evan's* book, *Waka Taua* (The Maori War Canoe). *'When starting out, the crew first had to get the waka up to cruising or planing speed. This was accomplished by three deep, strong strokes, called whainene, followed by up to 40 sprint strokes, or pine. The whainene effectively pulled the waka from the water's grip, and the pine brought the vessel up to its optimum speed. When using the pine, only the bottom portion of the blade entered the water.'*

Other names given to particular paddling strokes as identified by *Evans* include the *Houti*, a deep stoke with maximum effort required; the *Hahama*, used in rough or choppy conditions being a light, fast stroke with only the lower portion of the blade used; and the *Ha* stroke, which called for the paddler to give maximum effort every second stroke and only half of this for the remainder.

An early European account of watching waka racing in New Zealand recalls...*the natives were shouting Hoea, Tiaia, Pehia, Ana Kumea roughly translated, these words mean, "Pull, Stick it in, drag it along, press it down, haul it along.'*

Interestingly, it's not uncommon for Tahitian crews to paddle only 10-12 strokes per side, to avoid lactating and keep the arms fresh. Elsewhere, 14-18 strokes per side is more common. Many things in Tahiti and her islands are approached with a great deal of difference. While Tahitians are well known for their excellence in sprint racing, they are true masters of ultra-marathon length events where no relief paddlers are permitted.

Anglo Tahitian-Hawaiian Stroke

***Outrigger Australia* in full flight Hamilton Island.**

Today's wa`a paddling stroke is the result of being passed through the hands of many thousands of paddlers Pacific wide and beyond - even to the native American Indian. But as covered in Significant Interventions, some influences have been greater than others in terms of their direct effect on the wa`a stroke specifically. Whereas river canoe paddling technique encouraged direct drive downwards in the stroke throughout its length, the Australians modified this with the introduction of surfski paddlers. They placed greater importance on an aggressive entry followed by powerful rotation around the spine so the larger muscles of the body effected the pull through torque. They also locked their elbows during this twist, bending them towards the mid and latter part of the stroke.

Comparisons

In making comparisons with a sport such as Olympic canoeing, we must never be misled by the fact that this discipline is essentially flat water oriented. Therefore, it is easier to analyse and establish a definitive paddling technique. On the other hand, wa`a paddling is concerned with paddling in a variety of conditions. It encompasses both flat water sprint racing and open ocean paddling which is complicated by a number of natural variables including the wind, and wave and tide action.

How do you come up with a defined paddling technique for each of these extremes? Rough water paddling dictates, through constant irregularities of the ocean environment, that, each stroke is marginally and sometimes grossly different to account for the constantly changing conditions.

While flat water sprint racing technique may be easier to define, we need be careful not to compartmentalise this technique, believing it to be applicable also to rough water ocean paddling. Flat-water sprint racing is practiced in a relatively stable environment, where adverse wind and currents tend to be avoided, while the open ocean is anything but stable.

Technique - The Quest for Perfection

Technique and its analysis is an intellectual process that demands complex thought processes. In order to become a technically advanced paddler, you need to apply yourself to consider just what makes efficient paddling. Facts without thought can be dangerous and often misleading. If someone has told you to paddle in a certain way, with no explanation or reason given, then you have no knowledge as to why you are doing it. This often makes you less inclined to continue. On the other hand, if you are informed about why a certain action will have an effect on wa`a speed or paddling efficiency, your understanding will motivate you to use that technique, especially if you see and feel improvement.

Leverage itself is a complex subject. One of the things that makes efficient and consistent wa`a paddling technique so challenging is that (unlike rowing which uses a fixed oarlock so the point of rotation of the oar is fixed) managing a wa`a paddle is subject to gross inconsistencies created by the paddler. These inconsistencies relate to the grip on the paddle shifting, biomechanical movement and control of the paddler's entire body during each and every stroke. Needless to say, developing a technique and style, that is most efficient and ruthlessly consistent for you, in any given paddling condition, is paramount. This is truly only attainable with practice.

Employing incorrect technique has obvious downsides. These become clearly apparent through poor wa`a speed, a tendency to fatigue quickly and an inability to keep in time with other paddlers. Less obviously, and even more importantly, you need to understand that wa`a paddling will, if practised enough, mould or sculpture your body shape through muscle growth and definition. Over time, incorrect technique develops

inappropriate muscle groups and can lead to injury.

In this regard, video recordings of your paddling technique are most beneficial, providing one of the fastest ways of improving your technique. Detailed analysis can be made of the way in which you apply yourself and individual nuances (your style) can be examined, encouraged or criticised then reapplied, filmed and re-analysed. Once good technique is established, it pays to watch that video many times over so you can re-run those images in your head as you paddle – creatively visualising an efficient technique.

Comparisons with Olympic canoeing can provide us with some understanding of the variety of paddling techniques used. Two primary techniques relate largely to the degree to which the paddler bends from the knee and hip during the stroke, while the movement of the upper torso remains essentially the same in both. These are referred to as the static lower body frame and dynamic lower body frame techniques.

Static and Dynamic Paddling Techniques

Spend any time watching wa`a crews and you will notice how some paddlers remain relatively upright during their stroke cycle. They rotate only in a twisting fashion from the hip and waist with a dropping of the upper shoulder to plant the blade. Others rotate and lower their entire torso, low to the gunnel, seemingly pushing the blade in somewhat more energetically, returning to a more upright position at the exit phase of the stroke. This in some regard defines 'traditional' paddling technique.

Dynamic Paddling

Dynamic technique incorporates leg movement as well as that of the torso and because of this it is also referred to as inertia transfer technique. Dynamic technique relies on a substantially greater amount of the body weight during the pull. There is a reliance not only on upper torso rotation but on a thrusting motion from the hip and knee, where body weight adds inertia (forward energy).

There is active movement of the upper body in the stroke. The body is leant into the stroke at the reach phase of the stroke, with a bending and twisting at the waist. This is generally practised by smaller paddlers, women and juniors aged paddlers.

The body should bend forward from the hip/waist in combination with torso rotation and a slight degree of bending and straightening of the leading leg; the offside leg is

A perfect example of dynamic paddling technique in action. *Jo Jo Toeppner, OffShore California,* stands only 5' 4" but packs a hell of a punch with each stroke as she applies not only upper body strength but also body weight. By bending forward at the waist to maximise reach and by marginally twisting the upper torso then unwinding through the stroke, body weight is applied to the pull. The energy created is then transferred downward, through the seat and legs, into the canoe. Below *Kirsti Holmes* (Australia) in full reach.

bent with the foot a long way underneath the seat. This allows for greater reach and utilisation of body weight. By straightening the leg during the power phase of the stroke, we emulate dynamic or inertia paddling technique to some degree. This being said, the dynamic technique is by nature technically harder to perfect. The timing is critical and it is not suitable in all circumstances. It is therefore preferable to learn the static technique first.

High, top arm action ensures the elbow is raised above the level of the head. The upper torso dips low in order to achieve maximum application of body weight during the power phase of the stroke. The lower hand is positioned approximately one hand span from the neck of the blade.

One of the obvious problems that comes to mind with the dynamic or inertia technique, is that such large movements by several paddlers creates a potential for longitudinal and lateral instability in the wa`a. This could cause sink and rise both lengthways and sideways in time with the forward and backward motion of the paddlers. This is undesirable as it increases then decreases the wetted waterline length, causing the wa`a to be subjected to varying degrees of resistance and theoretically diminishes its glide and 'boat-run'.

The stroker is using a dynamic paddling technique, rotating and leaning way forward. Seat #2, a taller paddler, is somewhat more static relying on a longer torso and arm length to provide reach. Right: Both paddlers seemingly 'throwing' themselves into the reach and entry. This style of paddling has similarities with the traditional Hawaiian technique.

It is critical that the paddler rotates from the waist, while lowering the leading shoulder to ensure smoothness in this motion. This technique is predominantly used by shorter, lightweight paddlers and generally more used by women than men. Single-bend paddles are better suited to this style of paddling.

Static

Static technique requires that the lower frame, below the hip, remains stationary while the upper torso leans forward and rotates. This is the only movement. Static technique relies solely on the power and weight of the upper body to pull the wa`a through the water. Predominantly this is an upright paddling position, suited to tall individuals who have plenty of leverage and upper body strength. Generally speaking, tall paddlers, both male and female, tend to adopt a more upright, or static paddling technique. The lower hand is placed relatively high up the shaft which maximises the leverage potential inherent in their height. This requires added strength but when you are six foot plus, it is generally available. Both double and single-bend paddles work well for this technique.

Hawaiian paddlers, *Robbie Harrison* and *Marc Haine* (both over six foot) apply a static technique with upper torso rotation from the waist, while remaining relatively upright. Extra weight, strength and leverage allows for this technique.

This static technique requires the lower hand to be positioned at least two hand spans up the shaft for added leverage and reach i.e. higher up than when using the dynamic technique. This requires greater effort to maintain is but more achievable for taller, stronger paddlers.

Seat #3 is paddling with a slightly more dynamic paddling technique, while the seat #4 paddler remains more upright, using a static approach.

Mixing Dynamic and Static Styles

Whether there should be a mix of the two styles within the same wa`a is largely a matter of discretion. If you have a mix of light and heavy paddlers, tall and short, then a mix of styles at work in the wa`a generally works fine, provided that it does not affect the timing and rhythm. It is important that those who do employ the dynamic technique, in particular, do it well.

With regard to synchronicity of technique and maintaining uniformity within a six person wa`a, it is essential that coach and crew agree upon a given technique or combination. Failure to do this could result in different techniques causing problems with the timing and rhythm. All paddles used by a crew must also be uniform in design concept, though naturally they will vary in the length of the shaft.

At its highest level, outrigger wa`a racing is a technical endeavour which demands some intellectual effort and thought. Failure to analyse paddling technique and your individual style, will drastically limit your potential. Thinking your way to more effective paddling is better than embarking on a mission of frenetic fitness and (often misguided) strength programs. Real progress only occurs through understanding what it is you are setting out to achieve.

Understanding Some Fundamentals

'This may come as a surprise, but canoe and kayak paddling, together with rowing are the only sports where all participants are required to do the same thing, all at the same time. Well, unless you include bobsledding and anyway, that's on hard water!'
Terry Wallace.

There are some fundamentals paddle skills, commands and seat position rolls you should know. With regards to paddle skills, while this is generally termed 'technique', the 'how to' element of paddling, this will ultimately be affected by your individual 'style'. Your style, is an unavoidable consequence of your unique biomechanical and physiological make-up, which need not be a hindrance to sound technique, indeed some paddlers excel at being less conventional than others. Provided sound principles are being met then there is no reason why good should not make for a good paddler.

A the same time, you will need to consider how efficient your technique is - maximum return on minimal output equates to efficiency of energy expenditure. Paddling drills are a great way to learn biomechanical movement. It is important that you understand some basic theory regarding the stroke and how this converts into moving the wa`a forward. **Facts without thought will slow your learning process.**

Sit and Switch

The Sit and Switch technique is used for wa`a paddling to avoid fatigue building up on one side of the body. It is highly effective for this form of endurance paddling. Knowing when to change paddling sides is an art and not always determined by fatigue levels, though its preferable to change before fatigue and lactate build up occurs.(See 'Calling the Huts')

Essentially a call of 'hut' is made on the penultimate stroke, as it enters the water - you take that stroke, then another, then change sides in unison. The number of strokes per side can vary, with as few as 10 and up to 25, depending on the circumstances.

Below: seat # 5 has changed early to protect the ama. Seat # 5 need not adhere to the call and must act instinctively or at the command of the steerer.

Seat # 1 is the most forward paddler.
Seats # 1, 3, 5 paddle on the same side.
Seats # 2, 4 paddle together on opposite sides to 1, 3, 5.
Seats # 1, 2 change sides when rounding markers to assist steerer.
Seat # 5 may change sides randomly to protect the ama from capsize.
The steerer paddles and steers on either side as required.

General Terms for *Noho* - The Seats

Seating positions within the wa`a can be thought of in terms of fractional components;

Sixths	**The individual paddler and their unique role.**
Thirds	**Paddlers forward, middle and rear of i`ako**
The Sum of the Whole	**The entire crew.**
Forward Paddlers	**Set the pace and cadence.**
Middle Paddlers	**Provide power and stability.**
Rear paddlers	**Provide power, steering and stability.**

Terry Wallace, from the island of Hawai`i, provides traditional insight regarding seating positions. '*The seats have different names according to where they are located within the canoe. The following are Kona generic terms and may be different on other islands.*'

Noho `Ekahi (noh-ho eh-kah-hee) Seat #1

Also called *Mua* (moo-uh) which means front or forward. Also called *ka`i* (kah-ee) - the leader of a procession and *Hana Pa`a,* which literally means steady work. This is not a power seat. Sets the pace of the stroke. Should know instinctively whether the pace is 60 strokes per minute, 70 strokes per minute, or whatever. Also helps steer from the front, especially during sudden changes of direction by reaching with the paddle *kahi* (kah-hee = cut) and executing an *uni*

(oo-nee), levering the blade into the side of the wa`a. (Note: some call uni, 'u-nay', but there is no such word or pronunciation in the Hawaiian language.)

Must be constantly alert to what is ahead; swimmers, rocks etc. Depending on the team, mua sometimes calls changes. Will often call a change of stroke timing, faster or slower. *Mua* must keep strokes straight back as opposed to following the contour of the canoe to avoid turning the bow. This allows the steerer to paddle more and steer less.

(Must be self motivated, posses the ability to stay focused, be sensitive to the nuances of the canoe's travel and speed over the water, and its interaction with the water relative to wind, waves and current altering the stoke rate to suit. An aerobically demanding seat, strokes are generally of lighter build than others in the wa`a.)

Noho `Elua (noho eh-loo-uh) Seat # 2

Means second. Assists by coaching #1 with timing. Assists turning canoe from the front when necessary. When the wa`a is stationary, keeps left hand on front i`ako to avoid *huli*.

(Must be well disciplined in matching exactly the entry and exit phase of the stroke paddle. Any variance in timing, will cause paddlers along one side of the wa`a to be either slower or faster than the other. Must be able to encourage the stroke. Calls the time when paddlers change paddling sides with the call of *hut*)

Noho `Ekolu or (noho eh-koh-loo) Seat # 3

Sometimes called *Kahea* (kah-hay-uh) which means caller or announcer. On some teams *`Ekolu* calls changes. Part of the engine room with power. Concentrates on moving the wa`a forward.

Noho `Eha (noho eh-hah) Seat # 4

Means four or fourth. The other part of the engine room. Also concentrates on moving canoe forward. Often *Ke ka,* the bailer in long distance races. When the wa`a is stationary, places left hand on rear i`ako to keep from *huli.*

(Occupied by the heaviest, strongest paddlers, these seats are often referred to as the power seats, the engine room. Seat # 4 is generally responsible for the bailing of the wa`a.)

Noho `Elima (no-ho eh-lee-mah) Seat # 5

Also called *Pani* (pah-nee) or steerers substitute or assistant steerer. Keeps a vigilant eye on the ama. May have to sacrifice body by jumping on rear i`ako to keep canoe from *huli*. Often bails - *Ke ka*. Helps to steer when required, usually in large waves. Would take over steering if *ho`okele* is unable to steer or man overboard!

(Another power seat, number 5 will often bail when needed and provide some steering assistance for the primary steerer in extreme cases. Also known as the keeper of the ama, ensuring that the ama remains safe. In rough waters, the paddler can choose to remain on the ama side rather than change sides on the call and steer if needed.)

Noho `Eono* (no-ho eh-oh-no) Seat # 6 *Ho`okele or steerer.

Sometimes called *Papaki`i* (papa-kee-ee) literally means sit flat. Uses a different paddle from the rest of the crew called *uli* (oolee). Be careful with this word! It is pronounced differently from the word *ule* (oolay) which means penis. The captain of the wa`a. Keeps *poe wa`a* (crew) moving forward and focusing on the job. Must be constantly alert to all conditions affecting the wa`a including wind, waves, and other wa`a. Also paddles whenever possible.

(The steerer's role is vital to the safety and well being of the wa`a and crew. They are, in legal terms, the captain and therefore must take responsibility for many issues of safety in terms of the navigation and handling of the wa`a. The prime motivator in the wa`a, they need to develop a keen sense of understanding of the nuances of the wa`a and how it interacts with the ocean.)

Think Your Way to Better Paddling

There are literally hundreds of texts in existence which describe the basic mechanics of the forward stroke as it applies to wa`a paddling. While paddling is very much a physical activity, the world's best paddlers, without exception, apply a good deal of thought and mental calculation to each and every stroke they take. They are perceptive to the progress of the wa`a and its glide through the water either by feel or in relation to a competitor or perhaps a land based object.

The most fundamental understanding you need to firmly establish in your thinking is that you will not be pulling the paddle through the water towards you. You will be pulling your hips up to the blade and with it, the wa`a. In terms of creative visualisation, think of your wa`a on rails and the paddles are a series of poles cemented into the seabed. You are going to reach out, grab a pole and pull yourself up to the pole, pulling the wa`a along with you. Like most things, there are efficient ways to do this and not so efficient ways.

Purchasing a Paddle

Purchasing a paddle is a significant event and this should be done with consideration to club / team protocol regarding technique taught and preference. Discuss it with your coach or experienced paddlers, ie single or double bend. Don't rush into this and ensure in the learning phase that you have a well designed paddle of appropriate length. It is an unfortunate reality that many novice paddlers are expected to learn with club paddles which are often utterly ineffectual and therefore discouraging.

Blade Width

Generally speaking, a larger blade area (Width 9.25"-10") is preferable when learning in order to 'feel' resistance without having to apply bucket loads of power. Small blade areas (Width 9.25" downwards) as used by many top crews, require explosive power and fine control for maximum results. The optimal blade size you can 'handle' is directly proportional to your body weight and strength (strength endurance not 'raw' strength) and this then relates to whether you are paddling distance or sprints.

The blade acts in the water as an 'anchor' and depending on a number of factors, there should be little or no slippage of the blade through the water. The shaft is used for leverage in relation to the placement of the hands and the application of force. The blade is anchored and the objective is to pull the wa`a up to the blade.

Smaller, lightweight paddlers and in particular women and juniors, will tend to favour smaller blade areas, while larger, heavier individuals will tend to favour larger blade areas. Some paddlers prefer to 'rate high' (strokes per minute) and will choose a smaller blade area, while others who prefer a slow rate will choose a larger blade area. This can be a facet of relative levels of fitness, age or genetics, i.e. fast or slow twitch muscle types in particular. Regardless, team wa`a paddling requires synchronicity of timing - paddles in and out together.

For **distance paddling** shorter paddle lengths (total length of shaft and blade) provide greater leverage in relation to their centre of resistance and are therefore easier to use over extended distances and times. Smaller blade area and greater angle relative to the shaft are preferred. Shorter paddle lengths allow higher stroke rates to be achieved. For **sprints,** longer shaft, larger blade area and less angle relative to the shaft can be used.

Holding the Paddle

Grip the lower shaft approximately one hand span up from the neck of the paddle. Place top hand on grip. Lower hand can be raised or lowered in some paddling circumstances, usually no more than two hand spans up from the neck. Fingers should be spread marginally and the shaft only very lightly gripped. Don't squeeze as this will increase fatigue in your forearm. The shaft should be neither too wide nor too narrow. As your strength and experience increase, it's possible to move your lower hand further up the lower shaft to increase potential leverage. Greater experience will lead to your moving your grip on the shaft to suit the conditions.

In this image, high, lower hand placement is being used to maximise leverage inherent in the length of the shaft. Small blade areas offer less resistance and drag. The shorter blade height naturally tends to allow the lower hand to be higher up on the shaft relative to the neck of the blade. The paddler maintains a grip distance between grip and lower hand that is approximately shoulder width.

Phases of the Forward Stroke

The key components of the forward stoke can be broken up into 6 distinct phases;

1. Set Up / Windup	**Maximum rotation / reach prior to blade entry.**
2. Entry	**Placement of blade in water.**
3. Catch	**Loading of the blade.**
4. Pull Through / Power Phase	**Pull applied to the blade.**
5. Exit	**Removal of blade from water at end of stroke.**
6. Recovery	**The swing through to set up.**

Commands

Wind Off	**Stop Paddling**
Paddles Up	**Stop Paddling**
Reach Out	**Get Ready [Set up]**
Kaupe	**Reach Out**
E ho'omakaukau	**Get Ready**
Ko	**Pull back the blade**
Imua	**Paddle**
Push	**Paddle Hard**
Go Now	**Paddle Hard**
Back Paddle	**Reverse Paddle**
Hold Water	**Brake Stroke**
Draw Left/Right	**Draw Stroke [Seats 1 and 2]**

Drills

Dry Land Session

Wa`a can be raised on tyres. Paddlers in seats # 1 through 6 and set up in an appropriate manner, with paddles left, right, left, right along the wa`a. Paddlers reach out (correct their posture - ensuring legs are correctly positioned as well as their grip on the paddle). When set, proceed to make the call of Paddle. Watch and make corrections as needed. Practice the sit and switch. Have paddler's take turns in calling the *hut*.

Waikiki Surf Club **junior training day.**

Pendulum Drill

Paddle is swung forward as per the recovery phase, lower hand releases mid-way and paddle continues forwards controlled by the top hand only. Continue through recovery motion, paddle will swing away from paddler then return where it is 'caught' with the lower hand and the stroke taken again repeated. This works on fine-motor skills and control of the paddle and the recovery phase. Can be done on dry land or water.

Paddling One Side
Have paddlers, all on one side of the wa`a, paddling in unison. Good for emphasizing timing, entry and exit phases of the stroke.

Ballet
Pause at the set up, emphasis on correct start /end position of stroke and timing and length of stroke.

Eyes Closed
Emphasis on timing and feel for boat run and movement.

No Huts
Paddlers count and change on a given number of strokes (no caller). Discipline training and concentration.

Notes on Coaching

In a coaching situation, it would be preferable prior to going on water to have ensured that the basic rigging process, lifting and carrying procedure has been taught and demonstrated. Prior to moving to actual paddling technique tuition, capsize drill should also be taught first. From a coach's standpoint, you will be able to assess the confidence of the paddlers in such a situation and it allows the point to be made that this is a water sport and that wa`a do capsize.

These pre-requisites are largely concerned with safety and therefore preliminary introductory skills. Some clubs as a matter of course require a 'swim test' and won't just accept your word that you can swim.

Sequential Methodology: As in most forms of teaching and learning, a logical progression is required moving from simple to more complex tasks. In this case, you are progressing from basic gross motor control to the finer points of refinement, to ultimately strive for greater efficiency. Remember, facts need thoughts behind them for true learning to occur.

Demonstration is the best way to illustrate good paddling technique in combination with video footage. Have this available as a resource, run it and point out key components of the stroke. Move from this to demonstration within the wa`a (land based or on water).

Demonstrate the five phases of the wa`a paddling stroke with explanation about the nature and purpose of each. Remember, fact without thought will not stimulate understanding.

South Head, Hamilton Island, Australia. At this level of paddling in these conditions, clear communication from the steerer or between paddlers could be critical. Key words are essential in keeping communication brief and to the point. Failure to keep power to the blade is also a critical error. Total commitment is required without hesitation.

The Importance of Leg Work

While strong legs are essential, they are little use if you cannot effectively brace yourself in the seat. Being unable to lock-in and drive the energy down into the wa`a is essential. Sit at an angle so you are facing marginally outward, between 5° and 10°, away from the side you are paddling on. This has the effect of pushing the upper part of your hip against the wa`a hull, while on the non-paddling side your thigh can brace up against the hull. (Padding on the inside of the wa`a can prevent chaffing.) This method also prevents the paddler from over-rotating at the end of the stroke and as a result pulling too far back during the power phase of the stroke. It also increases the paddler's reach at the entry point of the stroke.

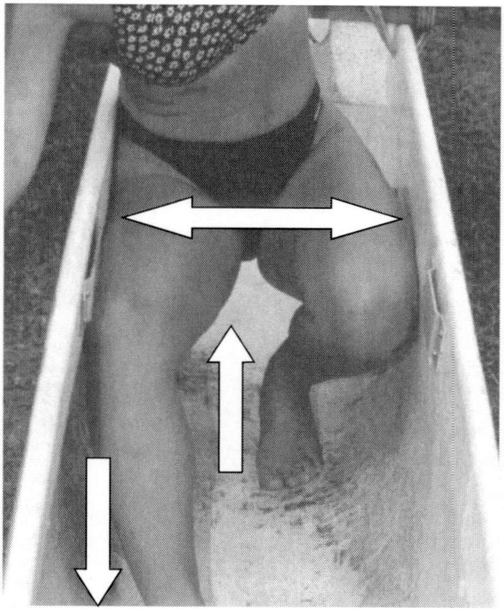

The paddler is seated 'square' on the seat and is bracing herself by forcing both legs apart and against the canoe hull.

The front foot supports the body during the reach.

The rear foot should transfer the bulk of the residual drive from the power phase (pull) to the hull floor in a backwards direction, driving the hull forwards. Most of the energy transfered from the paddle terminates at seat level.

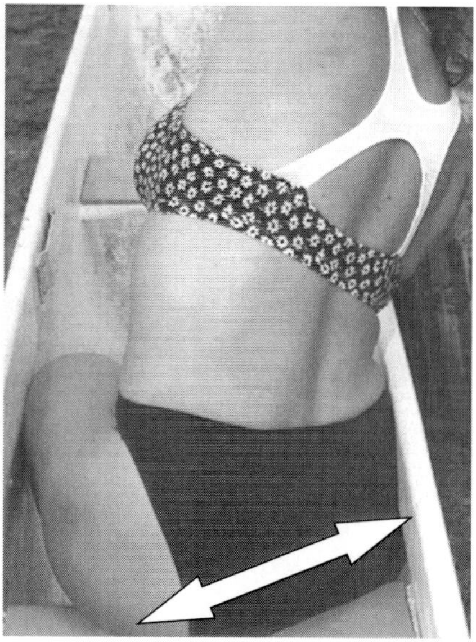

Paddler has altered position to be sitting 'angled' on the seat. This provides greater support from both sides of the canoe against outer leg and bottom. Greater forward reach can also be achieved without having to hyperextend.

In the case of the six person wa`a, paddler body weight and the energy transference along the paddle, down the arms to the seat, is dissipated down the legs through the feet and out the floor of the wa`a. Therefore, the legs play an important (often overlooked) role in team wa`a paddling. The feet must have good traction and be firmly braced so energy transfer to the canoe is maintained and not wasted.

This has been increasingly acknowledged and many paddlers' training now involves leg work (bike riding or running) to strengthen leg muscles. Strong legs are essential in ensuring that the energy in pulling the canoe up to the blade is transferred to the canoe hull through the seat and legs. Legs should be proportionally as strong and fit as the upper body. This isn't to say the legs have to be big, as this will only add additional body weight which is not always desirable. Your legs and seat provide the 'gearing' which connects the horsepower from your blade to the wa`a. Strong, fit legs are essential and must not be overlooked in a paddlers training regime. Weak legs can be the weak link between upper torso strength, powerful technique and energy transference to the wa`a.

Palau Art

The Forward Stroke

Many arm-chair theories regarding the va`a paddling stroke exist yet they rarely considered the issue holistically. Dragon boat or C1 forward stroke theories certainly take into consideration the craft, the paddle and the paddler, yet when this cross-flow of opinion is dragged screaming into the context of the va`a, essential differences seem lost in the translation. They are mutually exclusive to each other, unique, different, in short they are poles apart.

Biomechanically Speaking

The most powerful muscles used in the va`a paddling stroke are your back and shoulders, particularly the fan-shaped *latissimus dorsi,* the *erector* muscles running along the spine, the *deltoids* and *trapezius* muscles of the shoulder. The smaller muscles of the arm such as the *biceps* and *triceps* are used predominantly in the initial pull phase of the stroke, with the greater portion of labour and power ultimately been transferred by torque created by twisting around the spine with the larger muscle groups. This is especially true when using a single bend paddle and the correct technique to match.

Va`a paddling is an endurance sport and you require these larger, stronger muscles to do the bulk of the work as they will 'tire less' than the smaller arm muscles. Consequently, in describing the va`a stroke, emphasis is placed on using these larger muscle groups. Muscles not involved in actual paddling should be relaxed. While adverse body motion is not as obvious in a team va`a, if enough paddlers perform adverse body motion, it will affect the run of the va`a'. Smooth transmission of power in the stroke is essential.

Lanikai **powering along the Tahitian coastline, *Heemoana Va'a* Race.**

***Lanikai* paddling in Tahiti.**

The Tahitian Factor

The va`a stroke continues to evolve today. While traditional dogma and views on paddle design have slowed its evolution, the pace has picked up again because of cross-over between paddle sports and globalisation. Throughout time, one constant has remained; the abyss between the Tahitian way of thinking and that of the rest of the world. You can't overlook the Tahitian's preference for the double-bend paddle, the technique they use, the belief that a paddle with considerable flex is actually 'OK' and ultimately their entire mind set towards training, competing and winning.

Following the 2006 Moloka`i Hoe, held in relatively calm hot and humid conditions, *Lanikai* steersman *Jim Foti* commenting on the Tahitians win, *'That was a crushing, Tahiti is back.'* *Shell Va`a* crushed the course record and the other 101 teams in the field crossing in 4:46:04. *Hititoa/Erai* came in 2nd with a time of 5:00:27. The winning margin of 14 minutes and 23 seconds is the largest gap between 1st and 2nd places since 1962 (when *Waikiki Surf Club* beat *Lanikai* by 15 minutes). 'What *Shell Va`a did today is unheard of,' Outrigger Canoe Club* steersman *Karel Tresnak Jr.* said. *'Today was not supposed to be a fast one, and they blew everybody away. There was a really good field this year and how far ahead they were from the rest of us is crazy.'* *Raromatai* placed third in 5:00:43, giving the Tahitians a sweep of the top three places for the second time in Moloka`i Hoe history. In 1976, Tahiti teams took the top four places.

Set Up | Entry of Blade (Single Bend)

The beginning of the stroke cycle or set up contains a great deal of coiled energy that is created during the recovery motion. The set up is the moment just prior to the entry of the blade into the water. Sometimes, particularly in flat water paddling, it can incorporate an almost undefinable pause. As you move from the set up to the entry, the position of your body and legs remains more or less unaltered, contact of the blade with the water is achieved predominantly by lowering the leading arm.

The set up position ready to enter the water. The set up must contain residual energy generated as a result of the recovery phase (swing through from exit).

Maximum lower-back arch and rotation (twist) around the spine I 1 I chest is canted strongly forward I 2 I reach with lower shoulder which is lowered towards the gunnel I 3I upper shoulder moves back to angle the blade, top elbow is raised but level with head and 1/3 flexed I 4 I lower arm is slightly bent - not straight, chin and gaze remains up, lower arm moves down to bring about entry I 5 I

The leading leg corresponding to the side you are paddling on, must be extended with approximately a 45° bend at the knee, foot placed firmly on the hull floor. The purpose of this leg is take the weight of the upper body as rotate forward during the set up and reach phase of the stroke.

The opposing leg should be bent with your foot underneath the seat. The primary purpose of the rear foot is to brace and push against the pull generated by the force acting against the paddle. This will feel like a backwards force which translates into forward energy to the wa`a.

The buttocks are your primary connection with the wa`a and therefore you must be seated firmly and marginally angled into the stroke.

Lower hand on the shaft should be at least one hand-span up from the neck of the blade. This can be increased to two or three depending on your height and strength. Taller and or strong paddlers sometimes prefer a higher hand grip to increase their leverage.

During the 90s, the lower arm was straight however recent studies advocate that a marginally bent elbow provides greater stability for the paddler and greater control of the blade. It is also essential that the top arm is bent at the elbow so the grip of the paddle is closer to your body, ensuring that the blade angle is increased.

Entry - Ensure clean entry into water with minimal splash.

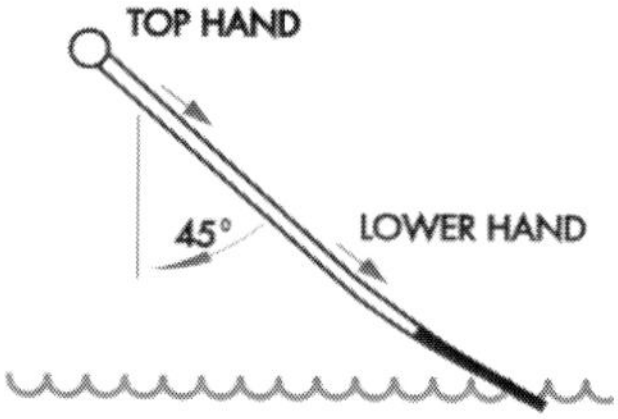

Catch - Considered the most critical part of the stroke, the initial 'loading' of the blade with pressure. Notice direction of pull of lower arm, marginally downwards creating 'lift' of the hull and forward drive.

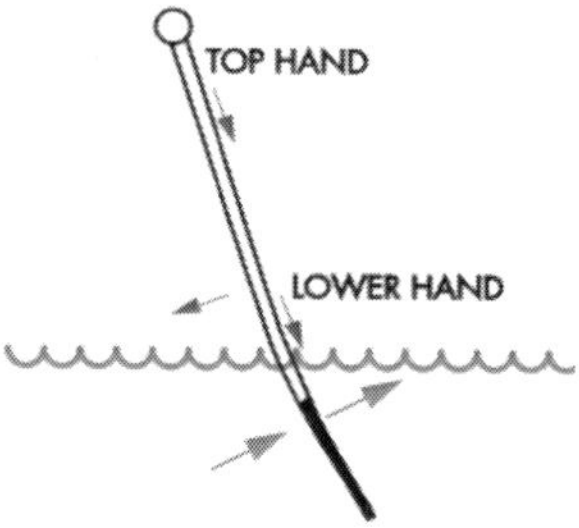

Pull (Vertical Shaft) - Pull is created by 'unwinding' of the torso around the spine delivering 'torque' to the blade face. Top and lower hands are effectively 'hand over hand', power is generated more significantly by body rotation, not direct pulling by the arms. Shaft is vertical, but the blade still offset to the degree inherent in the paddles design.

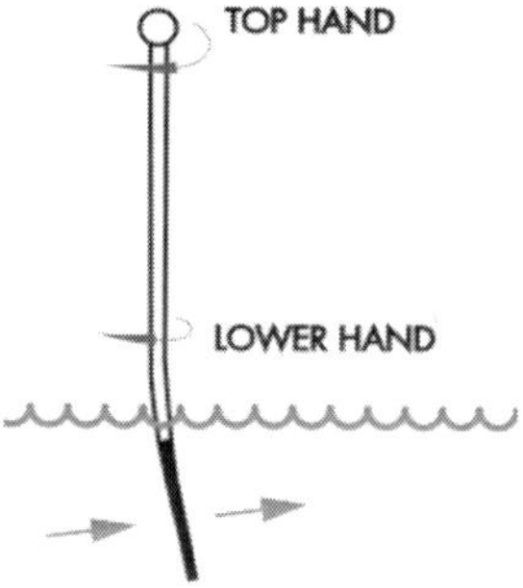

Pull - (Vertical Blade) When the blade is vertical, maintain by continuing to rotate the body as this is when it is best positioned to generate forward propulsion. When it moves past vertical, its time to commence the exit. (Solo craft benefit by a slightly longer 'push phase' past the hip - also can be beneficial when pushing down into swells in team canoes).

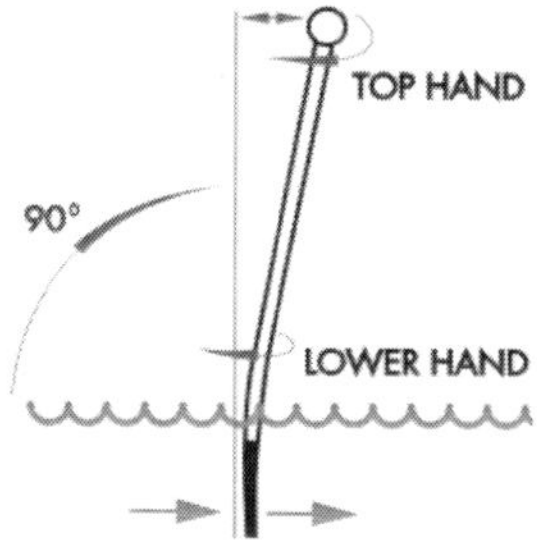

Exit - Avoid 'pushing' forward with the top arm and pulling upwards with the lower as the resulting force acts to pull the hull downwards.

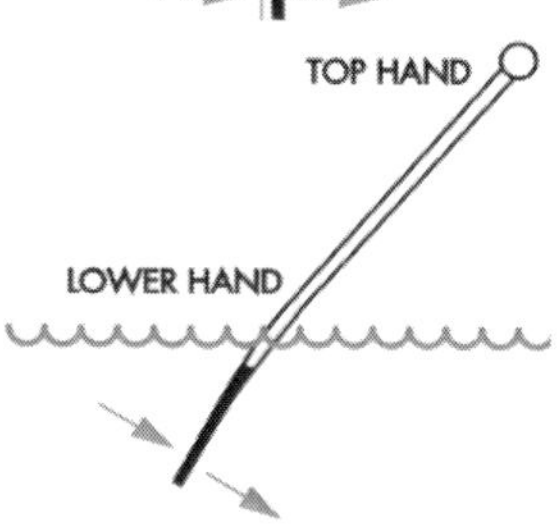

Extend the paddle as far forward as possible. In the beginning of the stroke, most of the potential power - 80-85%, is in front of you. The blade tip touches the water and enters as a result of the lower arm moving down (paddlers who free-fall from the shoulder to enter the blade are using a 'dynamic' paddling technique). Ensure a 'clean' entry with minimal splash. Just prior to the *catch*, the *latissimus* muscle is stretched and the 'rubber-band affect' of this stretch together with pulling with the lower arm is the first force that propels the va`a.

Set Up Common Errors

If we assume the set-up phase of the stroke is the first cycle of the forward paddling stroke, it's safe to say that if it goes wrong here, the flow on will directly affect the quality of the next phase; the entry. The following is a list of common errors associated with this phase of the stroke.

Arms and Hands

Lower arm too straight
Top arm elbow too straight or high - can occur if paddle length is too long
Hands gripping the paddle too hard
Upper elbow angled excessively down or up
Incorrect lower hand position on the shaft - too high, too low
Paddle not angled perpendicular to the water and parallel to the va`a.

Posture/Body

Sitting too upright
Leaning too far forward
Hunched shoulders
Lack of rotation - very common
Sitting too square on the seat
Excessive lean out from side of the va`a.

Avoid bending or hunching your middle and/or upper back. The small of your back should be slightly arched for the entire stroke, straightening only on the exit. The net consequence of ensuring this posture is that greater power can be contributed to the downward drive on the blade by the core muscles of the upper body.

Head/Neck/Face

Head hanging down, gaze focused down
Tense neck
Tense facial muscles/clenched teeth.

Legs

Feet not braced on the floor of the va`a
Front on-side leg not semi-extended
Off-side leg not bent and foot braced.

Entry Phase Common Errors

The entry phase of the stroke is very controlled yet dynamic. The paddle is neither smashed into the water nor delicately placed, you need deliberate purpose, commitment and precision. An understanding of what it is you need to achieve is essential. Poor entry will doom the rest of the stroke. The key element here is to ensure the blade does not take air down with it. Ensure that no effort is made to pull before the blade is fully buried in the water.

Arms

Upper arm pushing forward before contact with water, so the blade is moving backward at entry.

Paddle Not Parallel to Va`a

Dragon boat and other canoe sport paddlers suggest that the paddle should enter parallel to the hull so the blade tip is entered square on and directly downward. The common practice of *feathering* the blade during the recovery phase of the va`a stroke by an inward rotation of the wrist and rolling relaxation of the lower shoulder, permits the blade to be sliced in sideways at the point of entry. It then becomes parallel with the hull as the paddle moves through to the catch. The advantage of the blade being entered progressively from one corner, rather than flush with the surface of the water is that it produces a cleaner entry with less chance of aeration occurring along the length of the blade.

Additionally, the width of the va`a often makes it difficult for all but a few to achieve a hand-directly-over-hand, parallel entry of the blade relative to the hull. Its fine for narrow, solo craft, but to advocate this as a technique for a team va`a is to fail to factor in the craft itself and the limits it places on technique.

Here we see *Kai Bartlett* slice the blade in sideways as opposed to square on and parallel to the va`a hull; a common technique applied to the entry phase of the va`a stroke.

Posture/Body

Failure to drop the shoulder and lower arm to push the blade deep.
Excessive lean over the gunnel
Early rotation causing the paddle to move backwards prior to entry.

Timing

The entry of the paddle sets up the timing phase of the stroke. While gross errors of timing between paddlers will be obvious, often they are marginal and hard to detect. You can implement drills to improve and reinforce the need for good timing; paddlers counting out, "one, two, three, four" with each entry for example. Team paddling is like a tug of war, to be effective, everyone must pull together.

The Catch - 'Applying Pressure'

This is the shortest phase of the stroke and the most perplexing as it is sometimes confused with the 'entry'. Ultimately it is as it suggests; the exact moment when the blade is fully submerged and catches or grips the water. This requires that water is 'pressured' against the blade face. The term *lock* and *load* provides a good visual parallel. The blade has been placed, locked into position, then *loaded* - immersed in water and under pressure. No pull, no catch. The quality of the *catch* is largely determined by the quality of the entry and the manner in which power is applied to the blade - and the design merits of the blade itself.

Many experts suggest the catch phase is the most important and dynamic part of the stroke. No matter how hard you rotate, pull and drive, if the blade has poor catch - grip on the water, it will simply slip backwards and fail to pull the va`a up to the blade.

The blade can be anchored or braced against the water once fully submerged. It is still being directed in a downward motion by the top and lower arm, shoulders, upper back and the body's rotation.

Catch is achieved by a synchronised pull with your lower arm and rotation of the torso from the hips so you unwind from the reach position. The paddler's centre of gravity is marginally lowered as the blade travels close to and nearly parallel with the va`a. A solid catch is essential for the next phase of the stroke to ensure the maximum use of the power-face. The power-face is essentially 'primed' to take the load that will be transferred to it during the power phase of the stroke.

Catch Common Errors

The catch is the first true 'feel' phase of the stroke. A poor catch as opposed to a good one 'feels' very different – a concept newcomers often struggle with. Experienced paddlers know the value of good catch and can quickly recognise how effective they have been in achieving it. A good blade shape is a key element. The potential for a good catch is only as good as the quality of the entry. The blade must be nearly free of air along both faces. Newcomers can benefit from larger blade faces which offer more resistance and drag, so they can feel this loading of the blade. Small blade faces require greater precision of placement and power in order to achieve adequate catch.

Arms
Lower arm bends - pulls, too early in anticipation of the pull
Upper hand pushed prematurely over the lower hand.

Posture/Body
Applying power to the paddle by early rotation, thereby rushing to the power phase
Excessive lean over the gunnel
Failure to commit fully to the stroke.

Legs
Legs not braced.

These common errors affect the blade's performance in terms of its potential to anchor solidly against the water. Rushing to the power phase of the stroke before establishing a good catch will negate the effectiveness of the power phases to come. An entry that enters the blade into the water quickly and cleanly, applying downward motion of the lower arm and downward drive by the top arm so the blade is fully immersed, followed by torso rotation, will ensure the best results.

Depth-charging the blade into the water will simply cause large amounts of air to be pulled down and around the blade, meaning it will not have a solid mass against which to pull. A poor catch is obvious if the blade creates plumes of water and spray at the point of entry, which is often a result of the paddler executing the forward stroke prior to contact with the water. These poor habits must be eliminated early. A common drill for this phase of the stroke is having the paddlers paddle quietly, best practised in flat, still water.

Poor catch when paddling a va`a from a stand-still is common as paddlers rush to the power phase prior to loading the paddle correctly. This is usually characterised by large amounts of splash at the entry and exit of the blade.

The Pull (Power) Phase

An estimated 80-85% of the forward power is generated during a mere 7-8" of pull, originating from the point of entry. The notion of 'surprising' the water should be emphasised, so the torque of the body and pull of the lower arm can be executed in an explosive yet smooth manner. This quick and sudden compression of the power-face against the water provides little escape time for the water to flow off and around it - this is especially critical with smaller blade faces.

Parallel Pull
The width of the va`a can be problematic in achieving a direct hand-over-hand vertical and parallel pull through and indeed this is not the best biomechanical position from which to generate maximum torque and power. Some marginal offset is achieved as it permits greater power to be generated from the body's rotation which is transferred to the blade. This is where surf-ski and kayak paddlers excel in using this technique because it is a natural extension of the kayak stroke. However,

ensure your stroke does not *sweep* away from the side of the va`a as this will diminish the forward propulsion and make life difficult for the steerer.

Getting 'Over' the Stroke

Creative visualisation or at least having a sense of what you are trying to 'feel' during the power-phase of the stroke is a valuable tool in self analysis.

You want to have the idea of pole-vaulting yourself over the top of your paddle. The grip needs to be in front of you, so as you sense you are working from 'behind' the paddle and your top arm will tell you a lot about whether you are achieving this, especially when the shaft is vertical.

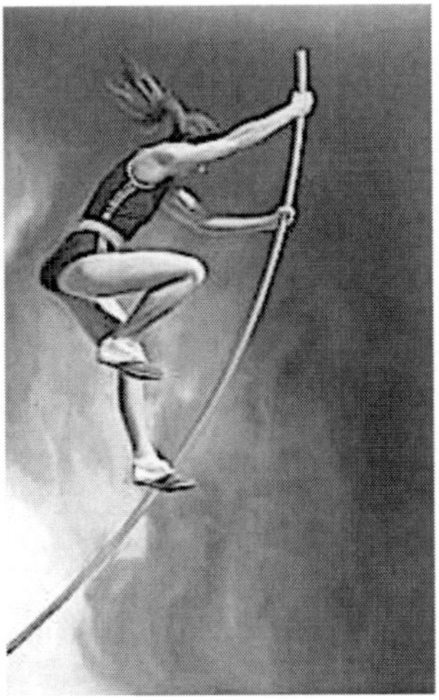

A paddle that is too long in the shaft will fail to give you this feeling, as your top hand will be too high above your head. From this position you cannot achieve this sensation. This is one reason why overall paddle lengths have reduced over time. Another reason is preventing shoulder injury often caused when the top arm has to work too high above the head when the shaft is vertical.

Pull is initiated by the lower arm, originating from the elbow and leading shoulder, wrist and forearm remain strong following a natural path of travel | 6 | Avoid simply 'pulling back' in a linear line. Direct the pull in a downward and backward trajectory. Your upper arm | 7 | keeps pressing down, not pushing forward and remains bent. Try to keep your upper hand angled back toward you for as long as possible to keep the blade angled forward to improve power transmission and increased lift for a longer period of time. Once your 'upper' and 'lower' hand are nearly 'hand-over-hand', | 8 | the body rotates around the spine, utilising the larger muscles of the upper body | 9 | Bending of the lower arm ceases momentarily to transfer torque from your body to the blade.

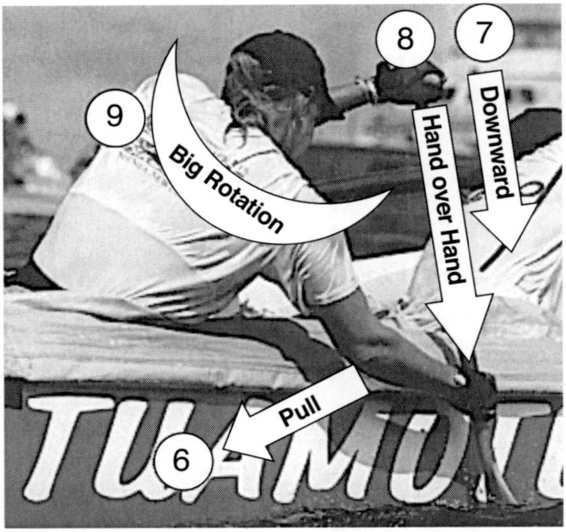

The abdominal muscles play an important role in 'squeezing' and rotating the body, the *latissimus dorsi* is the major muscle group in controlling the pull of the

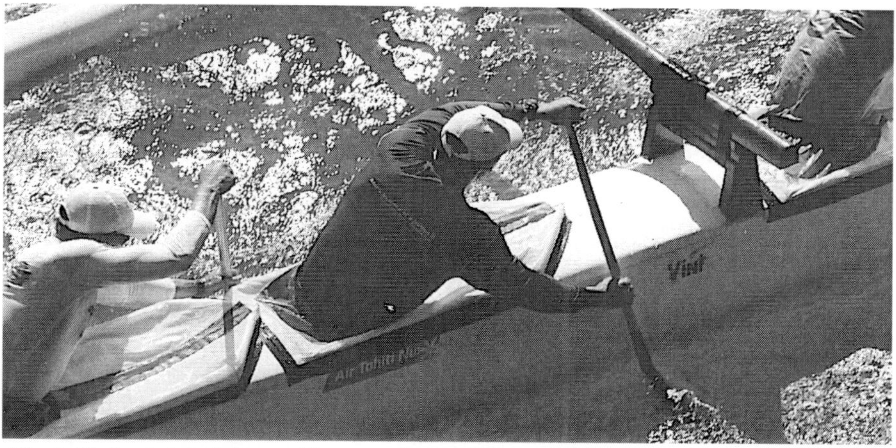

The initial catch is followed by a period of 'lift' as the angled blade is pulled down and back. Once hand-over-hand, the body then begins a powerful rotation until the shoulders are square-on.

Concentrate on keeping your top hand (10) working in small circular motions in front of you, Note top hand is level with lower shoulder (11) indicating correct paddle length, reach and blade depth in combination. Once the va`a has been pulled up to and well past the blade's vertical position and it is nearly level with your hip (12) the lower elbow will naturally bend (13) your wrist and shoulders will relax, the top hand grip should be just level or below the sternum (14) and your shoulders just past 'square-on' (15). The blade is then sliced up and outward from the side of the va`a. *Chris Maynard.* Marquesas Islands.

blade. Aim to keep your upper and lower hand, hand-over-hand and lower back arched for as long as possible while rotating around your spine to ensure maximum time and effectiveness in pulling.

Avoid moving your body excessively forward as this will encourage 'push'. The lower small of your back should remain arched. As the torso 'unwinds', your leading shoulder moves back, while your offside shoulder moves forward, until the shoulders are square and the chest vertical. Once the shaft moves past vertical, as a result of the va`a being pulled up to it, your lower arm will naturally need to bend at the elbow and the top hand should be almost level with your sternum. This signals the end of the stroke.

Lift

When the initial pull is applied to a blade with a 10-12° angle, lift is the result with greater amounts of forward drive being generated as the blade moves through to almost vertical. This lift effect has become increasingly recognised as critical.

There is now increased emphasis on the pull being considered in terms of moving downward and backward while attempting to keep the blade face angled for longer and keeping this lift happening for longer. As the blade moves to vertical, emphasis is then placed on rotation around the spine to generate torque. Consequently, we can talk in terms of a lift phase which then transfers to a drive phase.

Once the blade is vertical, your lower arm ceases to pull, the top arm's downward push is reduced and your body continues to rotate around your spine, providing power to the blade. Your lower arm elbow will naturally bend when it is no longer effective when the blade reaches your hip and the exit is initiated.

Top Arm

A common error is to push forward with your top arm. This causes the blade to move to and past vertical prematurely. Little power is gained by pushing forward with the top arm. Pushing forward is only truly effective with a double-bend paddle at the point at which the shaft is almost vertical. Your top arm must push down at the early part of the power phase as this acts on the angled blade, which in turn causes an equal and opposite reaction providing lift and drive forward.

Vertical Positioning

As you begin to rotate/unwind and apply pressure to the blade face, the shaft will quickly move from almost vertical to 10-12° offset forward. When this position is reached, no pushing and loading of the paddle in a downward manner should continue, only rotation and torque around your spine, using the larger muscles of your upper back, shoulders and *latissimus dorsi*.

Power Phase Common Errors

Arms

Lower arm pulling too early, rushing the stroke
Pushing paddle too deep
Continuing to push paddle deep once shaft is vertical
Pushing forward with top arm (single bend)
Upper hand pushed prematurely over the lower hand on shaft
Jerky pulling of the lower arm.

Pushing the top hand forward so it passes over the lower hand of the lower shaft, prevents the blade being vertical for long enough. This indicates poor rotation and is often used as a way of avoiding pressure experienced during the subsequent rotation and pull. Keen to avoid pain and suffering, many novices use this technique. Competitive paddling demands strengthening of both your body and mind.
Paddlers will sometimes continue to generate downward thrust past the vertical and fail to rotate and pull back, driving the paddle deeper than required and generating little or no forward power. Timing and execution of the transition between catch and the power phase is critical. Do not bury the blade much beyond the shoulder of the paddle.

Posture/Bend
Back too straight
Hunched over
Insufficient body weight applied to paddle
Rotation of upper torso not coinciding with gradual lift of the body as it moves to being square on, affecting energy transference along the shaft through to the paddler's body.
Power applied only after the blade has travelled past vertical
Paddle driven deeper as it passes knee and hip, as body leans over gunnel.

Legs
Poor leg drive.

The Exit Phase

The lower arm bends progressively as the va`a is pulled up to the blade. Ensure leg drive and transference of energy through your buttocks and feet to the va`a is in a forward direction, with stability around your trunk and spine. Soon after the shaft passes through the vertical, your lower elbow will want to bend, this defines the end

of the power phase of the stroke. Tension is released from the body and the exit phase of the stroke can begin. In flat water conditions, a clean whirlpool, nearly free of air bubbles should be all that remains after the exit. This indicates that a clean entry and good catch was achieved at the beginning of the stroke cycle and that the exit was executed at the correct time.

Upper arm is near straight and hand is level with or just below the sternum (15) The upper torso should now be almost upright, shoulders square (16) relaxed lower and upper wrists (17) and shoulders. Lift then slice the paddle out of the water and away from the va`a as it reaches the hip, using the lower arm, rolling the elbow outward (18). Note that continued pulling at this point will turn in to a push and pull-down, the reverse of the forces at play at the beginning of the stroke. These are counter-productive.

It is universally agreed that the paddle should leave (exit) the water soon after it has reached the hip area. This ensures that you avoid the push and loading of the paddle, which serves only to pull the va`a down and create drag on the paddle.

The action which the paddler uses to exit the paddle is commonly executed in two very distinct ways. It is best if there is an uniformity between crew member's exit action as there is on entry and the entire stroke. Variances in exiting styles can cause timing issues at the worst level and looks untidy from an aesthetic viewpoint.

Exit Phase Common Errors

As you rotate, apply power and move through the power phase, the blade naturally moves past vertical and is inclined backwards. Your lower elbow will naturally find its own limits and begin to bend as the blade passes your knee, the blade exiting approximately level with your hip.

The blade is now angled toward the rear and in an upward trajectory. While at the front of the stroke this created lift, it now has the opposite effect. It will pull down on the va`a if you continue pushing and lifting, which causes it to slow as the run or glide is hindered. Consequently, pulling must cease and the blade either lifted directly up or out to the side if using the more popular feathering technique.

Posture/Body
Paddler fails to rotate body
Paddler over-rotates so their torso now faces outward on paddling side.
Arms
Slow exit of the paddle causing drag
Paddler pushes and lifts paddle past the hip, scooping the water, pulling wa`a down
Paddlers exiting at different times.

Exit and Recovery Techniques

There is a rule of thumb which goes that, 'the recovery phase of the stroke is near twice that of the actual stroke itself.' This rule does vary depending on which style you develop, as the Tahitian style often appears near equal proportions as against the Hawaiian which is closer to the 1:2 ratio.

At the moment the exit is commenced, paddlers have two options. They can either lift the paddle directly up and carry the blade in an 'up and over' motion through the recovery phase; or they can initiate a motion which exits the paddle out from the side of the va`a using an up and outward rotation of the lower shoulder. This effectively slices the blade sideways out of the water, and commences **feathering** of the blade even before it completely exits the water. The blade then travels in a low sweeping arc over the water.

These two styles are overtly different and constitute a major variation in technique which has a direct affect on the recovery and entry phases of the stroke.

Sideways Exit and Feathering. This is achieved by rotating both your wrists inward once the blade is totally free of the water, leading arm bending and angling out, away from the side of the va`a and a lifting and rotating your shoulder outward.

Slicing the paddle up and out from the side of the va`a, employing a low swinging recovery while 'feathering' the blade. Top arm remains low at the exit and the paddle is swung forward as the body rotates through the recovery, the lower arm extends outward and the top arm travels up to bring the shaft upright. In contrast

to 'lifting and carrying' the blade forward, the majority of the work carried out by the body's rotation.

Your lower shoulder begins to relax as the blade begins its exit. Your elbow, as it continues its bend, is relaxed and angled out from the side of the body, while the wrist is relaxed as the blade begins to exit the water outward from the side of the va`a. Your lower and upper wrists roll over and inward as they relax so the blade face begins to open out into the feathered position for the commencement of what can be called the air transfer phase. Once free of the water, the paddle commences a low arced trajectory across the water in a 'c' shape away from, then back to the side of the va`a in a feathered position to reduce the effect of wind resistance.

As a consequence of this low arced recovery, some paddlers will tend to 'slice' the blade into the water sideways, as opposed to a more 'vertical' downward entry. This can create a smoother, cleaner placement into the water, as air is less likely to be trapped on the back of the blade.

Parallel pull, sliced exit away from hull, 'feathered' paddle, lower elbow marginally bent, top arm low, forms a 'D' shaped pattern; entry, pull, exit, recovery, entry.

At the mid point of the recovery - usually twice as long as the stroke itself, the upper arm reaches its highest point and your body begins to move from vertical into a controlled rotation around the spine, so your leading shoulder begins to move forward and down Your body remains relaxed and the shaft should be almost vertical, close to the hull of the va`a. Your lower and upper wrists begin to prepare the paddle for entry once the set up has been reached.

Lifting and Carrying the Paddle Squarely Forward.

The paddle is lifted directly up at the exit, a consequence of the paddler having rotated to nearly upright - chest vertical, shoulders square, and through a lifting up action of the lower and top arm. Once free of the water you should carry, not swing, the paddle along the va`a gunnel, rotating mid-way to the set up and entry once again. The paddle is not rotated with the wrists, remaining 'square on'.

This has been common in the Tahitian stroke using double-bend paddles, though in recent times there appears to have been some modified, with a greater degree of feathering at the exit and greater swing. You will end the stroke sitting almost straight up as the paddle is lifted up out of the water. Some feathering of the blade is initiated by rolling your wrist, the arms carrying the paddle forward together, with the twist or rotation of your body coming reasonably late in the movement. This square recovery is common to dragon boating.

Flicking

When using the sliced exit avoid *flicking* the blade by over working the top arm wrist action. This can spray the paddler's seated behind you and can fill the va`a with water when covers are not being used. While some advocate this flick believing it contributes to forward propulsion, it actually creates *drag* as the paddle is effectively *loaded* when it should be empty. As the paddle leaves the water, it is essential to relax to allow tension to leave your body and to ensure a more fluid recovery phase. This is your chance to breath in.

Recovery Phase Common Errors

Arms

Lower elbow and wrist not relaxed, should turn inward
Top hand wrist not relaxed and failing to control paddle when feathering
Exit is jerky
Leading arm too low

Posture/Body

Upper body excessive movement
Paddle carried back too low and hits the water during the swing back
Paddle carried too high back to set up phase during swing back
Relaxing, letting go of tension and remembering to breath are all vital elements of the recovery phase. This is a time to focus and concentrate in a relaxed state during the move through to the set up phase. The smooth action of your recovery is essential to avoid unnecessary downward pressure on the wa`a. Your pull has set the wa`a in motion, it is important you don't interfere with this.
Smoothness and fluidity needs to be emphasised.
In flat water, practice by having the blade face skim over the top of the water during the recovery phase when *feathering* the paddle.

Timing

In a team va`a, the *timing, cadence* and *rhythm* of the *entry,* power and *exit* phases need to be as synchronised as possible. This discipline needs to be reinforced and adhered to as it is one of the most important factors in generating good hull speed.

While the stroke sets up the stroke rate, each crew tends to have an optimum average stroke rate. Several timing drills can be practised either on land or on the water. Having everyone paddle on the same side can emphasise this, while at the same time practising smooth and quiet paddling.

Double-Bend Paddle Technique

The difference between single and double bend paddle technique could be considered subtle, but in truth the power-phase, exit and recovery in particular is as different as the paddle itself. The additional bend in the upper shaft provides a crank which, when the shaft is almost vertical, provides you with a degree of mechanical advantage. (See also pages 259-260)

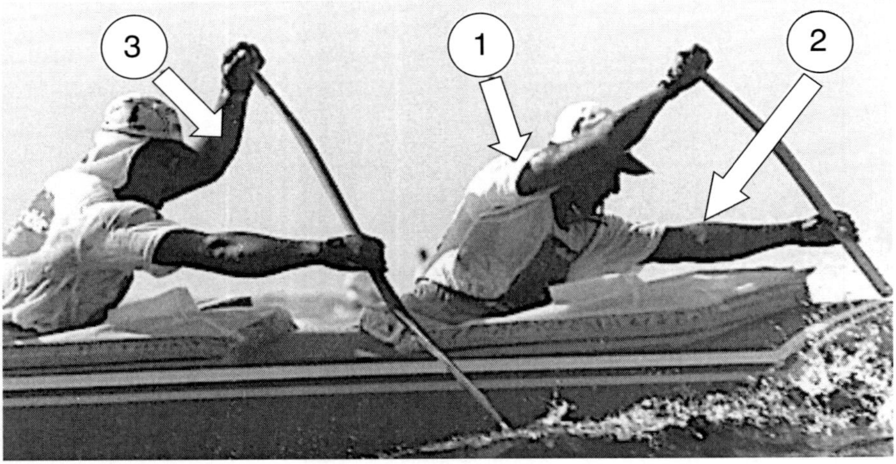

Set Up and Entry of the Blade

Your body is leaning forward, but the degree of body rotation is less than when a single bend paddle is used. Chest is canted forward, lower shoulder dropped toward gunnel, upper shoulder moves further back than with single-bend because of the additional upper bend placing the handle further back toward you. Avoid over-rotation I 1 I Lower arm tends to be straight to account for reduced rotation in achieving good reach, I 2 I chin and gaze remains up, lower arm moves down to bring about entry, top elbow is often angled marginally down, I 3 I shoulder remains as low as possible, top arm is 2/3 flexed because of additional crank in upper shaft.

Because of the added bend in the top portion of the shaft, placement is largely controlled with the lower hand. In addition, the top hand is further back relative to the top shoulder because of the angled crank.

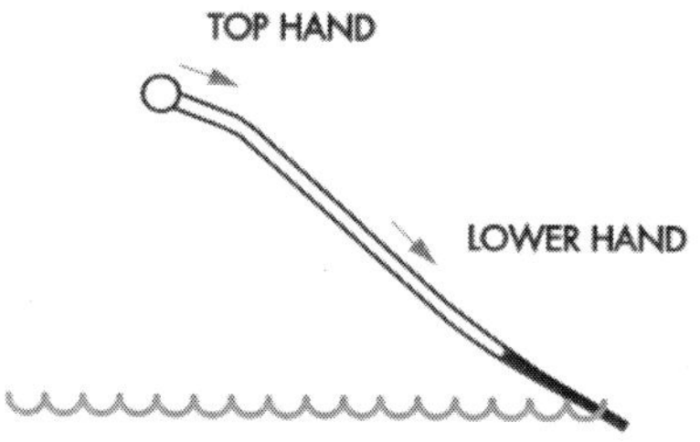

Similiar technique for the catch phase as per single bend, initiated by pulling and bending of the lower arm with lift generated at the front portion of the stroke.

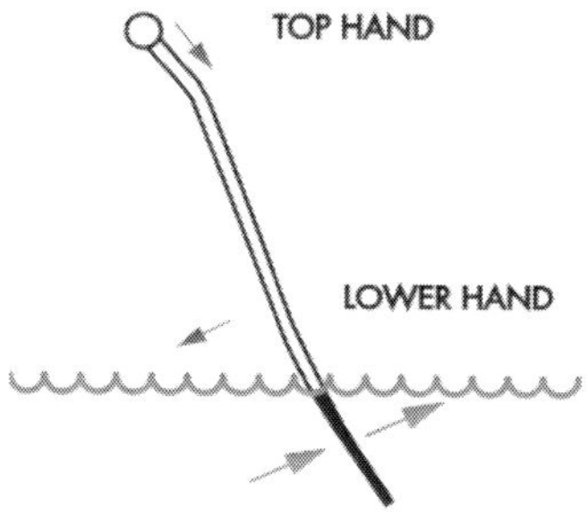

As the blade enters the vertical phase of the stroke (vertical shaft), in contrast to the single bend technique, the paddler pushes forwards momentarily with the top arm in order to take advantage of the crank. This coincides with pull from the lower arm.

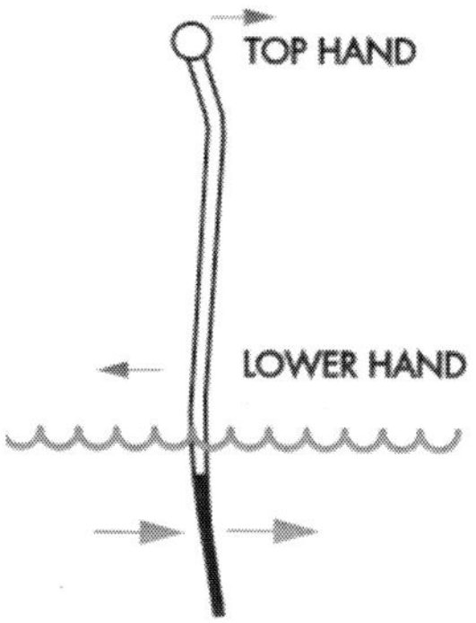

Some rotational movement is used late in the pull phase combined with continued pulling and pushing via the arms.

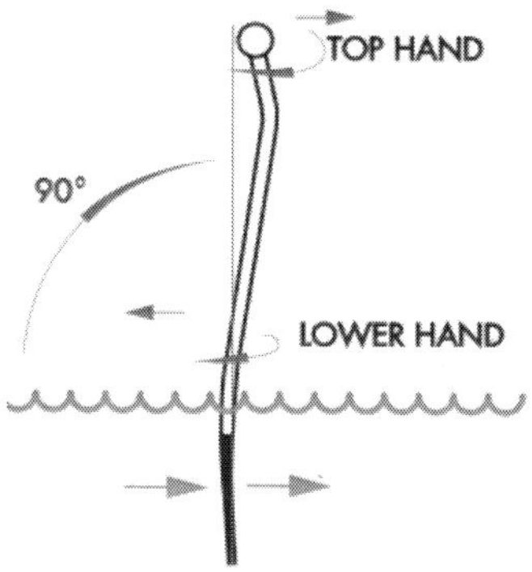

Poised for entry, paddlers remain reasonably upright in their paddling posture - a traditional Tahitian characteristic, with only marginal lean forwards, relying on good twist and lower arm extension for maximum reach. The top arm, is bent at the elbow and points downwards, with top hand above head height.

At the set up phase of the stroke, the paddler enters the blade via equal downwards thrust into the water using top and lower arms until the catch phase is reached immediately after. The paddler then rotates or unwinds keeping top and lower arms locked briefly, with top and lower hands moving at equal speeds, top arm moderately driving downwards and across the body, lower arm locked, moving in syncronicity with the paddlers natural body rotation.

Catch As for Single-Bend.

The Power Phase

As for single bend technique up until the point when the shaft is nearly vertical. At this point | 4 | push forward with the upper hand while pulling back with the lower hand | 5 | This is a short, sharp, powerful movement, done while rotating around the spine | 6 |. See also Page 258-260.

At the mid-point of the stroke, with blade nearly vertical in the water, the effectiveness of the double bend paddle comes into its own. Your lower arm is now bent to an almost 45° angle and the top arm remains, with elbow cocked, in a marginally downward angle. The paddler now goes through a transition, where you actively 'pull' with the lower arm and at the same time 'push' forward with the top in one short powerful burst. In doing this, the 'crank' within the upper shaft is used to good effect.

Immediately towards the end of this 'power' phase of the stroke, the lower arm is very much bent and the exit from the water is quick and near hip level. Interestingly, many top Tahitian crews, tend to 'lift' the paddle out of the water, implementing very little 'feathering' of the paddle. Both top and lower arms then carry the paddle forwards in unison, with the twist or rotation of the body coming reasonably late in the movement. The paddler ends the stroke, sitting almost straight up as the paddle exits the water.

The bend that exists in the double bends shaft, three quarters the way up or so, is often referred to as a *crank* and with good reason, because in real terms that's exactly what it can be for the paddler. Provided it is a well designed double bend, this crank or fulcrum point can act as an addition lever in providing drive and power to the blade.

Exit Phase

It is not uncommon for this stroke to travel further than past your hip as a consequence of this push from the top arm. The inherent flex in the shaft as is common to double bend paddles of French Polynesia, seems to negate some of the issues of pulling the va`a down. At the end of the stroke, your top arm is straight and parallel with the gunnel.

Lift the blade from the water when it reaches your hip - continued pulling will become push and lift, pulling the va`a down. Because your lower arm pulls and the top arm pushes to use the upper crank in the shaft, it is better if the blade is lifted up first when level with the hip rather than sliced outward away from the va`a. Commencement of feathering can occur once free of the water, chin and gaze remain up and forward.

Recovery Phase

Team Shell Tahiti, **lifting and carrying the paddle more squarely forward, using predominantly a high vertical lift of the top arm, bending of the lower elbow. The movement is very economical in terms of overall body movement; most of the work is done by the arms.**

Common Errors

Same as for single-bend technique, but also failing to synchronise push with top arm and pull with lower arm when the shaft is almost vertical and continuing to pull and push for too long past vertical, pulling the va`a down at the back of the stroke, are the most common errors.

Working With The Ocean

Surfers surf ocean ground swells generated by distant storms which pitch and break over the shallow water. While ocean paddlers pursue a completely different ocean energy; wind generated surface waves or 'wind swell' often referred to simply as the 'sea'. Conditions permitting, you may end up chasing both ground swell and the surface wind formed waves.

Downwind Paddling Defined

The term paddling 'downwind' is as it suggests paddling with the wind behind, chasing a moving or following sea. The experienced paddler reads the ocean as a series of ever rising and falling peaks and troughs or 'bumps' into which they steer their craft, attempting to remain on the 'fastest' sections which provide the most assistance - the downward slope or forward face. As a snow skier might move left and right to carve a path between the bumps as they ski down the mountain, the ocean paddler seeks a similar path. In the context of a team va`a, this skill comes down to the steerer.

The art of remaining in the fast section of these bumps or 'runners' requires the paddler to remain alert, anticipating or seeing where one section is diminishing and another is forming. The goal is to ultimately 'connect' or 'link' these newly forming sections to maintain maximum assistance and speed, a term sometimes referred to as 'connecting the dots'. As a consequence, in the case of downwind paddling, the fastest way between two points is rarely in a straight line. Importantly, when moving at speed on a va`a, it's not so much what's behind you that matters, but what's in front. This is again in contrast with the surfer who goes from a stand still to be lifted and pushed from behind.

While smaller surface wind waves and swells are a localised phenomenon, the larger ground swell can reside below and between. These are caused by distant powerful storms and are often mere decoys in terms of where real gains in speed can be found.

Though the ground swell encountered far from shore in deep water will often be moving at a greater speed than that of the surface sea, they are generally difficult to catch because they are not as steep as the 'sea' on top. However, if the distance between the ground swells is short and the incline steep, this could change your tactics.

Technical Aspects

When paddling downwind following a 'running' sea, knowing when to paddle hard and when to back off are key skill elements. In the case of a team va`a, this requires the 'stroker' to alter their stroke rate in response to the ever changing dynamic of the craft's interaction with the ocean's irregularities. The lead role the stroker must play in this situation is critical. The ability to deliver varying power, increased stroke rates per minute and different technique to achieve effective speed gains is a true skill

The trigger to change any single or multiple aspect of technique or application, can be either a visual response in seeing the runner forming ahead in the form of a trough or a 'feeling' when the craft begins to drop at the bow and lift at the stern. Ultimately, this all becomes academic if the 'steerer' fails to 'set-up' the va`a and hold it within the runner while searching for the next. The rest of the crew must also respond accordingly, in time and with full commitment.

It's all in front of you, odd as this may seem. Your focus needs to be on what's ahead, reading the constantly changing shape of the ocean. Interpreting what's going on immediately ahead of you and reacting accordingly is to acknowledge what is going on behind.

In this sequence, *Outrigger Australia* are putting the hammer down looking ahead, knowing that significant gains in speed are about to be had.

These skills transcend true explanation. They must be learned by experience and represent team work and co-operation of the highest order which separates top crews from the mere average. The single best way to acquire these response based skills is by spending time on a solo or duo va`a or surf-ski.

While the steerer has the most technical of all seats within a team va`a, the stroker has the most demanding and technical of the paddler seats. This is the case whether in a calm or rough water environment. If your weak link is situated at either end of the va`a, your potential is immediately compromised.

The stroker must remain resolute and confident, continually biting away at the ocean, reading its nuances immediately in front and below their blade. It is the steerer's role to maintain the whole balancing act, keeping the va`a steady between the curvatures of the ocean, keeping a broader view and continually setting up to take advantage of the ocean's energy. In this respect, both stroke and steerer work in close harmony - almost unwittingly and especially as they spend more time together.

The position of stroke requires great concentration at all times. Since they also dictate to the paddlers behind them, faults of the average strokers become very obvious. Many choose to 'switch off' and simply swing away. They take the attitude that because they are 'up front', others must follow, pure and simple.

Psychologically, it's a tough position with no paddle to follow. It's just you, the bow of the va`a, the ocean and five sets of eyes looking to you to perform. You can't hide up front and if the crew feels your stroke rate is too slow, too fast, or too short, there's always someone there to remind you; and sometimes impatiently if you fail to deliver what's wanted.

In this image, the larger undulating ground swell is clearly seen, the 'sea' or lumpy messy chopped up surface water is what we need to be concerned with as it opens and closes, rises and falls. This is the good stuff which needs to be used in order to keep the va`a travelling at optimum speed.

In terms of fine-tuning a crew's stroke rate, cadence, reach, entry and exit points of the stroke itself, the stroke holds the key, provided the paddlers are willing to follow and are concentrating. Beyond this, their ability to make adjustments to these primary technical facets is a skill requiring time to acquire in as many ocean conditions as possible.

Ocean solo va`a or surf-ski training is invaluable in cultivating an intimate knowledge of the ocean, paddling skills and the ability to rely upon self knowledge, fuelled by confidence on the water. Knowing when to vary the stroke rate and its length out-front is only acquired by paddling all points of the ocean; across, into and with, so you learn to mix up your stroke to get the most out of the ocean and your craft. In this respect, these are the primary skills you must have as a stroke or you'll remain average and in doing so, handicap your crew's performance.

This knowledge is paramount and having the confidence to deliver it in a va`a at all times in harmony with the shifting ocean is vital. Your crew cannot continually tell the stroker what's needed, that's up to them and they will be judged accordingly.

Many crews have been frustrated by a stroke with poor technique who is not able to adapt and 'milk' the best of the ocean and their crew. The stroke should not assume this position as a 'power-seat' but more one of stealth and finesse, and never with the attitude of a headstrong maverick. A good stroke learns to blend and get the most out of the 'power-seats' behind them in any circumstance.

Going Long - Going Short

The stoker must strive to ensure optimum performance from the paddlers behind, especially in terms of uniformity of reach, timing and 'rating'. Their head-space must be pre-occupied with ensuring they are getting the most out of the crew. A common problem originating from the stroker is when they consistently fail to provide adequate 'reach' out front. If the stroker 'shortens' their reach or rating, this will be copied and have an immediate ripple effect along the entire length of the va`a.

Strokers are often built more for endurance than strength, whereas the 'power-seat' paddlers are amongst the biggest and tallest. In this regard, a stroke must always 'think tall', keeping reach to a maximum and allowing these taller paddlers to use their leverage effectively. Tall paddlers have a

dislike for paddling 'short' and the stroke must always oblige. One interesting and often overlooked aspect of 'short' paddlers is that many still have a long torso and arms, so when seated they are quite tall in the seat relative to their height. This means they are quite capable bio-mechanically of delivering a long reach and plenty of leverage.

In recent years, with the introduction of the *Mirage* va`a in particular, there has been a shift in placing heavier paddlers in the stroker's position, to 'weight' the bow in the case of chasing runners and even when punching up-wind to reduce the pitching of the va`a. The decision to do so is governed by prevailing conditions and varying abilities of the crew.

While keeping a 'long out-front' style is essential, there are times when you will want to shorten up. This is a skill which takes time to develop and is a 'feel' orientated skill. Done well and at the appropriate time, your 'power-seats' will tolerate this for short periods of time. 'Going short' is demanding in terms of its application and only the stroke can dictate when to use it, otherwise the va`a will quickly fall 'out of time'.

A shortening of the 'reach' provides you with a brief opportunity to; increase the va`a hull speed through increased stroke rate; maintain speed in adverse situations such as paddling against strong tides and shallow water (where the hull is sucked down - interaction); or push over the face of a swell. It can also be used in short bursts to catch up and overtake another va`a, working on the basis of; on every *hut* called, the first six strokes will be of this nature, for the next four *huts*, for example.

Perhaps the most common example of its application is from a standing start where the stroke-length is initially short and deep, progressively lengthening out as a steadier pace is established. The skill here is in having excellent paddle control so the blade is buried cleanly, ensuring it 'bites' before power is applied and that the exit is clean. Washing machine starts may look good, but are totally inefficient!

While the 'longer' stroke is appropriate for consistent 'distance pace' paddling, when a short burst of speed or additional power is required, marginally shortening the reach and 'depth-charging' the paddle can effectively accelerate the va`a. Working within a burst of six to ten strokes seems most effective. You can go for more, but you want to avoid 'burning the crew' and to provide just enough lift in power to achieve your objective. This can be alternated between *huts*, left and right to keep fresh arms.

Paddling Upwind

Upwind stroke rates are naturally diminished as a result of wind resistance and pushing against oncoming waves. The preferred technique is to ensure a long reach, keeping technique smooth, maximising blade time in the water, pouring on the power, and maintaining a quick recovery. Stronger, heavier crews often benefit from this approach. Lighter crews, including women and juniors, often apply a long reach, short pull back and fast recovery, keeping the stroke rate quite high. This is done because of a lack of power and if the stroke is 'laboured', the va`a has greater time for the forward momentum to diminish.

Out in the Ocean and Providing Variety

The most common time to vary long and short reach is when chasing 'bumps' on the ocean. A following sea continually accelerates and decelerates the progress of the va`a as it travels down the swell and at times 'stalls' in the trough when it buries into the back of the wave ahead. During the 'lull', where the va`a falls off the runner and labours in the trough, is a good time to 'shorten up'. You want to apply plenty of power, driving deep, depth charging your stroke for a short period of time, to 'prime' the va`a for the next drop in. Naturally your stroke rate slows marginally, proportional to the va`a hull speed, so you compensate for this by pouring on the power. As the va`a drops in and gathers speed, the stroke is 'lengthened' out and the stroke rate increased proportionally to match the va`a hull speed.

It's crucial that the crew follows the stroker's lead, that they understand the dynamics at play and know that the change is only temporary. Their knowledge of 'working the ocean' is also very important. In short, the 'collective knowledge' is what counts. Strokers who insist on being totally inflexible regarding stroke rates and length miss the point or simply don't have the experience to deliver what's needed. Flat water paddling calls for a consistency of stroke length and rate. But even in this situation, variation will break the monotony and provide bursts of speed in between the 'distance pace'.

The rougher the water the greater the change needed to blend with the conditions. A stroker that fails to blend with the conditions is failing to account for the variations and the opportunities presented to them. This is both tedious and frustrating for a crew wanting to 'chase bumps'.

Physiological Aspects

Chasing 'bumps' is essentially a series of 'sprints' or 'efforts' followed by 'recovery periods' culminating with the 'set distance' or 'marathon pace'. While it would be easy to think of a race such as the Molokai to O`ahu as a marathon event, in reality it's a continuous series of sprints.

In such conditions, it's important to remember that bursts of 'effort' for long periods of time are neither possible nor profitable and learning to change is essential. Rest periods, or at least periods at a steady pace must be balanced between these bursts and surges in power and effort. *Fartleck* training methods are well suited for this type of racing.

During these bursts of 'effort', heart rates increase and the lungs scream for air, placing high cardiovascular demands on the body, as opposed to the slower and more sustainable rate.

Mental Attributes

A stroke must be highly competitive. If the stroke 'throws the towel in' when the going gets tough, more on the mental plane than the physical, you're in trouble. When a va`a threatens to overtake during a race situation, the stroke must maintain composure, deliver good reach and rating, and consider how to best deal with it. Going that few extra inches in the reach out front will push everyone else to do the same. Increasing the rating can help also, maintaining good reach, but at all costs you've got to hang in and throw the challenge back.

Keep your technique sound, use the ocean where you can and take the crew with you. Don't be distracted by other va`a in close and tight racing situations, or be distracted by the cadence of their stroke rate. Keep your head in your va`a and encourage the best from your crew.

Weight Distribution

Getting your weight as far forward as possible on the seat is a crucial element when chasing bumps. Get your butt on the edge of the seat to weight the va`a forward, this will also assist with your reach and twist.

Blade Depth

The depth at which you bury the blade should vary in certain circumstances. When the va`a is *bogged* or when you want to pour-on the power in flat water, burying the blade deep and clean is vital to maximise blade grip, creating potential for maximum effectiveness during the 'power phase' of the stroke. In this instance, you can *choke down* on the shaft of the paddle to roughly one hand span up from the neck of the blade. When the va`a 'breaks free' from the current or begins to surf down a wave, you can *choke up* on the shaft. When the va`a begins to 'surf' you can simply 'tap' the va`a along, burying the blade so the upper shoulders of the blade are visible. This enables a higher stroke rate with less 'effort' and constitutes a 'rest period'.

When the Call for 'Upping' the Rate Comes

Potential stroke rate is directly proportional to hull speed. All paddlers need to understand this. When the middle seats call out to 'pick the rate up' and the stroker is struggling to respond, merely burning up, consideration of the dynamics at play are required.

Firstly, a stroker cannot make a significant difference to hull speed by pulling harder than anyone else. Often when they try, the rating slows, technique suffers, or early 'burn-out' occurs. It must be a collective act of team synchronicity, everyone pulling harder and in time to generate increased hull speed, so a higher stroke rate can be achieved. For significant increases in ratings, there must ultimately be a significant increase in hull speed.

A commonly overlooked factor is that along the length of a 43' va`a, paddlers at the front, middle and rear are all in different sections of water (in terms of open ocean conditions). The stroker may be buried in the back of a wave where water particles are 'reversing'. The middle seats may be on the crest of the wave where water particles are revolving in the same direction as the va`a. In this instance, the stroker struggles to 'turn-over' their paddle quickly, whereas the middle seats are being assisted and therefore find the 'turn-over' easy and hence their demand for an increase to the stroke rate.

Swell Dynamics

If the va`a is following the direction of travel of the swell it's easy to see at what point the water is circulating either with or against the va`a relative to where it is positioned. The same is also true when punching against an oncoming wave.

The va`a moving in the same direction as the wind and swell will tend to *rock* back and forth between the swells as it stalls and accelerates.

Water particles perform a circular motion as a wave passes without significant net advances in position. The motion of the water is forward as the peak of the wave passes, but backward as the trough of the wave passes, arriving again at the same position when the next peak arrives. While there is a slight advance of the water with the wave, the advance is small compared to the overall circular motion. In this context, it's easy to imagine water travelling in reverse and counter direction of travel to that of the va`a in the case of the bow of the va`a being buried in the back of the wave ahead.

The circular motion of water particles on the back face of the swell ahead are moving counter to the direction of the va`a which slows its progress. Ideally, you want to avoid this 'stalling' situation as much as possible, having enough speed and inertia to 'push' over or through the back face of one wave and onto the forward face of the one ahead.

When the va`a stalls, the bow raises and the stern falls. You will feel the drag and slowing of the va`a as the bow section pushes against the opposing rotational movement of water particles on the back face of the swell ahead. The va`a breaks free as the incline increases and the bow drops further, and the push from the front face of the wave through the rotational motion of the water, travelling in the same direction as the va`a, takes affect.

Those seated aft would be experiencing 'assistance' as the water is circulating in a forward direction. In any event, throughout the length of the va`a paddlers are experiencing different stages of wave action, which translates directly to the feel within the blade itself. Develop a mental picture of what is going on within the water relative to where you are on the wave. When the va`a plunges into the back of a wave ahead, the water level is often at gunnel height, if not swamping, making turning the paddle over quickly and exercising good technique nearly impossible. In this instance, the stroker tries to maintain a good rate by not burying the blade deeply, keeping the entry shallow, and working the surface only. Keeping the rate up is essential as the power-seats behind want the rating up while they are in a 'fast' section of the wave, ready to power-up.

Tricks of the Trade

When the crew wants a higher rating, but seem incapable of providing the extra hull speed, one option is for the stroker to *shorten up*. But this will just upset everyone, so don't be tempted. You can bury your blade less deeply and resort to a light 'tap' which works reasonably well and enables a faster pull back keeping the reach and pull back the same length. Or you can opt to simply increase your recovery rate.

The problem with the latter is that it tends to create 'timing' problems, so you're often best to resort to the light 'tap' method. A 'quick `n light' technique is often very effective, where you decrease power application, length of pull-back and blade depth, therefore increasing stroke rate. Practising this with your crew is essential and a very worthwhile technique to have at your disposal. This is counter to the 'long and strong' approach.

Do Strokers Always Dictate Stroke Rate?

Many things dictate stroke rate. You will have your established 'base rate' or the rate at which your crew feels most comfortable for extended periods of time, then everything in between. Given 'clean' water, without the influence of adverse wind, waves/swell, current or shallow water, the 'base' rate is easily established. Once external factors come into play, the stroke-rate becomes dictated by these. Shallow water will slow your rating, as will adverse wind, while chasing a runner or travelling with the flow of a strong current, will all increase your rating as hull speed increases with the assistance. This being said, in an interesting juxtaposition, a knowledgeable, strong crew behind the stroke can make all the difference, often dictating the rating.

On many occasions, just staying in touch with what you feel through your butt, is as good a way as any. Listen with your head too much and you can loose the 'feel'. If you can feel a surge of power kicking in, with a good crew you can be sure they are onto something and want just that little more, so you up the rate and at times its as if you're staying with them, rather than the other way around. This is an important lesson to learn and the payoff for paddling with exceptional paddlers always hungry for more canoe speed. Don't fight what they want, work with them, not against them. When they put the hammer down, the wheels have to turn a little faster.

Timing Problems

There are many points at which *timing* becomes a problem, most noticeably at the entry, exit and recovery phases of the stroke. Some paddlers demonstrate a very fast, snappy recovery phase, feathering the paddle very efficiently during the swing back, while others prefer and are only capable of a much slower recovery, with a more pronounced high swing back to the set up phase. This presents a problem straight away. An often overlooked consideration is that of 'fast' and 'slow' twitch muscles and the relationship between them.

Fast Twitch Muscles. The purpose of this type of muscle is to provide rapid movement for short periods of time. Fast twitch muscles do not use oxygen - they use *glycogen*. Reactions using *glycogen* require *anaerobic enzymes* to produce power. *Glycogen* is stored in the muscles and liver, and is synthesised by the body using *carbohydrates*. There are also two types of fast twitch muscles. These two types of fast twitch muscles will function during moderate and maximum muscle effort. Fast twitch muscles provide you strength and speed.

Slow Twitch Muscles.
As their name indicates, these fibres have a slower contraction time. Slow twitch muscles use *oxygen* for power and have a predominance of *aerobic enzymes*. These types of muscles are large muscles found in the legs, thigh, trunk, back, hips and are used for holding posture.

Individuals, genetically, have more or less fast twitch muscle. In many instances, strokers have a high percentage of 'fast twitch muscle' which means that they are capable of delivering very high stroke rates when required. Interestingly, even with 'speed' training, there can only ever be minimal gains in fast twitch muscle groups, as little as 5%.

Some argue that it's only crucial that the power-phase of the stroke is in time throughout the crew. Va`a paddling is very much about 'power up-front', so the 'pull' becomes the primary driving force as opposed to the 'push' out the back. Strokers need to have excellent paddle skills and be very accurate technically. While the stroke generally dictates the rating, they will be out of time if they fail to 'blend' with the needs of the crew or the 'run' of the va`a.

Calling The 'Huts'

In 1948, the *Sit and Switch* style of paddling was developed by *Eugene Jenson* for va`a racing while training for the 800km Bemidji to Minneapolis race. The call of *hut* is the cue to switch paddling sides. The sound is easy to make as it requires pushing air out of the lungs which, when under physical strain, takes little effort on the part of the caller.

It's one of those things that is apparently so easy to do. No one ever tells you how to do it and it is taken for granted that anyone can do it. In reality, it's a skill, an important detail which, like all the other details that go together to make a successful, well oiled crew, has the potential to either hinder or help you. As always, the tougher the race conditions the more crucial this calling becomes and the more expert you need to be in order to do it right.

Sit and Switch

Paddlers paddle on opposing sides of the wa`a, in sequence from the front i.e. stroke on the left, # 2 on the right, #3 on the left and so on. Paddlers alternate sides to alleviate fatigue and keep their arms fresh. This style of paddling is often referred to as the 'Sit and Switch' method. Other va`a disciplines employ this method however within outrigger paddling, it is key to much of the structure of things.

The Novice Caller

The first question which always comes to mind is how many strokes should be taken before the call is made. Novice callers often adhere to a rigid number between 14 and 16. In some parts of the world, Tahiti for example, calls on 8 and 10 strokes are common. Religiously, the caller will count in their heads until the magic number comes up. They are often quite anxious, hoping they don't loose count or their breath (whichever comes first) while trying to deal with everything else going on around them.

Being a novice also often means that their arms are going to want to fall off a lot earlier than those of experienced paddlers. Pain thresholds are generally lower in novices, so the need to change takes on great urgency after only a reasonably small number of strokes. However, it's also common for novice paddlers/callers to focus so much on their paddling that they forget to call.

The Experienced Caller

In contrast, the experienced paddler and caller, relies more on a time frame as opposed to counting. Once you've called the switch for a while, the tedious and religious adherence to counting is and should be disposed of, replaced by an internal and intuitive 'body and head clock'. You instinctively know when the time has come to call and you also know that calling on a set number is to be avoided.

Your 'body clock' will tell you 'hey buddy - change!' and your 'head clock' will balance this out against your assessment of the way in which the va`a is travelling i.e. are you about to drop in on that swell you've been chasing and is this such a good time to call it?

You may well have taken 18 strokes on the one side, but then all of a sudden you're in the drop in zone and you figure just a few more big ones and over you go. So you hold out … 20, 21, 22, 23 … then you find the va`a racing down the face, *Hut!* and you power up with fresh arms. This behaviour could wear out a novice and maybe the crew wouldn't have the power to pull over and drop in anyway.

This briefly defines the major differences between the novice and the experienced caller. Overcoming the issues facing the novice requires time in the va`a, knowledge of the ocean and a genuine feel for the canoe and its nuances. A novice paddler cannot be expected to understand all this initially, but there are certain qualities which they will need to get started.

The Importance of a Consistent Sound

A caller should have a good strong voice and be able to call the *Hut* in a consistent manner in terms of its sound. This is a tough sport and a weak call does little to inspire the rest of the crew. It must be uplifting and strong, and sound like you mean it. Keeping the call short is also important, *Hut* as opposed to *Huuuuut*. If you prolong it, it tends to begin at the entry phase of the stroke and end at the exit which confuses the issue, especially if the stroke rate is high. Call it just prior to the entry phase of the penultimate stroke (last but one), short and sharp, keeping the tone consistent.

Some callers fool around with the call so we get *hut, huuut, yep, hike, yooooh* etc. I guess whatever you decide to call is OK, as long as everyone else is familiar with it and you're consistent. Consistency and strong tone becomes especially important when you are with a crew that likes to chat as they paddle, or you have someone keen on being the loud mouthed motivator or when we get calls from the steerer to 'up, up' the rating.

Much like a penguin which recognises its mothers call amongst all the others screaming, everyone can then at least listen for that one recognisable and distinctive call despite the other voices. (Excessive talking in the canoe is a factor more associated with novice crews.) If the call keeps varying how can you listen for it?

Besides the caller, there is always the need for a second 'talker' in the va`a. They are the one who motivates, calls the rating up, or asks for more power. At this point, it can become confusing if the call for more power, or higher rating sounds much like the callers *hut* such as 'up, up!'.

An effective technique I have seen in Tahiti is a whistling system, normally used by the steerer. When they want to 'up' the rating/power, a whistle is given to pass this on, normally two short whistles by the steerer. It's effective and cannot be confused with any other sound or request. You hear the whistles and react accordingly. This system can naturally be modified to include, a one, two or three whistle system to indicate a number of different requests.

As a tip, it can often pay when paddling without covers to call down into the hull of the va`a. This allows the sound to travel along the length of the va`a, acting like a sound box. This is particularly helpful in strong winds.

When To Call

When the conditions are dead flat, or when sprint/regatta racing, adherence to a set number of strokes per side without variance can be detrimental to overall performance. You may want to vary things somewhat, especially at the beginning and end of the race. Faced with a neck and neck finish, with only metres to go, do you call a *Hut* or go for broke?

In ocean conditions, the caller must learn to feel when the va`a is 'stalling' or 'accelerating' accordingly. Calling a change during the stall phase of the va`a run, during the chase for 'bumps' is totally appropriate. As the va`a falls off the swell and decelerates, and the wave moves from under you, it's time to 'power up' with fresh arms, dig deep and prime the va`a for the 'drop in'. Depending on the duration, you may call another change during this stall phase however the va`a only tends to stall briefly (depending on the horse power of the paddlers and the size/steepness of the bump).

As the va`a picks up speed again, and the nose drops in and the tail gets a lift, you'll notice the stroke rate pick up. This is not the time to call a change. At the critical part of the 'take off', much like a surfer paddling ahead of the wave, if you momentarily take the power off by changing sides, you're likely to miss your opportunity.

Calling when chasing a running sea is a skill learned by feeling the va`a as it rises and falls, accelerates and decelerates with the ocean's movement.

Stay on the side you are and put the power on. If you get lucky and the va`a drops in and you take off, you can briefly remain paddling on the same side until you reach a point of terminal velocity, then call a quick change and chase the wave all the way.

As you see, you need to feel your way around calling the change to blend with the dynamics of the va`a's interaction with the ocean. You can so easily kill hull speed and miss opportunities if you fail to call correctly.

Calling At The Starts

Your crew will no doubt have its own system for starting. For our crew, the initial number of strokes on the starting side is pretty high and may go 18 before the call, or more. We work on the 'thrash and burn' theory. We just go for it and the call isn't made until the caller feels the va`a has reached just short of top speed. The harder we work, the faster we reach that point.

So Who Should Call?

A number of variations exist and each is open to some debate. Either way, once you are used to a particular method and as long as it works, it really doesn't matter.

1 Calling: It can be argued that the notion of stroke calling the '*huts*' makes good sense, after all, they are eyeballing the ocean ahead and below and can best see what is going on. They are setting the pace and feeling their way over the va`a. They are working within their own capacities, which in many ways dictates much of what goes on behind. They are also setting the pace.

This permits the stroke to dictate how they perceive things and can call accordingly. However there are drawbacks. It's a long way from the front of the va`a to the rear for the call to be heard well all the time. Therefore, some crews have used a system where # 1 calls '*Hut*' followed by # 2 calling '*Hike*', sometimes followed by the crew calling out '*Hoe*', so we get the call, '*Hut, Hike, Hoe*'.

This may work for some in some races. However, for longer change races it seems a trifle exhausting to have to call it this way for 5 hours or so! I'm not sure if any top level crews use this system. It seems to be a good base for novice paddlers to come to grips with the whole *Sit and Switch* issue.

2 Calling: Here there is a better chance of all paddlers hearing the call. As they already work closely with the stroke, it provides what is generally considered to be the best place from which to make the call. Of course the '*Hut, Hike, Hoe*' call can still be made from here.

3 Calling: Some crews use this position for calling, however they are not very well placed to read what's going on up front and its probably better that they focus on paddling and protecting the ama.

In summary, don't underestimate the importance of calling the switch. It takes practice to learn to call 'instinctually' rather than 'mechanically' without variation. Vary your calls to suit the canoe's travel and the limits of your crew to get the best from both.

Bailing

A va`a bailer, *ka wa`a* (Hawai`i) or *tata* (French Polynesia) is a vital piece of safety equipment for the va`a paddler. Throughout Oceania, bailers were designed and constructed in a number of ways but they were always carved from wood.

No mechanical bilge pumps are permitted in racing va`a, with the exception of sailing va`a. There are no commercially available hand held bailers, so it is common practice for clubs to make there own – usually cut out from large plastic bottles and similar in shape to a traditional bailer.

Ideally, each va`a needs a minimum of two bailers and these should be attached to the va`a by a lanyard so that in the event of capsize the bailers remain with the va`a.

Bailing is one of the single biggest neglected concerns and it is a skill that many outrigger canoe paddlers lack. Bailing is seen by most to be a waste of time, incorrectly believing that it's better to keep paddling to keep up the speed. However, the very thing that will contribute to an ultimate decrease in the speed of a va`a is the 30, 40, or 60lbs plus of water sloshing around underfoot.

The Importance of a 'Dry' Va`a

You don't have to be a rocket scientist to figure out that carrying any significant weight over and above the va`a and its accessories equates to increased drag, The hull sinks deeper, increasing the wetted surface area and leading to increased friction or drag. Yet many crews pull up after a race, tired, complaining the va`a felt like a brick, with the hull floor ankle deep in water.

'Ah, but we do bail!' you say. OK, but how often? The next biggest neglect of crews is to not bail frequently enough, bailing only when the water is up around their ankles.

1" (20mm) of water spread over the length of a six person va`a weighs around 100-kg (200lbs+), the weight of a passenger.

A dry va`a is paramount. Starting that way and keeping it like that is crucial. Bailing regularly must become part of your team's regime when training so it becomes second nature. Bailing is as much a part of canoe paddling as is getting wet. Crews with skilled 'bailers' ensure the va`a remains light which helps to keep the crew fresher for longer.

Some years ago when the sport had been in Australia for around ten years, questions were asked about fitting battery driven pumps into va`a, similar to the standard equipment on Australian Surf Boats. Fortunately, the argument over the need to keep bailing manually and traditionally won. However, in Hawai`i, manually operated bilge pumps and through the hull self bailing devices are permitted on sailing canoes in order to maintain high levels of safety.

Keep the va`a as dry as possible. Bail small amounts frequently rather than large amounts occasionally to keep the average weight of your va`a as light as possible.

Bailer Design and Types

Every va`a must have a minimum of two bailers attached by a lanyard and hung on a bracket adjacent to seats # 3 and 4. Bailers are an essential item of safety and a va`a should never leave shore without them!

The ability to bail well is a learned art and you will need to have the right type of bailer to do the job. A bucket sized bailer is more of a hindrance than a help. More, in this case, is not necessarily better. It's just too big to be effective. It may be of some use if you completely swamp or capsize.

Under normal paddling conditions, bailers are used by one individual (usually seat # 4) removing unwanted water to keep the va`a as light as possible, while the remainder of the crew continues to paddle. Bailers should be small and easy to manage as their main use is in the collection and removal of relatively small amounts of water - but not always.

Efficient bailing requires an efficiently shaped bailer. It must have a thin lip so it can literally scoop the water up from the hull floor as you drag it along the bottom and it needs to have a handle so you can get a good grip on it. Bailers shaped from plastic (5ltr chlorine bottles or similar) which when shaped, hold around 2ltrs are ideal. Carry a minimum of two, positioned on a hook forward of seats # 3 and 4 and on the right hand side of the va`a.

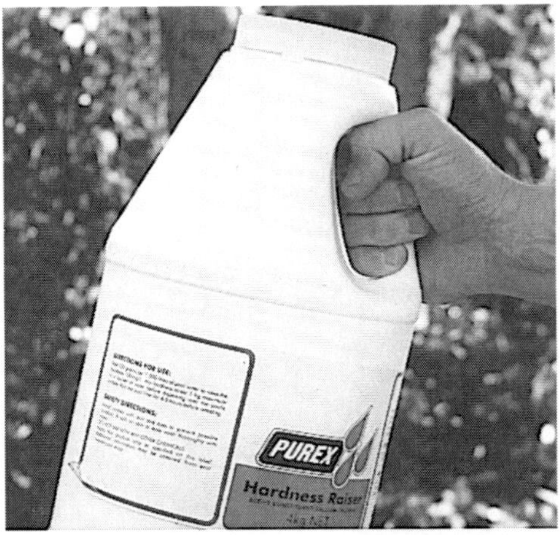

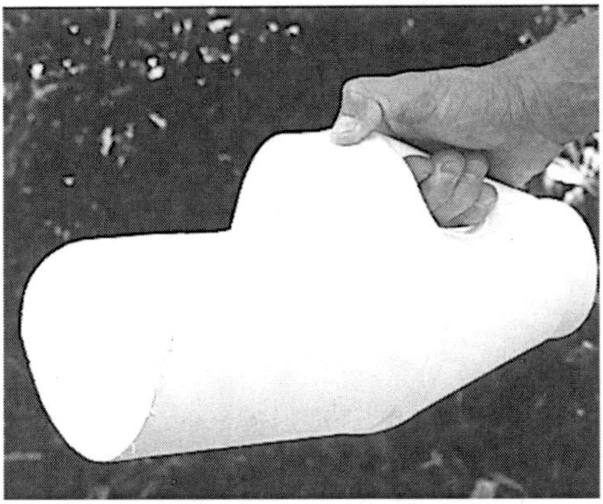

Today's bailers are best shaped from plastic containers similar to this. Using a sharp knife, a bailer approximating the traditional shape can be created. The thin flexible lip is excellent for sliding along the floor and 'scooping' up the water.

Have a look at the design of the traditional bailers fashioned across the Pacific from timber and use them as a guide when you create your own. The bailers you use should be sufficient for paddling Moloka`i or lining up for a sprint race. You don't need bailers to be proportionally larger or smaller relative to how rough the ocean is.

A large bucket just isn't efficient or effective. It cannot be effectively scraped along the hull floor as the lip tends to be too fat to get that last half inch of water out. At the other extreme, when trying to bail out mega amounts of water, the bucket is simply too heavy to be practical. You want to be able to scoop up the water quickly and off load it quickly

In addition, a bucket sized bailer becomes even more of a problem with covers on. Often, the covers reduce the space to such a minimum that it's hard to get the bucket to squeeze into the space and nearly impossible to get even a quarter full bucket out!The very point of using the smaller sized bailers which are efficient and shaped ergonomically is so you can biomechanically undertake the task well, while allowing for a good stroke rate! Speed is the key to good bailing. You have to do it quickly, so the job is done and you can get back to paddling.

Traditional hand carved bailers.

Which Seats Bail

Water collects or 'pools' primarily in seats # 3 or 4 conforming to the hull's rocker curvature. Water will move to the 'belly' of the va`a and this can vary between va`a designs. For example, *Hawaiian Class Racers* are straighter in the mid section. The water collects between seats # 3 and 4 in almost equal proportions, so who bails depends on hull trim - crew weight etc. However, in *Force Fives* and *Bradleys*, the water tends to collect further back at seat # 4 as with the *Mirage*. Seat # 4 is generally your primary bailer. Tahitian designed va`a also vary according to design.

Bailing using a larger bucket in calm conditions, seat # 4 sits up the gunnel and paddle is simply place on the floor to the right and braced with the leg. Below this, bailing from seat # 3 seated on the gunnel. Bailing Practice at the local swimming pool.

Bailing Practice

Bailing must be fast and efficient, and the entire process can be practised beach side. Simply add water to the va`a and practice all of the procedures you would go through if on water and paddling.

Communication

Prior to bailing, you must call out *'Four bailing on the next* (next *hut*)' or something similar - which means, that when the next *hut* is called you will be bailing. When the *hut* is called, call out *'Four bailing!'* and proceed to go through the process. When you are finished and you are back paddling, call out *'Four paddling!'* or similar so the others know there is a full crew paddling once again. Without this level of communication, it is extremely frustrating for the paddlers forward of seat # 4 who can't see what is happening - but they will feel the va`a slow and the drag increase!

With Covers - Unzipping

Holding the paddle in your left hand, unzip carefully, without rushing, to avoid jamming the zipper! You may need two hands, one to hold the flap aside depending on the design. Once unzipped, brace your paddle and with your left hand keep the cover open and pulled upwards to prevent water coming in over the left gunnel. Reach in with your right arm and grab the bailer from its hook.

What to do with the Paddle When Bailing?

Without covers, your first task is to secure your paddle. One method is to place the paddle upright, blade on the hull floor, on your left-hand side. Use your thigh to brace it against the side of the hull. Don't just drop it on the bottom of the va`a. This should be the procedure whether paddling with or without covers, though you could also brace the paddle on the right hand-side depending on conditions. The calmer the seas the easier it will be to manage your paddle, but even in calm water it will tend to want to slide along the va`a floor and fall. There are practical reasons for having the paddle on the left, as you will want to keep your weight on this side and it is generally an easier position from which to jam the paddle against the hull as you apply pressure.

Positioning Yourself to Bail

You can either remain in your seat or sit up on the left gunnel of the va`a. You will automatically create instability in the va`a when you stop paddling and start bailing, so you will need to be concerned with the ama and keeping the va`a stable. Sitting on the gunnel will cause the ama to compress and while this makes a more stable canoe, it will slow it down even further.

Sitting on the edge of the left gunnel, the right hand bails while the left holds the paddle and covers open. This is a Tahitian va`a and the space within the 'cockpit' area is tight.

You can either remain seated or sit up on the left gunnel of the canoe. You will automatically create instability in the va`a by ceasing paddling and bailing, so you will need to be concerned with the ama and keeping the canoe stable. Sitting on the gunnel will cause the ama to compress and while this makes for a stable va`a, it will slow it down even further.

Scoop the water up quickly and with minimal movement, throw the water more or less directly upwards, using the wrist to flick the water out. Avoid using big arm and shoulder motions. Do not 'pour' the water out over the side. This is slow and inefficient. Throw it out. Be sure to not throw it behind you and onto seat # 5. Consider wind direction.

Bailing should be done with the right hand, while the left hand is on the gunnel and or holding the cover open. Bailing with the left hand could create greater instability as you would need to lean right in order to reach in and bail.

Speed is essential to successful bailing. You must use a properly shaped bailer which can be scooped along the hull floor, passed between paddler, seat and covers with ease and 'flick' the water skyward. Large 'bucket' sized bailers are hard to manage and snag on the covers.

Speed is the Key

Bailing is something you need to do quickly, very quickly. In some respects, you're less concerned with how much you take with each scoop, though clearly it must be a significant amount, than the speed with which you do it. Fast bailing rates will clear the va`a quickly, whereas being slow and methodical just means the va`a has a cover open longer, potentially allowing more water to pour in over a longer period of time.

Bailing frequently means that the covers are only going to be open for short periods of time as you will only have a

Bailing when punching upwind can sometimes result in more water entering the va`a than you can bail. Wait until conditions improve. Photo *Harvie Allison*

small amount to get out. Don't delay too long! Bailing should not last for more than 60 seconds, around 4 *huts* or so. More than this and you can assume you have allowed too much water in the canoe or perhaps your technique is too slow and needs work.

When to Bail

Some crews will wait to hear the steerer call for bailing. Others will rely upon the paddler in seat 4 to bail when they think it appropriate. Knowing when it is appropriate to bail is a skill. Communication is very important.

If you are paddling on a long upwind stretch and taking in lots of water, you will need to bail frequently. It may pay for the steerer to veer off from head on wind to reduce the pounding while you bail and also lessen the load on the paddlers. With covers - do not leave them open for too long if very rough. Better to bail frequently and over a short duration, than waiting until you need to bail lots of water, which will take longer. Without covers - in extreme circumstances, you may need to be bailing continually until out of the worst of it.

If you are on a short upwind section, you may be able to leave the bailing until you turn to come back downwind or across wind as the loss of a paddler upwind can cost you a good deal of speed.

When all is considered, bailing when paddling upwind can often be the best time to bail if conditions are not too extreme. Bailing when paddling downwind presents some interesting ideas; if following a big sea or even chasing steep runners, the added weight of some water at the front of the va`a can actually assist the inertia and ability to 'drop in'. However, there comes a point when there can be too much water, so you will need to gauge this carefully.

During change-over races, when a fresh paddler enters the canoe at seat # 4, they can check if bailing is required.

Some crews prefer to have seat # 4 bail just prior to exiting the va`a, so that when they exit, the va`a is 'dry'.

When Not to Bail

There are certainly inappropriate times to bail as in the case of paddling with covers on. Every time you open the covers, you increase the potential for taking on more water. If you are in an extremely rough section of water, in short steep fast moving confused water, paddling upwind or being hit side on for example, opening the covers to bail could allow more water to enter the va`a than you can possibly keep up with. This could actually create a dangerous situation. In this instance, it would be best to wait for smoother water or a point when the va`a changes course so the angle at which the water is striking the va`a is improved.

Steerers may need to alter course to keep the va`a drier for a period of time, so the covers can be unzipped and bailing can be done! This is especially true if paddling without covers and you are taking on huge amounts of water. Maintaining your course and bailing can be a waste of time in this instance. You may have seats # 3 and 4 bailing in extreme cases.

Bailing the va`a when you only have a quarter of a mile to travel, you're neck and neck with another va`a and the hull is full of water probably means you've left it too late. Bailing at this point will probably cost you the race and odds are you have failed to keep up with your bailing duties. Now the entire crew is paying the price, which emphasises the need to bail early, when you only have a small amount of water underfoot.

In the first 20 to 30 minutes of the start of the Moloka`i race the va`a remains 'dry'. Then you hit Lauu Point and take a pounding through the slop, all of a sudden you're taking on water and you need to think about bailing. Where your competition is, is irrelevant because there is a long way to go and a dry va`a is a light va`a, your paddlers will definitely thank you for it.

Factors Affecting Water Entering the Va`a

Entering paddlers always bring water in with them. The type of clothing worn in particular will have a strong bearing on just how much they bring in with them, neoprene and super absorbent materials especially.

Baggy or super absorbent clothing worn by paddlers entering the canoe from the water in a change-over race can bring in excess water. Tight fitting, quick drying, low absorbent materials are preferable. They will also make it easier for you to get into the va`a as the water you bring in on your clothes will be weighing you down as you make your change. You can experiment with various clothing to see just how absorbent they are.

Other factors affecting water entering the va`a include;
Pounding up wind | Poorly fitted covers | Poorly designed covers | Covers not zipped up properly | Relief paddlers entering the va`a | High winds | Rough Seas | Not zipped up properly

Entering paddlers bring water with them. The clothing they wear can make a big difference as to how much this is. As an individual and as a crew take this into consideration.

Without Covers

Water enters the va`a gradually from spray and from any angle. Upwind is particularly critical. When paddling downwind, the va`a can bury at the front and water often pours in around seat # 1. Additionally, if the va`a stalls in the trough of a wave, the water can pour in at seats # 3 and 4.

Note: Steerers can reduce the amount of water entering the va`a by taking a line which reduces swamping. This is often achieved by angling the va`a roughly 10° off-line of directly on coming waves when heading up wind.

Bailing After Capsize

After a capsize in rough conditions, once you have recovered the va`a but the hull is still full of water, you may need to re-capsize the va`a and recover it once more to see if you can release more water from the hull. If you have covers on and this is the case, it can be extremely difficult to remove the water during the righting process (see Capsize).

Capsize - Causes, Prevention, Recovery

The capsize of a wa`a is a very significant event, and the manner and speed with which the crew deals with it is critical. Though va`a are prone to capsize, the reality is that even when well rigged, capsize is nearly always due to the fault of the crew.

This sequence (Hamilton Island South Head) show seats 1,2 draw stroking on the right to avoid submerged rocks. At speed, draw strokes should be replaced with a bow post stroke (uni on the left) to steer the wa`a right. Seat 5 should have reacted to this and been on the left to protect the ama.

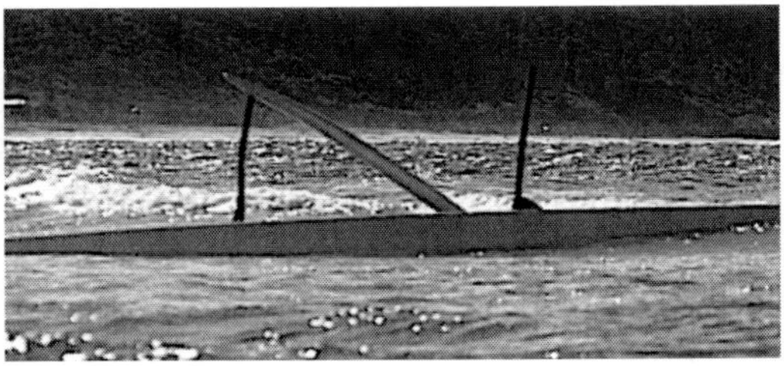

Capsize can cause damage to the wa`a outrigger assembly. When recovering the wa`a, it is critical that as it is righted, the ama is not allowed to land heavily. This can split it along its seam or tear apart the rigging.

Capsize - Who's to Blame?

by Kawika Sands

This examines the assignability of 'blame' when it comes to a *luma`i* (capsize) often referred to inaccurately as a *huli*.

There you are, skimming along without a care in the world, except for the water near the va`a. You reach for the water again when you notice that it seems higher on one side than the other. By the time you feel your seat tilting, you catch a glimpse of the ama, then someone yells *Ama*!, and over you go. What usually happens next is a lot of finger-pointing.

In the long run, it doesn't really matter what the circumstances are. Everyone almost instinctively looks at the steerer. In light of all the other things, he or she must assume responsibility. While this might seem unfair, it's part of being the back seat driver.

Culpability

Seat # 6 ± 50%

Seat # 5 ± 28%

Seat # 4 ± 6%

Seat # 3 ± 5%

Seat # 2 ± 6%

Seat # 1 ± 5%

The first thing you notice here is that the blame is shared by the entire crew. Then, that # 5 has the second largest share. I assign some responsibility among the crew because they can collectively both help cause a *luma`i* or prevent one. By paddling incorrectly or on the wrong side, it makes the steersman's job more difficult, causing him to steer more on one side or even too late.

You might notice that I've assigned # 2 and 4 only slightly more 'blame' percentage. More because without a *luma`i* line, (tipping string) these two paddlers are in the best position to place a hand on the i`ako and lean left to counter the ama's momentum. On the other hand, their primary job (like # 1 and 3) is to move the wa`a.

Seats # 5 and 6 are supposed to keep it afloat. As if # 5 doesn't already have enough to do, his nick-name is *Keeper of the Ama*. This is in reference to the fact that they are in the best position to keep an eye on the ama and call for assistance to keep it down. They are closest to the steersman and can be easily warned of quick changes in direction (particularly toward the right). It is important that # 5 has steering experience. This experience helps him anticipate and co-ordinate with the steersman.

Each time a steersman proves himself, that trust grows into respect. That trust/ respect is what will keep the team together in a crisis, but then, it's a two-way street. The thick skin is priceless when things don't go as planned!

The 50% formula I suggested is merely a starting point. If conditions are particularly tricky, if a paddler strokes on the off side, when he should be on the ama side, if # 5 is not watching the ama or has not come to the point where they know (without being told) when to stroke/lean/poke on the left or shout 'Ama' in time, then yes, it is fair to place less responsibility on the steersman for a capsize. On the other hand, learning how to read the sea and other conditions, strategy, tactics, manoeuvring, and so on are the steersman's responsibility. A good # 5 (and # 1 through 4) can make an incredible difference.

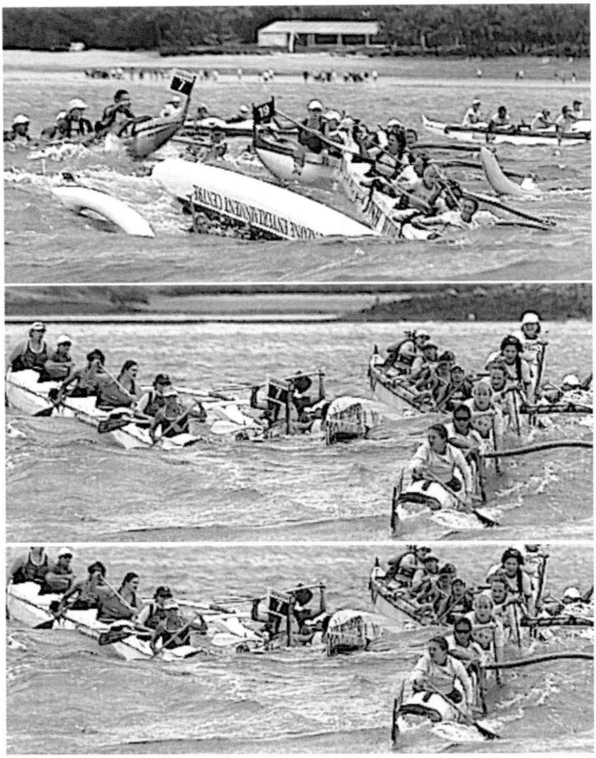

However, it is also fair to say that with good training and practice, a strong even stroke along the wa`a can allow the steersman to 'fly' the ama, therefore decreasing drag. If a quick manoeuvre by the steersman is required, without speaking a word, the crew may be able to compensate.

'Your comments about the peperu, steerer (Tahitian) being responsible for the flip are most relevant. I have always tried to train my crews to be responsible for the trim of the va`a. The peperu is responsible for the correct course and the optimal speed of the va`a in relation to the existing sea conditions.

In order to perform this function, it is imperative that the crew maintains a neutral steering bias that will enable the steerer to do his job. I have attempted radical and abrupt steering manoeuvres that have resulted in a luma`i. I have also attempted the same manoeuvres with a different crew that have not resulted in a huli because the crew had the knowledge and experience to compensate for the correction and negate it. Therefore, it is the responsibility of the whole crew to work together to optimise the performance of the va`a and avoid a disaster. It is always a pleasure to work with a crew that is in tune with a steerer who is searching for the right angles that will optimise the speed of the va`a. It is ultimately the responsibility of the steerer to assess the abilities of the five people in front of him and not to attempt manoeuvres which are beyond their abilities to adjust to.' Tom Conner - Winner of over ten Moloka`i races.

Capsize is more often than not due to error on the part of the paddlers and or the steerer than simply because of rough water. Wa`a can tolerate extremely rough waters and in the hands of an experienced crew, the wa`a generally remains safe and stable. The only real risk is one of swamping, where the water pours in over the gunnels or over the splashboard. In many strange and unpredictable ways, a wa`a is often most unstable when stationary.

Despite the focus on 'human error' being the cause for capsize, a poorly rigged wa`a i.e. one which is inherently tippy, is the second major factor which increases the possibility for capsize. Rigged correctly, the wa`a itself is a remarkably stable craft.

Preventative Measures to Consider

Some of the thinking on preventative measures for capsize are somewhat dated. Much of the normal reaction to a wa`a in the process of a capsize encourages paddlers # 3, 4 and 5 in particular, to leap violently to the left to put weight on the ama in a desperate attempt to grab the i`ako to push it back down. This is too obvious a response and in many respects the reaction from inexperienced paddlers.

In the paddler's attempts to save the ama, they inadvertently move their body weight to the right - arms outstretched to the left, the bulk of their mass often ends up further to the right, negating much of their efforts. A more advanced reaction of the experienced, skilled paddler is to react by bracing the wa`a with their paddle, by placing the blade flat down on the water surface to their right and pushing down hard, while moving some weight to the left. Paddlers braced out on the right, in a sense create a secondary safety ama countering the roll of the wa`a.

Tipping or *Luma`i* String

A tipping string rigged approximately 1m from the hull, between the two i`ako, can be used as a brace. Paddlers # 3 and 4 lean left and brace against the string. This set up, has its merits, though the paddlers need to practice using the string to good effect. Its not a given that just because there is a string upon which to lean, that you will prevent a capsize. Remember, the better option at speed could be to brace right.

Seat Reactions and Roles

Seat # 1 - **Sit back and see what happens!**

Seat # 2 - **Can lean back and place left hand on the i`ako. Alternatively brace right.**

Seat # 3 - **Can brace right or 'kick' body weight right. Reach behind grab i`ako, use tipping string.**

Seat # 4 - **Can brace right or 'kick' body weight right. Lean left, reach for i`ako, use tipping string.**

Seat # 5 - **The 'keeper' of the ama. Their job is to work with the steerer to protect the ama and keep the wa`a level and safe. Seat # 5 can react by coming across to the left and perform a quick bracing stroke to pull the ama down or reach for the i`ako itself.**

Seat # 6 - **May need to keep steering or react to save the ama by bracing left.**

There are a variety of options which can be taken. Experience decides which is best.

The Steersman

by Al Ching

When a wa`a flips, the blame is usually focused on the steersman. Some steerers seldom flip while others can't be trusted in flat water. While the list of things to learn will last a lifetime, a little at a time can be practised.

One of the biggest advantages an experienced steersman has is recognising when and how to steer through situations that may cause the wa`a to flip. A novice will not readily recognise potential danger and will not know how to deal with it. Making the correct decision is sometimes a gamble, making you look like a hero or a scapegoat. However, there are times when even the best will go over. Sometimes the ama will go over so fast that it is difficult to save it. Explaining it to the crew is even more difficult.

Aspiring students need experienced steersmen to coach them constantly in order to improve quickly. Nevertheless, coaches do not have much time for personal training and spend more and more time with paddlers as the season wears on.

I try to spend time with steerers and talk about what we are doing right or wrong. I feel it is the least understood position with the most to learn. We run drills, watch occasional videos and aim for small personal goals. Of all the positions, # 6 can make the most noticeable change in hull speed. Yet some coaches invest the least amount of time with it.

In rough water, there are particular angles that may cause the wa`a to flip if the steersman is not careful. When the ama begins to rise and the front of the wa`a is hooking left and diving, it could spell trouble. At this point, the steerer should already have sensed or recognised what is probably going to happen and their paddle should be in the water on the right (to keep the wa`a straight) his body leaning left with the left arm out as a counter balance. If the steerer's reaction is too slow and the ama is suspended, airborne, he should switch to the left side of the wa`a as fast as possible and anchor the blade in the water with both hands as he may be the only one able to save the wa`a.

Steering on the right with two hands on the shaft could be very risky in rough seas, because if the ama goes up, you're trapped on the right with both hands and your paddle in the water. You have no way to counter balance to help you recover. It would be wiser if to use the right hand to steer right and keep the left hand free to counter balance. This will also allow you to react quicker to get back to the other side.

Lanakila steersman *Joshua Crayton* encourages good balance from his crews. He expects everyone to sit up and not lean to the left or right when it gets rough. If the ama comes up, they push it down with their hips and never break rhythm. Most of them are kayakers and don't panic when the ama gets airborne. *Joshua* also rigs the ama using the standard 72" front and 73" in the back. It's far enough out to allow sufficient time to react if it becomes airborne. Their primary goal is to paddle, undistracted by the ama. To prepare them for big races, he plans practices that expose the crew to the roughest water to chase down swells and ride bumps. He knows that a well-trained crew will make it easier to control the canoe and keep it straight and level.

It's good to ask questions. Set some easy goals. Never be satisfied for very long. There are no short cuts. The more time spent steering, the better you will become and the better choices you will make. Experience and repetition are still the best teachers. Steering is a talent many can learn but only a few will become proficient. It should be considered as one of the ultimate challenges in paddling.

Hesitation Leads to Capsize

The sequence to capsize normally follows that as the ama lifts and the canoe reaches what is called in technical terms, the *Moment of Statical Stability* or the *Righting Moment* where the force involved in returning the hull to an upright position reaches a point of equilibrium - a factor concerning the weight of the canoe bearing down through its centre of gravity, multiplied by the righting lever force. At this point, the wa`a will more often than not regain stability, momentarily, which is your window of opportuntity to prevent capsize. A violent capsize, due to the forces involved, will bi-pass this phase and no moment of statical stability will be reached.

One of the most common causes which leads to capsize is the hesitation of the paddlers to take that next stoke following the ama lifting. Inexperience will cause you to either exit the blade then hesitate or swing through the recovery phase, pause in anticipation and contribute to the fate of the wa`a. If, without hesitation, you commit fully to the next stroke and bury the blade as if your life depended on it, the crews combined forces will compress the ama back down - most of the time and in combination with seats # 3 and 4 nudging their hips left to prevent the ama raising further – or bracing right.

Dry Land Capsize Drill

Paddlers can go without experiencing a capsize or going through a drill for many years. But this is a water sport and it's good to be reminded of that once in a while. Capsize drills provide an opportunity to appreciate the limits of the stability of the wa`a and how to carry out a self rescue technique, to right the wa`a and empty the water from the hull. A capsize is a pretty dramatic occurrence and therefore not something which paddlers relish. It's not fun or necessarily a natural part of a paddlers experience as it is for surfers to fall from their surfboards.

As part of club policy and exercising a duty of care and risk management approach to the sport, carrying out a capsize drill should form part of a logical sequence of being introduced to the sport. The coach can access the paddler's confidence in the water and their swimming ability. Formalised swim tests should already have been carried out.

As quirky as it may seem, there is merit in running through a dry land capsize drill, providing a capsize occurs due to too much body weight being transferred to the right side of the wa`a, in combination with the steerer *poking* on this side and assistance from a wave travelling left to right.

An (old) upturned wa`a on dry land, provides a good prop for demonstrating the procedure for recovery; i.e. position of paddlers, collection of paddles, the calling off of names, positioning of the wa`a relative to conditions and how to get into position to set up for righting the wa`a. In the old days, Hawaiians reviewed righting a wa`a - *ho'olana,* procedures with a model wa`a and this can also be used today. Speed of recovery is the key element. The longer the recovery takes, the more likely the hull will be full of water as air trapped in the hull escapes and is replaced by water. The rougher the water, the quicker this process occurs.

Recovery Without Covers

Capsize drills for newcomers should be carried out in flat water. Consider the conditions, i.e. air and water temperature, and have paddlers dress appropriately; neoprene vests for example to keep warm. Prior warning needs to be given so the paddlers can bring appropriate clothing and towels etc. with them.

Speed is of the essence. There's only a small window of opportunity to recover the wa`a so a minimal amount of water remains in the hull void.

Air trapped within the hull void when upside down will keep the hull high off the surface of the water, but will be replaced with water as the air escapes causing the hull to sink deeper, making the righting process more difficult. Rough water allows air to escape and water to enter at a quicker rate.

It has been suggested that the wa`a be positioned so the swell is striking the ama side, with paddlers swimming the nose and tail around. This loses precious time and forms part of a second phase attempt if the initial righting process is unsuccessful or if the wa`a is totally swamped i.e. the upturned hull trapped air content has been mostly lost.

1. Ensure the wa`a is a safe distance from obstructions (moored vessels, buoys etc) allowing for any drift due to wind or current.

2. Have the paddlers lean to the right to initiate a stationary capsize.

3. Seat # 2 and 4 need to ensure that they push forward off the hull to be away from the i`ako as they impact the water.

4. Paddlers should keep hold of their paddles and not discard them.

5. Establish a quick head count. The *buddy system* can be used so # 1 and 2 check they are safe and together then # 3 and 4, etc. Report head count to steerer, who now oversees the righting process. Missing paddlers are generally trapped within covers. Look for cause and rectify immediately (jammed hydration system, jammed zipper).

Use drastic action if paddler needs to be released. Grab and physically pull them out.

6. Seat # 3 and 4 pass their paddles to paddlers 2 and 5 respectively. Seat # 3 and 4 then climb up on the i`ako onto the hull, spin over and place their feet on the *maku* (i`ako overhang) while reaching over to grab the i`ako.

7. Steerer, # 1 and 2 swim around the ends of the wa`a or under and assist by pushing up on the i`ako and ama. On a count of 'three' or similar, it is important the paddlers synchronise their pull and push over. It may take a couple of attempts. Before attempting to recover, check no swimmers or obstructions are in the path of the returning ama.

Important; The paddlers on the hull, as they roll with the wa`a, need to brace the i`ako before the ama makes contact with the water, rather than continue to pull down on the i`ako. This prevents the ama landing too heavily.

9. Though the method shown here may work with a smaller surfing wa`a as in this demonstration, for a larger six person wa`a, the method is impractical. The method used here, relies partly on the wa` a rising and falling with the oncoming swell striking the underside of the wa`a hull.

If the Hull is Near Full

In the case of the hull being nearly full and water continuing to pour over the gunnel, you will have to capsize the wa`a and begin again. Swim the wa`a into position so the ama is down swell. Right the wa`a but only to the point where the ama is vertical and

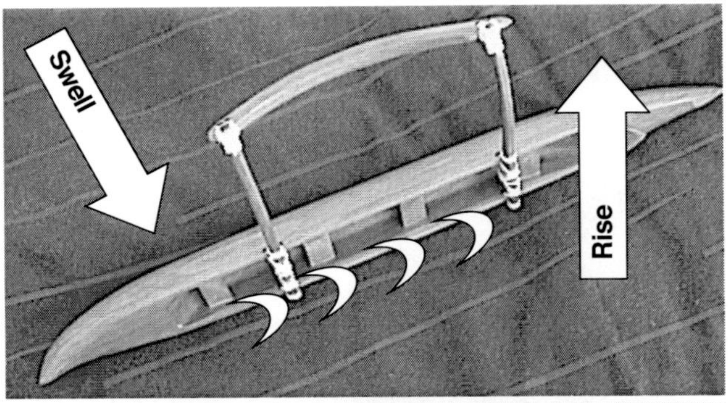

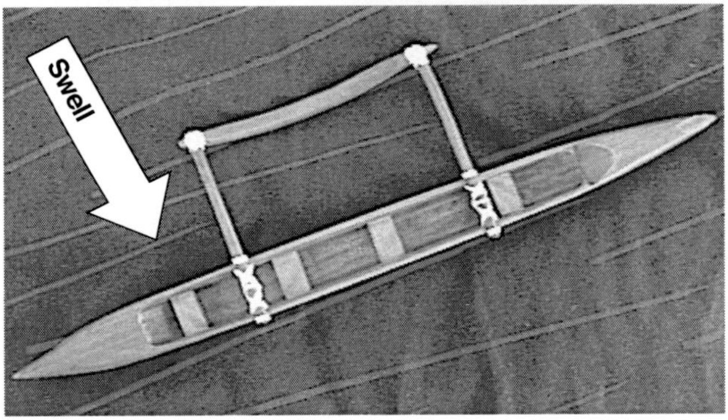

If the hull void is full and there are no covers, you can stagger the righting of the wa`a so as to 'empty' some of the water from the hull void. Right the va`a so as the hull void is on the down side of the direction of travel of the waves and hold in position. The hull will rise and fall and as it does so water will enter when in the trough and spill when it rises up on the crest.

The secret is to release the wa`a (cushioning the ama) at the crest of a suitable swell, when water has spilt out of the hull void.

the wa`a on its side. The hull will rise and fall with the passing of the swells and water will pour into and out of the hull. When at the top of the swell, water will pour from the hull. Time it right so that at the peak of the rise, you let the wa`a continue over to be recovered.

'When the ama is in the air prior to righting the wa`a, this is the time when as much of the water in the hull should be spilled out, to you give you some bailing room. Water can be spilled out by having all available parties putting upward pressure on the hull in an effort to lift it out of the water while the ama is in the air' Tay Perry.

Once the wa`a is righted it will be in the preferred position, with the ama into the swell. If you have covers and the hull is nearly full, you are going to find it very difficult to be successful using this technique, but it's worth a try. A last ditch effort could involve removing the central cover in order to allow the water out.

'Holding the wa`a broadside to the weather is better than into the weather - wind and swell. As a wave travels the length of the hull, it spills into the wa`a on both sides of the hull if held directly into it. While broadside is no guarantee, the odds for success are better.' Tay Perry.

A capsize with the swell coming from behind or in front must be recovered quickly. The seal is being broken between gunnel and the water, allowing water in and air out. Swim the wa`a broadside to the swell with the ama down swell, when you need to re-capsize to flush water out. Speed is the key.

It should take less than a minute, 30-45 seconds if you think and act quickly, this is not a good time to procrastinate.

Once the wa`a is recovered from this position it will not be at an ideal angle relative to the swell. You can have swimmers position the wa`a so as to be broadside to its direction of travel.

A delayed recovery in rough water with covers, can lead to so much water entering the wa`a that it becomes trapped within the hull. In some situations, the wa`a will need to be capsized and compressed air from a dive tank used to displace the water as was used ultimately here off Moloka`i.

①
②
FILL CANOE WITH AIR,
DISPLACING THE WATER.
THE CANOE WILL RISE

After Righting

Once the wa`a has been righted, the hull void will generally be either half, three-quarters or nearly full. Optimally half full will provide the best scenario, however three quarters is more likely. In the case that the righting process has been delayed and the waters are rough, the hull may be nearly full; if so do not have paddlers enter the wa`a, as you will need to re-capsize.

With the wa`a now in an upright position, the next phase involves the bailing out of at least one-quarter of the water before all six paddlers may re-enter the wa`a.

1. Your two lightest paddlers should enter from the middle of the wa`a - ama side and commence bailing while remaining four paddlers maintain the stability of the wa`a.

2. Have 2 paddlers add downward pressure to the mid section of the ama only.

Common faults which lead to the wa`a taking on further water over the gunnels is caused by the swimmers holding on to the bow and stern or arms wrapped around the manu pulling the extremities down, further lowering the freeboard of the hull which is already reduced by the waters content. Stress the need to avoid doing this.

The remaining swimmers therefore should apply minimum pull down weight on the wa`a while the bailers reduce the water content to allow the freeboard to increase. They should tread water and not cling to the wa`a. Another possibility is to have remaining paddlers swim the wa`a around so it is broadside to the weather. Paddlers can enter the wa`a when only a quarter full, paddles are handed along, and seat # 4 continues to bail while others begin to paddle.

Towing a Wa`a

Towing an wa`a requires understanding of the way in which a wa`a handles under tow and the structural features of the wa`a hull. Failure of the skipper of the boat who is providing the tow to carry out the correct method of lashing the wa`a, can result in unnecessary structural damage.

Lashing the towline around the front seat is a classic mistake and in any sort of swell the seat is unceremoniously ripped from the wa`a. How a wa`a is correctly towed is something a paddler should know. Don't rely on the boat skipper knowing the first thing about towing a wa`a, it could be the first time they have ever seen one. If this is the case, the wa`a captain, generally the steerer, should take control and supervise the lashing procedure to ensure that the wa`a is towed in a safe manner.

The most suitable line for towing is nylon, because it is exceptionally strong and has the greatest stretch properties of the synthetic cordage, stretching 30-40% before its breaking point. Its inherent stock absorbing qualities protect the structural elements of the wa`a; a stiff rope will put a good deal of extra strain on the wa`a.

You will need to have a length of cord that is just over twice the wa`a length, i.e. 24 metres (80ft). This ensures that the energy transfer from the tow boat back to the canoe is spread over this distance and that the canoe is away from the boat's wake. However, we are considering ideals here and often you will have to make the best of what the towing boat skipper has on board.

Lashing Procedure - Creating A Towing Bridal

1. Start by taking a turn around the hull and pass the ends of the rope through the forward i`ako lashing holes and tie off using a bowline under the wa`a. This helps to lift the wa`a while being towed. This bowline is one of the most useful of all maritime knots and one of its great advantages is that it will not tighten severely under pressure and can easily be undone after towing.

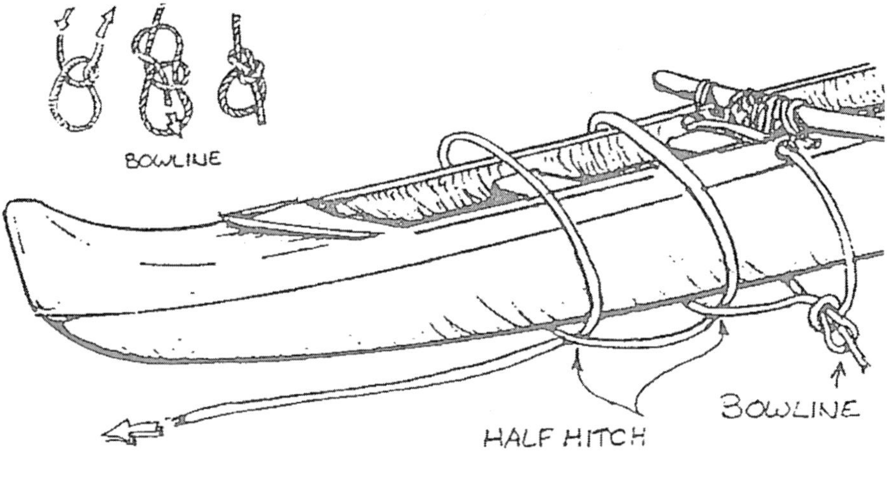

2. Loop the rope around the forward section of the wa`a over the area of seats # 1 and 2 to create two giant sized half hitches. This is important because when the wa`a is towed, the bow would otherwise tend to wander from side to side, resulting in the wa`a travelling sideways, broaching and possibly flipping.

Paddlers should not sit in seats # 1 and 2 and while paddlers could sit in the remaining seats, remember that unnecessary weight in the canoe will add strain to it during the towing process. You can have paddlers sit at # 3 and 4 to act as ballast and stabilise the wa`a, or have the steerer in place to ensure the wa`a holds a straight course, or all three. Whether you have paddlers in or out will be a factor that will have to be determined given the situation, based on sea conditions, the nature of the towboat and the condition of the wa`a and paddlers.

This simple method will ensure that the wa`a holds a straight course when being towed, the rigging remains intact during the towing process and that the strongest elements of the wa`a are being used for the towing process.

Alternatively
One way of tying off a towing line to a wa`a is using the i`ako. In this instance, two separate lines have been used. The primary attachment simply attaches to the i`ako and the loop passes under the hull.

To this, a secondary line is attached which passes over the top of the hull in a large half-hitch and the rope then travels under the wa`a to the tow vessel.

Below: Towing bridal lashed to a Tahitian va`a. Tow line is secured around raised stanchions.

Change Overs

Distance races that incorporate change-overs add a dimension to va`a racing that is totally unique to the sport. It adds a dynamic that gives it a hardcore edge, an element of danger and intensity which increases the potential for error, putting added pressure on everyone from coach to paddler through to the support boat driver.

Beyond the physical elements that change-overs demand, there is also a good deal of strategy involved which highlights the different levels of professionalism and preparedness between crews. Many races have been lost through poor management and strategy even though on paper the crew appeared to be a 'winning combination'.

It calls for an increased level of athleticism and strength, and often challenges you to overcome any fear of the ocean as you leap off your support boat into water that is sometimes thousands of feet deep, way beyond the continental shelf. All you have to do then is negotiate the swells and driving wind, sight the va`a, set up for the pick up, reach for the va`a - weighing well over a thousand pounds, travelling sometimes at considerable speed - and haul your butt in as fast as you can.

Change-overs in paradise. Raitea, French Polynesia.

The actual act of getting into the va`a is, without a doubt, the hardest part to do well. For women it is generally more challenging than for men; an issue of upper body strength. Men can usually pull themselves 'up and in' in one movement, whereas the ladies often stop half way and then swing their legs around. But it's fair to say that some guys have problems and some women make it look easy.

Many factors make up a good change including a good sense of timing, swimming ability, co-ordination, strength and an understanding of the mechanics of what it is you are trying to achieve. At times you need a cool head and if you hesitate, you're lost, as you only get one shot at it.

Creating a Change Chart

Steve Scott, one of _Outrigger Canoe Club_ Hawai`i's most successful coaches, talks about change-over races.

When creating a change chart, select a change crew on the basis of how they fit together. Seat # 1 and 2 must work well together and in a 9 person race, I would select two strokes and three # 2s, leaving me with three remaining specialist paddlers seats # 3, 4 and 5 and a steerer. These paddlers would only ever rotate between these seats, the others can sit anywhere they are needed but will always ultimately rotate to be working as a pair in seats # 1 and 2. In the case of a ten person team, you can have three specialist strokers.

When you're dealing with a 9 person race, everyone is going to have to sit in at least two seats and you'll need a minimum of two strokes and three seat # 2, then everyone else can sit in the remaining seats. What's crucial is having the match up between # 1 and 2, so # 2 matches up with the stroke. This is the most critical combination. If you can figure this out as a place to begin, then # 3, 4 and 5 can hopefully just slot in and follow.

Of course each stroker has a marginally different rhythm and technique, and some adaption process is going to have to occur with each change of stroke. What you want to do is minimise this, so you need two strokes who are similar in style and pace, if possible.

You can of course have a situation where both of your strokers end up in the wa`a. This is not ideal and of course the one not stroking is going to have to exit, rest, then enter again. This means that the present stroker will need to be in for a long period of time beyond the 12-15 minutes I usually work on. Strokes are the ones who get burned out quickest. It's mentally and physically tough.

If you want to relieve the steerer at some point, this will need to be factored in. The steerer may want to come into the wa`a to paddle for a time. Either way, you will need to build in a contingency, as many steerers will say they can go the distance, then find they need a break. You are best therefore to always have two steerers, a primary and a secondary and this will ensure that you are covered in case of injury, exhaustion or sickness.

On the first change, you're normally looking to change the stroke as a priority, along with # 4 and 5, but not necessarily all at that same time. I try to keep # 2 and 3 in, because # 2 has to combine with the stroke and from there change # 2 and 3. #1, 3, 5 and # 2, 4 combination. For the most part, # 2 is going to stay in longer to make it an easier transition, so # 2 can blend with # 1.

Creating a change chart is one of the most complex and challenging tasks which a paddler or coach can attempt. You should stick to it as closely as possible and only make amendments if there is injury or sickness preventing a paddler making a change. From a time point of view, opinions vary. It's fair to say that if a particular crew is cranking along making distance on other canoes and it's time for the call, you may want to leave it a while.

A coach's assessment of who is burning out and needs the rest is a very strong factor. Their knowledge of the individual paddler's capabilities is essential and paddlers should communicate to the coach how different combinations are working and how they are feeling.

In the case of most female change races, you will have 10 paddlers, 9 for men. Your aim is to select a crew based on individual *ability*, *fitness* and *skill* levels. But it is just as important to consider how the paddlers 'fit together', as pairs and as a blend of six, with the specialist seats # 1 and 2 being key elements.

Having at least two or even three paddlers who can 'float' between seat positions, is a great advantage, which will allow for the inclusion of specialist paddlers to rotate primarily within a limited range, i.e. seats # 1 and 2. Moving paddlers between seats while maintaining the highest possible average hull speed is your goal. This can only be achieved if you know your paddlers well, both their strengths and weaknesses. Anomalies will include;

upwind and downwind sections, rough water and smooth. You may need to move your paddlers to suit because of issues of ability or *trimming* the wa`a.

Your Seat Five Paddler

In a rough water race, your seat # 5 will need to be a competent steerer and confident in rough water. They should also show initiative in assisting the steerer when required. They may need to be in this seat at pre-determined sections of the race, which means you'll need to estimate the time when you will need them in this seat. A good example is the 42km race at Hamilton. You may estimate that at 1hr 10mins your crew will be heading towards Pentecost Island on the upwind leg and you want your most reliable seat # 5 in position to assist the steerer for as long as possible. Or in the Moloka`i to O`ahu race as you pass Lauu Point and head into open water, you decide this is where you will need your strongest seat #5 to be.

Preparing a Working Chart

You will need to draw up a simple grid, which will include from left to right;

Column 1 Row Detail	**Time** *Begin at 0 then incrementally in minutes* 0-30mins-45mins-50mins-55mins-1:05mins etc.
Columns 2-7 Row Detail	**Seat # 1 through to # 6** *Name paddlers in each seat at that point* Smith, Brown, Jones, Alan, Aitkens, Russell,
Columns 8-11 Row Detail	**Rest** *Name paddlers who are out of va`a at that point.* Jackson, Green, Anderson (+1 if ladies crew)

Even before you have decided upon the final crew, you can begin putting names on the grid – sometimes if you are short on paddlers, you will need to do this and fill in the blanks as you progress.

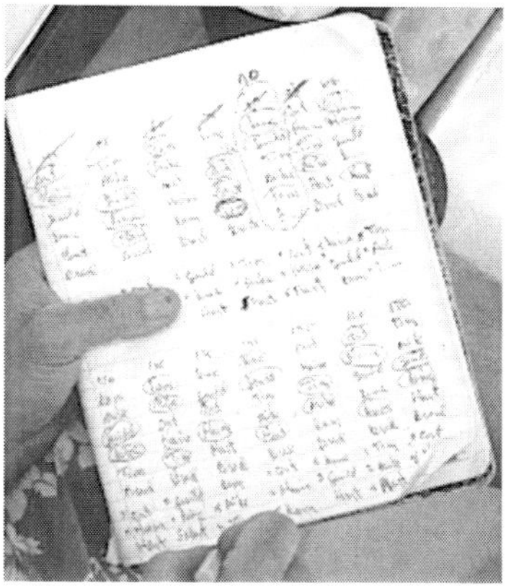

It's worth noting, that while your chart is a key element, there are times when through injury, fatigue, missed changes, poor combinations, or radical changes in conditions, that you will need to improvise and make decisions based on instincts. At times like these, the chart may become a liability not an asset. You must always be prepared to be flexible. Knowing your paddlers well is essential. Observing particular combinations and making mental notes are key elements in implementing a change in strategy of combinations during the race.

While you can create a change chart which will run for the entire race (and beyond in the eventuality the race takes longer than expected) this is often a nearly impossible task due to a number of factors. The more experienced the crew, the greater the number of races they have shared, after a few hours of racing, much of the sequence of changing becomes clock-work.

Many teams will only create and use a chart for the first two hours or so, after which they will revert to making the decision to change as they see fit. Sometimes paddlers will be asked if they want to stay in the wa`a or get out! Others in the support boat will often be keen to get in, while some may need some extra time out. The longer the race, the more complex this issue becomes.

An Example Change Chart

Looking at a change chart from *Outrigger CC Hawai`i* from the 1996 Moloka`i race, only the first change consists of a 3-person change, followed by a 2, 2, 1 format. Seats # 2, 4 and # 1, 3 changed as pairs, followed by a single seat # 5 change.

1st CHANGE: Seats 1, 3, 5
2nd CHANGE ONWARDS: 2/4, 1/3-5, 2/4, 1/3/5, 2/4, 1/3/5, 2/4, 1/3/5, 2/4, 1/3, 5/6

A repeated 2/4, 1,/3, 5 sequence broken on the 16th change with the inclusion of a steerer change at approximately 2hr10mins. Steerer exits, seat # 5 moves to steerers seat and a fresh seat # 5 enters, with a # 2/4 change to follow and the primary steerer, returning after approximately 10mins rest in a single paddler change.

AFTER STEERER CHANGE SEQUENCE: 1/3/5, 2/4, 1/3/5. 2/4, 1/3/5. etc
Changes on this chart are being made every 5 minutes, paddlers come into the wa`a, remain for 2 changes, on the 3rd they exit, giving them an average of 15 minutes in the wa`a.

Paddler	Seating	Primary
Courtney Seto	1/2/4	1
Billy Pratt	1/3/4	1
Marc Haine	2/3	2/3
Marc Rigg	2/3/5	2/3
Chris Kincaid	1/4/5	4/5
Clayton Chee 'floats' between	1/3/4/5	3/4
Chris Black 'floats' between	2/3/4/5	5
Walter Guild	3/4/5	5

Seto and Pratt share the bulk of the stroking, Haine and Rigg the bulk of seat # 2, 3 time, Kincaid, Black and Guild dominating seat # 5, Kincaid and Chee dominate seat # 4, Chee also spends time in seat # 3.

Change Chart Manager

The change chart manager/coach on the support boat acts as the time keeper and is the general in charge of running the change-over sequence. In rare cases, if you do not have someone taking charge of the chart, the paddlers will have to follow the chart themselves with assistance from the boat driver!

You will need a 'chart manager' who is methodical and not prone to sea-sickness! This is a common problem, yet it is often overlooked. You want to be sure that you don't loose your essential link between the chart and the paddlers. Without a chart manager, unless your crew is very familiar with the system and sequences, your race could get ugly and confusing. Your best change chart manager is an experienced paddler!

Start your watch with the start of the race. Ideally, if you have done your sums right, your first change will coincide with the chart time! Some races allow for the first change after a pre-determined time, others on pre-determined arrival point. Make sure you check this!

Time Issues

Most races will have either a pre-determined time after which changes can begin, or a particular point which must reached before changes can begin. Once you have made your first change, the entire process is ultimately at the discretion of your change chart manager/coach, who can either religiously stick to the chart, or improvise as required. It is important that paddlers know what is going on, therefore ensure good *communication*.

Changes usually occur for each paddler approximately every 12-15 minutes and in a particular sequence. Changes will tend to be initiated every 5 minutes in order to move through the available paddlers and to stick to the paddler time limits. However, this will depend upon how many paddlers you are changing each time over a given duration. In the case of a women's ten person crew, if you changed four paddlers in one go, followed by a single change 5 minutes later, you would not need to make another change for another 10 minutes.

Keep in mind, that while a change race covers a long distance, the race can be considered as a series of short hard efforts followed by a rest. While the generally accepted time stint is 12-15min maximum per paddler, little experimentation has been done regarding loss of time, energy and distance travelled by extending these times to longer stints; i.e. 20 minutes or more.

Energy expended during exit and entry to a wa`a, the loss of wa`a speed, and increased water entering the wa`a are all factors which suggest that the more frequently this occurs, the greater the room for error and the greater the cumulative effect. However, few crews are brave enough it seems to try something different. Apart from the generally accepted rule applying to when the first change can be made, there are no rules concerning when or if a change should be made. Cold water changes, in particular, can be very energy sapping both while in the water and when on the support boat as the body consumes energy just keeping warm.

For example if a crew is travelling well - why make a change. As radical as it may seem, if you are involved in a change-over race such as Molokai`i to O`ahu or the Hamilton Cup, it is not compulsory to make any change-overs whatsoever, as long as you have relief paddlers available, which is an odd irony.

Religious adherence to changes is fine, as long as it is not to the detriment of the crew as a whole. Why make a change if the current crew is catching runner after runner and overtaking others? It should cross your mind to leave that crew as is, until it becomes apparent a change is required.

Dummy Changes

This is a ploy used at times when two crews are racing neck and neck, and the changes are being closely monitored between each and often mirrored. It is used more often towards the end of a race. The support boat will tell it's paddlers it is going to make a *dummy drop off*. The support boat will then travel ahead and make a drop off of paddlers, and the wa`a goes through the motion of approaching the paddlers for a pick up and can even mimic unzipping. The opposition crew. seeing this, makes their own move to make an actual change. The crew making the *dummy-change* then paddles past the relief paddlers and as the opposition crew makes their change, they have to paddle hard to gain ground.

Race Start

In relation to how to begin a race, I believe you need to load it up with your best crew and keep it that way for as long as possible. Getting the best advantage at the start is crucial. While others are making their first change, if you can delay your change and get a few boat lengths on them, so much the better.

Practising with particular combinations is important so paddlers have confidence in the format. The change chart is your blueprint for making the combinations work. Over the years, *OffShore California* ladies have changed one paddler at a time, whereas I like to change two, sometimes one.

Recently, there has been a move to do a two person change but keeping the entering paddlers spread quiet a way apart. So rather than being two or three feet apart, they may be as much as two canoe lengths apart. The idea is that you minimise the slowing effect on the wa`a and keep more paddlers paddling at any one change.

Remember, the change chart is your blueprint. But if a combination is working well and the wa`a is flying, you might want to just let them go a bit longer. Ultimately there is a great deal of intuition at play which creates a variety of race strategies.

The Australian men's teams in a 9 person crew tend to follow a 2 and 3 person changing sequence, i.e. changing seats # 1, 3, 5 and # 2, 4. Other men's crews use two, 2 person changes, followed by a single change and then repeat the format.

Using a two person change as an example, *Outrigger Australia* have experimented in the past with spreading the two paddlers very wide apart, so the relief paddlers enter the wa`a separately and have less impact on the speed of the wa`a They used this in the 1997 Molokai race to good effect, when conditions were calm. The normal procedure however, is to have all relief paddlers enter together.

In the case of single changes, there is always the potential for the wa`a to have too much speed and inertia, especially when in a following sea and the paddler fails to hang on! Take this into account.

Towards Race End

Towards the finish of the race, if you've been following your change chart, you will have hopefully estimated your finish time. Generally, you won't always finish with your strongest crew, not without major changes which can be a risk. Towards the end of the race, there can be some very critical times with *Make a change or hold off,* kind of decisions, especially if it's close. Every time you make a change, you're going to lose one or two seats of wa`a length on your opposition, and that's if it is a good change.

If you're down to the wire with only five or ten minutes remaining, you've got your best crew in the wa`a and you're duelling with another, would I make a change? Tough call. I would have to consult with the paddlers. If they felt strong, then I guess I would leave it. If we didn't have our strongest set up, or if one of the paddlers was suffering, then a single drop off would have to be a seriously considered option.

Other Concerns Regarding Seat Positions

There are many views regarding how best to effectively alternate paddlers. Many factors need to be considered from the point of view of the paddler's individual ability, fitness and suitability to different seats.

Consider how seat # 5 works with the steerer, especially when help is required in rough water. Consider body weight, so when you need to add 'weight' to the front of the wa`a or 'lighten' it, depending on upwind or downwind legs, you will have this information available.

Weighting the wa`a up with heavier paddlers in a following sea can pay off in certain conditions and certain wa`a designs. Too much weight may lead to constantly burying the nose of the wa`a, slowing progress and increase the risk of stalling and excess water finding its way into the wa`a. The *Mirage* wa`a for example, has been designed so it can accommodate greater weight in the bow with less chance of burying due to increased volume and improved rocker line.

When punching upwind, you may want to keep the bow of the wa`a from constantly pitching up and down, slowing progress each time the wa`a rises and falls. It may pay to weight the bow to reduce this motion and to encourage the wa`a to punch through, as opposed to going up and over. This tends to be preferable in steeper, shorter, smaller, choppy waters.

Support Boats

Beyond key elements of boat handling, the support boat must be suitable for the task. It should have cover for the paddlers; shade from sun or adverse conditions and adequate space to safely stow all drinks, supplements and paddlers gear. Ensure the boat is powerful enough to cope with the load and that getting into the boat from the water is easy and safe. Some races have minimum boat standards.

Dealing with Your Support Boat Driver

The hire of a support boat is often expensive. Though the support driver is the Captain, it's your money, your race and therefore state what you expect. I have had some blinders! Drivers fishing during the race, boozing, breaking down, arriving late, not arriving at all, utterly incompetent, rude, unhelpful, dim witted, arriving with a boat load of buddies 'along for the ride' and a suntan.

You are entering into a contractual arrangement and you must be confident enough to call the shots in regards to how you want things done. For many drivers, its a cash-windfall and a good day out. For you, you've trained your arse off, made a huge commitment financially and otherwise to be in the position to race. Don't let your driver or the boat you hire blow it for you.

Dealing with support boat drivers can be very difficult and frustrating. You must explain clearly what you need to have happen, ensuring the safety of your paddlers, the wa`a and other water users. They are an important part of your 'Team' and race strategy.

Support Boat Positioning

Support boat drivers need to cause minimum disruption to the crew with regards to their boat's wake, noise and fumes. When the call is made for a change, they are generally behind the wa`a and they need to take as wide an arc away from the wa`a as possible on the non-ama side. You don't want a whole lot of wake on the ama side which can jeopardise the paddlers and possibly swamp the wa`a.

A support pulls up along side a wa`a on the non ama side to provide the steerer with water. Alternatively, have a swimmer pass up supplies.

Below: When coming along side to announce changes, approach on the right, off-side. When going ahead, leave at 90° and make a wide arc upto 500m ahead. Paddlers hate engine fumes and backwash.

As you come across, you want to go up and back at a slight angle, rather than straight across the path of the wa`a, this will help minimise wake. You want to line up the drop relative to the direction the wa`a is travelling in and this can take on a number of factors.

When the support boat needs to communicate with the steerer, the support boat approaches the wa`a from the non-ama side, level with the stern and at least 10m distance and informs the steerer of the seat numbers to be changed. This can be done by megaphone, yelling or even with numbered cards. The message, if verbal, is usually repeated and the steerer acknowledges that they understand the call by either waving, nodding, yelling back 'Got it', or giving the thumbs up.

When following your crew, remain behind or to the off side of the wa`a, far enough so as to avoid fumes, excess noise and boat wake affecting the crew - and others. Make sure you don't provide wake-riding waves to your opposition. Take notice of other crews around you. Experienced steerers will look for any assistance they can get, so don't let them use your boat wake to their advantage.

Support Boat - Positioning for the Drop

The support boat then falls back and remaining on the non ama side, travels directly outwards at 90° for at least a few hundred metres. They then make a wide sweeping arc to be ahead of the wa`a by at least 500 metres or so. The support boat then needs to slowly time a drift across the path of the on coming wa`a, to be in alignment when approximately 150m away.

When to Jump

During the time it takes for the support boat to move ahead into position, the steerer informs the crew of the changes i.e. *Changing # 1, 3, 5 - # 1, 3, 5* which is then repeated by seat # 3 to ensure that the forward seats have heard the command.

Relief paddlers must be ready to enter the water on the command of the steerer, who waves their paddle or arm to signal they have seen you and it's OK to enter the water. Alternatively, the coach or paddlers can determine when to jump off the support boat if experienced. However, the key issue is that the steerer has identified the support boat.

In the confusion, it is easy to loose sight of your support boat. Critically, the support must be stationary and engines in neutral both at the time of exit of relief paddlers and pick up of exited paddlers.

You can make the drop directly in the current path of the wa`a, or you can make it in relation to where the canoe should be headed; that's to say you know the steerer will be bringing it back around to a particular course.

A coach can also drop the paddlers off at some other spot to initiate a large deviation of course, if you think the wa`a needs to be headed in a different direction. This forces the issue and the steerer has no option but to change course. Don't make it too radical.

Some steerer's like to control when relief paddlers enter the water, and waive their paddle in the air to signal when they should enter. This can be important at critical times when negotiating shallow waters and rocky shorelines where the steerer is trying to get the best angles.

Relief paddler with arm raised to signal to the steerer their location.

Enter the water in sequence so seat # *1* would be *last* into the water for a # *1, 3, 5* change. Swim quickly into position, space out to the correct width between seats and ensure you form a neat line. Raise your hand and wave if necessary to improve the steerer's bearings.

When in the Water

One of the crucial elements is in the spacing of the swimmers waiting to get into the wa`a. If you have more than one trying to get into the wa`a at one time, the wa`a slows down more. So you want to avoid having two or three relief paddlers grabbing the wa`a at the same time. If you have # 4 and 5 making the change, they need to be about one seat apart. Getting this right is crucial.

As the wa`a approaches, with 15m or so to go, it is critical that you are swimming towards the wa`a at approximately a 45° angle, not treading water with your legs below you!

The Steerers Approach

The steerer maintains the wa`a roughly ama width out from the paddlers, so the paddler has room to swim in. If the steerer aims the wa`a directly at the swimmers, the swimmer has to back up which will cause their legs to drop underneath them.

Exiting Paddlers

If your *hut* caller is exiting, ensure a relief caller takes over before the paddler exits i.e. if # 3 was calling, seat # 2 should call out *2 has the huts!* and they then take over. Once the change has been made, # 2 and 3 can communicate and seat # 3 can take over.

When you unzip the highest numbered paddler unzips first. When unzipping, do not rush as this can lead to jammed zippers! If you need two hands, then do so. Either way, unzip methodically even if things around you are going crazy.

Communication breakdown. Paddlers should be exiting at the same time. Swimmers # 1 and 2 have not reached their entry points yet, but seat # 4 swimmer is about the grab the gunnel. Their legs are directly below them which will hinder their entry. Photo *Chris O'Kieffe*.

For entering paddlers, its off putting to find your seat still occupied! Lock your paddle in, then roll out leaving a couple of seconds space between you and the entering paddlers.

When to 'unzip' can be determined by the steerer calling out in the first instance *5 unzip* which is followed by seat # 5 calling out, *5 unzipping, 5 paddling*, followed by the next highest seat numbered paddler following sequence, say seat # 3 then 1.When it's your time to exit the wa`a, the steerer can call out *Paddles up!* which is the command to fix your paddle into the paddle holder - methodically. *Out*! is the call to exit.

For the exiting paddler, it's really important they anticipate and time their exit well in relation to the change. They must allow enough time for the entering paddler to grab and enter the va`a where there's an empty seat, and not end up face an exiting paddler still sitting there.

Exiting paddler should roll out of the wa`a on the non-ama side and must not push off the hull floor with their legs as this can literally push the wa`a sideways towards the entering paddlers which could be disastrous, this is especially the case in seats 1 and 2. Exiting paddlers need to exit together to avoid landing on each other. Paddlers must exit in such a way to minimise the effect on the wa`a speed.

The entering paddler is under a lot of pressure. They can be nervous and cold, they have adrenaline running through them, and are in a very different state to the exiting paddler. If they come face to face with the exiting paddler still in their seat, the wheels are going to fall off straight away as they will hesitate and lose momentum.

Entering The Wa`a

Because men generally have greater upper body strength, they can get themselves up out of the water and into the wa`a relatively easily. Though not all do! For the ladies, it's crucial to perfect the technique and develop the strength to get their body below the waist, out of the water in one motion. This minimises the net drag component which is what slows the wa`a down the most. *Pull-ups* are one of the easiest exercises to use for improving muscle strength for this, as well as *lat' pull* downs.

If only the feet are trailing, that's better than the whole lower half of the body. Once the upper body is up and over the gunnel, it's a question of rotating or swinging the butt and legs around into the seat, grabbing the paddle, zipping up and paddling.

Sharon Attelsey demonstrates a common way for women to approach the problem. This requires an explosive release of energy by pulling with the arms shoulder width apart. In one motion, the body is twisted as it exits the water and the butt swung around and over the gunnel. With a moving wa`a, your legs should be out behind you as you swim in to meet the wa`a while kicking. This twisting motion needs to be executed quickly so the inertia of the pull up and the twist all becomes one. Failing this, your full body weight exerts itself on your arms for too long and you can crumble under the effort. Once you're around and your butt is over the gunnel, legs on the gunnel, the rest is easy.It's just a question of swinging your legs over and sliding down into the seat.

Men for the most part have greater upper body strength and consequently their technique is often smoother and quicker, they are very often less flexible, so ideas of 'cocking' the leg up and over the gunnel to haul themselves in, is generally not an option, just a last resort. The paddler must grab and pull in one motion using the inertia from the wa`a to help lift them out of the water.

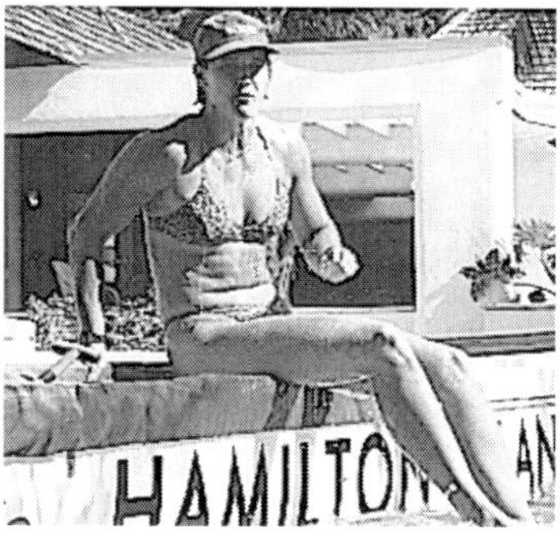

Swim into Your Change

One of the most common recurring problems is when the relief paddler reaches for the wa`a and their body is too vertical, feet directly below them. You need to have your legs out behind you, so when you reach up and pull, the legs can follow easily. When your legs are directly below, they end up pulled under the wa`a, which is really hard to recover from. The inertia is gone. It has to be a one-motion deal, there are no second chances.

Mindy Clarke **demonstrates what happens when your legs end up vertical and not out behind you. Your legs get pulled under the hull and it becomes very difficult to recover. This situation spells disaster however you look at it. The wa`a's inertia which you could have used to help pull you in, is now gone. Your body is now dragging through the water, nearly bringing the wa`a to a dead stop, your paddling mates want to beat you over the head with their paddles and your coach is burying his face in his hands as another wa`a passes by! Because your arms are bent at the elbows, it's nearly impossible to pull yourself in and often the only way to resolve this is to straighten your arms out and pull up again, incorporating powerful leg kicks to help you up.**

Water-polo players can get way out of the water just by the motion of their legs under the water. I believe entering paddlers don't often use their legs to good effect. Driving with your legs can make a huge difference in ensuring your body gets out quickly. Enter at an angle, not straight up.

Mindy **shows a common 'leg-over' technique. The right leg is hooked over the gunnel to give purchase and the body is lifted and rolled up and into the wa`a. Paddlers can sometimes end up prone, looking forwards which then requires some effort to recover from.**

Running your hands along the side of wa`a is not always a good idea, as it generally means you are stationary. The first point of contact with the wa`a should be the gunnel, with both hands firmly grabbing hold. If you do run your hands along the wa`a hull, keep your legs out behind you.

Simultaneously kicking with your feet and pulling inwards then pushing upwards with both arms in one movement is the key to getting out of the water quickly. You only have one clean shot at it. If you fail to get your hips up on to the gunnel and your legs free of the water in one motion, you are going to have to do some serious improvising to recover.

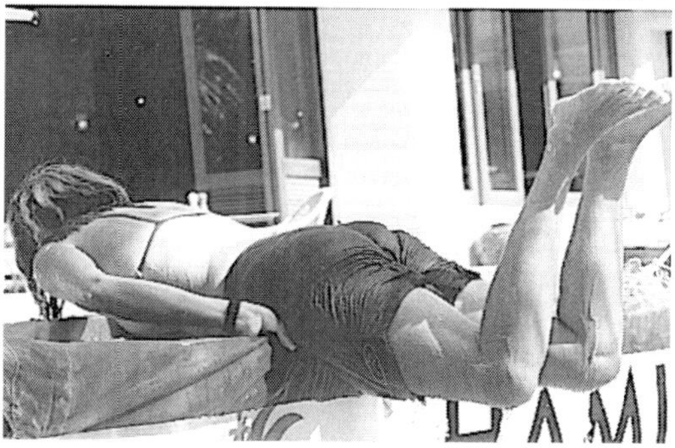

***Mindy Clarke* demonstrates what to do if you end up half in and half out. Get your legs up and out of the water so the wa`a does not come to a standstill.**

If you are struggling during practice to get into the wa`a, practice by wearing small swim fins, the type used for body boarding. You will find the extra speed from kicking will help get you up. Preferably, practice without the covers on. Getting your flipper past the covers can be interesting.

Pulling off good change-overs is crucial and on occasion we get situations where we have good paddlers who are lousy at changes. But you have to go with the good paddlers as they spend more time paddling than changing and hopefully they'll make up for the change-over errors!

Pick Up of Changed Paddlers

A rope with a small buoy attached thrown to those entering the support boat can assist them and is preferable than the driver attempting to get 'close'. Allow paddlers to climb aboard without 'pulling' them in as this can lead to injury.

Zipping Up | Bailing

The fundamental basis of what we're trying to do is to get relief paddlers into the wa`a as quickly as possible, without slowing the progress of the wa`a. Regarding the covers, when paddlers enter the wa`a, they need to get zipped up and paddling as soon as they can. Strokes lost, slows the wa`a. The lowest number zips first. The front of the wa`a is wetter than the rear. On rare occasions if you find yourself in calm water, there may be no need to zip up for your stint - experience will dictate what you decide.

Remember, whenever you make a change, you're taking in water with you. As seat # 4 is the primary person doing the bailing, when they make a change, the fresh paddler, while the cover is open, should bail if it needs it. They need to check each time they enter the wa`a as a matter of habit to save them having to unzip and bail, re-zip and begin paddling again.

Time in the Support Boat

Making the most of being OUT OF THE Va`a by Jo Lukins

Jo Lukins is a sport psychologist working in North Queensland, Australia.
She lectures at James Cook University in the Institute of Sport & Exercise Science and School of Psychology.

The changeover race brings an interesting component not experienced in any other type of outrigger competition. Time out of the va`a during competition. Typically in long distance races, individual paddlers will spend some proportion of the race out of the va`a and in a support boat. Clearly this initiative comes about by the physiological needs of the body to re-hydrate and replenish vital energy sources, What some paddlers fail to recognise, is that this time is also a good opportunity to re-focus the mind.

In land-based sports such as tennis and volleyball, the suggestion has been made that winning or losing the next point is largely influenced by what the athlete does in between points (both physically and psychologically). Similarly when given a break in an outrigger canoe race, how that time is spent will greatly influence the energy and determination a paddler takes with them, back into the va`a.

The mindset of the paddler is an important concern. For example, paddlers in the support boat realising their va`a is not doing as well as they expected, may spend the changeover time with thoughts of, 'it could have been different' and 'we're not going to do it'. Such a mindset is likely to leave the paddlers feeling negative, perhaps causing them to develop a self-fulfilling prophecy where their diminished effort results in the unsatisfactory placing they knew they were going to get!

Compare that example with the paddlers who use the changeover period to create the ideal mental platform for the next stretch of paddling. These athletes appear confident, in control, and portray an image of composure to their team mates. Success thrives on success, and a successful team generally consists of athletes who believe in their own ability.

To maximise your efficiency during a changeover you must give yourself the best possible chance of preparing for the next session in the va`a.The following are psychological skills that you may find useful when trying to obtain a positive mindset.

Closure

Paddlers cannot compete in the past or paddle too far into the future. Therefore, to maximise the likelihood of success, individuals must paddle focusing on the task at hand and the current stretch of water.

I know of many paddlers who will divide a changeover race into sections. Closure cannot occur until the paddler has considered and analysed what occurred in the previous stretch in the va`a If the paddler and team were performing well, they can use that information to reinforce their confidence in both their ability and race strategy. If the team has lost distance on the water, then they must be able to turn that negative into a positive. For example: 'yeah, we're further behind team x than we'd want to be right now, but our rate is good and the power feels strong – we're following our race plan, we can do it'.

The paddler should consider, thinking briefly about what has been done well and where improvements can be made and then focus the rest of the time thinking about what they will be doing next, and how to achieve it. Unfortunately, not everything is under the athlete's control (Strong head winds, opposition va`a's etc).

These uncontrollable events can distract the athlete's focus away from the relevant thoughts about achieving the pre-race goals. A useful phrase I have used with athletes is to repeat the mantra 'right here, right now'. This also works as a distraction technique which will block out anything that has happened in the past and stops the athlete from getting too worried or focused on sections of the race which are too far ahead.

One way of dealing with these issues is to use a technique called 'Parking Thoughts'. Just as the thought suggests, having a mental location where problems can be left, and dealt with at a later date. For example, paddlers may imagine putting a collision with another boat inside a 'mental black box' that cannot be opened until the race is over. The reality is that energy spent dwelling on that incident is a waste, so by using the black box and bringing closure, you can continue on preparing for the race.

Arousal Levels

For the next step, paddlers need to maintain a level of physical and mental arousal that allows for calm, clear thinking and be energetic enough to maximise their performance. The energy levels needed to be most focused and ready to exert maximum performance, and how to produce that energised state.

Many different techniques exist for controlling arousal. Relaxation (controlled slow deep breathing) can be used to calm down an over aroused state, whereas, increased arousal can be generated by sharply increasing physical activity (push ups). When paddlers have reached a state of optimal arousal (or activation) then they should begin to consider their goals for the next paddling session.

Concentration

Athletes are usually always thinking, however, they're not always concentrating! The key is to be able to focus and concentrate on the right thing at the right moment. Paddlers can optimise their concentration by knowing from the outset what has to be done and by being able to focus whether they are working towards that goal, or whether the plan needs to be modified.

Keeping in touch with your personal and team goals for the race is often a useful strategy to achieve utmost concentration. Paddlers who have planned their goals for the race, written them down, and kept them specific, measurable, and realistic are setting themselves up for success.

Creative Visualisation

Paddlers can visualise exactly what and how they are going to achieve the goal of their next paddling session. Visualisation allows an athlete to experience success in their mind, by preparing the body for its next activity.

For Example, it may have been pointed out to you in the support boat that you need to lengthen your stroke. Spend a few moments seeing your blade in the catch position with a long reach.

Visualisation is the result of 'what you see is what you get'. An athlete who thinks about failure is setting themselves up to achieve it. Therefore, the successful athlete is the one who not only wants to achieve success, but can see themselves achieving it.

Positive Thinking and Communication

The advantage to the break in a changeover is being able to communicate with others. If the coach is in the support boat, the paddler has a unique opportunity to get feedback on their performance and to plan for the paddling ahead.

Good communication with the coach or the person organising the changes is crucial to gaining the most from the break. My experience with athletes tells me that the majority of athletes are most responsive to instructions which are both specific and positive. Whilst I've paddled with people who respond to abuse and negativity, frequently this will be draining on the team. It is crucial that prior to the race, the team is aware of the type of communication needed.

The key to any self-talk by the athlete is to remain positive. This is probably one of the greatest skills an athlete can develop. When an athlete is positive, their self-esteem and confidence will increase, allowing them to best maximise their potential.

Using cue words is a useful strategy for helping a paddler to develop a desired mind-set. If you are feeling like you need to relax 'Calm' may be the word you need. If you need to get energised. 'Fire up' may be the phrase you need. The mind and body are highly responsive to the words we use, so in your pre-race preparation and training, experiment with words which will lift you to the level you need.

Summary

Teams who wish to be successful need to consider every facet of the changeover race. The time in the support boat following the changeover typically receives little attention. However, it is my belief that this time can make a crucial contribution to the success of a team.

Preparation for how this physical and psychological recovery time will be spent needs to be considered by all team members, coaches and support boat crew. If you can be mentally strong in the support boat, this will transfer back into the va`a.

In summary, when in the support boat: Quickly reflect on what's been working and where improvements can be made. Then move your focus to 'right here, right now', stay in the present 'Park' any negative or irrelevant thoughts. Keep your arousal at an optimal level. Concentrate on what is relevant, keeping positive and using visualisation.

Psychological skills are like any other skills, they need to be developed and practiced so they become an integral part of performance. Practice these techniques in your training so you can utilise them during competition.

Crew Selection

No matter how fair and reasonable the system may be that the coach has in place for determining crew selection, someone will always feel hard done by when left out of a crew. It is important that the coach be able to justify their reasons as they refer the paddler back through the selection criteria. If you have no system in place, you fail to create an insurance policy which you can use and refer back to when explaining your final cut.

Of all the tasks a coach performs, the most difficult and criticised is their selection of a crew. Those chosen will thank you for it, while some of those left out may feel a range of emotions including humiliation, disappointment, resentment, frustration, confusion and anger, to name just a few.

But many of these emotions can be softened provided a coach is honest, open and presents a solid blueprint for the selection process early in the season. Being left out of a crew will naturally evoke certain emotional responses from the individual, but these need not be negative, more a wake up call to train harder, focus more, and develop new skills and new attitudes to rise above the disappointment.

However, if as a paddler you feel the system is not being exercised fairly, then you may feel that no matter hard you work and improve, it will make no difference; these are very destructive and detrimental feelings.

Strength of character is a vital part of being a successful va`a paddler as the act of paddling is as much a test of the mind as it is of the body, it continually presents challenges - giving you the opportunity to improve yourself.

On the face of it, you can understand the intensity of disappointment someone feels when left out. After all, if you have devoted several months or more of early morning sessions, gym work and early nights, sacrificed social events and even sometimes your relationships with others, you can feel a little justified in being peeved.

From both the paddler's and the coach's viewpoints, establishing criteria can lend itself to pitfalls and criticism. It must be watertight, devoid of any ambiguity and above all, relevant and exercised with complete fairness. If not, it could become a hangman's noose and not the escape clause the coach had hoped for.

Crew selection has truly been a soul destroying task for some. I have heard stories of utter despair at failing to be selected, especially for races such as Moloka`i were paddlers often paddle long after the season is finished in order to have a chance of making the cut.

The toughest situation arises if the coach's partner or close friend is vying for selection and they have to 'drop' that person. Sometimes it's a gut wrenching, no win situation.

Let's begin with a possible crew selection criteria. The best example for this is an old but very good one, presented by *Offshore California* used during much of their multiple Moloka`i winning years. I have tried to update it a little and provide some concepts for both the paddler and coach to consider.

Photo *Chris O'Kieffe*

Selection Chart

A chart will be kept showing who is considered on the first team and who is considered 1st, 2nd, 3rd in line thereafter. This information will be available to you, so that everyone knows where they stand. You deserve to know. If there are enough paddlers available, a second and third team etc. will be charted.

This sounds pretty reasonable and as it says, 'You deserve to know'. I suppose if one were to question this at all, you may be concerned with creating a 'pecking order' or 'hierarchy' so everyone is aware of their 'place'. On

the other hand, it's honest and forthright and va`a paddling is a hard sport, so if you can't deal with it, then perhaps this sport's not for you?

Ideally, this hierarchy chart should be concerned with seat allocation and which paddlers are next in line relative to that seat. It's easy to forget that we are not up against six others, but merely one or two others in relation to our 'specialist' or 'preferred' seat.

Ability

There is simply no way around it, some people will just be able to pull a va`a better than others no matter how hard they try. While these people are valuable to the team, this is not the only deciding factor in being selected.

Ability in this instance is being presented in broad terms as it simply states 'able to pull a va`a better than others' which appears somewhat ambiguous. For example, it does not say for how long, i.e. endurance. However, it seems to imply a multitude of attributes coming together to make he or she of greater overall 'ability' than the next paddler.

Perhaps 'ability' in this case, should be the sum of the whole, so that when you add in all *physiological* and *biomechanical* factors you need to consider, we end up with a formula which states:

Strength + Power + Speed + Endurance + Timing + Technique = Ability

Strength

How 'hard' someone can pull the va`a through the water in such things as an OC1 and OC2 as well as paddling buckets will be a consideration.

We need to be very careful when we talk in terms of strength when we relate it to va`a paddling, which after all is a very physical sport concerned primarily with endurance. 'Strength' has a number of definitions when talking in terms of physiology.

Maximum Strength is defined as the maximum amount of force an individual can produce within a given movement of unlimited time, i.e. power lifting.

Explosive Strength is concerned with the maximum amount of force that an individual can produce in a short amount of time, i.e. the first few seconds of a race.

Reactive Strength is measured as the body's ability to absorb heavy impacts or landings and involves the muscles *extending* before being *contracted* with great force. Paddlers do this each time they rotate and reach forwards (extend) and after the *catch phase* of the stroke, they pull - *contract,* the muscles.

Sustained Strength enables an individual to maintain maximum forces over several repeated *contractions* or a single *contraction* over a long duration. Va`a paddlers, must maintain near maximum forces or *contractions*, often for very long periods of time and therefore this is a vital component to their performance. This could also be considered as *Strength Endurance*.

The point of defining these facets of *strength* is so that a coach and paddler can clearly see the value in each and how it pertains to the sport. Of all these facets of strength, maximum strength would seem to be of least importance and therefore a coach should be careful to devise sport specific measures of *strength tests* which relate to va`a paddling.

A forgotten term in this instance is **Power.** The most successful canoe teams on the water the world over are essentially *Powerful* and have high levels of **Power to Weight Ratio** i.e. relative to their weight, they are extremely powerful. Excellent levels of *sustained strength* amounts to a powerful athlete as they can continually repeat a near maximum force for a considerable period of time.

This has a multiplying effect, so a 75kg individual may be considered more 'powerful' than a 100kg body-builder. For example, a 75kg paddler who performs 30 chins ups repeatedly equates to 75kg x 30 = 2250kg while the body-builders who manages 15 only equates to 100kg x 15 = 1500kg.

Pulling buckets or resistance type tests are rarely used these days as the risk of injury fails to justify the purpose of the test and as already pointed out, this sort of test falls short of any genuine selection criteria specific to outrigger canoeing. In physiological terms, the sport is not about who is the strongest, but more about who can maintain *sustained strength* relative to their *power to weight ratio* for the longest period of time.

OC1 Time Trials

OC1 and OC2 tests have certainly increased in validity as a method of crew selection over recent years. For a brief spell, some teams, including *Faa`a* of Tahiti and *Lanikai* of Hawai`i, used OC1 race-offs and testing as key deciding factors in crew selection. This view has been moderated somewhat, but still remains an important factor in crew selection.

While the merits of determining *ability* cannot be denied through OC1 results, you need to be aware of the pitfalls when using this as a primary factor in crew selection. It's true to say for example that certain individuals perform better in a 'team' situation than they might in an individual pursuit. The willingness to avoid letting the team down, the pleasure in being an integral part of a working whole, and the sense of responsibility placed upon the individual to excel are all factors which make it possible for some individuals to perform at much greater levels of intensity when working for and with others rather than purely for themselves.

Some successful OC1 paddlers fail to blend well with crews and have a problem with timing and working in with others. Perhaps this is a factor of personality more than anything else. Simply dropping an OC1 test on paddlers, where 'x' are proficient and 'y' have never been on one, doesn't seem altogether fair, especially if the test is in open ocean conditions. If, on the other hand, it is the coach's policy that all their paddlers must become proficient on an OC1, then the test takes on more validity as all paddlers gain proficiency.

Without doubt, all OC6 paddlers should be spending time paddling an OC1, it's simply the single best way to become a more proficient paddler while improving ocean skills. Unwillingness to spend time on such craft perhaps shows an unwillingness to go the extra distance. While there are crews winning with non-OC1 paddlers, you have to ask how much faster and more skilled could they be if they were?

Endurance

How long you are able to keep up a high level of effort will be a consideration. No matter how strong you are, you have to put out effort for the entire race.

This encapsulates a va`a paddler's essence and relates back to our *Sustained Strength* issues. This must be near the top of our selection process. The use of a *Concept 2 Ergo* with paddling adaptor will certainly answer some questions a coach may have about a paddler's endurance levels.

Timing and Technique

How well you follow others in the va`a with good form (so that others following you will be more effective) will be a consideration. No matter how strong you are nor how well conditioned, if you're *timing* is off, you are not contributing effectively to the effort. A Tug of War is a great example. If ten people pull at the same time, they will be more effective than if each of them pulls at a different time.

Poor timing can stem from a lack of *discipline*, a lack of *natural rhythm* and *cadence,* pushing too far back in the stroke or entering too early, or being in a canoe full of *fast twitchers* or *slow* as the case may be and you are the complete opposite. It could just be that poor *technique* is affecting your *timing*. While poor timing is a frustrating issue for some, it can generally be fixed with guidance from the coach.

Technique, of course, is the shared responsibility of the coach and paddler. The coach must teach, demonstrate and advocate a particular technique and strive to have all his/her paddlers as uniform as possible. Some paddlers will naturally have greater degrees of *natural biomechanical ability* than others. *Idiosyncratic styles* also need be considered, as *ideal technique* is often modified through variations of individual style, which can prove to be just as effective.

Attitude

A person can have a bad attitude and still paddle well, but that negative attitude will carry through the va`a. Some will feel intimidated, some mad and the crew won't feel like pulling the va`a for you. A team that likes each other will work harder for each other.

Attitude is an extremely vital factor in selection. From the coach's perspective, this is often the difference between their job being an easy one or a painful one.

Some individuals object to being coached, as bazaar as it may sound! You pick them up on points, you make suggestions, you try to reinforce issues and the paddler seems to almost resent you for it. Clearly this sort of paddler is not a *team player,* possibly low on self esteem or perhaps there is a clash of personality. Perhaps the coach's bedside manner leaves something to be desired? Either way, it's a no win situation, which needs to be talked out and resolved, face to face on neutral territory.

Paddlers who respond well to coaching, listen and appear willing to learn at all times and put ideas into practice make ideal students. In addition, a happy go lucky, easy going nature is a blessing in a highly competitive person. But to be truly 'liked' by all, to be a motivating, invigorating individual ensures that this paddler will always have a positive affect on those around them. Potentially speaking, a happy crew is always going to have a greater chance of achieving its absolute best as it won't be weighed down by negative ballast!

Participation

Above are the main considerations of securing a seat in the va`a, but you need to understand that if one seat is open and two paddlers of equal ability and attitude are available, the person who gives more of themselves to the club's effort will usually get the seat. Not whoever is the nicest to coach gets the seat!

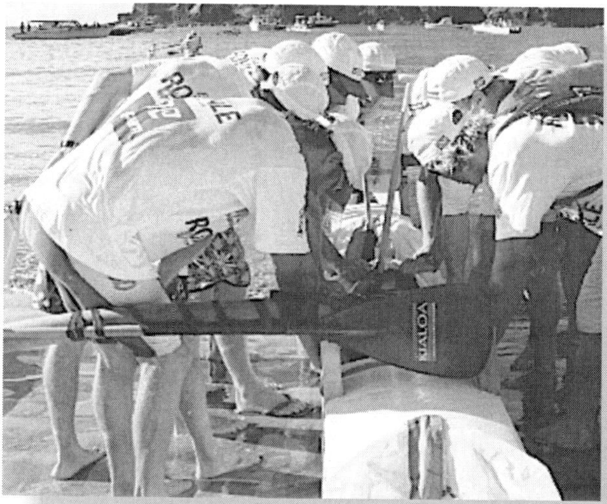

If push comes to shove and you need some sort of deciding factor, this may as well be it. Let's face it, coaches are human beings and thereby fundamentally flawed. Chances are, nine times out of ten, they will pick their personal favourite, because all other available selection criteria have been apparently exhausted. Or have they?

At the end of the day, what is wrong with the coach having the final say? After all, all other criteria are essentially external forces, tangible and documentable, so why shouldn't they be able to give the final nod to Bill or Beth? Well, as long as you have a good reason for it beyond, 'Bill gave me a good deal on a stereo' or 'Beth has beautiful eyes' then perhaps you're covered. Importantly, always have a damn good reason you can validate and that it relates to va`a paddling!

Selection Tools

**Changing paddler combinations within the va`a,** is without doubt a vital selection tool. It concern issues of *blending* and involves moving paddlers between va`a, within va`a and between different seats to arrive at the most effective blend for the crew. The process can take quite some time and should be continued throughout the season as paddlers continually 'evolve'. During the season some paddlers will improve, some will simply not making any progress at all and some will go backwards through over training or injury - which the coach need recognise.

What paddlers need to recognise is that when they are being moved around, they are being 'tested'. Everyone's seat is up for grabs, or at least that's how it should appear, otherwise where's the incentive to improve or keep performing?

Time trials can be used with this process, but generally speaking, over any distance increases or decreases in va`a speed can be observed, especially with more than one va`a on the water.

Good blending is vital. It brings together many vital aspects of creating a fast and efficient canoe. The coaches must isolate individual abilities, physical attributes and the suitability of each paddler to each seat.

At the higher levels of va`a paddling, each seat becomes increasingly *specialised,* so we can ultimately look at *blending* in variety of ways; in sixths, the individual paddlers themselves, in thirds, separating the va`a into the front section, seats # 1 and 2, mid section, seats # 3 and 4 and rear section, seats # 5 and 6.

We can consider how seats # 1, 3 and 5 and seats # 2 and 4 blend as they will be paddling on the same sides as each other and finally we can consider the entire six paddlers and how they all come together to make up the entire crew.

Individual Effort | Training Performance

A paddler's willingness to push hard for every session goes a long way. Some paddlers run hot and cold which does not inspire the coach with confidence.

OC2 / OC1 Competition

OC2 paddling provides a way of pairing off paddlers into their respective seat combinations. It is also an excellent way of developing timing and technical skills. OC1 competition is great for assessing an individual's paddling abilities. In open ocean conditions, it is an excellent way of understanding the paddler's ocean skills in terms of handling rough water, identifying 'runners' and being confident in these situations. If, as coach, you value this highly as a selection criterion, then you must make it clear and encourage all your paddlers to be actively involved in paddling OC1's. Otherwise, non OC1 paddlers will be disadvantaged, no matter how good they are in a team va`a.

Feedback from Team Members

Asking paddlers you have confidence in about the selection of others, can certainly help you make hard decisions but be careful of their own bias. It pays to consider their feedback carefully before acting on it, if at all.

Feedback from Other Coaches

Some input from other coaches may be of value, but once again, be careful who you speak to and how you interpret their views.

Attendance

We will not make attendance a factor by itself. A person can show up for every practice, but never put in any effort. But it will be hard to apply any of the other factors if you are not there!

Attendance is a big issue. Suppose a hardcore, surf lifesaving competitor cannot make it until mid outrigger season. Should they be allowed to arrive one day and expect to take over someone's seat who has been there from the start of the season and attended every session? Once again, if you allow this, you need to make it clear to your paddlers at the start that this will be happening.

No paddler, if available, should think they only need turn up to the sessions they feel like. This comes under *Bad Attitude*. Those who make paddling part of their a lifestyle should be rewarded accordingly and not treated thoughtlessly, brushed aside by prima-donna, part time outrigger canoeists - male or female, who arrive demanding and expecting to be in the top crew.

In terms of updating this original blueprint for crew selection, which was clearly very successful, helped by good genetics and a good deal of work by the likes of *Billy Whitford*, here are a few revised concepts.

Realistically, I think the coach needs to make it clear what is expected of their paddlers in terms of crew selection without necessarily having to list 'why' they will be selected, but clearly state some basic philosophies behind what is expected.

Outrigger canoe paddling is as much a test of strength of character as it is of mind and body. Every training session, every race day presents a test. Crew selection by the coach is made easy if you fall short of these expectations, live up to them and crew selection becomes increasingly more challenging.

Attitude

Be mindful of your *attitude* towards others, yourself, the va`a, your sport and your outlook on life. Never be too proud to ask for advice nor offended when it is given voluntarily. Your positive outlook will always make a va`a feel lighter and more buoyant.

Develop Your Paddling Skills

Develop a willingness to become a highly skilled paddler. Recognise that even after a lifetime of paddling, you will still be left with many unanswered questions. Outrigger va`a paddling is an *art form,* not just a sport. Your willingness to *develop, nurture,* investigate and constantly improve by training on other available forms of outrigger va`a craft will reinforce that willingness.

Strength of Mind and Body

Know that outrigger va`a paddling is a *tough* sport. It takes great strength of mind and body to excel. *Nurture* this *strength* so it is visible to others and yourself. Become an inspiration. These qualities will become valuable assets to yourself and others, and will be highly regarded.

Flexibility, Power, Endurance, Speed, Strength

These five principal factors relate to fitness and while they can be improved by va`a paddling alone, they can be vastly improved if worked on outside the va`a by additional activities. Improvement in these five areas will ensure you achieve your best. Paddlers who pursue these ends, by and large out perform those who do not. Therefore, it becomes a *self fulfilling* process which will become obvious as the season progresses. 'Random tests will be made during the season and paddler's performances will be documented. Improvement over time will be expected.'

Make a Difference

Make a difference each and every time you get in the va`a to ensure you gain recognition for your ability. This ability will not go unrecognised. Be courageous enough to graciously challenge another for their seat, actively or passively. *Honour* and *respect* are at stake, tread carefully and challenge only when the moment seems right. Such challenges must first be discussed with the coach who will have the final say on the situation. Your intentions must be made known.

Ocean Skills

Where possible, forge a relationship with the ocean and the waters you paddle in. At its highest levels, outrigger va`a paddling is an ocean sport. Learn how the ocean moves and learn to use it to your advantage. While talking to others who understand the ocean is helpful, true understanding comes only through *feeling* and *experiencing* the *oceans* many *moods*. Paddling an OC1 is the single best way to learn.

Blending

The *blending* of paddlers within a va`a to achieve maximum hull speed over a defined distance, will be established by interchanging paddlers seating positions, within and between va`a on the basis of *abilities, technical merits, fitness levels, attitudes* and how that paddler ultimately *blends* as a whole within the va`a. Rise to the challenge and recognise your opportunity to make a difference. Such exercises will be carefully monitored and feedback can be gained from other paddlers and coaches.

Final Crew Selection - Race by Race

If you are selected to be part of a *first crew*, treasure it, for it is always available to others who may want it more than you do. For the moment, you have earned it, defend it at all costs. From here there is only one way you can go.

If you are selected to be part of anything less than a *first crew* member, you too should treasure your seat for there are also others who may want it more than you. Take heart and be optimistic that the opportunity is always open to move upwards. Take this attitude and your seat will be safe. Crews will be selected race by race according to distance, conditions, availability and the factors listed.

Pay Your Dues

Make sure you are a paid up member. *The Club* takes a dim view of those who *freeload* and shun their financial responsibilities. Only paid up members will be considered.

Conclusion

Whatever you decide upon, it must be fair and reasonable and be shown to bring you and your crews success to whatever degree you deem it so. The thoughts and concerns of your paddlers will be many and varied. Your concern is on being the *best* you can be for all of your paddlers. Work hard, *earn respect* rather than demanding it.

Risk Management

Outrigger canoeists have been extremely fortunate in terms of avoiding tragedy, though there have been incidents. Death from *hypothermia* occurred in Oxnard, California in 1999. Inappropriate clothing, cold water and inexperience contributed to the deaths of two paddlers in only 45 minutes when their va`a over-turned and became disabled.

Without the benefit of statistics, *heart failure* seems to be the most common cause of death while paddling. For some die-hard paddlers, perhaps it's the noble way to shoot off this mortal coil. To what extent such cases were avoidable, I am not sure.

Each year, several V6 and W6 sink to the bottom of the ocean or get smashed on a reef. One reason for the limited loss of life could be that the vast majority of those participating in the sport are in tropical to sub-tropical climates, 20° north and south of the equator, in warm Pacific waters. *Hypothermia* is of course possible in even the warmest of waters.

However, the sport's track record would probably be much worse today if it weren't for the fact that its formative years were predominantly in Hawaiian waters. Many of these paddlers are experienced water users and good swimmers. This though is changing as we see the sport move to new parts of the world including Europe, Japan, Canada's Pacific North West and into East Coast USA. A capsize in these cooler waters can be fatal in a relatively short period of time.

Heat exhaustion and dehydration are major concerns in hot, humid tropical climates. Adequate hydration before, during and after is a critical element of safety.

The reality is that no matter where you live, risk is present at all times and in varying degrees. As the sport grows, so will the diversity of individuals participating and with it, the increased 'odds' of 'death by misadventure'. If there is one overwhelming misconception about the va`a by those who try it for the first time, it's that they fail to realise that capsize does occur and they think that in some way va`a paddling is less 'risky' than other paddle sports.

As the sport expands, the need for appropriate *safety* and *risk management* concerns need to be developed and nurtured by coaches, clubs and paddlers. This will help ensure that new paddlers are made aware of the risks, provided with the skills to avoid unnecessarily risky situations, or if an incident does occur, how to deal with it appropriately.

In short, it is essential that the risks to both paddlers and other water users be minimised through responsible, thoughtful actions before, during and after paddling. By implementing *Prior Risk Management Procedures*, the highest level of safe, responsible practice is in place and minimises the risk to all concerned, both on and off water. Taking the *safe* option is not to suggest we avoid pushing paddlers or equipment to their limits, but simply that it is done within safe limitations.

Many areas of risk management can be identified. An obvious place to begin would be consideration of the equipment. Equipment failure would seem relatively rare in the sport, but when it does occur, it can be disastrous and on occasion life threatening. The *cause* and *effect* of such equipment failure can be attributed to a number of factors, which more often than not are completely avoidable.

Duty of Care

Duty of Care reinforces the need to keep others safe. Coaches need to pay particular attention to this issue, as must more experienced paddlers in safe guarding those with less experience. Ultimately, it centres on the notion that 'you' will act in a safe and responsible manner in order to ensure the safety of others.

If you think your wa`a can take repeated bashings like this then you're mistaken and clearly not the owner who has to dish out the dosh to fix it. That being said, some levels of structural damage are simply not repairable.

Wa`a Equipment

One of the first places to begin your session, prior to warm up, is checking your equipment. Whether using one wa`a or more, it needs to be checked. This should become a ritual that is carried out before and after every session. These checks should go beyond just the va`a and its components, and should include all equipment to be used during the session.

Factors Affecting Equipment Condition

Inappropriate usage (ignorance/negligence)
Wear and tear (usage)
Abuse (negligence/neglect)
Age/Environmental (time)
Poor manufacturing (negligence)

Of these factors, it's safe to say that only wear and tear and age factors are innocent issues of unavoidable damage, though equipment deterioration from UV exposure can be slowed with the correct precautions. Inappropriate use and abuse will speed up the 'ageing' process. If this is combined with poor quality manufacturing, the equipment's tolerance will be lessened and could lead to an early demise, essentially putting at risk everyone who uses the wa`a.

Inappropriate Usage

The wa`a and outrigger assembly, including the rigging have their limitations and pushing them beyond that limit can lead to damage. One of the most significant causes of damage is caused through 'surfing' the wa`a on pitching waves, launching out through breaking surf, or paddling over large waves.

Not what this style of wa`a is designed to cope with. Expect a loss of longitudinal strength, cracked lashing holes, broken seats and more. In time, repeated abuse of the va`a in this way will effectively break it.

This is not really what it was designed for. Repeated violent capsizes and paddling over large oncoming waves and landing heavily off the back, leads to a progressive weakening of the structural integrity of the wa`a. In time, its 'longitudinal' strength is lost and the hull loses stiffness. Seats become cracked, the spreaders often develop weaknesses and all components of the wa`a and its outrigger assembly are progressively or sometimes abruptly compromised.

When the i`ako come under stress, delamination between the timbers can occur (this can also be due to poor manufacture). These too become flimsy, losing their integrity. The ama, possibly the most 'fragile' of all components, comes under enormous strain and many fail to absorb even with minor damage, often breaking clean in half.

Purpose built 3 and 4 person surfing wa`a that are 22 – 26' in length as opposed to 40 – 45' and are built tough with exaggerated rocker and width, strengthened i`ako, ama and rigging. They are manoeuvrable and purpose built for surfing.

The lesson here is simple. Use the wa`a within its intended design limitations and it will serve you long and well. Go beyond this and you can expect damage and reduced longevity. Remember the designers' adage 'Form and Function'.

Wear and Tear

Even if equipment has been used in the way the designer and manufacturer intended long term use will lead to wear and tear. Some components of the wa`a and its rigging are particularly 'at risk' from wear and tear. On occasion, wear and tear occurs within a short period of time due to poor rigging techniques and inappropriate material being used and therefore, time is not the only enemy.

Abuse

If wear comes from use, abuse generally comes from simple ignorance. Outright abuse of equipment essentially means mishandling the wa`a and outrigger assembly in some way; dragging the wa`a up on the beach, across rocks and debris, ramming other va`a, dropping the wa`a rather than placing it, sitting on it and so forth. Some steerers use the va`a as their own personal battering ram, which is unacceptable.

Abuse is avoidable, practised by those ignorant of the respect which should be a natural extension of handling a wa`a. Most of the 'abuse' of a wa`a occurs in the intermediate stages of on water paddling; launching, retrieval, storage and handling, though inappropriate usage could also be considered a form of abuse of equipment.

Age

Age takes its toll. Exposure to the elements over a period of time will ultimately lead to a breakdown of materials. Fibreglass va`a are in simple terms, plastic. Constant, prolonged exposure to the sun, especially in tropical climates, will lead to deterioration of the gel, resins and fibres.

Preventative measures can be taken in the form of covers or housing for the wa`a traditionally called a *halau* in the Hawaiian Islands. Timber i`ako will, in time and without appropriate maintenance, shed their protective coating and in some cases laminated i`ako may delaminate. Inherent stiffness will, over time, turn to increased pliability (flex) and lashing pegs can work loose or wear away. All elements of the va`a and its associated components are under threat from age and only regular maintenance will ensure its seaworthiness.

Poor Manufacturing

Poor quality workmanship unfortunately is purely a factor of human error from the outset. The most dangerous issue is that the canoe and its components may appear new and therefore strong and sound, yet underneath many flaws can lurk and only reveal themselves during use. Close *quality control* inspections prior to clubs making the final payment, along with a manufacturers guarantee seems to be the only means of safeguarding the investment.

Wa`a Components to Inspect

Bungs

Many fibreglass wa`a have a bung placed at the lower centre portion of the bulkhead wall to allow air pressure to be released from the bulkhead itself. This practice is seen less in newer va`a designs. Bulkhead walls have been thickened and no bunghole is added to make a totally watertight void. Some manufacturers drill a small breath hole on the very top extremity of the manu or bulkhead to allow air to bleed as opposed to expanding with nowhere to go.

Unfortunately, bungholes often create more problems than they solve. Nylon threaded bungs wear reasonably quickly and need to be replaced yearly. In addition, sand particles trapped around the thread act as an abrasive when tightened and loosened, causing rapid wear, and leading to leaks. Sand trapped between the threads also causes water to leak through to the bulkhead.

A common problem occurs when the thread is striped. The solution for many is to tighten it until it 'jams' which is no solution at all. The 'female' component screwed to the bulkhead itself presents a problem because it is more often than not screwed or riveted to the bulkhead wall and siliconed. Screws become loose, silicon degenerates and water passes through into the bulkhead.

The extremities of many ama also include a bung. Bungs are in place to regulate *air pressure* and only in adverse situations are they there to let water out. When on-shore, all bungs must be loosened so the air within the cavity can escape as it heats and expands during the day. Trapped, expanded air will effectively put pressure on all the joins and internal walls, and cause stress and possible cracking to external gel coats or in the worse case, cracks to the outside.

An ama can be damaged if the bung is screwed on tightly and the hot air which is trapped inside cools too quickly when placed in the water. Small pin-prick holes can begin to weaken the walls and it may ultimately take on water much like a sponge. Place the va`a in the water for a few moments and then tighten the bungs.

It is common practice with surf-ski and kayak paddlers to blow air into the hull cavity until it fills and is under pressure, then replace the bung. This practice can create a 'rigid' hull which flexes less in rough water and can prevent 'creasing'. This practice is quite different as air blown into the cavity is not 'hot' and will therefore not cool and contract as will hot air. Air has been forced in under pressure. This practice can be used on the ama and OC1's and OC2's, but is rarely done.

After paddling, always release the bungs. If there is any water whatsoever within the cavity, you must assume either there is a problem with the male/female component of the bung assembly, the integrity of the ama or the bulkhead itself. Water trapped within hull bulkheads commonly leads to the growth of algae.

Bulkheads

The sealed bulkhead void at the front and rear of the canoe has been added on fibreglass wa`a, (absent on koa wa`a) in order to provide buoyancy to the wa`a in the event of a capsize. This is the wa`a *life jacket*. Inspect the entire area, under the hull, over the bow and stern covers, manu and the bulkhead walls themselves, including the bungs.

If there are more than two holes present on the bulkhead, water is able to enter and air escape creating the potential for the bulkhead to fill completely with water and loose all buoyancy. The area within the bulkhead can be considered 'negative buoyancy' in view of the fact that it is the 'air' alone providing the buoyancy. If the bulkhead has only one hole, water will enter until the air pressure is 'equalised'. Then no more water can enter as the air has effectively 'compressed' with no where to go.

Most wa`a manufacturers rely upon the fact that in the event of capsize trapped air within the bulkhead will provide the buoyancy. But this is a somewhat optimistic short term view as with time, it is not uncommon for additional holes to be created somewhere within the bulkhead. Many va`a have been lost because water fully replaced the air within the bulkhead, causing the va`a to become irretrievable or simply sink.

The only sure way of retaining this 'buoyancy' in the long-term is through the placement of some form of 'positive buoyancy' within the void. One of the most effective ways to do this is imply adding tightly sealed 1ltr and 2ltr plastic bottles. These durable 'trapped air containers, ensure that the void cannot be replaced with water, thereby safeguarding buoyancy even if the bulkhead is damaged and allowing water to enter. Note; bottles should be replaced periodically as they can implode and deteriorate.

Adding 'Sealed Air Containers' to Wa`a Bulkheads

***by Al Ching*, Redondo Beach, California**

A good idea in safeguarding and preventing the loss of a wa`a is to fill the wa`a bulkheads - tanks, with empty plastic drink bottles which paddlers discard daily. The bottles are also very light and pose no problem as far as adding extra weight. At any marine hardware store - yacht chandlery, you can pick up a round 'hatch-cover' - inspection hatch, for around US$12. They can be installed easily onto the bulkhead in approximately 30 minutes. Be sure to purchase the 'screw-on' hatch-cover design as opposed to the 'press-on' on variety as they are much easier to open and close.

Purchase a hatch-cover opening large enough to accept a 2ltr bottle. It's possible to fit roughly 40 x 2ltr bottles into an average forward bulkhead and just a few less in the rear. Allow more for some of the larger wa`a. Everyday after practice, simply remind paddlers to put their 'empty, tightly sealed' plastic bottles into the bulkhead.

Each of these bottles becomes an individual air tight container. They should also be replaced and checked for leaks periodically. Some bottles have lasted a long as three years and more without leaking.

Once the bulkhead voids are full, its a good idea to leave the bungs - if they are fitted, on each bulkhead open, as this will insure that no water will accumulate within the bulkhead and will drain into the body of the wa`a where it can be bailed out. This will not float the wa`a any higher than if they relied upon the trapped air within the bulkheads only. However, the bulkheads can be severely cracked and leaking, but it won't matter, as the individual bottles will keep the wa`a afloat for many hours even in the roughest of seas until help arrives.'

Gunnels

The upper edge of the gunnel suffers from the impact of paddles, being tied down on trailers and excessive longitudinal movement (twisting) of the wa`a hull. Particularly prone are the areas adjacent the lashing holes and in some wa`a, depending on how they are manufactured, areas where joins have been made.

Warping and *bulging* of the gunnel are common signs of water uptake. Many manufacturers use timber along the length of the gunnel that is sandwiched between fibreglass. Often this wood is inexpensive and not of marine grade so cracks in the gunnel leads to water absorption. Increases in hull weight can often be attributed to this absorption and in the worse cases I have heard of up to 60lbs of water being retained by these lengths of wood. Foam sandwich gunnels are far superior.

Manu

The raised extremities of the wa`a front and rear, are prone to impact during paddling and transportation and should be checked for cracks and splits. Underneath this area is a watertight bulkhead. Holes and cracks which allow water to enter and air to escape can lead to water filling this space during a capsize.

Splashboard

The splashboard is a vital safety component of the wa`a and serves to keep water from pouring over the front of the wa`a and into the hull. These are attached to the rear of the bow cover - *kupe ihu*, in a variety of ways. Some are a part of the mould, while some are attached separately, with screws, rivets and silicon or fibre-glassed in position. Screws work loose, silicon degenerates, and fibreglass can weaken and develop cracks.

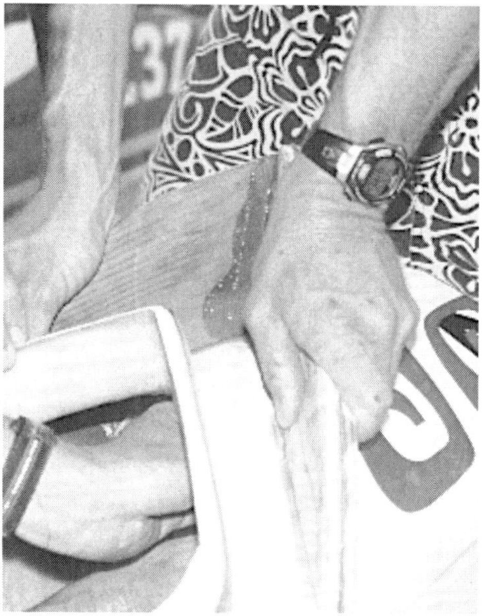

Underneath this area is a watertight bulkhead. Holes and cracks which allow water to enter and air to escape can lead to water filling this space during capsize. Ensure that where the splashboard is attached is firm and repair any apparent holes or cracks which pass through to the bulkhead below. Also check the splashboard for any damage.

Lashing Holes

Check for stress fractures around the holes and ensure there are no sharp edges which can cut into lashing ropes or rubbers.

Hull Floor

The hull floor surface copes with a great deal of wear and tear. Sand left in the wa`a causes the non-slip coating on the surface to wear and ultimately produces a smooth, slippery surface making it difficult for the paddlers to grip with their feet. Ensure paddlers remove sand from their feet before they enter the wa`a.

Surfboard wax can be used to improve grip where there is a smooth surface, however the best solution is to reapply non-slip paint - marine grade. Check for cracks which may appear through the centre-line of the hull floor. Leg drive is crucial to efficient paddling therefore good grip underfoot is paramount and ultimately a safety issue.

Seats

Check for signs of cracks and fractures where the seat joins the hull, both above and below. Keep in mind that the seats act as thwarts or hull braces and therefore take the weight of the paddler and the longitudinal twist and torque of the hull. Weakened joins will contribute to increased 'longitudinal movement of the hull' - twist, and will affect hull speed and performance. Also check the seats themselves. If padding has been added, replace when worn.

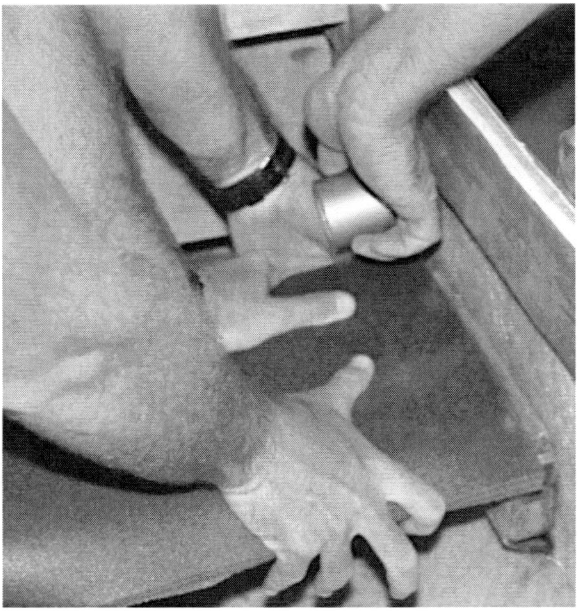

Spreaders

The spreaders, where the i`ako attach to the wa`a, absorb a great deal of torque and leverage, and need to be checked thoroughly. This isn't entirely possible with rigging and i`ako attached, however where the spreaders join the hull presents the area most likely to suffer damage. The spreader is often made of timber and then laminated in fibreglass.

I`ako

The i`ako are generally laminated timber. Laminates can split apart and the varnish or epoxy coating once worn or burned off by the sun causes the timber to be exposed and no longer sealed. Check the point at which the i`ako leaves the wa`a's side travelling toward the ama, the point of maximum curvature - where the laminates most often divide and the lashing peg/s at it's extremity, if added.

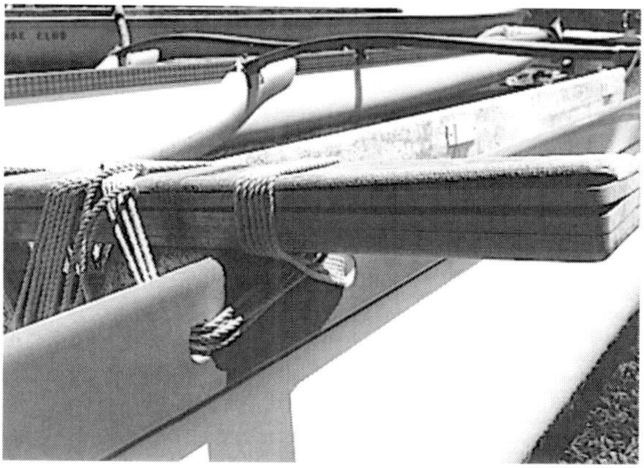

Delamination between the timbers.

Ama

The ama is vital to the wa`a' safety. Check the seams where the top and bottom are joined, check bung and i`ako mounts, and lashing holes in particular. To check that the ama is airtight, remove the bung (if included) and blow repeatedly until the air is under pressure, have someone listen and check for air leaks. This is also a good method for removing a certain amount of water from inside. Blow until it becomes hard to continue, then release the air. The pressure will force the air out and some water at the same time.

Rigging and Other Items

Checking the rigging prior to paddling is crucial. Never assume it is firm, simply because it was the day before. Rigging can be tampered with and can also work loose or begin to deteriorate. Quality rigging materials will not make up for poor rigging technique and visa-versa.

Cotton Sash

Cotton is one of the most popular rigging materials used when rigging with the Hawaiian *Diamond Weave* method. Being organic, it is prone to reasonably rapid deterioration. Black staining on the cotton indicates *rotting* and will also cause *powdering* between the fibres. Check that it has not stretched and loosened the weave. Check for signs of abrasion where it passes through the lashing holes.

Check the firmness of the weave and the finish, both where the i`ako joins the spreader and the i`ako joins the ama. Replace cotton or re-rig if necessary. Always rinse with fresh water after each session.

Rubber

Rubber degenerates very quickly under strong UV and wears quickly. Ensure it is always very tight and finished securely so it does not unravel. Always rinse with fresh water after each session. Replace rubber if perished or re-rig if loose.

Snap-Lashes I Ratchet Straps
More common these days are snap-lashes or heavy duty roof rack straps. Check webbing for abrasion, nuts and bolts for damage or rust, and ensure there is very high tension applied.

Emergency Rigging
A spare set of snap-lashes or lengths of rubber can save the day.

Duct Tape
Taking heavy-duty tape in the wa`a is a simple precaution and often worth its weight in gold. It can be used to secure loose rigging, a cracked ama, split manu, sharp gunnels, damaged paddles, seats, bailers, navigation lights and all sorts of things. Attach it to the i`ako by taking a few wraps.

Covers
Covers are an essential part of safety equipment, though generally not thought of in this way and rarely added for training purposes, which is odd. The fact is, covers should be used at all times in open sea conditions which present any threat to swamping or capsize, yet because of time it takes to attach them, this is rarely if ever the case. In cold climates, covers protect the paddler's lower body from wind chill and in most paddling situations from spray water entering the wa`a.

Covers should be checked to ensure an adequate seal and security, and in particular, zipper and Velcro fasteners examined for ease of use. Replace or repair faulty elements.

Wearing of a Personnel Floatation Device (PFD) is mandatory in some parts of the world. Check with Harbours and Marine Coast Guard or Club.

Bailers
Bailers are an essential item and a wa`a should never be on the water without them. A minimum of two with at least a 2ltr capacity, scoop shaped with a handle. These should be hung on the side of the wa`a by brackets, not rolling around on the floor. They should be secured with a lanyard so that in the event of capsize, they remain with the wa`a.

Spare Paddles
A spare paddle is always advisable in case of loss or breakage. It can be attached to the rear i`ako with the blade over the wa`a grip

towards the ama, lashed using a length of rubber which begins out from the grip and is wrapped progressively towards the lower shaft of the paddle, finished off using a quick release knot. Do not use duct/carpet tape to attach a paddle as it is hard to remove. Steerers sometimes carry a spare blade behind their seat.

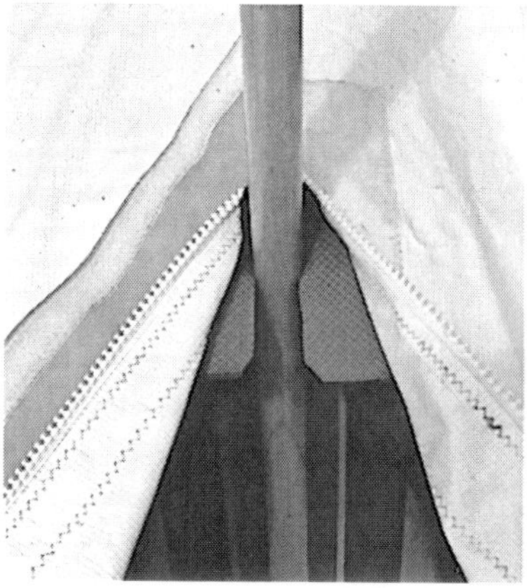

Paddle Holders
Ensure paddle holders when fitted to *hoops* function efficiently. Some clubs fit paddle holders to the hull wall when racing without covers such as in the Catalina race in California.

Club Paddles
In the case of club paddles being used, ensure they are in good condition as they are often more of a liability than a workable tool. Ensure novices have the correct length paddle. Check that your own paddle is in good working condition. Paddles with *splits* should be dried out and repaired as injuries can occur if they snap while paddling.

Additional Equipment / Requirements

In some areas of the world, local *Harbours* and *Marine Authorities* insist on a minimum of safety equipment to be carried within the wa`a and these can include; *V-Sheet, PFD's, Sea Anchor* and *Flares*. There are many small items that can be included which could 'make the difference' in an emergency situation and depending on your storage arrangements within the wa`a you can determine what you can comfortably carry.

Lifting and Carrying

Trolleys
Trolleys can be considered as a *safety* item as they can reduce and prevent *back injury* and in some cases, damage to the wa`a

The potential for injury is high when lifting and carrying a wa`a because of its weight and length. Ideally, all paddlers should be lifting the wa`a from the middle section and not at the ends. Ensure *bent knees* and a *straight back* when lifting.

Selecting Club Venue

Unfortunately, there could be inherent dangers residing in the venue from which you run your club. Across the globe, outrigger wa`a clubs are based in absolutely every imaginable venue; car parks, yacht clubs, motor boat clubs, private canal and beach homes, rowing clubs, public beaches and parks, vacant land, under bridges and idyllic beaches. Storing 45′ wa`a is no easy task and in areas such as Japan and New York, where space is at a premium, finding a venue becomes one of the hardest factors in beginning and maintaining a club.

However, if we have to go looking and had a wish list, the following factors should be taken into consideration. Some are general while others concern the safety of the equipment and security of the paddlers themselves.

An interesting metal device which slots over the *muku* (short overhang) and provides the paddlers with a suitable purchase point on the non ama side. Carrying the wa`a by the seats can damage them.

Available Space

Does the venue provide adequate space for storage and manoeuvring of wa`a to and from the water? Will it allow for growth of your club?

Security

Security issues are paramount. You have invested and will continue to invest in expensive equipment. Vandalism and interference with wa`a is not uncommon.

Arson has been a problem for some clubs and sometimes you are left wondering if it was premeditated. Simple vandalism against the wa`a seems less common, but broken bottles and trash can be thrown into the body of the wa`a, drunks sometimes urinate inside them, rigging can be tampered with and children, in all their innocence, love to climb all over wa`a.

On rare occasions canoes are stolen. *Lock* wa`a up using lengths of plastic covered wire, passing through the lashing holes of the wa`a and securing to a tree, fence, weights etc. It all makes life more difficult for would-be vandals. If you are within a *lockable* compound, that's even better. If there is a security company who patrols the area, contact them and supply your after hours number in the event of any problems promising them some form of reward for helping out. An additional safety concern is whether or not the venue provides a *safe* environment to be in at all times or are their times of possible risk, i.e. being in the venue late in the evening for individuals or small groups.

Exposure
Ideally you want to be away from high exposure areas. Advertising your wa`a is not always a good thing, especially within cities. If wa`a are located on busy main roads and thoroughfares the risk of vandalism seems to increase, more so in areas where outrigger wa`a are a novelty and less common.

Noise
Excessively noisy venues make on land sessions difficult and unpleasant, during peak hour traffic especially.

Parking
As your club grows, you will need adequate parking space. If car pooling is not possible, then two wa`a equates to twelve cars and so on. Can paddlers park somewhere close to the venue. Will they disturb residents at 5-am in the morning? Will cars take up the residents usual parking spots?

Accessibility
Is the venue accessible all the time, or is it closed at certain times of the year? Can adverse weather make it impossible to access? Can all car types get to the site, or is it a goat track for off-road vehicles only?

Trash Can
Can club rubbish be disposed of or will you need to supply your own and chain it up somewhere or need to take your rubbish with you?

Council By-Laws
Universally, local councils have rules concerning land use. It pays to find out what your limits are as far as use of the land you are interested in. You may need permits. Often you will need to plead your case with the powers that be. Always talk about 'youth programs' and so forth to help them see the value in what you are doing not for yourselves, but the community.

There is one club I know of that paddles their va`a around and collects trash once a month. They collect bucket loads of rubbish and make sure the press hears all about it, it helps them promote their cause and shows that they care about the waterways.

Access and Foreshore Obstructions

Great land space is one thing, but can you launch and retrieve wa`a easily? Can you use a 'dolly' if you want? Consider the immediate area where the wa`a will be stored, the foreshore and below high tide water line. Does it have potentially dangerous obstructions; oyster beds, cables, pipes, waste materials, etc.? Will you have to wear steel capped boats in order to walk around safely, or will bare feet be OK? Will the unpleasantness of it simply make it unbearable or can you organise your members to clean the place up?

Low Water Access

In tidal areas you must consider the water levels at both high and low tides, as well as the *Spring* and *Neap* tidal ranges. How far out does it go? Ask a reliable local. Can a 45' wa`a be comfortably carried/wheeled that far and could a 'dolly' be used?

Club Box

Is it possible to leave a club box on site, containing spare paddles, bailers, etc.? A club box means that some items of equipment are available to paddlers at anytime as opposed to only one member having all the club paddles, the rigging materials, navigation night lights, bailers, etc.

Notice Board

Can a notice board be put up displaying training times, messages, phone numbers, race results, regatta dates, emergency numbers, safety issues, meeting dates, etc.? The Club Notice Board can form an extremely important role in club proceedings and communication if used correctly. Without a formal clubhouse or if club has limited social activities, members will get together only at regattas and meetings.

Lighting

Is there suitable lighting on and off the water, within launching/recovery/ storage areas? Fumbling around in the dark is no fun and can lead to accidents - at least some form of lighting is important.

Proximity to Risk Establishments

Locating adjacent to night clubs and bars can present a problem after hours, when intoxicated partiers may find amusement in vandalising canoes. Even being near busy high schools can be problematic.

Permanency

Just how permanent is the land you are using? Is it going to be developed soon? Moving club venues regularly is possible but somewhat disturbing. Try to find an area which allows some permanency so you can build up an infrastructure around the site together with community support.

Freshwater Facets/Taps

Access to fresh water is a bonus so the wa`a and equipment can be rinsed and water bottles/hydration systems filled. You may need to supply your own hose.

Boat Ramp

Can a support boat be launched from a trailer and recovered easily?

Site Water Safety

Once the land meets all or most of your needs, you then need to consider what will become 'home-waters'. These are a number of things to take into consideration;

Tides/Tidal Range

Tides can be considered as the periodic rise and fall of sea level and it is the tidal range which you are most concerned with. Excessive tidal ranges can make your training entirely dependant upon times of high and low water, and incoming and outgoing tides. Timing your outward and return times could be crucial.

Tidal Streams

You will need to educate yourself about the tidal streams and the direction in which they flow when flooding (rising) or ebbing (falling), so all paddlers (especially steerers) are familiar with the dynamics of water flow within the area.

In addition, being aware of the strength of the tidal flow is crucial as this could present some limitations as far as the course that is steered. In some areas of the world, such as the waters which separate Australia from Papua New Guinea, within the Torres Straits, the strength of the tidal flow is more like a river than the ocean!

Currents

Currents relate to large bodies of water which move in relation to seasons and are less of a concern in general, but some understanding should be encouraged.

Underwater Fixed Obstructions

These include man-made objects such as bridges, pontoons, mooring buoys, channel markers, underwater cables, pipes, as well as natural ones such as reefs, coral outcrops, rock ledges, tree stumps, sand spits etc. All can be dangerous and should be noted and avoided.

Wave Action

Large onshore waves will make launching and returning to the shore hazardous. Will your activities be limited by prevailing wind directions, strengths and ground swells? Does the beach gradually shelve or does it drop off suddenly? Visit the area during a variety of weather/sea conditions to make an assessment.

Water Traffic

Other water users can present a risk to your va`a and other water craft. Is the venue close to shipping lanes, ferry routes, trawlers and/or other recreational water users such as water skiers, sailboats or yachts? Check it out on a sunny weekend and consider what it would be like in the peak of summer during holiday times. Steerers will need to be very aware of their legal requirements and of local harbour and marine regulations.

Pollution/Out-fall

In some cases, you should be concerned about areas where there is a known pollution problems. In some areas of the world I have visited, Hong Kong being one

Top: A New Zealand set up carrying two fully rigged waka ama.

Australian trailer, capable of carrying six wa`a and all associated equipment. Fully laden this make a substantial road vehicle which needs to be towed with due care.

Below: Tahitian Style

of them, pollution levels in some areas are such a concern that many paddlers suffer a variety of infections, in particular skin and eye problems. Additionally, the wa`a and rigging absorb oils and pollutants which makes it paramount to clean all equipment - and oneself, immediately following all on water sessions.

Trailers

Wa`a trailers come in a variety of forms designed to carry different numbers of wa`a, rigged or unrigged. Loading and securing va`a and equipment is critically important, using the correct securing materials. Ensure the trailer is well maintained, checking tyre wear, brakes, lights and mounts.

Ocean Dynamics

Wa`a paddling is predominantly an ocean sport and with its growth, paddlers are venturing further into open ocean conditions and races are becoming more challenging, both for team wa`a and singles. Paddlers need some understanding of ocean dynamics as a matter of safety.

Studying oceanography includes land-forms and their effects on wave formation (points, spits, bars, reefs, river entrances, open beaches, open ocean), wave structures (plunging, spilling, surging), different rip currents caused by wave action (permanent, fixed, flash, travelling), beach types which in turn have an

effect on wave types (dissipative, long-shore troughs, low tide terrace beaches and reflective), ground swells, wind chop, wind against tide and wind over tide.

Wa`a of the six-person type are not surf craft. They are designed to perform within a variety of sea conditions including flat water, chop and larger sized ground swell or surging type waves. Placing the wa`a in areas of plunging or dumping wave action is especially dangerous to both the paddlers and the wa`a , placing enormous strain on the rigging. Even small waves of this nature have a huge capacity for damage. Specialist 4 person wa`a constructed specifically for surfing are the best things to use.

Short, steep wave action as one might find in shallow bays with strong local winds, or in areas of shallow water with strong tidal streams, where wind against tide causes this effect, stress the wa`a, its component and its rigging. Constant jarring and pounding of the hull and ama causes excess torque and strain to be absorbed by the ama, i`ako rigging and spreaders. The rigging can work loose or worse still break under the constant movement. Lashing holes, mounting points, spreaders and i`ako are all at risk.

Strong winds complicate the issue and add increased stress due to the wind. In addition, the va`a can take on a great deal of water without the presence of spray covers.

Maritime Rules

Steerers in particular, but preferably all paddlers, need to have some basic understanding of the rights of way rules as they apply to harbours, harbour entrances and open ocean situations. Being able to identify channel markers is also essential. This information is freely available and should be taught to paddlers as a matter of club policy.

Clothing Concepts

Is your clothing adequate for the air and water temperatures, and the duration of the session? Does it offer suitable movement or will it cramp your style! In addition, consider protection from the sun.

Paddling with no shirt from a man's viewpoint, undoubtedly provides a great feeling of freedom and expresses the primitive element of the sport. Just be aware of the damaging effects of ultra-violet exposure - sun, and the benefits of wearing appropriate long sleeved UV resistant, lightweight clothing.

The need for appropriate clothing that provides effective protection from the elements fall into the area of risk management, as inappropriate clothing can be hindrance and a danger. First and foremost, there must be an understanding of the relative differences between air temperature (factoring in any wind chill) and the water temperature.

While the air temperature may not pose any threat, extremely cold water has the potential to kill in only a short time, therefore paddlers need access this risk and dress appropriately. This scenario presents the most difficult in terms of choice; dressing for warm air temperatures, in the knowledge that the water temperature is low enough to be pose a danger if immersion occurs for any length of time. Spring is a notoriously dangerous time of year in many places, where air temperatures may by high, but water temperature is still low.

Technological advances in performance, technical clothing in recent years, though sometimes expensive, offers paddlers the ability and freedom to paddle near all year round.

Whatever is worn, paddlers need to retain flexibility and freedom of movement, particularly in the shoulders and arms. Without this, the paddler is at risk of cramping and will be hindered in performing the paddling stroke effectively or for any period of time. The paddler should neither overheat or be allowed to cool down to the point of discomfort.

The internal organs around the area of the *kidneys* are prone to cold and must be protected when either the air or water temperature or both pose a danger. Other areas of the body including the arms, chest and entire torso must of course be covered.

To reduce wind chill, a thin lightweight nylon jacket can be worn over the top to provide a final barrier. The advantage of layers is that they can be removed to suit the comfort of the paddler as they or the air warms.

The wa`a spray cover should be worn in the case of cold climate and weather conditions. The paddler's body heat becomes trapped inside the hull, warming the lower limbs and reducing wind chill, immersion and excess water along the hull floor.

Specialist cold water/ climate paddling clothing can be purchased from paddling outlets. Some of the best paddling clothing for such conditions can be bought from white water rafting/ canoeing outlets who stock hi-tech garments that are specially designed. Some of these are 100% water tight, sealed around the wrists, neck and waist with rubber gussets.

Polypropylene Tops Either long or short sleeved, purchased at outdoor adventure shops, provide adequate protection on cool days, worn next to the skin. Offer some degree of splash protection.

Wool Tops Breathable and useful as undergarment or for use in moderately cool climates. Can be worn in combination with polypropylene layer.

Neoprene Vests Lightweight (2mm) neoprene vests (sleeveless) worn next to the skin provide excellent insulation to the back, chest and stomach. Combined with a polypropylene top, this adds addition insulation.

Neoprene Short Sleeve Shortie Half leg designed wet-suit of 2mm thickness. Ensure that it is designed for surfers and has ample freedom of movement under the arms.

Neoprene Shorts Lightweight (2mm) neoprene shorts provide warmth in the groin region and some comfort against the seat. These can be worn in combination with a neoprene vest.

Steamer Tops Specialist canoeing and kayaking shops in cool to cold areas often stock specialist white water clothing. Sealed neoprene/ rubberneck, wrist and waist gussets provide effective seals against the water while a waterproof material designed to be a loose fit cover the arms and body.

Cotton Lycra Shorts - leggings and tops Cotton lycra is worn more often by women than men. Its fashionable look and array of colours make it an attractive paddle material. Provides some insulation and protection from UV rays, has the advantage of being very flexible, allowing the paddler freedom of movement.

Nylon Spray Jackets Lightweight nylon jackets can provide effective wind barriers. Keep pockets zipped up and hoods rolled up, in the water these can be a hindrance.

Board Shorts Available at any surf shop, these are practical in warm water/ air locations and are hard wearing. Quick dry material recommended.

Padded Board Shorts Regular board short with neoprene padded seat area.

Rash Shirt Short – long/short sleeved nylon, polyester or lycra, are popular for providing some insulation on cooler days. They provide excellent freedom of movement and varying protection from UV rays. Some offer *wicking*, i.e. they are breathable and allow the skin to dry out.

Cap/Beanie 25 % of body heat is lost through the head. In cold weather and high wind, a beanie style hat is a definite recommendation. In times of extreme heat and glare, a peaked cap reduces glare in the eyes and keeps direct sun off the head and face.

Gloves Worn to protect hands against blisters and abrasion or to protect from the effects of cold (sometimes as protection from sunburn). Gloves can be either of a light leather material as used by dinghy sailors, neoprene or cotton lycra. It is essential that the gloves are very flexible and that the paddle can be felt through the material. Gloves can be a great hindrance if not selected properly. Specialist paddling gloves can be purchased at better canoe and kayak stores.

Neoprene Boots Keep feet warm, protect against sharp objects such as oysters, coral, rock, glass, etc.., and can also provide some traction on the hull floor. Neoprene style footwear, with appropriate non-slip sole, are essential when cold climate paddling. Numb feet are highly uncomfortable, tend to lack traction, prone to pain at the slightest knock and distract the paddler's attention away from paddling.

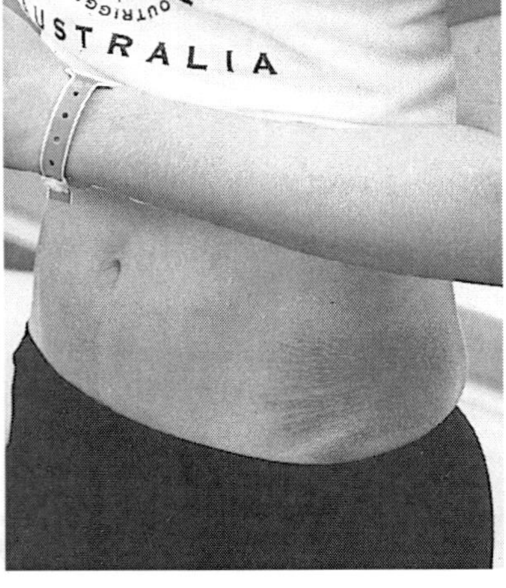

Sunglasses Specialised ocean sports sunglasses and goggles protect the eyes from the damaging effects of UV rays. Common problems are *fogging* on the inside of the lenses and *crystallisation* on the outside. These can be countered to some extent by liquid products which add a protective water proof film to the lenses. Ensure you wear a 'retainer' to prevent loss in the event of capsize and secure fit when paddling. Polarised lenses are preferable.

Covers can cause severe rash when paddled without a shirt so ensure you are protected.

Road Trips

One of many factors making participation in this sport so enticing, addictive and alluring is the uniquely beautiful locations where it is practised. In so many ways, the sport allows you to combine overseas travel, vacation time and sport all in the one package in a way that few others can emulate. Additionally, the strong cultural affinity the va`a commands in many areas of the Pacific makes the experience educational and culturally enlightening.

Fundamentally, travel to new venues to compete provides a uniquely profound prism of experiences, which opens your mind up to the world, new friendships and greater affinity with the sport as a whole, taking your participation beyond the physical to a very much higher level of awareness.

Possibly the most confusing issue is in choosing which event to go to, made all the more difficult when many of the most appealing events all seem to fall one after the other (or even on the same day) at around the same time of year, notably through September and October. California's *Al Ching* reinforces this issue, *'This drains the attendances to all the races. Races have become so popular that clubs have to make choices to conserve their energy and flow with their training schedule. Of course there is the small matter of finance we have to contend with. Before the explosion of the sport, we had fewer choices and attendance was huge.'*

This has been a growing problem for some time as the sport has grown and expanded. By some perverse failure to see this an issue, associations and race organisers seem happy to keep compounding the problem, unwittingly but ultimately creating an atmosphere were one event is now having to compete against another, especially in view of attracting overseas crews.

Mere mortal's bank accounts are limited and finite and therefore selecting which event to invest in is a critical issue. If it weren't, the advice would be, pack up and hit the road from September to the end of November and enjoy the premier events of Hawai`i, Tahiti, Micronesia and end it with a flurry in the Cook Islands. The best advice I can give is 'don't get tunnel-vision'. Make sure you try them all rather than becoming locked into returning to the same event year in and year out as many paddlers do.

Welcoming dance on the remote Marquesan island of Ua Huka.

When travelling to

more remote areas, do so in the company of low maintenance individuals content just to be in the moment, happy to experience new sights and cultures without judgement. Don't expect the best equipment and do expect inconveniences all of which will add to your 'Road Trip' experience. To quote *Tom Conner* from a paddlers perspective, '*It's how you deal with the obstacles (in life) and how you react to them which counts the most*'.

When in the Marquesas on one occasion, the va`a supplied to the Australian crew was so woeful, that it took an entire day to repair the seats and make a new splash guard from wood scraps and this va`a was in good shape compared to the one they were supposed to use. The ama and i`ato arrived late in the day on a ferry from a nearby island, while in the meantime, all other (local) crews were rigged and sorted and home relaxing. Sabotage? No, not at all, because at the end of the day the locals were doing all that they could with what they had. Circumstances 'in the islands' often take an odd direction and rarely resolve themselves quickly, directly or as you would like them, but amazingly ultimately seem to fall into place, even if in 'island time'.

French Polynesia

There are so many reasons why, as a paddler, you should make the effort to visit French Polynesia to experience va`a paddling and its culture at its best. Yet ironically, Tahiti remains to paddlers especially those of European decent, from Pacific Rim countries and even Hawai`i as somewhere revered, mysterious, often referenced but rarely visited.

It seems incredulous that on the one hand much is made about respecting the culture of the sport, yet many paddlers seem squeamish in actually fully diving in and embracing it, preferring a thin veil of euro-centricity to gloss over any real or genuine cultural depth, hence why paddlers of European decent from around the Pacific feel far more comfortable visiting and competing in Hawai`i where competitors are largely of similar ethnicity and where much of the cultural aspects seem at times eroded. In Tahiti, the competition is indigenous and of a very high level.

That paddlers the world over would continue to invest their money by re-visiting the same old races, year in and year out seems a narrow interpretation of what the sport offers. Issues of language barriers, expense, equipment worries, competition levels and the mystery of it all, seems to intimidate would-be visitors, to the point where 'xenophobia' seems to set in. Those paddlers who have made the journey and embraced the natural beauty and felt the passion for the va`a which emanates from the paddlers and the communities of the islands, can be said to be enlightened individuals, who doubtless no longer question why the paddlers of French Polynesia excel on so many levels within the context of the sport.

The most spectacular va`a races in the world happen right here and the only reason they are not judged so, is due to a general lack of press and exposure, keeping these events all but a mystery. The October **Hawaiki Nui Va`a** is a three day event, begins from the island of Huahine, crosses to the island of Ra`iatea 48km away, then 26km to the island of Tahaa and finishes on the final day with a 60km race towards the most mythical and stunning of all Polynesian islands, Bora Bora. It is in short, the most spectacular va`a race on earth, without equal anywhere.

The **Heiva Va`a** races and the 86km change-over race depart from **Tahiti around Moorea** and back are held in July during the month long festivities of the Heiva Festival. In June there is the **Heemoana Va`a** race, chasing the big South swells, born thousands of kilometres away in the frigid waters of the Antarctic, the same swells that create those big waves for *Teahupoo's* world famous surfing ASP contest, *Billabong Pro*. It's a 60 km change-over race with 9 men paddlers, which begins from *Teahupoo*, where the only road around the island comes to a dead end. The race ends at the opposite end of Tahiti, to the West in Punaauia.

And, if you are into rudderless V1 paddling how about the **Aito** race in Tahiti where over 600 paddlers line up on the start line or the **Super Aito** from Moorea to Tahiti, a 36km ocean race?

Then there's the Marquesas, one of the remotest island groups on the planet. The **Vakauhi Race** between Ua Huka and the fabled isle of Nuku Hiva covers 35miles of deep cobalt blue ocean and epitomises the primal elements of the origins of the sport; the Jurassic park of va`a racing as you paddle between island mountains that are emerald green, wind worn and wiry, arriving to the sound of beating drums and chants, you feel like warriors returning after battle.

Hawai`i

The Hawaiian Islands offer a wide variety of events and in recent years the proliferation of OC1 and OC2 races in particular have increased paddler-traveller numbers greatly to the islands during April-May. Notable relative newcomers are the **Maui to Moloka`i Challenge Race,** which is rated as one of the best direct downwind courses in the world and the **Kauai World Challenge** which has risen to be one of the world's most prominent due to the professionalism of its organisers, incorporating lead up races during the week before the main event, which follows the coastline and involves beach changes.

Longer running events such as the **Kaiwi Challenge**

Honaunau Bay 'Place of Refuge' where the women finish and the men begin the paddle back to Kailua. Dawn breaks in Kailua Kona Hawai`i, the starting point of the *Queen Lili`uokalani* race.

Hale O Lano starting point of the Na Wahine O Ke Kai and Molokai Hoe.

(Hawaiian Island Paddlesports Assocation) a 39mile race between the island of Moloka`i and Oahu held every year in May and the **Moloka`i Challenge Solo** (Kanaka Ikaika) races remain pinnacle distance events.

The island of Kauai ranks as one of the most scenic in the world and each year paddlers from the Hawaiian Islands and abroad gather on Kauai for the **Kauai Na Pali Challenge Race,** which departs from the beautiful town of Hanalei on the North Shore and around the Na Pali. Crews pass some of the most beautiful coastline in Hawai`i; majestic cliffs, sea caves and arches. The race ends on the West Side of the island at *Waimea Plantation Cottages*.

In the lead up the Molokai to Oahu races, the distance season beginning around August offers a variety of races, including the ***Duke Kahanamoku*** put on by *Lanakai CC*, the **Dad Centre Race** run the *Outrigger CC* and the ***Henry Ayua* Memorial Race** staged by *Hui Lanakila*.

Traditionally the 42mile women's September **Na Wahine O Ke Kai** and the mens in October.

Molokai Hoe are regarded as pinnacle OC6 open ocean change-over events raced between the island of Molokai and Oahu across the Kaiwi Channel and dubbed the unofficial 'world championship' events in this discipline. These events tend to lack somewhat in the socialising stakes as its predominantly all about the racing, but offer challenging open ocean racing.

In contrast, the two day September ***Queen Lili`uokalani*** event, the *Largest long distance race in the world* as it boasts, is truly a great Hawaiian experience, where socially, culturally and competitively the event offers it all. Held on the island of Hawai`i from the town of Kailua, the setting is languid, tropical and laid back. The 18 mile women's course follows the coastline to Honaunau, known as the *Place of Refuge* in ancient times and the men paddle the course back to Kailua later that day. The following days races include DC12, OC1 and OC2 craft.

California

California has an ambience all of its own, uniquely different from the Hawaiian scene. Although there are strong bonds between the two states, there is a curious

tension which exists between the differing sub-cultures of the va`a. It was possibly spurned ever since Californians flopped a mould from the Hawaiian koa *Malia* and began churning out fibreglass wa`a, setting in motion the globalisation of the sport on many levels; akin perhaps in the same way as Tahitians recoiled when Anglo-Hawaiians moved the goal posts and instigated specification rulings in the late 1970s.

Two primary distance races come to mind on the Californian racing scene. **The Catalina Classic** founded in 1959 is a 30 mile change-over race between Newport Beach and Avalon on Santa Catalina Island - women / mixed, followed the next day by the men's return. Conditions are generally flat to moderate, the water on the cool side if you are from the tropics but the air temperature is generally very pleasant. Just as well to take some lightweight thermal tops just in case.

Generally speaking if, Molokai is a 'steerers' race, this is a 'paddler's' race as conditions often do not present well for assistance. Socially, the atmosphere feels typically 'laid back' Californian style and very enjoyable. Historically this stretch of water, the San Pedro Channel, is Californian's nemesis crossing as the Kaiwi Channel is to Hawaiians. The Catalina OC1 / OC2 race is also a highlight on the racing calendar.

Not as well known, the **Whitey Harrison Canoe Classic** is a 20 mile change race run by *Dana Point OCC* which has become a classic event and historically significant. It was named after *Lorrin "Whitey" Harrison*, who learned to paddle and make wa`a in Hawai`i in the 1930's. Women race in the morning followed by the men in the afternoon. This long distance race begins just outside Dana Point Harbour, turns

Hamilton Island Rocks! Evening aerobics and hydration session. Below: Catseye Bay Hamilton Island. Below this, Gold Coast Cup Australia.

around off Main Beach in Laguna Beach and finishes at Doheny Beach. This event is historically very central to Californian wa`a paddling and racing largely due to the influence and charismatic personality of *Harrison*.

Australia

Australia's premier event is the June/July **Hamilton Cup Race** known as the 'paddle and party hard' event, this 4 day event crams in everything for everybody. OC1 and OC6 events over sprint courses, longer races over 16km and change-races over 42km. The 42km Hamilton Cup race itself is one of the leading prize money events, with AUD $100,000 distributed throughout a wide range of place-getters. The event is held on Hamilton Island in the Whitsunday region of North Queensland. South East winter trade winds are common which often means very changeable weather from balmy to cool, calm to very windy. Course changes are not uncommon.

The 42km event is considered by many as tougher than the Moloka`i to O`ahu race on a good day, as there are long up-wind legs, heavy currents and short steep choppy waters to contend with. This course is very demanding on the steerer as you attempt to take the best line between islands and negotiate currents. Significantly, the event is also well known for its professionalism and organisation.

Of notable mention is the **Gold Coast Cup** race in April / May, which begins at Greenmount and travels North to Southport. Not as well known or long running as the Hamilton Cup, the Gold Coast Cup offers, when conditions permit - South East trades, Australia's best downwind distance change-over event. Socially lacking in any atmosphere, the event is all about the paddling. Australian crews use the event sometimes as a build up to the Hamilton Cup event. The Coffs (Harbour) Coast Cup race also offers a great weekend of racing, held early in the year.

New Zealand

New Zealand predominantly has a great love of sprint / regatta racing, in contrast to Australia where the reverse is true. **The Hauraki Hoe** event in March is New Zealand's longest running change-over event, which leaves from Auckland Harbour and makes its way out and around the outer islands within the Hauraki Gulf. It can be a gruelling event in big seas. Water temperature is cool, cold if you're from the tropics and the air temperature can also be cool at this time of year. It is a very scenic race and very low key which is regrettable as it has great potential.

The **Tauranga Harbour Challenge** is possibly New Zealand's best attended event, comprising of a 26km W6 race as well as W1 and W2 races over 16km. Socially it offers a good opportunity to really get to meet New Zealand's best paddlers while enjoying the evening events which can extend to Fijian *kava* parties, Hawaiian *Hula*, Tahitian singing and English pub songs. Tauranga is on New Zealand's East Coast of the North Island. Racing is predominantly in sheltered waters.

International Va`a Federation World Sprints

Held every two years by varying host countries, the IVF World Sprints are a truly international occasion bringing va`a paddlers from around the world together. From a cultural perspective, the event is very rewarding as Pacific nations, Pacific Rim,

European and South American paddlers come together. Sprint racing in V6, V12, V1 and V2 - rudderless, does not appeal to all, especially those paddlers more driven to compete in open ocean conditions and in this respect the event tends to reinforce the notion of sub-cultures within the sport; flat water and rough water ocean paddlers. That being said, many of the worlds best va`a paddlers attend the event, revelling in the social atmosphere, the racing is great but its all about the people at these events on so many levels. The organisation tends to be inconsistent between events which can be frustrating, but all in all, it provides a great celebration of the va`a sport with flag bearing ceremonies and different va`a cultures proudly sharing their dance, song and ceremony.

The **Fiji International** held in April in Nadi is continuing to expand as a good value for money, feel good event. The October **Micronesian Cup** events held alternatively in Guam, Saipan and Palau offer a genuine grass roots event, low key, sociable and highly enjoyable. The Guam Cup is also a great event staged in October and held in a fantastic location.

The Cook Islands, November **Vaka Eiva** event is gaining great support and offers a great variety of events including racing around the island of Rarotonga. The **Rio Va`a** event held in Rio De Janiero Brazil is growing in popularity and offers a unique opportunity to visit and compete in a truly vibrant part of the planet.

New Caledonia continues to pursue ultra distance events, seemingly wanting to out - do the Tahitians, but seem to struggle with consistency despite great efforts. While in Europe the sport is soon to explode with races such as **La Porquerollaise** (Toulon), the **North Sea Outrigger Canoe Championships** the **Internationaux du Va`a, Rallye De La Baie Des Phoques.** Much of this is due to Tahitian paddlers serving national service in Southern France. They have managed to bring va`a with them, courtesy of the French Navy and now manufacturing has begun in various part of Europe.

Other races include the **Statue of Liberty Race** in New York which provides va`a racing in one of the most unlikely venues. Canada's **Gibson Race** is hailed as uniquely scenic and a must do event, while there are also uniquely different races such as the race from the island of Bimini Atoll to Florida.

Micronesian Cup